Lecture Notes in Information Systems and Organisation

Volume 64

Lecture Notes in Information Systems and Organization—LNISO—is a series of scientific books that explore the current scenario of information systems, in particular IS and organization. The focus on the relationship between IT, IS and organization is the common thread of this collection, which aspires to provide scholars across the world with a point of reference and comparison in the study and research of information systems and organization. LNISO is the publication forum for the community of scholars investigating behavioral and design aspects of IS and organization. The series offers an integrated publication platform for high-quality conferences, symposia and workshops in this field. Materials are published upon a strictly controlled double blind peer review evaluation made by selected reviewers.

LNISO is abstracted/indexed in Scopus

Alessio Maria Braccini • Jessie Pallud
Ferdinando Pennarola
Editors

Technologies for Digital Transformation

Moving Towards the Future of Organisations

Springer

Editors
Alessio Maria Braccini
Department of Economics and Business
Tuscia University
Viterbo, Italy

Jessie Pallud
EM Strasbourg Business School
Strasbourg Cedex, France

Ferdinando Pennarola
Department of Management and Technology
Bocconi University
Milano, Italy

ISSN 2195-4968 ISSN 2195-4976 (electronic)
Lecture Notes in Information Systems and Organisation
ISBN 978-3-031-52119-5 ISBN 978-3-031-52120-1 (eBook)
https://doi.org/10.1007/978-3-031-52120-1

This Springer imprint is published by the registered company Springer Nature Switzerland AG
The registered company address is: Gewerbestrasse 11, 6330 Cham, Switzerland

Contents

Technologies for Digital Transformation. Towards the Future of Organisations 1
Alessio Maria Braccini, Jessie Pallud, and Ferdinando Pennarola
1 Digital Technologies and Digital Transformation. 2
2 Emerging Digital Technologies and Organisations. 2
3 Researching Technologies for Digital Transformation 3
3.1 Exploring Emerging Technologies 4
3.2 Exploring Implications of Emerging Technologies 5
References. 9

Part I Exploring Emerging Technologies

Manufacturing SMEs and Artificial Intelligence: Between Promises and Paradoxes 13
Aurelio Ravarini, Fatema Zaghloul, and Emanuele Strada
1 Introduction. 13
2 Digital Technology and SMEs in Italy 14
3 AI Applications in Manufacturing 15
3.1 AI in the Manufacturing Industry 15
3.2 AI Applications in Manufacturing: The Main Use Cases 16
3.3 Barriers to AI Implementation 17
4 Methodology 18
5 Initial Findings 19
6 Discussion: Between Promises and Paradoxes 23
7 Conclusion 24
References. 24

Investigating the Artificial Intelligence Debate in Organisation and Management Studies . . . 27
Marco Smacchia and Stefano Za
1 Introduction . . . 27
2 Theoretical Framework . . . 29
3 Research Methodology . . . 31
4 Descriptive Bibliometric Analysis . . . 32
5 Topics Exploration with Co-word Analysis . . . 37
6 Conclusion . . . 43
References . . . 44

Do Forecasting Algorithms Need a Crisis-Mode? Machine Learning Based Sales Forecasting in Times of COVID-19 . . . 49
Tobias Fahse
1 Introduction . . . 50
2 Conceptual and Theoretical Background . . . 51
2.1 Machine Learning for Sales Forecasting . . . 51
2.2 Data Drift and Structural Breaks . . . 52
2.3 COVID-19 Stringency Index . . . 54
3 Methodology . . . 55
4 Data and Artifact . . . 55
4.1 Data Set . . . 55
4.2 Algorithm: OLS Model . . . 56
5 Results . . . 57
6 Discussion and Conclusion . . . 61
References . . . 62

Artificial Intelligence in Information Systems Research: A Socio-technical Perspective . . . 65
Dorsa Safaei, Kazem Haki, and Jean-Henry Morin
1 Introduction . . . 66
2 Research Background . . . 67
3 Research Method . . . 68
3.1 Literature Selection . . . 68
3.2 Analysis Framework . . . 69
4 Results . . . 71
4.1 Current State of Research . . . 71
4.2 Socio-technical Analysis of Current Studies . . . 73
4.3 Machine Learning Constituents . . . 75
5 Discussion and Conclusion . . . 76
References . . . 79

Blockchain and Lending Process Efficiency in the Banking Industry . . . 83
Elena Bruno and Giuseppina Iacoviello
1 Introduction . . . 84
2 Literature Review . . . 85

3 Methodology and Research Design 89
3.1 Initialization Phase. 90
3.2 Data Collection Phase 90
3.3 Discussion Phase 91
4 Empirical Research: An Italian Case Study 92
5 Discussion and Conclusion. 93
References. 96

Under Pressure: Strategic Choices and Contextual Trade-Offs of SMEs Facing Industry 4.0 Implementation 101
Anastassiya Zabudkina, Olivier Lisein, and François Pichault
1 Introduction. 101
2 Theoretical Background 103
2.1 Industry 4.0 103
2.2 SMEs and Their Specific Features. 104
2.3 SMEs in the Context of Industry 4.0 105
3 Methodology. 106
3.1 Data Identification and Selection. 106
3.2 Data Coding and Analysis 108
4 Results. 109
4.1 Pressures in the Inner Context of SMEs 109
4.2 Pressures in the Outer Context of SMEs 113
4.3 Strategic Choices of SMEs 114
5 Discussion. 115
6 Conclusion 118
Appendix. 119
References. 121

Part II Exploring Implications of Emerging Technologies

The Context Sets the Tone: A Literature Review on Emotion Recognition from Speech Using AI 129
Fabian Thaler, Maximilian Haug, Heiko Gewald, and Philipp Brune
1 Introduction. 129
2 Background and Related Work 131
2.1 The Concept of Emotions 131
2.2 Recognizing Emotions Using Artificial Intelligence. 132
2.3 Emotion Recognition Through Speech Analysis. 132
2.4 The DSR Framework. 133
3 Methodology. 134
4 Results. 136
5 Discussion. 137
5.1 Practical Implications 139
6 Limitations and Further Research. 140
7 Conclusion 140
References. 140

Understanding the Links Between Neuroscience, Physiological Tools and Stress, with the Eventual Neuroscientific Impact of Culture, in Organizational, Managerial and Information Systems (IS) Fields Through a Social Network Analysis . . . 145
Raffaele Silvestre and Mauro Romanelli
1 Introduction . . . 146
2 Research Methodology . . . 150
2.1 Data Collection . . . 151
3 Results . . . 153
3.1 Dataset Analysis . . . 153
3.2 Citation Analysis . . . 154
3.3 Co-citation Analysis . . . 157
4 Discussion . . . 157
5 Research Implications . . . 160
6 Future Research and Limitations . . . 162
References . . . 163

Digitalize Thy Place: Benefits and Challenges in the Development of Smart Destinations . . . 167
Sara Nicoletti, Francesca Capo, and Lorena Maria D'Agostino
1 Introduction . . . 167
2 Theoretical Background . . . 169
2.1 Digital Tourism and Smart Destinations . . . 169
3 Methodology . . . 170
3.1 Data Collection . . . 170
3.2 Data Analysis . . . 171
4 Findings . . . 174
5 Conclusion . . . 180
5.1 Discussion . . . 180
5.2 Potential Solutions and Implications for Policy Makers and Managers . . . 181
5.3 Contributions and Limitations . . . 182
References . . . 183

Digital Transformation and Dysfunctions: Case Study of a Japanese Leading Technology Company, Analysis from Socio-Technical Approach . . . 185
Soen Hayashi
1 Introduction . . . 186
2 Theories . . . 186
2.1 SEAM Theory . . . 186
2.2 STA Theory . . . 187
3 Research Method . . . 187
4 Case Study: Digital Transformation and Business Reforms of OMRON . . . 187
4.1 SINIC Theory: The Compass for Corporate Development . . . 188
4.2 The Concept of 'Big Company Diseases' . . . 189

4.3 OMRON's Business Reform 189
4.4 The Implementing Digital Transformation of OMRON 189
5 Analysis of the Interviews. 190
5.1 Problems of Communication and Teamwork Within the Department. 190
5.2 Problems of Coordination and Cooperation Between Departments. 191
5.3 Outside of Organization Issues and Supply Chain Management 191
5.4 Many New Product Developments Are Carried Out Every Year, but Often There Are Too Much Emphasized on Technologies and Functions. 192
5.5 In Terms of Organizational Structure, There Are Many Middle Management Layers in Each Department 192
6 Discussion. 192
7 Result 194
7.1 Social Factors. 194
7.2 Technical Factors 194
8 Conclusion 194
References. 196

Digitalization, Online Services, and Entrepreneurial Environment in the Italian Smart Cities' Transition 197
Filippo Marchesani and Federica Ceci
1 Introduction. 197
2 Literature Review 199
2.1 Smart City and Digital Advance 199
2.2 Digitalization and Entrepreneurial Environment. 201
3 Methodology. 202
3.1 Sample and Variable Description. 202
3.2 Analytical Approach 204
4 Results. 206
4.1 Cluster Analysis. 206
4.2 Predictive Validity 209
5 Conclusion and Discussion. 210
References. 211

Exploring the Evolution of Digital Transformation Research in Non-profit Organisations: A Bibliometric Analysis. 215
Michele Cipriano and Stefano Za
1 Introduction. 216
2 Theoretical Background 217
3 Research Method 218
4 Results. 220
4.1 Descriptive Analysis 220
4.2 Conceptual Analysis 227

5 Discussion and Conclusions 231
References 232

How to Unlock the Value of Your Data: Six Design Guidelines for Implementing Data Strategies 239
Jörg H. Mayer, Marc Lanzerath, Juliane Wutzler, Reiner Quick, and Marcus Peruscha
1 Introduction 239
2 Literature Review 241
3 Method 244
4 Artifact Description 245
4.1 Why Are Companies Implementing a Data Strategy Now 245
4.2 Which Functions and Departments Need to Be Involved 246
4.3 How to Translate Data Strategies into Action 247
5 Evaluation 249
6 Discussion and Conclusion 251
References 252

Data-Driven Failure Management: An Ontology-Based Speech Recognition App for Failure Capturing in Manufacturing Processes 257
Philipp Scharfe, Heiner Ludwig, Katja Bley, Martin Wiener, and Thorsten Schmidt
1 Introduction 258
2 Foundations and Related Work 259
2.1 Manufacturing Processes and Existing Solutions for Failure Data Collection 259
2.2 Typing-Based Vs. Speech Recognition-Based Solutions 260
2.3 Ontologies as Data Model 261
3 Research Approach 261
4 Design Requirements and Principles 263
5 Artifact Instantiation 265
5.1 Data Storage: Ontology-Based Data Structure 265
5.2 Speech Recognition-Based User Interface 267
5.3 Data Retrieval Tools 268
6 Artifact Evaluation 268
7 Discussion and Outlook 270
References 271

Evaluation of Innovativeness as the Success Factor of Innovative Start-Ups: Evidence from Literature 273
Francesco Bellini, Fabrizio D'Ascenzo, Irina Gorelova, Adriano Fabbri, and Giuseppe Ventrice
1 Introduction 274
2 Research Methodology 275
3 Results and Discussions 279

3.1 Propensity for Innovation 280
3.2 Open Innovation 281
3.3 Sustainability 283
4 Conclusions 284
References 285

A Bibliometric Analysis of FabLabs Research 289
Rocco Agrifoglio, Concetta Metallo, Roberta Oppedisano, and Maria Ferrara
1 Introduction 289
2 FabLabs 290
3 Research Methodology 291
4 Descriptive Statistics 292
5 Results of the VOSviewer Co-occurrence Analysis 294
6 Conclusion 296
6.1 Cluster 1: FabLab Drivers and Consequences 296
6.2 Cluster 2: FabLab and Learning Process 296
6.3 Cluster 3: FabLab and Digital Manufacturing Processes 297
7 Limitations and Future Prospects 297
References 298

The Metaverse: Digital Innovation in the Fashion Industry—A Systematic Literature Review 301
Grillo Michelle and Bonomi Sabrina
1 Introduction 301
2 Fashion and Digital 303
2.1 Fashion and Virtual Platforms: From Game to Metaverse 303
3 Fashion and Digital Innovation: State of the Art 305
4 A Systematic Literature Review 306
4.1 Methodology 306
4.2 Results 308
4.3 Content Analysis and Discussion 315
5 Conclusion 325
References 325

"Look! This Is the Future of Cardiology": Institutional Work and the Making of Telemedicine in Healthcare 329
Alberto Zanutto, Enrico Maria Piras, and Diego Ponte
1 Introduction 330
2 Contribution of Institutional Work 330
3 Methodology 332
4 Findings 334
5 Discussion 336
6 Conclusions 337
References 337

Technologies for Digital Transformation. Towards the Future of Organisations

Alessio Maria Braccini, Jessie Pallud, and Ferdinando Pennarola

Abstract Digital technologies have a profound influence on organisations, continuously producing transformative impacts. Unlike conventional technologies, digital counterparts extend beyond specific functions, permeating the entirety of organizational dynamics, especially influencing core processes like sense-making and decision-making. The forefront of technological development is characterised by emerging digital technologies like blockchain, artificial intelligence, robotics, and the Internet of Things. These technologies, while promising innovation, introduce uncertainties in organizations' digital transformation paths, with impacts difficult to predict. The chapters within this exploration summarise the varied insights—empirical, conceptual, and theoretical—offering a comprehensive perspective on the intricate implications and roles of emerging digital technologies within the realm of digital transformation.

Keywords Digital transformation · Emerging digital technologies · Artificial intelligence · Blockchain · Internet of things

---

A. M. Braccini (✉)
Università degli Studi della Tuscia, Viterbo, Italy
e-mail: abraccini@unitus.it

J. Pallud
EM Strasbourg Business School, Strasbourg Cedex, France
e-mail: jessie.pallud@em-strasbourg.eu

F. Pennarola
Bocconi University, Milan, Italy
e-mail: ferdinando.pennarola@unibocconi.it

A. M. Braccini et al. (eds.), *Technologies for Digital Transformation*, Lecture Notes in Information Systems and Organisation 64,
https://doi.org/10.1007/978-3-031-52120-1_1

1 Digital Technologies and Digital Transformation

Technology has consistently been a strong driver of transformation in the processes of organising production and economic activities in history. Innovation and continuous change of technologies afforded long-lasting cycles of development of economies and organisations. The benefits of technology innovation frequently spilt out of the focal setting of adoption, with cross-industry and economy-wide impacts [1, 2]. Indeed, continuous, and generalised development of technology brought improved work and life conditions, larger distributed welfare, scientific and economic breakthroughs and provided continued support for further technological development. Such phenomena are even more visible when *technology* is *digital technology*, which besides producing all the above-mentioned outcomes, turned out to be the strongest transformative agent for organising and organisations [3].

But digital technology is not just a diver of change. It is also an entity in continuous change, whose evolution and adoption trigger many implications for individuals, organisations, and societies. Digital technologies automate data and information processing, touching the foundations of the cognitive and intellectual processes—such as communication, information, and decision-making—that characterise human agency as individuals, and in institutions. Hence, digital technologies change the fabric of organising [3, 4].

Unlike traditional technologies that organisations have managed with waves of incremental or radical innovation and contributed to the development of processes, functions, or units, digital technologies' transformative power encompasses the entire organisation [5]. Digital technologies present in the form of interconnected systems of entities that offer action possibilities to individuals, teams, and organisations. They are applicable to the fundamental processes of organising sense-making, decision-making, and knowing, and are no longer confined within the boundaries of specialised IT departments but span across all functional areas in organisations.

In this landscape, emerging digital technologies are at the current frontier of technology development and pose significant challenges [6]. These digital technologies are on the rise, part of organisations' rapid and exploratory process of adoption. These emerging technologies trigger new affordances for organising, with opportunities and implications yet to be explored. Exploring emerging technologies and their role in the digital transformation of organisations is at the frontier of research on digital transformation, and it is the rationale that binds the chapters of this book.

2 Emerging Digital Technologies and Organisations

What do we mean by emerging digital technologies? The concept was first formulated in the EU debate on the regulation of a set of technologies that may sit on the brink of another leap forward in progress and prosperity with significant industrial and societal changes [6, 7]. In this book, we consider them as a set of digital technologies that promise significant innovation breakthroughs. At the same time, they are also not already sedimented and follow uncertain and risky evolution patterns. In spite of that, they have the potential to fundamentally shape all aspects of organising [8].

Emerging digital technologies are the result of recent innovation. Yet they are already out of laboratories. Organisations are using, exploring, and integrating them in processes and activities. The impact these technologies will have on organisations depends on the development trajectories of the technologies themselves, and on the characteristics of the organisational context in which they will be adopted, with trajectories hard to predict.

The most significant emerging technologies at the time of writing are blockchain, artificial intelligence, robotics, and internet of things. They necessarily go along with traditional digital technologies, but they all show peculiar characteristics that make them unique compared to other digital technologies, such as information systems.

Artificial intelligence, for instance, has the characteristics of autonomy. Designed to leverage the mass size of data being produced in decades by digital systems, artificial intelligence can now learn, summarise, predict, generate content, and make decisions autonomously. If artificial intelligence may empower human and organisational agency, improving decision-making, it poses a threat to potential lack of control by human agency, biased action, and arbitrary evolution.

Blockchain promotes decentralised, secure information storage and sharing among multiple actors. If blockchain promises secure and effective inter-organisational collaboration platforms and may constitute the digital backbone of mass-distributed systems, it may also potentially disrupt existing institutions leveraging on centralised control authorities.

Finally, more on the same line of thought, the internet of things and robotics promote a healthier and safer life for workers and people in general, enabling smart objects, smart cities and smart factories to warrant good production and quality of life [9, 10]. At the same time, they raise concerns of surveillance and privacy, they throw to the desk the long-standing conflict between labour versus capital and suggest implications on the future of labour in production [11].

Studying emerging digital technologies, and their implications for organisational digital transformation, along with the contextual conditions in which they are used, has merit and is necessary. In this regard, the chapters of the book tackle emerging digital technologies, or the phenomena developing around them, from different angles, and contribute with empirical, conceptual, and theoretical knowledge on exploring the implications and role of emerging digital technologies for digital transformation.

3 Researching Technologies for Digital Transformation

The chapters of these books were selected among the best papers presented at the 2022 edition of the Italian Chapter of AIS and collected on this topical book to provide an up-to-date overview of the research performed by scholars attending the Italian community of AIS on emerging technologies. The chapters underwent a double-blind review process and were included in this book to provide an interdisciplinary and multifocal perspective over technologies for digital transformation. In total 18 different papers are collected in this book, and they face technologies for digital transformation from two different points of view: the first group of chapters explore specific focal emerging technologies, both from an empirical and a conceptual point of view; the second group of chapters explore instead implications of emerging technologies for individuals, organisations, and industries.

3.1 Exploring Emerging Technologies

Chapters "Manufacturing SMEs and Artificial Intelligence: Between Promises and Paradoxes", "Investigating the Artificial Intelligence Debate in Organisation and Management Studies", "Do Forecasting Algorithms Need a Crisis-Mode? Machine Learning Based Sales Forecasting in Times of COVID-19", "Artificial Intelligence in Information Systems Research: A Socio-technical Perspective", "Blockchain and Lending Process Efficiency in the Banking Industry", and "Under Pressure: Strategic Choices and Contextual Trade-Offs of SMEs Facing Industry 4.0 Implementation" explore three specific emerging technologies: artificial intelligence, blockchain and Industry 4.0. Out of the three, artificial intelligence has got most of the attention from researchers as several chapters explore different dimensions of artificial intelligence applications.

In chapter "Manufacturing SMEs and Artificial Intelligence: Between Promises and Paradoxes", Ravarini, Zaghloul and Strada [in this volume] focus on the adoption of artificial intelligence by small and medium enterprises in the manufacturing sector, an area of research that has received relatively little attention by the IS discipline. Based on a multiple case study of three SMEs, their work highlights an articulated picture of AI adoption that differs from the profile traced by mainstream literature. They also identify a struggle of SMEs between the objectives of realizing the benefits of the investments and the actual capability of building the necessary organizational context for realizing the prospected benefits.

Chapter "Investigating the Artificial Intelligence Debate in Organisation and Management Studies" by Smacchia and Za [in this volume] still insists on the manufacturing sector, and particularly investigates artificial intelligence within the Industry 4.0 domain. They address the current academic debate on AI in the organization and management scientific literature. By way of a bibliometric analysis of 1102 articles published in academic journals, they map trends and topics of research as a starting point to deepen the knowledge of AI. Their results indicate a fervent and developing debate on the implications and on the issues related to the use of artificial intelligence.

In chapter "Do Forecasting Algorithms Need a Crisis-Mode? Machine Learning Based Sales Forecasting in Times of COVID-19" Fahse [in this volume] reflect on the forecasting capability of machine learning algorithms. Considering the importance that effective forecasting capabilities play for the management of organisations, Fahse focuses on the reliability of forecasts in uncertain times produced by the pandemic. By focusing on the performance of a sales forecast machine learning system for baked goods ad Covid-19 times, Fahse suggests adding variables to sales forecast models informing models on restrictive measures to contrast covid disease spreading, providing evidence of the improved forecast.

In chapter "Artificial Intelligence in Information Systems Research: A Socio-technical Perspective", Safei, Haki and Morin [in this volume] focus on the interdisciplinarity characteristics of AI research. They recall the organisational and socio-technical nature of information systems research, and they look at the IS literature to explore to what extent the study of AI is contributing to deepening the socio-technical understanding of AI-related phenomena. They conduct a systematic literature review informed by a socio-technical framework analysing work published in flagship IS journals. Their results reveal research focuses more on technology, tasks, and actors, leaving behind the environment and structural components, and not fully considering the interactions among all the components of a socio-technical view of AI.

Chapter "Blockchain and Lending Process Efficiency in the Banking Industry" focuses on the blockchain, while chapter "Under Pressure: Strategic Choices and Contextual Trade-Offs of SMEs Facing Industry 4.0 Implementation" on Industry 4.0.

In chapter "Blockchain and Lending Process Efficiency in the Banking Industry", Bruno and Iacoviello [in this volume] explore blockchain technology in the banking sector, addressing the dual perspective of innovation trigger and disruptive agent of this technology in this specific industry. Using a qualitative research approach that combines a literature review and a case study, they highlight innovation and improved effectiveness potential in banking processes, products, and services, particularly focusing on the potential tension between a distributed technology, and an industry that prefers centralised data storage and processing technologies.

Finally Zabudkina, Lisein and Pichault [in this volume] focus on Industry 4.0 in chapter "Under Pressure: Strategic Choices and Contextual Trade-Offs of SMEs Facing Industry 4.0 Implementation", addressing the implementation of these technologies by small and medium enterprises. They proposed a narrative literature review focusing on contextual enablers and barriers influencing SMEs strategic choices concerning Industry 4.0 implementation. Adopting an institutional approach, they propose a framework showing the division between environmental and organisational triggers leading SMEs to trade-offs regarding five dimensions of strategic choices for Industry 4.0 implementation.

3.2 Exploring Implications of Emerging Technologies

Chapters "The Context Sets the Tone: A Literature Review on Emotion Recognition from Speech Using AI", "Understanding the Links Between Neuroscience, Physiological Tools and Stress, with the Eventual Neuroscientific Impact of Culture, in Organizational, Managerial and Information Systems (IS) Fields Through a Social Network Analysis", "Digitalize Thy Place: Benefits and Challenges in the

Development of Smart Destinations", "Digital Transformation and Dysfunctions: Case Study of a Japanese Leading Technology Company, Analysis from Socio-technical Approach", "Digitalization, Online Services, and Entrepreneurial Environment in the Italian Smart Cities' Transition", "Exploring the Evolution of Digital Transformation Research in Non-profit Organisations: A Bibliometric Analysis", "How to Unlock the Value of Your Data: Six Design Guidelines for Implementing Data Strategies", "Data-Driven Failure Management: An Ontology-Based Speech Recognition App for Failure Capturing in Manufacturing Processes", "Evaluation of Innovativeness as the Success Factor of Innovative Start-Ups. Evidence from Literature", "A Bibliometric Analysis of Fab Labs Research", "The Metaverse: Digital Innovation in the Fashion Industry. A Systematic Literature Review", and ""Look! This Is the Future of Cardiology": Institutional Work and the Making of Telemedicine in Healthcare" focus instead on implications of emerging technologies integration covering the different aspects of new affordances and action possibilities of digital technologies (chapters "The Context Sets the Tone: A Literature Review on Emotion Recognition from Speech Using AI" and "Understanding the Links Between Neuroscience, Physiological Tools and Stress, with the Eventual Neuroscientific Impact of Culture, in Organizational, Managerial and Information Systems (IS) Fields Through a Social Network Analysis"), changes and transformations consequent to digitalisation (chapters "Digitalize Thy Place: Benefits and Challenges in the Development of Smart Destinations", "Digital Transformation and Dysfunctions: Case Study of a Japanese Leading Technology Company, Analysis from Socio-technical Approach", "Digitalization, Online Services, and Entrepreneurial Environment in the Italian Smart Cities' Transition", and "Exploring the Evolution of Digital Transformation Research in Non-profit Organisations: A Bibliometric Analysis"), value generated by digital technologies and digital data (chapters "How to Unlock the Value of Your Data: Six Design Guidelines for Implementing Data Strategies" and "Data-Driven Failure Management: An Ontology-Based Speech Recognition App for Failure Capturing in Manufacturing Processes"), innovations for organisations, markets and professions (chapters "Evaluation of Innovativeness as the Success Factor of Innovative Start-Ups. Evidence from Literature", "A Bibliometric Analysis of Fab Labs Research", "The Metaverse: Digital Innovation in the Fashion Industry. A Systematic Literature Review", and ""Look! This Is the Future of Cardiology": Institutional Work and the Making of Telemedicine in Healthcare").

Two chapters focus on new affordances and action possibilities of digital technologies.

In chapter "The Context Sets the Tone: A Literature Review on Emotion Recognition from Speech Using AI", Thaler, Haung, Gewald and Brune [in this volume] explore the literature on emotion recognition from speech using artificial intelligence, considering the crucial role that customers' emotions play in the service industry. They intend to focus on identifying feature types and emotion dimensions for emotional speech analysis. Their results show that these dimensions are not adequately covered in the articles they have analysed. Therefore, they develop three guidelines for future design-oriented research addressing emotion recognition.

In chapter "Understanding the Links Between Neuroscience, Physiological Tools and Stress, with the Eventual Neuroscientific Impact of Culture, in Organizational, Managerial and Information Systems (IS) Fields Through a Social Network Analysis", Silvestre and Romanelli [in this volume] perform a literature review to deepen the link between neuroscience, physiological tools, and stress in organisation, management, and information systems literature motivated by the fact that modern information and communication digital technologies can afford to collect and analyse neuroscientific data with the potential of improving research on organisational phenomena such as technostress.

Four papers explore changes and transformations consequent to digitalisation and integration of digital technologies in organisations.

In chapter "Digitalize Thy Place: Benefits and Challenges in the Development of Smart Destinations", Nicoletti, Capo and D'Agostino [in this volume] focus on digital transformation of the tourism industry and investigate how firms and territories may leverage digital transformation for the creation of smart destinations. Adopting a qualitative research design based on interviews of ten key informants, they explore the adoption of a hospitality data and intelligence platform, and how it can promote the development of the tourist destination. In their analysis, they reflect both on benefits—in terms of improved forecasting and decision-making possibilities, and increased partnership opportunities—and challenges for the tourism industry, especially referring to the lack of critical digital infrastructures, or digital competencies.

Chapter "Digital Transformation and Dysfunctions: Case Study of a Japanese Leading Technology Company, Analysis from Socio-technical Approach" by Hayashi [in this volume] focuses on failures of digital transformation process related to contextual organizational issues. The chapter explores a case study from a socio-technological point of view combining the theories of the socio-economic approach to management and the sociotechnical approach. The result of the work identifies organizational dysfunctions in terms of work fragmentation, lack of communication, and lack of coordination among team members due to a vertical and compartmentalized organizational structure. They also trace these dysfunctions to social and technical factors in play in the case unit.

In chapter "Digitalization, Online Services, and Entrepreneurial Environment in the Italian Smart Cities' Transition", Marchesani and Ceci [in this volume] focus on smart cities investigating the evolution of online services implementation in cities over the years, and the impact on the entrepreneurial environment. Using panel data based on twenty Italian cities over a period of 11 years, the chapter identifies two clusters of online services implementation: in transition and developed. The two clusters are then related to the characteristics of the entrepreneurial environment. The results of the work show that the digitalization of services in smart cities is essential to create a favourable local environment for the development of entrepreneurial opportunities.

In chapter "Exploring the Evolution of Digital Transformation Research in Non-profit Organisations: A Bibliometric Analysis", Cipriano and Za [in this volume] focus on the trends of the digital transformation research, and identify a neglected area, that of non-profit organisations, in which they target their research efforts by performing a bibliometric analysis of the literature. They analyse 586 research articles selected from SCOUPS and published from 1983 to 2022 and identify trends and topics in this area of research. Their results show that most of the attention on digital transformation of non-profit organisations is concentrated in the past 4 years where 50% of the research papers they identified were published, and that the literature samples contains five clusters of papers addressing specific topics of digital transformation in non-profit organisations.

Two papers explore value generated by digital technologies and by digital data.

In chapter "How to Unlock the Value of Your Data: Six Design Guidelines for Implementing Data Strategies", Mayer, Lanzerath, Wutzler, Quick and Peruscha [in this volume] explore design principles to unlock the value out of data. Their work starts from the observation that organisations struggle to exploit the value of their data, and as such they shall define strategies and roadmaps for managing organisational related data. Leveraging on the results of experts' interviews, the authors propose six design guidelines for helping organisations implementing data strategies, applicable across industries and at all levels or the managerial hierarchy.

In chapter "Data-Driven Failure Management: An Ontology-Based Speech Recognition App for Failure Capturing in Manufacturing Processes", Scharef, Ludwig, Bley, Wiener, and Schmidt [in this volume] address the complexity of the manufacturing process, and their potential failures, focusing on data-drive failure management. They highlight the difficulties for many small and medium enterprises to leverage data-drive failure management due to the lack of relevant failure data. Adopting a design science research approach, they develop and evaluate a novel ontology-based speech recognition app that addresses key shortcomings of currently available solutions. Their work contributes with the identification of the design requirements and principles, and with the instantiation of these principles in an app prototype to collect failure data in the context of manufacturing processes.

Finally, four papers explore innovations for organisations, markets consequent to adopting and integrating digital technologies.

In chapter "Evaluation of Innovativeness as the Success Factor of Innovative Start-Ups. Evidence from Literature", Bellini, D'Ascenzo, Gorelova, Fabbri and Ventrice [in this volume] focus on innovative start-ups, specifically on measuring their innovativeness level. With a preliminary study, they aim at developing a framework that could be useful for assessing the innovativeness capabilities of start-ups.

Still on the side of innovation, Agrifoglio, Metallo, Oppedisano and Ferrara [in this volume] explore Fab Labs research in chapter "A Bibliometric Analysis of Fab Labs Research". They conduct an online literature search using the SCOPUS databased to explore the literature on community-based workshops and fabrication labs. They identify a dataset of 148 publications and perform a bibliometric co-occurrence analysis to identify clusters of research papers and discussion topics. They identify three clusters of literature, and per each cluster, they identify the topics discussed by the literature.

The work of Grillo and Bonomi [in this volume] in chapter "The Metaverse: Digital Innovation in the Fashion Industry. A Systematic Literature Review" explores digital innovation in the fashion industry, focusing on the metaverse. Relying on a systematic literature review, they explore the use of virtual world technologies in this specific industry. Their results unveil a plethora of industry interests, intersecting many enabling technologies, including virtual reality, augmented reality, blockchain, and non-fungible tokens.

Finally, in chapter ""Look! This Is the Future of Cardiology": Institutional Work and the Making of Telemedicine in Healthcare", Zanutto, Piras, and Ponte [in this volume] focus on the telemonitoring capabilities of digital technologies for telemedicine in the healthcare industry. Their work adopts a qualitative research design exploring the process that led from the first experimental adoptions to the final codification of a clinical service, unveiling a complex ecology of actors, knowledge, and practices that are necessary to institutionalise telemonitoring in healthcare organisations. Their findings highlight how the institutionalisation of change requires continuous tuning and transformation of everyday practices.

References

1. Göransson, B., & Söderberg, J. (2005). Long waves and information technologies—On the transition towards the information society. *Technovation, 25*, 203–211. https://doi.org/10.1016/S0166-4972(03)00115-9
2. Hanel, P. (1994). Interindustry flows of technology: An analysis of the Canadian patent matrix and input-output matrix for 1978–1989. *Technovation, 14*, 529–548. https://doi.org/10.1016/0166-4972(94)90152-X
3. Zammuto, R. F., Griffith, T. L., Majchrzak, A., Dougherty, D. J., Faraj, S., Dogherty, D. J., & Faraj, S. (2007). Information technology and the changing fabric of organization. *Organization Science, 18*, 749–762. https://doi.org/10.1287/orsc.1070.0307
4. Fulk, J., & DeSanctis, G. (1995). Electronic communication and changing organizational form. *Organization Science, 6*, 337–349. https://doi.org/10.1287/orsc.6.4.337
5. Vial, G. (2019). Understanding digital transformation: A review and a research agenda. *Journal of Strategic Information Systems, 28*, 118–144. https://doi.org/10.1016/j.jsis.2019.01.003
6. European Commission. (2019). Liability for artificial intelligence and other emerging digital technologies. https://doi.org/10.2838/25362.
7. Koch, B. A. (2020). Liability for emerging digital technologies: An overview. *Journal of European Tort Law, 11*, 115–136. https://doi.org/10.1515/JETL-2020-0137
8. Bailey, D. E., Faraj, S., Hinds, P. J., Leonardi, P. M., & von Krogh, G. (2022). We are all theorists of technology now: A relational perspective on emerging technology and organizing. *Organization Science, 33*, 1–18. https://doi.org/10.1287/ORSC.2021.1562
9. Margherita, E. G., & Braccini, A. M. (2021). Managing industry 4.0 automation for fair ethical business development: A single case study. *Technological Forecasting and Social Change, 172*, 121048. https://doi.org/10.1016/j.techfore.2021.121048
10. Margherita, E. G., & Braccini, A. M. (2020). Industry 4.0 technologies in flexible manufacturing for sustainable organizational value: Reflections from a multiple case study of Italian manufacturers. *Information Systems Frontiers*. https://doi.org/10.1007/s10796-020-10047-y
11. Bootz, J. P., Michel, S., Pallud, J., & Monti, R. (2022). Possible changes of Industry 4.0 in 2030 in the face of uberization: Results of a participatory and systemic foresight study. *Technological Forecasting and Social Change, 184*. https://doi.org/10.1016/j.techfore.2022.121962

Part I
Exploring Emerging Technologies

Manufacturing SMEs and Artificial Intelligence: Between Promises and Paradoxes

Aurelio Ravarini, Fatema Zaghloul, and Emanuele Strada

Abstract Driven by the growing availability and accessibility of data and processing power, businesses across all sectors are developing and implementing increasingly "intelligent" systems that are empowered by a wave of artificial intelligence (AI) technologies. This paper examines the state of AI adoption in small and medium-sized enterprises (SMEs) in the manufacturing sector, an area of research that has received relatively little attention. Three SMEs, whose main offices are located in Northern Italy, have been studied to understand how they deal with the issue of AI adoption and what problems they typically encounter. An articulated picture emerges where SMEs struggle between the desire to realize the promises of innovation and the ability to build the appropriate organizational setting to pursue it.

Keywords Artificial intelligence · Manufacturing · SMEs

1 Introduction

Research and applications that fall under the name of Artificial Intelligence (AI) are certainly not a novelty in the panorama of digital technologies. Due to the increasing availability of data, accompanied by technological advancements in computing power and data storage, AI is becoming a sought-after technology for the development and competitiveness of companies operating in various industries [1–3].

In a recent international survey, more than 75% of respondents reported that AI will revolutionize their organization over the next 3 years, and more than 60%

A. Ravarini (✉) · E. Strada
LIUC Università Carlo Cattaneo, Castellanza-Varese, Italy
e-mail: aravarini@liuc.it; estrada@liuc.it

F. Zaghloul
University of Bristol Business School, University of Bristol, Bristol, UK
e-mail: fatema.zaghloul@bristol.ac.uk

A. M. Braccini et al. (eds.), *Technologies for Digital Transformation*, Lecture Notes in Information Systems and Organisation 64,
https://doi.org/10.1007/978-3-031-52120-1_2

believed that, in no more than 3 years, AI will transform the industry in which they operate [4]. Another recent study highlighted that, in Italy, 88% of managers believed that investing in AI enables them achieve their growth objectives and almost all consider AI as a strategic factor [5].

The manufacturing sector is facing numerous challenges in which emerging technology plays an essential role: the growing importance of the production of products with added value, the sustainability of production processes, adapting to individual customer requirements, and responding quickly to market demands [1]. It is a context characterized by increasing product and process complexity, high variability of demand and customer preferences, and continuous pressure to remain competitive [6]. Research indicates that AI-based innovations are able to gather large amounts of data, obtained from numerous sources, and assist machines in making autonomous decisions, enhancing the flexibility of processes and circularity capabilities, in addition to addressing demand planning, inventory management, and quality control [7, 8]. Despite this recognition, most studies focus primarily on AI technologies implemented in the manufacturing industry (e.g. [1]), rather than on enablers and pre-requisites for adoption at a firm-level [6].

In addition, most studies on AI adoption are based on the context of large enterprises, which have a much easier access to financial resources and up-to-date managerial and technological skills. On the other hand, it is well-known that small and medium sized enterprises (SMEs) represent an essential and prevalent strength of many economies. The so-called "coming of the AI era" might, therefore, be an inappropriate generalization of a phenomenon which is, instead, constrained to a limited portion of the worldwide economy.

Therefore, this study explores the current landscape of AI adoption in a relatively less understood and examined research area: SMEs in the manufacturing sector. Adopting a multiple case study approach consisting of three SMEs, whose main offices are located in Northern Italy, we address the following research question: *What is the state of AI adoption in manufacturing SMEs?*

The remainder of the paper is structured as follows: the next section presents a brief background into digital technology implementation and SMEs in the Italian context, followed by literature on AI in the manufacturing sector, outlining the current discourse in this area and why the Italian context is chosen. Next, we outline the methodology. In the final sections, a synopsis of our initial findings are presented and discussed. We close with some discussion on the implications and concluding remarks.

2 Digital Technology and SMEs in Italy

SMEs (defined by the European Commission as having less than 250 persons employed, an annual turnover of up to EUR 50 million, or a balance sheet total of no more than EUR 43 million) are considered the backbone of the EU and, in particular, the Italian economy [9, 10].

The adoption of digital technology by Italian SMEs has developed at different speeds over the last few years. The Italian Institute of Statistics [10] reports that between 2016 and 2018, more than half of the companies with at least 10 employees made a decision to invest in technology. However, these investments were primarily aimed at the acquisition of infrastructures (such as cloud solutions, broadband access, etc.). The Covid-19 pandemic and the consequent lockdowns of 2020 forced companies to conduct all activities that did not strictly require in-person presence remotely, which resulted in (in Italy, like elsewhere) a massive and sudden (thus, unplanned) adoption of digital tools, mainly intended to support remote work. The period between the end of the toughest lockdown to today is recognized as a 'transition' phase, characterized by a degree of ambiguity and uncertainty regarding the impact of the pandemic on work and, consequently, on the digital tools that support it. With respect to infrastructure, in 2021 just over 60% of Italian SMEs had at least a basic level of digital intensity, placing them slightly above the EU27 average (equal to 56%). In the adoption of IoT systems, Italian SMEs are eighth in Europe, while in digital skills, Italy ranks third from last [10].

3 AI Applications in Manufacturing

In this section, a short overview of AI in the manufacturing industry is provided to present the research context, along with the primary application areas, and challenges associated with their adoption.

AI refers to the technologies that allow computers and machines to accomplish tasks that would ordinarily require human intelligence [11], essentially reproducing *what* humans can do and not *how* they do it. Early developments in AI, such as knowledge management systems [12, 13], and decision support systems [14], had limitations in terms of autonomy and learning capacity. With advances in processing, data availability, and technical methodologies, AI is now being used to create advanced innovations like cognitive robots [15], algorithmic intelligence [16], and autonomous agents [17]. IS scholars have studied the impact of emerging AI technologies in a variety of organizational settings to understand how they impact (1) process efficiency and decision-making quality (in terms of assisting/supporting human decision-makers, or replacing them) (e.g. [13, 18, 19]), and (2) the development of novel and innovative data-driven services and products (e.g. [16, 20]). However, the phenomena of AI adoption in SMEs is less well understood.

3.1 AI in the Manufacturing Industry

The significance of AI as one of the technologies underpinning the concept of smart manufacturing has been recognised by scholars (e.g. [1, 21]). In principle, an AI-based system can enhance organizational processes and efficiency, as well as existing products and services. According to Mittal et al. [4], two thirds of AI project implementations involve the automation and optimization of business processes. Furthermore, the use of AI in smart factories facilitates prompt decision-making based on historical and real-time data, with minimal human involvement.

A research study conducted by the Politecnico di Milano Observatory illustrates that the value of the Italian AI market in 2020 was worth 300 million €, of which 23% was destined for the banking and finance sector, followed by 14% in the energy/utility sector, 13% for manufacturing, 12% telco/media, and 11% insurance [22].

Lu [23] provides a comprehensive overview of the development and application of AI in various fields, but AI in manufacturing is only mentioned briefly. Furthermore, there is limited research concerning the adoption and impact of AI in SMEs and exploring this phenomenon at a firm-level [6]. While it is plausible that there is a significant gap with large companies, as is normally the case for the adoption of digital technologies, SMEs have different characteristics, including limitations in financial resources, skills and pre-existing digital technologies, which determine an adoption gap at least in terms of time and often also in terms of the benefits realized.

3.2 AI Applications in Manufacturing: The Main Use Cases

Reviewing the literature revealed that the most widespread applications of AI in manufacturing are in the context of maintenance, quality control, demand forecasting and production process optimization processes [6, 24]. It is in these areas that companies have a good availability of data necessary for algorithms. Furthermore, it is argued that the corresponding AI projects require relatively less in-depth expertise, are simple to implement and generate substantial benefits (including in financial terms) and are relatively easy to estimate in the feasibility study phase.

AI applications in other areas of manufacturing require greater effort, both in terms of economic and physical resources, which are recognized as difficult to implement in SMEs, and therefore, in general, are not widespread in this context.

Predictive Maintenance Predictive maintenance and its subdomain, i.e. the prediction of the remaining life of a machine, are the most common use case of AI in manufacturing, and are often also cited as prime examples of digitization via AI.

The implementation of AI in this process is a relatively easy application case due to the availability of optimal data already present in companies. In particular, the most widespread and used Machine Learning (ML) technique are linear regression models, to predict the residual life of a machine and classification algorithms to predict a failure in a defined period of time.

The analysis of the data collected by the sensors placed on the machinery enables the prediction of potential downtime and malfunctions and subsequently plan timely interventions [25]. In addition to minimizing downtime, there is also the possibility of reducing the costs associated with maintenance, consequently optimizing the frequency of maintenance interventions and increasing productivity.

Quality Control AI systems are able to detect anomalies in products compared to optimal results, using computer vision technologies. When a product is categorized as defective, the AI systems activate a signal so that the item is identified to make changes or to be discarded [6].

Applications in this area are widespread both to (a) reduce risks: non-compliance in products can lead to dissatisfied customers and/or fines, and (b) contain costs: diffusion of high-resolution cameras, together with visual recognition technologies, reduces inspection costs despite a high degree of precision in detecting defects throughout the production process.

Other Application Areas Among other various areas of application include demand forecasting and the optimization of production processes.

Demand forecasting using ML allows companies to predict consumer demand as accurately as possible. Applications in this area can generate cascading benefits in planning and coordinating areas such as sales, marketing, supply chain, customer management and finance.

The optimization of production processes is promising with respect to the achievement of sustainability objectives. In this context, process mining applications based on AI algorithms are spreading, aimed at identifying and removing bottlenecks within processes. The monitoring of the critical parameters of the production processes also allows the creation of high-quality products at moderate costs [26].

3.3 Barriers to AI Implementation

Despite the potential benefits that justify the implementation of AI-based systems, there are numerous elements that can jeopardize the success of an AI project in manufacturing.

With respect to Italy, studies indicate that most companies have not yet adopted AI initiatives [27], and of those that have, half were merely conducting proof-of-concept experiments, applying them to a few well-defined business processes [28]. Other studies demonstrated the difficulty, or at least organizations' mistrust, in translating AI promises into reality. For example, 77% of Italian C-level executives claim to encounter issues with AI adoption [5]. Claims of efficiency and transformation are usually not substantiated by measurable empirical evidence, making it difficult to determine to what extent, how, and why AI systems are being used, their impact on organizational and individual decision-making, and their ability to transform organizational processes. This poses a problem in determining how to evaluate the short- and long-term impact of AI from a social, economic, and political perspective [13].

Furthermore, a recent survey revealed that only 20% of Italian companies successfully completed AI projects. Despite having made progress in the management of their information assets, a precondition for the implementation of AI projects, it appears that Italian companies have room for improvement in the development of skills in the creation of a corporate culture that favors the growth and dissemination of such projects and in preparing the customer for new products and services [29].

From an organizational perspective, the main obstacles are represented by the persistent difficulties in managing data and integrating AI into existing business processes [4]. In fact, most companies continue to use "silo" structures, and the IT that supports them ends up being used to optimize individual organizational units. To effectively implement AI, however, an integration of business units is required; therefore, organizations need to redesign their operating model, taking into account the digital core that requires a transformation of organizational structure, culture, and power and control [30].

Other critical issues are related to the organizational implications of AI, to the human aspects that AI modifies. In applications where AI is a tool that does not replace, but supports the decision-making process [13], an obstacle is linked to change management: people with a more rigid mentality tend to resist accepting advice suggested by a machine. In other cases, AI technologies usually maximize the efficiency of operations by automating repetitive tasks [31], and consequently, the likelihood of jobs being lost or replaced is high [22, 24, 32]. This illustrates that the acceptance and adoption of AI applications can be affected by different cultures and personal values.

Another barrier appears to be related to the fact that the intention to adopt AI solutions is not accompanied by the definition of a well-defined path and objectives, such as the adoption of standardized execution processes to exploit the scalability of the AI, and management agreement regarding the AI strategy that should be adopted.

4 Methodology

Given the dearth of existing studies, we explore the current landscape of AI adoption in SME manufacturing companies in Northern Italy. This study adopts an interpretivist multiple case study approach [33], which is well-suited to exploring and understanding information systems (IS) adoption in organizations, as well as enabling cross-case comparisons to identify whether the findings can be applied to several cases or are idiosyncratic.

To facilitate the comparability of the case study findings, companies with similar characteristics were sought. Three SMEs were identified: two companies (one small, while the other medium-sized) in the taps sector, both located in the Cusio-Valsesia industrial district, and a small company in the personal protective equipment (PPE) sector. All three companies have a typical family management, even if the medium-sized company consists of a higher degree of structured organizational characteristics.

We interviewed five stakeholders across these three organizations. Drawing on multiple organizations allowed us to explore the phenomenon from diverse and multi-layered perspectives. To find knowledgeable informants, we adopted a purposeful sampling technique, followed by the snowballing technique [34].

The interviews were conducted with key figures within the company, including the Chief Executive Officer (CEO)/entrepreneur, to obtain an insight into the general vision of the company, the production manager as they are directly involved with the production processes, and the operators as they work closely with the processes analyzed. Each interview lasted approximately 45–60 min, was audio-recorded, transcribed and annotated. The research team met frequently during data collection for debriefings to evaluate the key themes that emerged from the data in order to assure trustworthiness and rigor and to create a contextually specific understanding.

A semi-structured interview schedule was followed which focused on aspects such as the organization's culture, technological capability, goals, and processes. The guide was developed and organized according to a structure derived from the analysis of the literature in the field of 'readiness'[1] in the adoption of digital technologies, and particularly that of AI readiness. Each section of the interview referred to a factor, consisting of a set of variables, as presented in Table 1. Given the diversity of participants, the interview guide consisted of slightly different sections that were specific and tailored to the participants' role and knowledgeability.

We complemented the interview data with secondary data such as internal documents (e.g. reports, business cases) to better understand activities and previous technology adoption and implementation within the organization.

Data collection and analysis were conducted simultaneously so understanding could emerge from the theoretical concepts and empirical content. Our coding procedure followed the logic of open coding, axial coding, and selective coding. Two authors independently analysed each transcript to ensure a reliable and systematic coding process. Following this, we contrasted and compared the codes to come up with a unified, yet evolving, code-book.

5 Initial Findings

Company X

Company X S.p.a is part of the Cusio-Valsesia district of taps. In this sector, it is the only European company with a fully integrated production cycle. The interview was conducted with two organizational roles: the Chief Information Officer (CIO) and the Chief Operation Officer (COO).

[1] Readiness indicates the state required to engage in a particular activity (i.e. the adoption of a specific innovation)

Table 1 The factors and the variables subject of the empirical study

Factor	Variable
Goal of the project	Company vision IT vision
Corporate culture	Change management Top-management support AI-Awareness Team
Task	Processes Requirements Documentation
Technology	Hardware capability Algorithm Software Capability Cloud Compatibility
Data	Identification Availability Finding Quality Management Privacy
Resources	Financial People Time
External Environment	Government Data

Adapted from [35–37]

It is a family-run company, established in the 1950s and now in its third generation, employing roughly 250 people, and an annual turnover, as of 2020, of over 76 million €, up 3.8% compared to 2019. It has an export of 78%, is present in 90 countries: Germany is the main market, followed by France, Australia and South Africa (BPER). The company is at the top of the category in terms of research activity and the degree of innovation of production equipment: 452 work centers, for a total of 2.8 million items sold per year.

The third generation has given an imprint strongly linked to technological innovation, but with an eye on specific characteristics of the work environment: "*in an AI project it is essential to consider the specific characteristics of the tasks and the individuals involved*" (COO)

Consistent with this approach, the company is conducting an AI-based pilot project in the field of demand forecasting, with the medium-term objective of increasing the efficiency of its business processes, enhancing the quality of the products offered and, hence, improving brand reputation. Another project involves the application of AI to enhance quality control, achieved by integrating computer vision technologies into existing processes. The company has not yet been able to make this second project operational due to technical problems, including the complexity of recognizing signs on reflective and chromed surfaces, for which the company has not been able to identify suitable cameras.

The first project is based on the Amazon Web Services (AWS) service: a relatively easy solution to implement because specific investments in hardware and software technologies are not required (the system is in-the-cloud), nor does it imply compatibility problems with pre-existing technologies. The organizational impact is also reduced: the solution does not require specific skills in using the service. As for the data, the solution is based on historical sales data, available internally. Data privacy is not a very relevant factor in this project as it primarily deals with sales data, which does not require protective measures. While the project can be completed with the available financial resources, it is unclear how long it will take for the pilot phase to become fully operational.

As the project is in the pilot phase, the company developed its own methodology to support change. The team dedicated to the project is an inter-functional team, which sees the IT and Operation department as protagonists, which are expected to be accompanied by external AI consultants, both to compensate for the limited technological skills, and as the solution identified so far is not considered entirely satisfactory by the company.

The identified solution therefore constitutes a first approach to AI as a tool for extracting relevant information from data and redesigning a business process of strategic interest. The success of this initiative is largely linked to its simplicity. As the CIO reported: "*since the company bases its success on Operations most of the workers are employed on operations-related tasks and have very limited skills in digital technology*", necessary to support the adoption of more sophisticated AI solutions. For projects of a more innovative nature, which would require ad hoc developed solutions, the company would not be ready: from an operational point of view, investments in new hardware and software resources and the development of technological knowledge for staff are required. From a strategic point of view, top management has not taken into consideration the possibility of a large-scale change and therefore processes are not studied with the aim of identifying the critical ones that could benefit from AI implementation.

Company Y

Company Y is a small company (employing roughly 50 employees) with headquarters in Lombardy, operating in the sector of tools, special equipment and PPE. The interview was conducted with the head of business development, who is also a member of the board of directors.

The company was born from a small family business which managed to grow and reach the fifth generation with a series of successes. The core business is integrated industrial distribution, followed by design and production. This is a B2B activity, in which the single order has a significant value. It follows the importance of establishing long-term relationships with the customer: the company has business relationships with over 3000 companies worldwide. Its competitive advantage therefore derives from its breadth of offering (the product portfolio includes 600,000 high-quality items), and the services provided to customers (pre-, during and after-sales).

Company Y has an open entrepreneurial mentality and is inclined to technological innovation. Some innovations have been implemented not only to enhance internal processes, but also in relation to the products and services offered, and increase their competitive advantage.

Despite declaring a significant interest in AI, the company has not yet implemented projects based on these technologies. The reason given by the head of business development is that "*an adequate AI application has not yet been found for the objective of internal improvement*". For example, one of the initiatives that was taken into considered was for an algorithm that predicts the financials at the end of the year, using a variety of heterogeneous data (including the management system, data on motorway traffic, exchange rates). After testing the solution, it was determined that it would not produce reliable and accurate results.

From the analysis of this case, the picture of a company well-prepared for the adoption of AI emerges. Top management has a strong propensity for technological innovation and is ready to invest in projects as long as they are consistent with the corporate vision. With respect to human resources, the company is aware of the fact that staff only have the necessary skills to complete the AI project, but not to be able to sustain it over time. For this reason, both training activities and the development of a methodology to support change are planned, to facilitate the implementation of new projects.

> The C-suite members have a strong inclination towards innovation, while the middle management is used to a more routinary approach .. that's why the former are keen to transmit trust into digital innovation to the latter.

Finally, from a technological viewpoint, the company has equipped itself with open and well-structured IS, thus reducing the risk of incompatibility with any future AI solutions.

In summary, the analysis demonstrates that the company has established plausible conditions for the adoption of AI. A possible explanation for the lack of implementation, even at a 'pilot project' stage, can be associated with the search for a very specific goal for the adoption of AI, to the point where it limits the capacity for innovation as it can result in overly restricting the choice of an application or initiative deemed adequate.

Company Z

Company Z S.r.l. (employs 50 people) specializes in thermostatic mixers and is now recognized for the quality of 'Made in Italy' and for innovation in the sector. The interview was conducted with the entrepreneur, who is also the founder of the company, and the general manager.

Despite having a management system and two manufacturing execution systems (MES) for sharing and analysis production data, the company is far from being digitalized. Furthermore, it appeared that the interest in undertaking technological innovation interventions on processes was secondary compared to product innovation, centered on design. The absence of AI projects is a direct consequence of this situation. However, the company has considered applications for predictive analysis of demand using customer data, but has not taken further steps, for example by creating a proof-of-concept.

The analysis of the case shows that the approach to AI is fundamentally conditioned by the lack of adequate personnel, who have the necessary technological knowledge in the AI field, but above all a vision on the possible uses and the related benefits. In this sense, the interest in evaluating AI solutions would seem unrealistic. According to the interviewee, "*the lack of interest in AI is not only a product of cognitive bias of the management, scarcely inclined to innovation, it is also due to our general lack of interest to the strategic impact of digital-enabled projects*".

However, it is worth acknowledging whether this strategy underpins the failure of digitization (generally, and in the direction of AI adoption) or, on the other hand, whether the small size of the company itself allows for effective management and efficiency without turning to the use of emerging technologies. According to the latter, evaluating AI has a rather purely reputational purpose: its only purpose is to communicate an '*image*' of an innovative company to partners and customers.

6 Discussion: Between Promises and Paradoxes

The aim of this research was to explore the state of AI adoption in Italian SMEs in the manufacturing sector. The analysis revealed that none of the three SMEs have turned to the AI applications that are cited in the literature as the most promising in the manufacturing sector. The preference for demand forecasting and process optimization over quality control and predictive maintenance could indicate that these latter two processes are either less strategically important or not complex enough to merit the sophistication of an AI algorithm in SMEs.

A second observation concerns the progress of the adoption of AI in SMEs. All three companies studied claim to be "*oriented*" towards AI for manufacturing. However, none of them have completed a project, and indeed, the smaller ones appear to be stalled at the evaluation stage. A possible explanation is the superficial knowledge of the technology, partially inevitable since it is an emerging technology. On this basis, managers are unable to fully identify the benefits, limitations and organizational implications of AI implementation. This general limit is amplified by the reduced availability of skills and financial resources, typical of small businesses. Therefore, investments are directed elsewhere; on projects whose benefits and relevance can be estimated, even in the short term, and the opportunity to exploit the promises of AI is lost at the root. This highlights that firm characteristics and organizational readiness influence the likelihood of adopting emerging digital technologies as suggested by Cho et al. [38] and Chatterjee [26], and hence, typically, larger firms appear to have an advantage in gaining considerable resources to leverage new technologies. Our findings support previous research (e.g. [39]) indicating that if adequate technical and financial resources, as well as trained employees, are available, adopting innovative technologies is not a problem.

However, it should be noted that the two small firms investigated in this research exhibit contrasting characteristics. These are very similar organizations (they operate in the same industry, in the same geographic area, and are of comparable size) and similarly declare an active interest in AI applications. Company Y, however, has laid the technological and organizational foundations to be able to move from the study phase of alternative solutions to the implementation of a project. Company Z, on the other hand, appears to be less prepared to face the complexity of an AI project: even if it identified a solution to be implemented, it would not have the necessary pre-conditions to mitigate the inevitable risk associated with an investment in an emerging technology. The company would thus find itself in the paradoxical situation in which the push towards technological innovation would itself be the cause of its probable failure.

7 Conclusion

This study addresses a topic that is as relevant as it is controversial. While the significant recent advances in digital technologies commonly identified with the expression "*artificial intelligence*" are evident, it is unclear in which areas they can generate benefits for organizations, and under what conditions. Like all emerging technologies, in reality, AI brings with it a significant dose of uncertainty about its effectiveness in any context. In particular, a technology that promises to improve organizational processes must take into account the typical characteristics of such processes, which vary considerably from sector to sector. Furthermore, the studies available on AI applications in manufacturing usually take into account large companies: extending their results to SMEs implicitly assumes that the very different conditions in which smaller companies operate have no influence on the impact of AI adoption. Given the importance of SMEs and their crucial role in economic sustainability, this study explored the current landscape of AI adoption in the context of three Italian manufacturing SMEs. On the one hand, the research illustrates the numerous potential benefits of AI in manufacturing and, on the other hand, reveals an articulated reality: SMEs struggling between the will to realize the promises of technological innovation and the lack of an adequate organizational setting to pursue it.

References

1. Zeba, G., Dabić, M., Čičak, M., Daim, T., & Yalcin, H. (2021). Technology mining: Artificial intelligence in manufacturing. *Technological Forecasting and Social Change, 171*.
2. Coombs, C., Hislop, D., Taneva, S. K., & Barnard, S. (2020). The strategic impacts of Intelligent Automation for knowledge and service work: An interdisciplinary review. *The Journal of Strategic Information Systems, 29*(4), 1–30.

3. Sharma, M., Luthra, S., Joshi, S., & Kumar, A. (2022). Implementing challenges of artificial intelligence: Evidence from public manufacturing sector of an emerging economy. *Government Information Quarterly, 39*(4), 101624.
4. Mittal, N., Saif, I., & Silverglate, P. (2020, 07). *Deloitte survey: State of AI in the enterprise, third edition: Thriving in the era of pervasive AI.* Retrieved from https://www2.deloitte.com/us/en/pages/about-deloitte/articles/press-releases/deloitte-survey-state-of-ai-in-the-enterprise-third-edition.html
5. Awalegaonkar, K., Berkey, R., Douglass, G., & Reilly, A. (2019). *AI: Fatta Per Scalare.* Retrieved from https://www.accenture.com/it-it/insights/artificial-intelligence/ai-investments
6. Kinkel, S., Baumgartner, M., & Cherubini, E. (2022). Prerequisites for the adoption of AI technologies in manufacturing—Evidence from a worldwide sample of manufacturing companies. *Technovation, 110.*
7. Li, B. H., Hou, B. C., Yu, W. T., Lu, X. B., & Yang, C. W. (2017). Applications of artificial intelligence in intelligent manufacturing: a review. *Frontiers of Information Technology & Electronic Engineering, 18*(1), 86–96.
8. Bag, S., Pretorius, J. H. C., Gupta, S., & Dwivedi, Y. K. (2021). Role of institutional pressures and resources in the adoption of big data analytics powered artificial intelligence, sustainable manufacturing practices and circular economy capabilities. *Technological Forecasting and Social Change, 163*, 120420.
9. Eurostat, S. A. (2017). *Your key to European statistics.* Retrieved from https://ec.europa.eu/eurostat/web/structural-business-statistics/small-and-medium-sized-enterprises
10. Istat. (2022). *Digitalizzazione e tecnologia nelle imprese italiane.* Retrieved from https://www.istat.it/it/files//2022/01/REPORT-ICT-NELLE-IMPRESE_2021.pdf
11. Kaplan, A., & Haenlein, M. (2019). Siri, Siri, in my hand: Who's the fairest in the land? On the interpretations, illustrations, and implications of artificial intelligence. *Business Horizons, 62*(1), 15–25.
12. Alavi, M., & Leidner, D. E. (2001). Review: Knowledge management and knowledge management systems: Conceptual foundations and research issues. *MIS Quarterly, 25*(1), 107–136.
13. Duan, Y., Edwards, J. S., & Dwivedi, Y. K. (2019). Artificial intelligence for decision making in the era of Big Data—Evolution, challenges and research agenda. *International Journal of Information Management, 48*, 63–71.
14. El-Najdawi, M. K., & Stylianou, A. C. (1993). Expert support systems: Integrating AI technologies. *Communications of the ACM, 36*(12), 55–103.
15. Aleksander, I. (2017). Partners of humans: A realistic assessment of the role of robots in the foreseeable future. *Journal of Information Technology, 32*(1), 1–9.
16. Günther, W. A., Rezazade Mehrizi, M. H., Huysman, M., & Feldberg, F. (2017). Debating big data: A literature review on realizing value from big data. *The Journal of Strategic Information Systems, 26*(3), 191–209.
17. Nunamaker, J. F., Derrick, D. C., Elkins, A. C., Burgoon, J. K., & Patton, M. W. (2011). Embodied conversational agent-based kiosk for automated interviewing. *Journal of Management Information Systems, 28*(1), 17–48.
18. Ghasemaghaei, M., Ebrahimi, S., & Hassanein, K. (2018). Data analytics competency for improving firm decision making performance. *The Journal of Strategic Information Systems, 27*(1), 101–113.
19. Dwivedi, Y. K., Hughes, L., Ismagilova, E., Aarts, G., Coombs, C., Crick, T., Duan, Y., Dwivedi, R., Edwards, J., Eirug, A., Galanos, V., Ilavarasan, P. V., Janssen, M., Jones, P., Kar, A. K., Kizgin, H., Kronemann, B., Lal, B., Lucini, B., ... & Williams, M. D. (2021). Artificial Intelligence (AI): Multidisciplinary perspectives on emerging challenges, opportunities, and agenda for research, practice and policy. *International Journal of Information Management, 57.*
20. Bardhan, I., Chen, H., & Karahanna, E. (2020). Connecting systems, data, and people: A multidisciplinary research roadmap for chronic disease management. *Management Information Systems Quarterly, 44*, 185–200.

21. Kusiak, A. (2018). Smart manufacturing. *International Journal of Production Research, 56*(1–2), 508–517.
22. Osservatorio Artificial Intelligence. (2021). *All-in: puntare sull'intelligenza artificiale per la ripresa del Sistema Paese*. Politecnico di Milano – Dipartimento di Ingegneria Gestionale.
23. Lu, Y. (2019). Artificial intelligence: a survey on evolution, models, applications and future trends. *Journal of Management Analytics, 6*(1), 1–29.
24. Margherita, E. G., & Braccini, A. M. (2020). Industry 4.0 technologies in flexible manufacturing for sustainable organizational value: reflections from a multiple case study of Italian manufacturers. *Information Systems Frontiers,* 1–22.
25. Hazen, B. T., Boone, C. A., Ezell, J. D., & Jones-Farmer, L. A. (2014). Data quality for data science, predictive analytics, and big data in supply chain management: An introduction to the problem and suggestions for research and applications. *International Journal of Production Economics, 154*, 72–80.
26. Chatterjee, S., Rana, N. P., Dwivedi, Y. K., & Baabdullah, A. M. (2021). Understanding AI adoption in manufacturing and production firms using an integrated TAM-TOE model. *Technological Forecasting and Social Change, 170.*
27. Morielli, M., & Galimberti, L. (2018). *Intelligenza Artificiale: Istruzioni per L'uso*. Retrieved from Accenture: https://www.accenture.com/it-it/insights/artificial-intelligence/artificial-intelligence-explained-executives
28. Fountaine, T., McCarthy, B., & Saleh, T. (2019). Building the AI-powered organization. *Harvard Business Review, 97*(4), 62–73.
29. Galasso, D., Micello, E., & Erba, S. (2020). *Artificial intelligence: Learn to fly! Osservatorio Artificial Intelligence*. Politecnico di Milano - Dipartimento di Ingegneria Gestionale.
30. Iansiti, M., & Lakhani, K. R. (2020). Competing in the age of AI: How machine intelligence changes the rules of business. *Harvard Business Review, 98*(1), 60–67.
31. Huang, M. H., Rust, R., & Maksimovic, V. (2019). The feeling economy: Managing in the next generation of artificial intelligence (AI). *California Management Review, 61*(4), 43–65.
32. Loureiro, S. M. C., Guerreiro, J., & Tussyadiah, I. (2021). Artificial intelligence in business: State of the art and future research agenda. *Journal of Business Research, 129*, 911–926.
33. Yin, R. K. (2013). *Case study research: Design and methods*. Sage.
34. Lincoln, Y. S., & Guba, E. G. (1985). *Naturalistic inquiry*. Sage.
35. Haren, V. (2018). *TOGAF version 9.2*. Van Haren.
36. Hughes, H. P., Clegg, C. W., Bolton, L. E., & Machon, L. C. (2017). Systems scenarios: a tool for facilitating the socio-technical design of work systems. *Ergonomics, 60*(10), 1319–1335.
37. Holmstrom, J. (2021). From AI to digital transformation: The AI readiness framework. *Business Horizons, 65*(3), 329–339.
38. Cho, J., DeStefano, T., Kim, H., Kim, I., & Paik, J. H. (2022). What's driving the diffusion of next-generation digital technologies? *Technovation, 119*, 102477.
39. Ransbotham, S., Kiron, D., Gerbert, P., & Reeves, M. (2017). Reshaping business with artificial intelligence: Closing the gap between ambition and action. *MIT Sloan Management Review, 59*(1).

Investigating the Artificial Intelligence Debate in Organisation and Management Studies

Marco Smacchia and Stefano Za

Abstract Nowadays, the number of organisations inside Industry 4.0 adopting new technologies based on Artificial Intelligence (AI) is continuously increasing. Scholars are not neglecting this phenomenon, investigating related topics, not only from a technological point of view but also in the organisational and societal domains. The goal of this paper is to provide a broad overview of the current debate on AI in organisation studies. To this end, we decided to perform a bibliometric analysis on 1102 articles published in journals belonging to organisation and management fields of the Academic Journal Guide. As a result, we identified a publication increase concerning societal and ethical issues about AI. Furthermore, through a co-word analysis, we mapped and described the main topics related to our research domain, finding that many of them are experiencing a period of renewed interest from academics. The following research is a starting point to deepen knowledge on AI and to find insights that could lead to new research opportunities.

Keywords Artificial intelligence · Bibliometric analysis · Machine learning · Co-word analysis · Organisation studies · Management

1 Introduction

The artificial intelligence (AI) debate started more than 50 years ago. More precisely, in 1956, during a conference at Dartmouth University, for the first time, the term identifying a technology able to simulate human intelligent activities was introduced [1]. Nowadays, after 50 years, AI remains a highly discussed topic in literature thanks to the rise of Big Data, the increased computational power at our disposal and the increasing importance of the digital transformation process [2].

M. Smacchia (✉) · S. Za
University "G. D'Annunzio" of Chieti-Pescara, Pescara, Italy
e-mail: marco.smacchia@unich.it; stefano.za@unich.it

A. M. Braccini et al. (eds.), *Technologies for Digital Transformation*, Lecture Notes in Information Systems and Organisation 64,
https://doi.org/10.1007/978-3-031-52120-1_3

Artificial Intelligence is defined as "a system's ability to interpret external data correctly, to learn from such data, and to use those learnings to achieve specific goals and tasks through flexible adaptation" [3]. Therefore, AI technology can simulate intelligent human behaviour by performing tasks that improve labour efficiency, reduce costs, enhance human resource structure, and create new jobs [4]. Currently, the AI applications used are defined as Artificial Narrow Intelligence (ANI), in which case the machine is able to replicate a task in a similar way to that of the human brain (e.g., Machine Learning). However, there are two further steps, namely Artificial General Intelligence (AGI) and Artificial Superintelligence (ASI), where the machine becomes self-aware and, respectively, equals and exceeds human capabilities [5]. Today, we are limited in using ANI applications (e.g. face recognition on social networks, smart speakers), but in the future, AGI and then ASI, defined as the "true artificial intelligence", could represent a further revolution for our society [6].

Artificial intelligence is among the most relevant topics of the last decade and is reshaping human interaction in various domains, from everyday tasks to working life [7]. AI could have internal and external implications for every kind of organisation. It allows improving both simple and complex tasks by reducing time and costs and impacting the relationship with external stakeholders [6]. Although the benefits of AI are many, the challenges it introduces are equally numerous. On the one hand, there are issues related to the adoption and implementation of AI technology, such as change in organisational process and culture, that takes a long time to be deployed. On the other hand there are social dysfunction problems that comprise privacy and decision-making process and issues related to talent acquisition [8]. Moreover, the implementation of artificial intelligence technologies and their adoption often lead to some forms of resistance from employees and managers [9, 10]. Many perceive AI as a possible replacement for their work, mainly when applied to solving analytical and communication tasks. In these cases, although AI is a continuous source of innovation, it could affect human employment and human behaviour [10].

Since the introduction of these new technologies, studies on the adoption of artificial intelligence have increased significantly, especially in recent years, fostering new theories and opening up further questions [7]. Although in the organisational sphere technology has been considered as one of the fundamental factors in shaping the forms of organisation and its functions, the number of studies investigating the impact of new technologies on organisational processes has declined over time, at least until the advent of the fourth industrial revolution.

Industry 4.0 represents the technological evolution mainly exploiting the concept of cyber-physical environment, where material/physical world is integrated with the virtual/digital space. To reach this goal many technologies like IoT, Cloud Computing, artificial intelligence and Simulation are becoming of utmost importance [11]. Starting less than a decade ago, the interest of scholars in such issues has increased, as well as the interest in investigating issues related to new artificial intelligence-based technologies within organisational environments [12]. For this reason, the aim of this paper is to identify the main issues and aspects analysed and discussed in the literature from a managerial and organizational perspective, without focusing on a specific sector or AI technology, differentiating this contribution from previous studies. Moreover, since artificial intelligence is an ever-evolving technology [13], we believe that cyclic studies can help to discover new insights within the specific field of study as well as to have an updated overview on the advancement of the literature.

In light of what is stated above, we believe it may be of interest to map and evaluate the existing literature [14] on the application of artificial intelligence solutions within an organisational context to identify new issues and research gaps that may lead to future studies. This study is a starting point to accomplish the main objective of the research. More specifically, we conducted a review of the literature concerning the discussion of AI issues in organisational settings to identify the main topics in order to develop a proper query for defining our initial dataset. Using the refined dataset, we performed a bibliometric co-word analysis since our scope is to build a conceptual structure of the domain by exploring the relationship between the contributions of our dataset [15] and since we needed to analyse a broad number of articles quantitatively.

2 Theoretical Framework

Since the studies concerning AI have increased exponentially in recent years, it is not surprising that systematic literature reviews and especially bibliometric analysis are widely used as review methods. Interestingly, the papers cover a broad range of topics, indicating that AI, inside the organisational setting, is being applied in different areas for different purposes.

Dhamija and Bag [16] performed a bibliometric analysis to review AI research in combination with operation management. They used WoS and Scopus as databases for the study and performed the analysis on 1854 articles published between 2018 and 2019. Results showed the presence of six interconnected clusters concerning AI technology in operation management. More specifically, the authors focused on sustainability issues relating to supply chain management. Reis et al. [17] explored AI advancement in the public sector by reviewing 74 articles. Their results showed a strong influence of artificial intelligence inside governmental organisations and differences between countries in AI development and implementation strategy. Verma et al. [18] reviewed 1580 papers published between 1982 and 2020 on the importance of AI in marketing. They explored the intellectual structure and trending topic with co-citation and addressed future research direction on the subject. Their findings highlighted an increase in publications and citations inside the debate. Riahi et al. [19] conducted a bibliometric analysis on AI applications inside the supply chain. They reviewed 136 articles written between 1996 and 2020. The results provide a framework for AI implementation inside supply chain processes. Finally, Wamba and Queiroz [20] provide a bibliometric review describing the relationship between AI and digital health approaches considering responsible AI and ethical aspects of scientific production.

The study was based on 14,128 articles written between 1977 and 2020. Their findings underline an increase of publications started in 2015. They also identify and describe the main topics related to digital health phenomena.

In Table 1 we compare the reviews to clarify better what is done in AI field and the approach that different authors have chosen to analyse AI studies. Differently from the other papers we use a similar framework of research to explore a broader domain concerning all kinds of organisation and management studies since this study is a starting point to identify the main topics concerning AI in this specific domain and assess which is the most relevant to investigate in further research.

Table 1 Bibliometric review on AI comparison

Article	Methodology	Focus	Findings
Dhamija and Bag [16]	Bibliometric Literature Review (Network analysis) 1854 articles published between 2018 and 2019	Review AI and related domains in combination with operation management	Identified six clusters that focus on predominant themes for present and future research
Reis et al. [17]	Bibliometric Literature Review and Content Analysis 74 articles published before 2018	Review of AI in government services: analysis of countries spending on AI and recommendations on areas to implement	Identified areas of research concerning the use of AI in the public sector and EU–USA policies comparison
Verma et al. [18]	Bibliometric Literature Review (Co-citation and Co-occurrence analysis) 1580 articles published between 1982 and 2020	Review of AI inside marketing sector	Identified most relevant sources and researchers in the field, along with relevant topic and future research directions
Riahi et al. [19]	Bibliometric Literature Review (Citation and Semantic analysis) 136 articles published between 1996 and 2020 (Same tool and process used)	Review of the application of AI in supply chain processes	The authors provide a framework to identify success factor for AI adoption inside supply chain processes, the identify also future research opportunities
Wamba and Queiroz [20]	Bibliometric Literature Review (Co-citation and Co-occurrence analysis) 14,128 articles published between 1977 and 2020	Review of the studies on Responsible AI inside digital health sector	Identified the main contributions, sources and trends in the field. The authors provide a framework that identified the most important field of research concerning the topic

3 Research Methodology

This contribution aims to explore and summarise the debate on artificial intelligence in organisation studies using a bibliometric approach. Bibliometric analysis quantitively explores and analyses a large volume of scientific data through a reproducible, transparent and rigorous method [21, 22]. Although the bibliometric methodology debate started in the 1950s, the proliferation of bibliometric review is relatively recent, especially in management and social science fields [22].

Since our goal is to inspect the relationship between our dataset documents and build a conceptual structure of the domain, we decided to perform a co-word analysis [15]. This method is based on the assumption that if words frequently co-occur inside documents, the concepts behind those words are closely related. The difference between co-word analysis and other bibliometric approaches like co-citation and co-authorship involves analysing the document's content [23]. Co-word analysis also allows us to discover interactions between different research domains by showing the main concept relationship between them [24].

The quality of keywords, the selection of the literature to analyse, and the statistical tools used to perform analysis are of utmost importance to obtain quality results from a co-word analysis [25]. To select the literature and conduct the study, we adapted the framework (see Fig. 1) suggested by Za and Braccini [26], consisting of a three-step analysis.

First, we had to set our dataset by identifying the appropriate list of journals to perform the query selecting the papers for creating our dataset. The Academic Journal Guide (https://charteredabs.org/academic-journal-guide-2021/) of the Association of Business Schools (ABS) provides a list of journals classified according to the field of studies to which they belong and their ranking. Concerning the areas, we considered those belonging to the organisational sphere, such as: "Entrepreneurship and Small Business Management", "General Management, Ethics, Gender and Social Responsibility", "Human Resource Management and Employment Studies", "Information Management", "Innovation", "Management

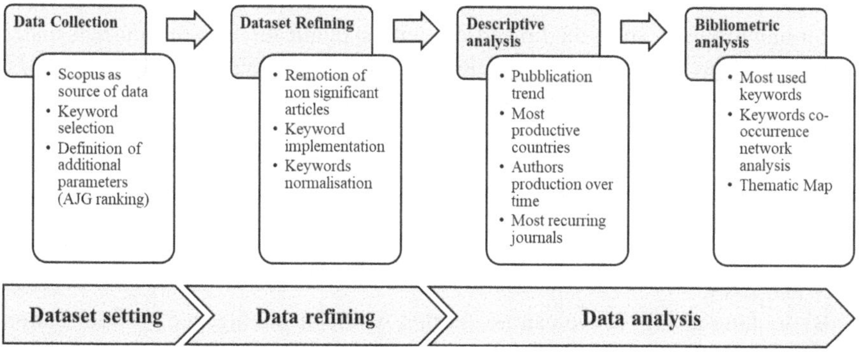

Fig. 1 Research protocol

Development and Education", "Organisational Studies", "Public Sector and Health Care", "Social Sciences" and "Strategy". For these fields, in order to focus on the most relevant results of the research debate, we considered journals with AJG ratings of 4* (grade 4 journals that are recognised worldwide as exemplars of excellence), 4 (all journals with a rating of 4 publish the most original and best-executed research) and 3 (3-rated journals publish original and well-executed research papers and are highly regarded). The data were collected within Scopus (https://www.scopus.com/) since all the journals we decided to incorporate into the search were available in the academic database. Specifically, we performed a query in which we included all the chosen journals by entering their ISSN code and the keyword "Artificial Intelligence". We did not use time or other restrictions. The query returned 1175 articles published between 1983 and 2022; citation and abstract data were exported in CSV format.

The subsequent step consisted of the data cleaning process; we first deleted the articles with no information (missing author, author keywords and abstract information) and integrated the author keywords in the papers where they were missing by cross-checking abstracts and indexed keywords. During this process, we also excluded articles with no reference to our research domain by looking at the title, keywords, and abstracts. At the end of the process, the sample was composed of 1102 articles. The last step in the data refining process was homogenising the keywords inside the dataset. All the keywords that indicated the same topic were replaced with a single word [21], the process was conducted and revised by both authors.

The subsequent steps concerning the data analysis were carried out using R and the bibliometrix package [27].

4 Descriptive Bibliometric Analysis

The analysis was conducted in February 2022. The dataset comprises 1175 articles, reduced to 1102 after the data refining process, published in 86 sources with an average citation per document of 30.9. The oldest article was published in 1983. According to Fig. 2, since the first article, annual publications in the journals under review have rarely exceeded 25 articles, with the only exception in 1994. In 2012 and 2013, there was an increase in publications to over 75 articles annually, but the trend settled once again between 25 and 50 articles in the following year. Finally, in 2021 there was a very significant increase in the number of published contributions to over 200, corresponding to 17.9% of the total number of articles investigated. The graph shows that this trend will likely continue in 2022, as the dataset was created in mid-February 2022, and the articles are only slightly smaller than the total in 2020 and 2019.

By looking at Fig. 3, we can assess that Artificial Intelligence in organisation studies is a topic with worldwide relevance. The graph shows the most productive countries, according to the authors' affiliation, and distinguishes between papers

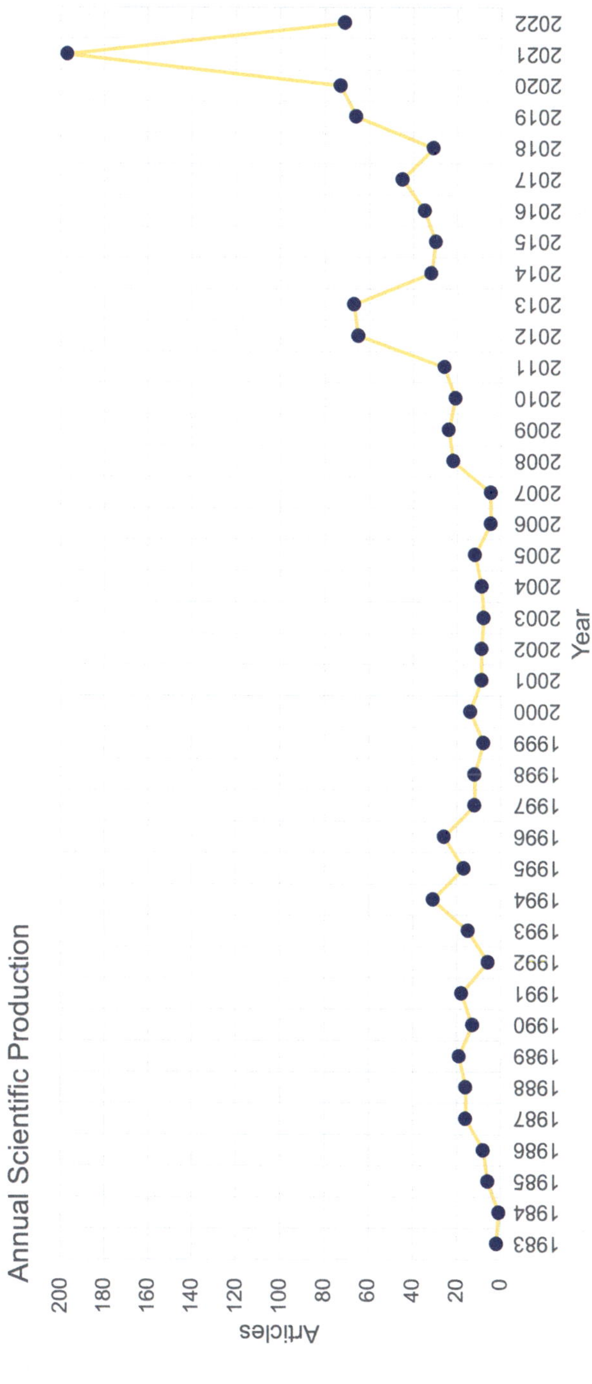

Fig. 2 Number of publications per year since 1983

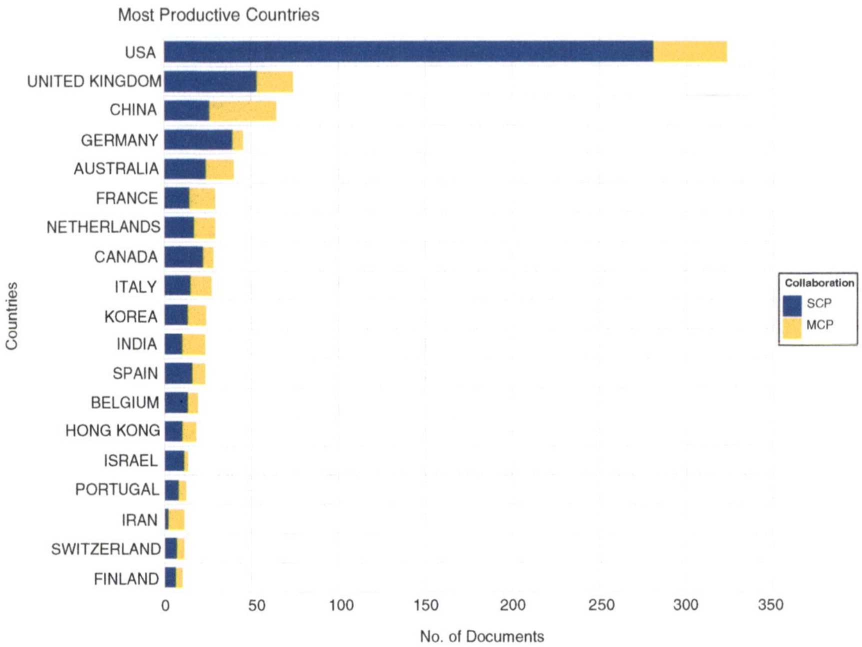

Fig. 3 Most productive countries

where the authors are from the same country (Single Country Publication—SCP) and papers whose authors come from different countries (Multiple Country Publication—MCP). By looking at the graph, the debate on Artificial Intelligence inside organisation studies is mainly developed in the USA. In fact, they have a greater number of publications concerning the other countries (323 papers). The United States is followed by the UK (74 papers) and China (64 papers). All the most productive countries have both single and multiple collaborations. It is interesting to note that China and Iran are the only countries where MCP are significantly higher than SCP, and China is also the second most collaborative region (38 papers) after the USA (42 papers).

In the analysis (see Table 2), we also considered the average article citation per country to assess better the impact of a specific country inside the scientific community. Interestingly, there is little correspondence between the number of articles published, the total citations and the average article citation. In fact, the US is the most productive country with the most citations, yet the average citation is higher in the Netherlands. Moreover, despite having one fifth of its publications, the other countries are very close to its average. This trend could be related to the high quality of the papers within the dataset, which were selected from the best journals (3, 4, 4*) in the AJG ranking.

Figure 4 represents the authors' production over time. The dot size expresses the number of published articles, while the intensity of the colour indicates the total citations per year. Over time, the two most productive authors were Chen H. and

Table 2 Total citations and average article

Country	Articles	Total citations	Average article citation
USA	323	12,335	38.19
United Kingdom	74	2344	31.68
China	64	1812	28.31
Germany	45	1014	22.53
Australia	40	841	21.02
Netherlands	29	1249	43.07
France	29	598	20.62
Canada	28	887	31.68
Italy	27	609	22.56
Korea	24	697	29.04

Delen D., with 8 and 7 articles. Chen H. published from 1994 to 2010, while Delen D. from 2011 to 2022. Chen H., Benbasat I. and Delen D. are also the authors that have the highest impact within the dataset, with an h-index of 8, 6 and 5, respectively. Benbasat I and Chen H. are also the authors with the highest citation count (956 and 941). Chen H. and Delen D. are also the authors that published the articles with the highest impact (659 and 384 citations). Both papers were published in the journal Decision Support System in 2004 and 2013. It is also interesting to note that, with the exception of Chen H., the articles that have had the most influence on the literature have been published in the last decade. Finally, similar to what is represented in Fig. 2, the results show how the topic interest is growing over time, especially in the previous 2 years.

Studies on the application of artificial intelligence-based technologies in organisational settings are published in various journals. In our search, we selected the best sources within the AJG ranking closely related to organisation studies. Table 3 highlights the journal with the higher number of publications concerning the research domain examined, the relative AJG ranking and the AJG field.

The most prolific journals are Decision Support Systems, with 362 out of the 1102 articles and Journal of the American Society for Information Science and Technology (JASIST), with 93 papers. The first four sources account for about 55% of the total number of documents, all belong to the Information Management branch, and all have a ranking of 3. Looking at the field of study and the journal ranking, we can see that most papers (770) belong to the Information Management category. The ranking of the ten most impactful journals also includes the *Journal of Business Research, Journal of Environmental Management* and *Risk Analysis* that belong to the categories *General Management, Ethics, Gender and Social Responsibility* and *Social Sciences*.

Of the 770 articles belonging to information management, 60 were published in journals with a rating of 4*, 51 in journals with a rating of 4 and 659 in journals with a rating of 3. It is very interesting to note that the second most prolific category is a social science, with 115 papers, of which two were published in journals rated 4*, 32 in journals rated 4 and 81 in journals rated 3. Moreover, most of the papers in this

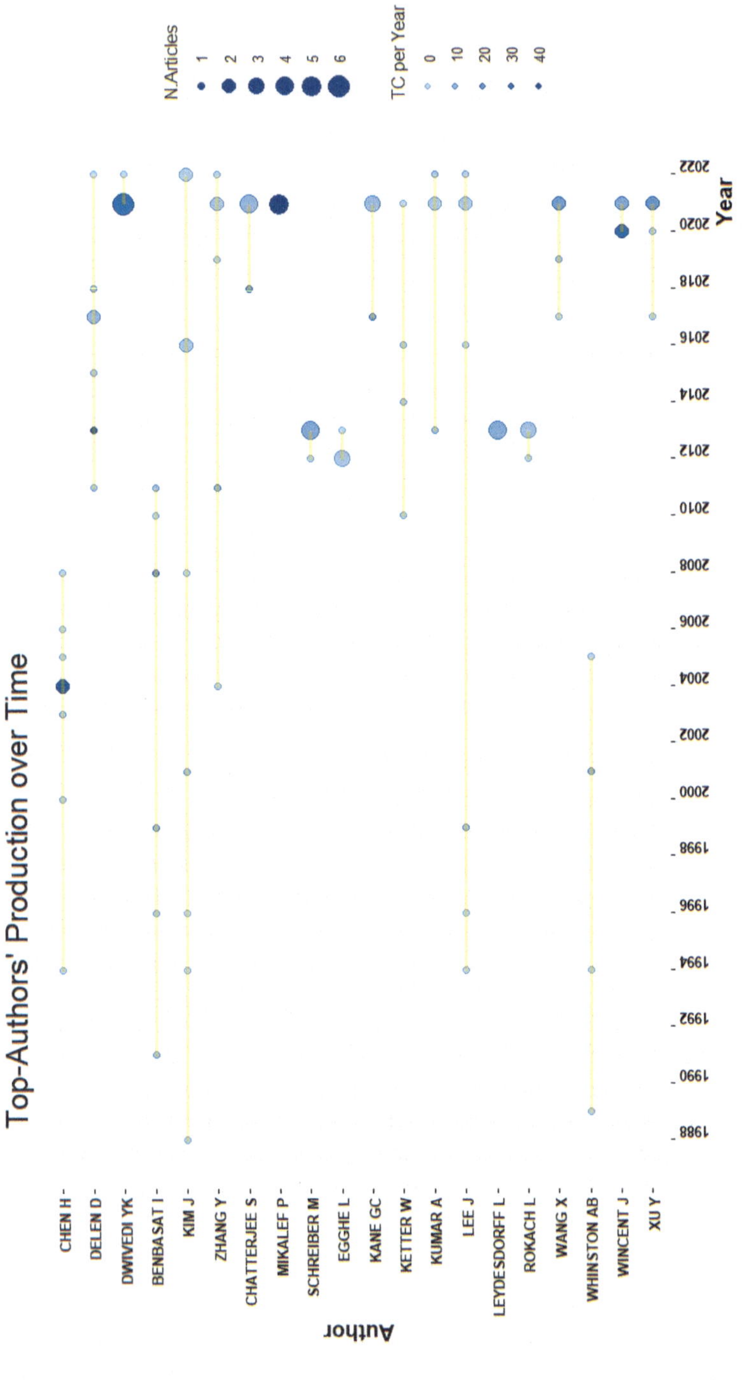

Fig. 4 Most productive authors

Table 3 Most recurring journals

Sources	Articles	AJG rating	AJG field of study
Decision Support Systems	362	3	Info. Man.
Journal of the American Society for Information Science and Technology	93	3	Info. Man.
Information and Management	84	3	Info. Man.
Information Systems Frontiers	66	3	Info. Man.
Journal of Business Research	57	3	Gen. Man., Ethics, Gender and Soc. Resp.
Information Systems Research	39	4*	Info. Man.
Journal of Environmental Management	31	3	Social Sciences
Risk Analysis	27	4	Social Sciences
Government Information Quarterly	23	3	Info. Man.
Journal of Management Information Systems	21	4	Info. Man.

field have been published in the last 4 years. The results could suggest that academics increasingly inspect AI's social and ethical implications inside organisational settings. This trend may be explained by several factors, such as the change in humans' perception of AI-related technologies.

They are moving from being seen as mere objects to being perceived as digital beings [28]. This phenomenon paves the way to new research frontiers where AI is compared to human beings. Another factor may be the acceleration of Digital Transformation in response to the Covid-19 pandemic that increased the positive perceptions about digital work [29]. Especially the last point could explain why the number of publications has also increased in *General Management, Ethics, Gender and Social Responsibility, and Human Resource Management and Employment Studies* fields.

5 Topics Exploration with Co-word Analysis

In this section, we explore the most relevant topics in our dataset by analysing the most recurring keywords used by authors. The analysis could provide insights into the most related topics to our research domain and their contribution to the literature. We divided the topic analysis into three parts:

1. The trend of the most used keywords.
2. Authors' keywords co-occurrences.
3. Co-words analysis by using the thematic map to draw clusters of keywords based on the centrality and density metrics.

The analysis started with the distribution of the most used author keyword with at least ten occurrences in the dataset (see Fig. 5).

After *artificial intelligence, decision support systems* is the most used keyword in the dataset with 217 occurrences, followed by machine learning with 97

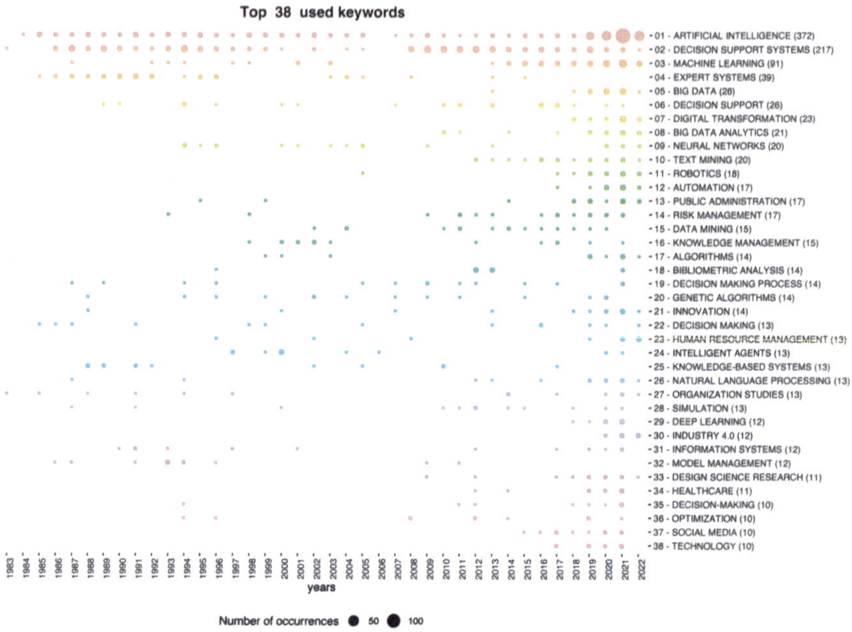

Fig. 5 Main keyword used in the dataset over time

occurrences. *Expert systems*, *big data*, *decision support*, *digital transformation*, *big data analytics*, *neural networks* and *text mining* complete the top 10 of the most used keywords with more than 20 occurrences (39, 26, 26, 23, 21, 20, 20 respectively).

By looking at the frequency of the ten most used keywords, it can be seen that most of them were used mostly in the last 4 years. For instance, the use of the keywords *artificial intelligence*, *machine learning*, *neural network* and *text mining* increased from 2019. The only keywords that go against the trend are *decision support systems*, *expert systems* and *decision support*. They were used the most in the period 2007–2013, 1985–1995 and 2010–2017 respectively. Finally, it is no surprise that *big data*, *digital transformation* and *big data analytics* are the most recent keywords. They have started to be used in the last decade.

For what concern the other 28 keywords, the frequency appears regular and in line with the annual production, with the majority of occurrences in the last 4 years. There are some exceptions, for instance, *intelligent agents*, *model management* and *knowledge management,* that were more used in the mid-1990s and early 2000s. The most recent keyword among the most used is *industry 4.0* first appeared in 2020.

The co-occurrence network (see Fig. 6) was created from the keyword that had more than ten occurrences. The nodes within the graph represent keywords connected to each other if they are both used in the same document (co-occurrence). The thickness of the ties reflects the number of papers in which the keywords pair appears.

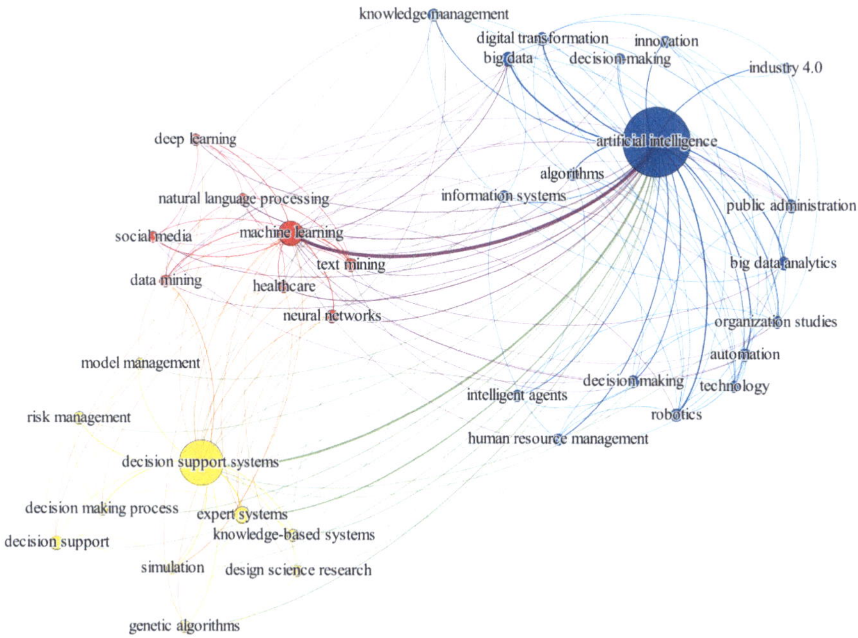

Fig. 6 Authors' keyword co-occurrence

By looking at the graph, we can see the presence of three different clusters strictly related between them:

- The blue cluster focus on artificial intelligence, the settings where AI is adopted and the related technologies.
- The yellow cluster refers to the decision support systems, where they are used and the systems in which they are implemented.
- The red cluster contains many technologies related to machine learning and two settings where ML algorithms are broadly used, such as social media and healthcare sectors.

To further explore the topics contained in the dataset, we created a thematic map [30]. The clusters shown in the map are based on the interconnections between keywords (co-occurrence network). Once the clusters are determined, they are distributed across the map according to two network parameters, *density* and *centrality*. The *density* represents the strength of internal connections between the keywords belonging to the same cluster and could be intended as a measure of the topic's development. The *centrality* is based on the strength of the external connection between different clusters and could be read as the topic's relevance in the entire research domain [30]. According to the different levels of the two measures, the map allows to define four different quadrants:

- Themes in the upper-right quadrant are known as motor themes (high centrality, high density). The clusters inside this quadrant are developed and important for the research.
- Themes in the lower-right quadrant are known as basic and transversal themes (high centrality, low density). These topics are important for the research domain, and they could be applied to different research areas.
- Themes in the lower left quadrant are known as emerging or declining themes (low centrality, low density). These themes are weakly developed or marginal.
- Themes in the upper left quadrant are known as niche themes (low centrality, high density). These themes are important inside their cluster but of limited importance to the field [31].

The thematic map (see Fig. 7) highlights the themes concerning the AI debate. The most populous quadrant is the one that refers to the basic/transversal themes. This is not surprising because most of the keywords are strictly related to AI and central to the debate since artificial intelligence systems will increasingly become an integral part of our lives [2]. Furthermore, these keywords refer to topics that are being applied to many research fields. For instance, most of the publications concerning *big data* and *machine learning* are from the last few years, strictly related and focused on different domains, such as the studies on unsupervised learning to enhance big data analysis inside the smart cities [32]. Another field refers to ML algorithms' reliability in monitoring the financial markets to counter money laundering and terrorism financing [33]. Obschonka and Audretsch [34] also discuss the

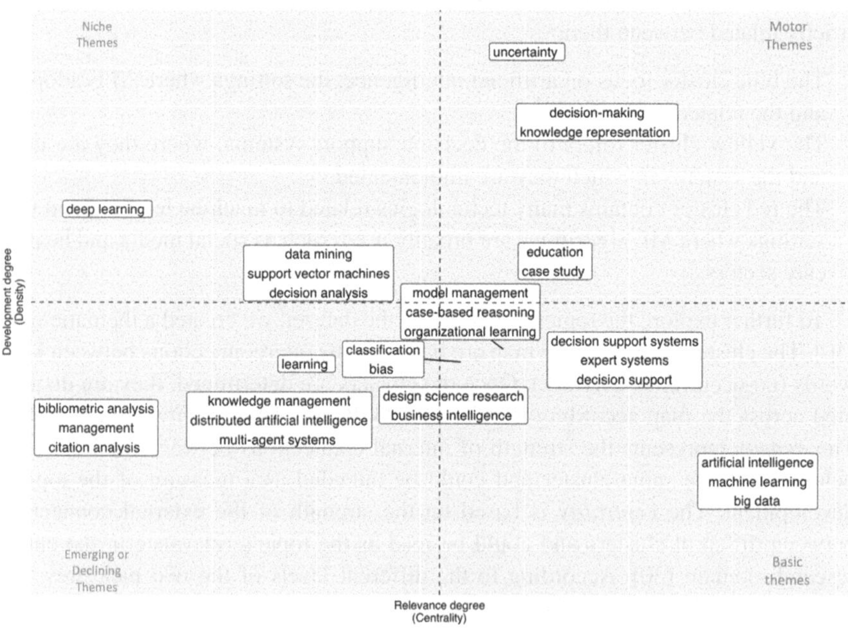

Fig. 7 Thematic map based on authors' keywords co-occurrence network

importance of the AI and big data debate inside entrepreneurship studies and their ability to change what has long been studied on the subject.

Similarly, the keywords *decision support systems*, *expert systems* and *business intelligence* are strictly related between them and used in different fields inside organisations [35]. DSS are used in many different settings, such as to reduce operability and maintenance costs in aircraft repair and maintenance process [36]. Furthermore, in recent years, AI technologies have started to be implemented within decision support systems. As a result, the latest generation of DSS can adapt in a better and efficient way internal and external stimuli, enhancing organisational learning. Like DSS, business intelligence organises and interprets raw data to make better and more informed decisions. They could be used inside the organisations to help employees and managers with different scopes, such as the inspection of foreign websites or social media analysis [35, 37, 38]. It is interesting to note that the topics that are declining over time, such as expert systems and intelligent agents, could experience a new period of development thanks to AI technologies that open the possibility of developing these systems further. For instance, Schuetz and Venkatesh [39] provide a research agenda about how Cognitive Computing Systems (CCS) could contribute to IS debate. Finally, it is important to underline the importance of the keyword *bias* when referring to AI. The use of AI and machine learning algorithms could lead to significant bias, more or less severe [40]. Many studies, especially in recent years, are focusing on this subject. An important field of research is related to contrasting racial and gender bias. Gupta et al. [41] contribute by examining how cultural values affect AI algorithms. They find that values such as collectivism, masculinity and uncertainty avoidance could generate bias concerning gender and racial discrimination in ML algorithms. Another decisive aspect is related to employee performance evaluation. In fact, biased or incomplete ML algorithms could perform less efficiently compared to older technologies, therefore is important to reduce the bias by considering domain expertise and specific skills that ensure the ability to use the technology [40]. It is also crucial to improve the quality of the communication between management and employees about the benefit, objectives and scope of AI applications [42].

With respect to the emerging/declining themes, we have paid more attention to the trend of the publication concerning the topics inside the quadrant to assess the novelty of the subject. Overall, the occurrences seem to be declining topics since most articles were published between the 1990s and the 2000s. But it is interesting to note that in the last 4 years, there have been many contributions related to the keywords inside the quadrant, and they are linked with trending topics such as sustainability, human augmentation and responsible AI. An example could be the keyword *learning*. Holm and Lorentz [43] conducted a case study on the effects of different types of AI applications on employees' skills in Denmark. Results show that AI has a positive effect on high skill jobs and a relatively adverse impact on the others, increasing inequalities in labour market. Di Vaio et al. [44] published a bibliometric literature review inspecting the relationship between AI and sustainable development. They focus on the role of *knowledge management systems* in the cultural drift toward the spread of AI for sustainable business models by identifying gaps for future research. Wamba and Queiroz [20] performed a *bibliometric analysis* on responsible artificial intelligence to explore the relationship between AI and the healthcare system. They provide a framework for AI technologies application inside the healthcare sector, underlining the advantages and disadvantages of AI-based health.

Finally, *management* is the keyword with the highest number of new articles. The attention and interest in artificial intelligence have increased among managers, but there is still empirical evidence. Brock and Wangenheim [45] provide a framework based on empirical evidence on successfully implementing AI in the digital transformation process. Raisch and Krakowski [46] study the relationship between automation and augmentation inside organisations. They argue that scientific AI research needs better capture social and organisational implications in management practices. Furthermore, as artificial intelligence is assuming an increasingly important role in decision making and analytical tasks, workers and managers must know how to take advantage of this transition by working side by side with AI and increasing their "emphasis on the empathetic and emotional dimensions of their work" [47].

Motor theme keywords, such as *decision-making,* are consistent with the quadrant description. In fact, artificial intelligence is mainly used to make decisions and research demonstrates that, in many cases, it is improving the quality of the decision-making process [48]. The importance of AI in decision making concerns many domains, from healthcare to HR management [49], and it will be of paramount importance for human intelligence augmentation [48]. The keyword *knowledge representation* seems to be well developed and declining since all the articles were published more than 20 years ago. On the contrary, the papers concerning *education* and *case study* are steadily growing. AI is a core concept in education. It could make the learning process more efficient and address social inequalities [50], and also help to organise operations inside schools and universities [51]. Case studies are strictly linked to management as empirical studies are crucial to better understand the impact of AI on organisations and society [35]. Finally, the keyword uncertainty represents a central theme in AI, especially in the last few years where the doubts regarding the benefits of artificial intelligence and ethical issues are increasing [28, 52, 53].

The last quadrant describes niche themes. Inside, we found many keywords related to AI and machine learning. For instance, *data mining* algorithms search for statistical patterns without specifying hypothesis a priori [54]. Nevertheless, discovering useful patterns is becoming more and more difficult as the data available are increasing. In this regard, Smith [54] identifies a big data paradox: "*It would seem that having data for a large number of variables will help us find more reliable patterns; however, the more variables we consider, the less likely it is that what we find will be useful*".

Similarly, support vector machines are ML techniques used for regression and classification analysis and for developing DSS based on imbalanced datasets [55]. *Decision analysis* (DA) is a form of decision making that involves the assessment of every aspect of the decision to have the best possible outcome. In the last years, AI helped to improve DA in many fields such as public policy, engineering, military and defence operations [56]. *Deep learning* (DL) is a subset of machine learning that can assist employees and managers in decision-making processes by increasing their analytical capabilities [57]. DL is used to develop prediction and classification models implemented in many areas, such as bankruptcy prediction and recommendation systems. This technology also had an important role as a support tool in containing the infection during the COVID-19 pandemic [58].

6 Conclusion

The paper investigated the existing literature concerning AI inside organisation and management studies. To achieve the objective, we performed a bibliometric analysis on a sample of 1102 articles articulated in two steps: firstly, we carried out a descriptive bibliometric analysis, and then we identified and mapped the main topics in our dataset through co-word analysis.

The descriptive analysis results show a growing interest in societal and ethical issues deriving from the use of artificial intelligence. This trend is confirmed by cross-checking the annual production and the AJG areas of the most impactful articles. It can be noted that there is a publication increase in fields such as *General Management, Ethics, Gender and Social Responsibility, Human Resource Management and Employment Studies* and *Social Sciences*.

The co-word analysis allowed us to analyse the recurring keywords used by authors in the dataset. The results show how most of the keywords have been used more in the last 4 years. This trend could suggest a new development period for the topic. The analysis of the thematic map also confirms these findings. Specifically, many topics, which have been studied for a long time, are recently experiencing a new interest from academics due to advances in the artificial intelligence field. For example, studies on DSSs based on AI technologies have significantly increased, and much emphasis is also being placed on the criticality of systems based on artificial intelligence algorithms and the social and work-related consequences.

Whereas other papers either deal with very specific topics or focus their analysis on a small number of articles, our research analyses a wide topic by considering a large number of articles. Therefore, our aim is to exploit this research's breadth to find the most important topics related to AI in management studies by using a similar research framework. This will be essential in order to pursue future studies that seek to map this field in more and more detail. We also used ABS's AJG ranking to filter within Scopus all articles from the best journals within the field of management studies. The use of this ranking allowed us to avoid applying additional filters on Scopus that could have affected the accuracy of our dataset.

This work has both theoretical and practical contributions. From a theoretical standpoint, the research, due to its broad scope, could provide a starting point to analyse the relationship between AI and organisation and management studies and understand the main topic concerning the subject. Furthermore, the paper describes the various topics related to AI, dividing them according to their importance within the research domain and their level of development. In this way, it is possible to have a clear overview of what has been done and the direction in which research is heading. From a practical point of view, the research aims to give insights into the use of artificial intelligence-related technologies and their criticalities. This study could help managers and policymakers willing to adopt AI technology, to better identify the AI-related issues to make better and informed decisions.

The study has some limitations. This research considers only journals rated 3, 4 and 4* of the AJG ranking that belong to selected areas. It could also be interesting to include the missing journals of AJG ranking with other conference proceedings that could present emerging topics that have not yet been addressed in the journal papers. Secondly, one of the aims of this work was to help us refine our query on databases. Hence future studies could use more specific keywords for literature search. The paper only takes into consideration co-word analysis using a thematic map and a co-occurrence graph. It could be interesting to use other methods such as multiple correspondence analysis (MCA) to further investigate the relationship between the keywords and also a co-citation analysis to explore the evolution of the knowledge in the community over time and what are the most influent authors in the debate.

References

1. Zhang, C., & Lu, Y. (2021). Study on artificial intelligence: The state of the art and future prospects. *Journal of Industrial Information Integration, 23*, 100224. https://doi.org/10.1016/j.jii.2021.100224
2. Haenlein, M., & Kaplan, A. (2019). A brief history of artificial intelligence: On the past, present, and future of artificial intelligence. *California Management Review, 61*, 5–14. https://doi.org/10.1177/0008125619864925
3. Kaplan, A., & Haenlein, M. (2019). Rulers of the world, unite! The challenges and opportunities of artificial intelligence. *Business Horizons, 63*, 37–50. https://doi.org/10.1016/j.bushor.2019.09.003
4. Duan, N., Liu, L. Z., Yu, X. J., Li, Q., & Yeh, S. C. (2019). Classification of multichannel surface-electromyography signals based on convolutional neural networks. *Journal of Industrial Information Integration, 15*, 201–206. https://doi.org/10.1016/j.jii.2018.09.001
5. Zhu, Y. Q., Corbett, J. U., & Chiu, Y. T. (2021). Understanding employees' responses to artificial intelligence. *Organizational Dynamics, 50*, 100786. https://doi.org/10.1016/j.orgdyn.2020.100786
6. Kaplan, A., & Haenlein, M. (2019). Siri, Siri, in my hand: Who's the fairest in the land? On the interpretations, illustrations, and implications of artificial intelligence. *Business Horizons, 62*, 15–25. https://doi.org/10.1016/j.bushor.2018.08.004
7. Makarius, E. E., Mukherjee, D., Fox, J. D., & Fox, A. K. (2020). Rising with the machines: A sociotechnical framework for bringing artificial intelligence into the organization. *Journal of Business Research, 120*, 262–273. https://doi.org/10.1016/J.JBUSRES.2020.07.045
8. Benbya, H., Davenport, T. H., & Pachidi, S. (2020). Artificial intelligence in organizations: Current state and future opportunities. *MIS Quarterly Executive, 19*.
9. Glikson, E., & Woolley, A. W. (2020). Human trust in artificial intelligence: Review of empirical research. *The Academy of Management Annals, 14*, 627–660. https://doi.org/10.5465/annals.2018.0057

10. Huang, M. H., & Rust, R. T. (2018). Artificial intelligence in service. *Journal of Service Research, 21*, 155–172. https://doi.org/10.1177/1094670517752459
11. Da Xu, L., Xu, E. L., & Li, L. (2018). Industry 4.0: State of the art and future trends. *International Journal of Production Research, 56*, 2941–2962. https://doi.org/10.1080/00207543.2018.1444806
12. Bailey, D., Faraj, S., Hinds, P., von Krogh, G., & Leonardi, P. (2019). Special issue of organization science: Emerging technologies and organizing. *Organization Science, 30*, 642–646. https://doi.org/10.1287/orsc.2019.1299
13. Lu, Y. (2019). Artificial intelligence: a survey on evolution, models, applications and future trends. *Journal of Management Analytics, 6*, 1–29. https://doi.org/10.1080/23270012.2019.1570365
14. Tranfield, D., Denyer, D., & Smart, P. (2003). Towards a methodology for developing evidence-informed management knowledge by means of systematic review. *British Journal of Management, 14*, 207–222. https://doi.org/10.1111/1467-8551.00375
15. Zupic, I., & Čater, T. (2015). Bibliometric methods in management and organization. *Organizational Research Methods, 18*, 429–472. https://doi.org/10.1177/1094428114562629
16. Dhamija, P., & Bag, S. (2020). Role of artificial intelligence in operations environment: a review and bibliometric analysis. *TQM J, 32*, 869–896. https://doi.org/10.1108/TQM-10-2019-0243
17. Reis, J., Santo, P. E., & Melão, N. (2019). Artificial intelligence in government services: A systematic literature review. *Advances in Intelligent Systems and Computing, 930*, 241–252. https://doi.org/10.1007/978-3-030-16181-1_23
18. Verma, S., Sharma, R., Deb, S., & Maitra, D. (2021). Artificial intelligence in marketing: Systematic review and future research direction. *International Journal of Information Management Data Insights, 1*, 100002. https://doi.org/10.1016/j.jjimei.2020.100002
19. Riahi, Y., Saikouk, T., Gunasekaran, A., & Badraoui, I. (2021). Artificial intelligence applications in supply chain: A descriptive bibliometric analysis and future research directions. *Expert Systems with Applications, 173*, 114702. https://doi.org/10.1016/j.eswa.2021.114702
20. Fosso Wamba, S., & Queiroz, M. M. (2021). Responsible artificial intelligence as a secret ingredient for digital health: Bibliometric analysis, insights, and research directions. *Information Systems Frontiers*. https://doi.org/10.1007/s10796-021-10142-8
21. Lamboglia, R., Lavorato, D., Scornavacca, E., & Za, S. (2020). Exploring the relationship between audit and technology. A bibliometric analysis. *Meditari Accountancy Research*. https://doi.org/10.1108/MEDAR-03-2020-0836
22. Donthu, N., Kumar, S., Mukherjee, D., Pandey, N., & Lim, W. M. (2021). How to conduct a bibliometric analysis: An overview and guidelines. *Journal of Business Research, 133*, 285–296. https://doi.org/10.1016/j.jbusres.2021.04.070
23. Callon, M., Courtial, J.-P., Turner, W. A., & Bauin, S. (1983). From translations to problematic networks: An introduction to co-word analysis. *Social Science Information, 22*, 191 235. https://doi.org/10.1177/053901883022002003
24. Cobo, M. J., López-Herrera, A. G., Herrera-Viedma, E., & Herrer, F. (2011). Science mapping software tools: Review, analysis, and cooperative study among tools. *Journal of the American Society for Information Science and Technology, 52*, 1382–1402. https://doi.org/10.1002/asi.21525
25. He, Q. (1999). Knowledge discovery through co-word analysis. *Library Trends, 48*, 133–159.
26. Za, S., & Braccini, A. M. (2017). Tracing the roots of the organizational benefits of IT services. *Lecture Notes in Business Information Processing, 279*, 3–11. https://doi.org/10.1007/978-3-319-56925-3_1
27. Aria, M., & Cuccurullo, C. (2017). Bibliometrix: An R-tool for comprehensive science mapping analysis. *Journal of Informetrics, 11*, 959–975. https://doi.org/10.1016/j.joi.2017.08.007
28. Dignum, V. (2018). Ethics in artificial intelligence: introduction to the special issue. *Ethics and Information Technology, 20*, 1–3. https://doi.org/10.1007/s10676-018-9450-z
29. Nagel, L. (2020). The influence of the COVID-19 pandemic on the digital transformation of work. *International Journal of Sociology and Social Policy, 40*, 861–875. https://doi.org/10.1108/IJSSP-07-2020-0323

30. Aria, M., Cuccurullo, C., D'Aniello, L., Misuraca, M., & Spano, M. (2022). Thematic analysis as a new culturomic tool: The social media coverage on COVID-19 pandemic in Italy. *Sustainability, 14*, 3643. https://doi.org/10.3390/su14063643
31. Aria, M., Misuraca, M., & Spano, M. (2020). Mapping the evolution of social research and data science on 30 years of social indicators research. *Social Indicators Research, 149*, 803–831. https://doi.org/10.1007/s11205-020-02281-3
32. Alahakoon, D., Nawaratne, R., Xu, Y., De Silva, D., Sivarajah, U., & Gupta, B. (2020). Self-building artificial intelligence and machine learning to empower big data analytics in smart cities. *Information Systems Frontiers*. https://doi.org/10.1007/s10796-020-10056-x
33. Canhoto, A. I. (2021). Leveraging machine learning in the global fight against money laundering and terrorism financing: An affordances perspective. *Journal of Business Research, 131*, 441–452. https://doi.org/10.1016/j.jbusres.2020.10.012
34. Obschonka, M., & Audretsch, D. B. (2020). Artificial intelligence and big data in entrepreneurship: a new era has begun. *Small Business Economics, 55*, 529–539. https://doi.org/10.1007/s11187-019-00202-4
35. Arnott, D., Lizama, F., & Song, Y. (2017). Patterns of business intelligence systems use in organizations. *Decision Support Systems, 97*, 58–68. https://doi.org/10.1016/j.dss.2017.03.005
36. Papakostas, N., Papachatzakis, P., Xanthakis, V., Mourtzis, D., & Chryssolouris, G. (2010). An approach to operational aircraft maintenance planning. *Decision Support Systems, 48*, 604–612. https://doi.org/10.1016/j.dss.2009.11.010
37. Abrahams, A. S., Jiao, J., Wang, G. A., & Fan, W. (2012). Vehicle defect discovery from social media. *Decision Support Systems, 54*, 87–97. https://doi.org/10.1016/j.dss.2012.04.005
38. Bhatt, G. D., & Zaveri, J. (2002). The enabling role of decision support systems in organizational learning. *Decision Support Systems, 32*, 297–309. https://doi.org/10.1016/S0167-9236(01)00120-8
39. Schuetz, S. W., & Venkatesh, V. (2020). The rise of human machines: How cognitive computing systems challenge assumptions of user-system. *Journal of the Association for Information Systems, 21*, 460–482.
40. Choudhury, P., Starr, E., & Agarwal, R. (2020). Machine learning and human capital complementarities: Experimental evidence on bias mitigation. *Strategic Management Journal, 41*, 1381–1411. https://doi.org/10.1002/smj.3152
41. Gupta, M., Parra, C. M., & Dennehy, D. (2021). Questioning racial and gender bias in AI-based recommendations: Do espoused national cultural values matter? *Information Systems Frontiers*. https://doi.org/10.1007/s10796-021-10156-2
42. Tong, S., Jia, N., Luo, X., & Fang, Z. (2021). The Janus face of artificial intelligence feedback: Deployment versus disclosure effects on employee performance. *Strategic Management Journal, 42*, 1600–1631. https://doi.org/10.1002/smj.3322
43. Holm, J. R., & Lorenz, E. (2021). The impact of artificial intelligence on skills at work in Denmark. *New Technology, Work and Employment, 37*(1), 79–101. https://doi.org/10.1111/ntwe.12215
44. Di Vaio, A., Palladino, R., Hassan, R., & Escobar, O. (2020). Artificial intelligence and business models in the sustainable development goals perspective: A systematic literature review. *Journal of Business Research, 121*, 283–314. https://doi.org/10.1016/j.jbusres.2020.08.019
45. Brock, J. K. U., & von Wangenheim, F. (2019). Demystifying Ai: What digital transformation leaders can teach you about realistic artificial intelligence. *California Management Review, 61*, 110–134. https://doi.org/10.1177/1536504219865226
46. Raisch, S., & Krakowski, S. (2020). Artificial intelligence and management: The automation-augmentation paradox. *The Academy of Management Review, 46*, 1–48. https://doi.org/10.5465/2018.0072
47. Huang, M. H., Rust, R., & Maksimovic, V. (2019). The feeling economy: Managing in the next generation of artificial intelligence (AI). *California Management Review, 61*(4), 43–65. https://doi.org/10.1177/0008125619863436

48. Metcalf, L., Askay, D. A., & Rosenberg, L. B. (2019). Keeping humans in the loop: Pooling knowledge through artificial swarm intelligence to improve business decision making. *California Management Review, 61*, 84–109. https://doi.org/10.1177/0008125619862256
49. Tambe, P., Cappelli, P., & Yakubovich, V. (2019). Artificial intelligence in human resources management: Challenges and A path forward. *California Management Review, 61*, 15–42. https://doi.org/10.1177/0008125619867910
50. Davies, H. C., Eynon, R., & Salveson, C. (2021). The mobilisation of AI in education: A Bourdieusean field analysis. *Sociology, 55*, 539–560. https://doi.org/10.1177/0038038520967888
51. Bailey, M. D., & Michaels, D. (2019). An optimization-based DSS for student-to-teacher assignment: Classroom heterogeneity and teacher performance measures. *Decision Support Systems, 119*, 60–71. https://doi.org/10.1016/j.dss.2019.02.006
52. Lundvall, B. Å. (2017). Is there a technological fix for the current global stagnation?: A response to Daniele Archibugi, Blade Runner economics: Will innovation lead the economic recovery? *Research Policy, 46*, 544–549. https://doi.org/10.1016/j.respol.2016.06.011
53. Weathers, D., Swain, S. D., & Grover, V. (2015). Can online product reviews be more helpful? Examining characteristics of information content by product type. *Decision Support Systems, 79*, 12–23. https://doi.org/10.1016/j.dss.2015.07.009
54. Smith, G. (2020). Data mining fool's gold. *Journal of Information Technology, 35*, 182–194. https://doi.org/10.1177/0268396220915600
55. Piri, S., Delen, D., & Liu, T. (2018). A synthetic informative minority over-sampling (SIMO) algorithm leveraging support vector machine to enhance learning from imbalanced datasets. *Decision Support Systems, 106*, 15–29. https://doi.org/10.1016/j.dss.2017.11.006
56. Cox, L. A. (2020). Answerable and unanswerable questions in risk analysis with open-world novelty. *Risk Analysis, 40*, 2144–2177. https://doi.org/10.1111/risa.13553
57. Shrestha, Y. R., Krishna, V., & von Krogh, G. (2021). Augmenting organizational decision-making with deep learning algorithms: Principles, promises, and challenges. *Journal of Business Research, 123*, 588–603. https://doi.org/10.1016/j.jbusres.2020.09.068
58. Piccialli, F., di Cola, V. S., Giampaolo, F., & Cuomo, S. (2021). The role of artificial intelligence in fighting the COVID-19 pandemic. *Information Systems Frontiers, 23*, 1467–1497. https://doi.org/10.1007/s10796-021-10131-x

Do Forecasting Algorithms Need a Crisis-Mode? Machine Learning Based Sales Forecasting in Times of COVID-19

Tobias Fahse

Abstract On average, algorithmic forecasts outperform human forecasts by 10%. This disparity increases further thanks to cutting-edge machine learning (ML) algorithms. As business decisions based on sales forecasting are regarded as particularly important and a variety of other activities rely on them, accurate sales forecasting is critical to companies' profitability. At the same time, being able to predict the next day's sales more accurately can significantly reduce food waste and help fulfilling sustainability. Thus, sales forecasting is one of the primary value propositions of artificial intelligence (AI). However, it is crucial for the acceptance and adoption of ML-based sales forecasting algorithms to perform reliably during pandemics such as the covid-19 pandemic. Although governments' containment measures highly impact the sales of a bakery's products, no study has yet scrutinized incorporating the stringency of containment measures as an input variable for sales forecasting. Hence, this paper examines the performance of a ML sales forecasting system for baked goods in times of covid-19 and proposes incorporating a covid containment measurement stringency index as an additional input variable to increase forecast accuracy in times of pandemics. This way, prediction accuracy increases by 4.61% on average. Consequently, a containment measures stringency variable should be used to increase accuracy in future pandemics. By simulating an upcoming pandemic, it is further demonstrated how learnings from the covid-19 pandemic could be meaningfully transferred. For this study, real data is used: A Swiss bakery chain provides real sales data covering 5 years including 2 years of the covid-19 pandemic.

Keywords Sales forecasting · Machine learning · COVID-19 · Containment measures

T. Fahse (✉)
Institute of Information Management, University of St. Gallen, St. Gallen, Switzerland
e-mail: tobias.fahse@unisg.ch

A. M. Braccini et al. (eds.), *Technologies for Digital Transformation*, Lecture Notes in Information Systems and Organisation 64,
https://doi.org/10.1007/978-3-031-52120-1_4

1 Introduction

In this paper, the usefulness of a covid containment measures stringency index to increase prediction accuracy of the next day's sales of baked goods is examined based on real sales data that is provided by a Swiss bakery chain.

On average, algorithmic forecasts outperform human forecasts by 10% [1]. This disparity increased further due to cutting-edge machine learning (ML) algorithms [2]. Business decisions based on sales forecasting are regarded as particularly important and a variety of other activities rely on them, accurate sales forecasting is critical to companies' profitability [3, 4]. At the same time, food waste is an increasingly significant challenge for society and is recognized by the United Nations as a sustainable development goal. Being able to predict the next day's sales more accurately can significantly reduce food waste and help to fulfill sustainability goals when applied in the food industry or in retail. According to the Swiss Federal Office for the Environment (BAFU), 2.8 million tons of food are wasted in Switzerland per year, which equals 330 kg per person per year, or about a quarter of the environmental impact caused by our food. Among all food categories, baked goods have the greatest environmental impact due to food waste [5].

The opportunity to increase sales by avoiding shortage and to reduce costs and food waste by avoiding overproduction calls for more accurate sales forecasting. Consequently, sales forecasting is one of the primary value propositions of artificial intelligence (AI) [6]. However, it is crucial for the acceptance and adoption of ML-based sales forecasting algorithms to perform reliably during pandemics such as the recent covid-19 pandemic. Restrictions like quarantines, mandatory home office or mask obligations highly impact the sales of a typical bakery's products and negatively affects the performance of ML models [7].

To the best of the author's knowledge, there are currently no studies that incorporate the severity of covid-19 containment measures into ML sales forecasting algorithms as an input variable. Several studies investigate how the covid-19 pandemic has affected sales forecasting and suggest novel algorithms to deal with the distortions [8–11]. For instance, the covid-19 pandemic affected the importance of feature variables: Comparing pre- vs. post-pandemic feature importance, features that negatively influence sales increased in importance in a study in the context of an online marketplace [12]. To deal with the distortions of the pandemic, one study incorporates expert opinions into a ML forecast algorithm [13], while another study adds flags to their data to indicate the different stages of the covid-19 pandemic (panic state, relief period after a wave, etc.), thus improving the prediction of monthly car sales [14]. However, pandemic containment measures were not considered in these studies.

To tackle the outlined research gap, this study examines the effectiveness of including a covid containment measures stringency index into a ML sales forecasting system to increase forecast accuracy in times of covid-19. For the elaborations, real data is used: A Swiss bakery chain provides transactional sales data covering approximately 5 years including 2 years of the covid-19 pandemic. The usefulness of the covid stringency index is evaluated based on the 15 best selling products of the largest branch of the bakery chain. First, for 13 of 15 products, the onset of the covid pandemic represents a structural break in the data. Second, it is shown that in case of a future pandemic, a restriction stringency variable should be used, as it increases the prediction accuracy by 4.61%. Third, situations in which a "pandemic variable" is beneficial or detrimental to the accuracy of forecasts are examined by simulating the start of an upcoming pandemic and comparing the ML system with and without considering the covid stringency index as an input variable. Fourth, this study shows how learnings from the covid-19 pandemic could be meaningfully transferred to an upcoming pandemic. These analyses are executed to answer the following research questions (RQ):

RQ1: *Does the COVID-19 stringency index improve 1-day-ahead forecasts in sales forecasting in the bakery domain?*
RQ2: *Can a pre-trained pandemic variable improve 1-day-ahead forecasts in times of pandemic?*

By answering these research questions, this paper contributes to practice by showing the usefulness of variables that measure the strictness of the government's containment measures as a reaction to pandemics in ML-based sales forecasting algorithms. This study contributes to theory by evaluating the degree to which ML based sales forecasting systems can be relied on in times of great societal change like pandemics. The robustness of such a system is critical for their acceptance and adoption.

The results indicate that a crisis mode is necessary to enable the algorithm to adapt to changing consumption behavior in times of pandemics but there is no need for practitioners to switch to full "manual mode" when a pandemic occurs.

2 Conceptual and Theoretical Background

In times of a pandemic, forecast accuracy declines due to changing importance of predictor variables and changing behavior of customers [7, 12]. This study investigates the effectiveness of a covid-19 containment measures stringency index increase forecast accuracy of ML sales forecasting models during the covid-19 pandemic. Consequently, three main topics are relevant: (1) Machine Learning for Sales Forecasting, (2) Data Drift and (3) the covid-19 stringency index.

2.1 Machine Learning for Sales Forecasting

Sales forecasting is the process of predicting future sales values using a model of historical data. Forecasting is critical for corporate strategy because many organizational choices are based on it [4]. As a result, effectively anticipating future sales based on historical data is critical to a company's success [3].

Most of a retailer's essential business functions, including manufacturing and procurement, supply chain optimization, marketing, and staff planning, require high precision sales projections [15]. It is difficult to manually handle procurement for all items in all locations since merchants routinely manage assortments with many distinct products. As a result, merchants rely on automated procurement systems, which rely on sales forecasts in turn [15].

During the last few decades, significant work has gone into developing and refining advanced information systems and the underlying mathematical models and algorithms for retail sales forecasting. In the past, specialized exponential smoothing models and ARIMA models were commonly used for sales forecasting, and they still perform reasonably well with minimum computing effort [16]. When the surrounding macroeconomic conditions are generally steady, classic exponential smoothing and ARIMA models are likely to be precise [17].

When consumer behavior is rapidly changing, however, recent research suggest that nonlinear models can outperform standard techniques in terms of prediction accuracy [15]. Different forms of neural networks [18], multilayer functional link networks [19], support vector machines [20], and decision trees are just a few examples [21]. Model training is computationally costly; hence such techniques generally have unfeasible resource needs [22].

The focus of this study is sales forecasting of baked goods in a medium-sized Swiss bakery. Whereas in retail sales forecasts might be needed on an hourly basis, for this project, predictions are needed at a higher aggregation level: the next business day's sales are most important for decision makers as they need to place an order for the next day at the production department at the end of each day. This leads to relatively lower amount of data points per product and per branch. In this context, with the provided data, a conventional time series approach like ARIMA performs almost equally well. More advanced ML models like neural networks can leverage their strengths especially with higher-frequency data. Against this backdrop, an autoregressive OLS model is chosen for the elaborations in this paper, as it requires few computational resources, and its interpretability allows for analyses which would not be possible with black-box models like neural networks or boosted tree models like XGBoost [23].

In addition, food waste is increasingly recognized as a social challenge. According to the Swiss Federal Office for the Environment, 2.8 million tons of food are wasted in Switzerland every year, which equals 330 kg per person per year, or about a quarter of the environmental impact caused by our food. The food category with the greatest environmental impact due to food waste is baked goods and overproduction is a main driver of food waste in the baked goods category [5].

2.2 Data Drift and Structural Breaks

The covid-19 pandemic has had great impact on the sales of the bakery chain at hand. Prior to the pandemic's start in March 2020, the branch sold on average 22130 baked goods items per month. During the pandemic, meaning from March 2020 until and including January 2022, the sales per month were 28,052 on average. This constitutes a statistically significant change of sales and promotes the assumption that the pandemic must be accounted for in a ML-based forecasting system. Figure 1 shows the total sales per month of the store and 15 products in focus of the paper. The start of the covid-19 pandemic is denoted by the vertical red line. The black line is the regression line for the pre-pandemic sales per month and the dashed line depicts the regression line for the post-pandemic sales.

Statistically significantly different slopes of the two regression lines indicate a structural break in the data and consequently the necessity to account for this break.

To test for a structural break in the data at the start of the pandemic in March 2020, the chow test performs a linear regression over all data points and each one over the data points prior and after the structural break point to be tested [24]. If the regression parameters of the joint regression equal the parameters of the two subsections of the time series, no structural break is detected, and the null hypothesis is accepted. Table 1 shows the results for the chow test performed on all 15 products in the data set.

As shown in Table 1, a structural break can be assumed for 13 out of 15 products on significance level of 0.001, for 1 product the significance level is 0.05. These results indicate that it is senseful to account for the start of the pandemic in March 2020 in a ML-based sales forecasting model.

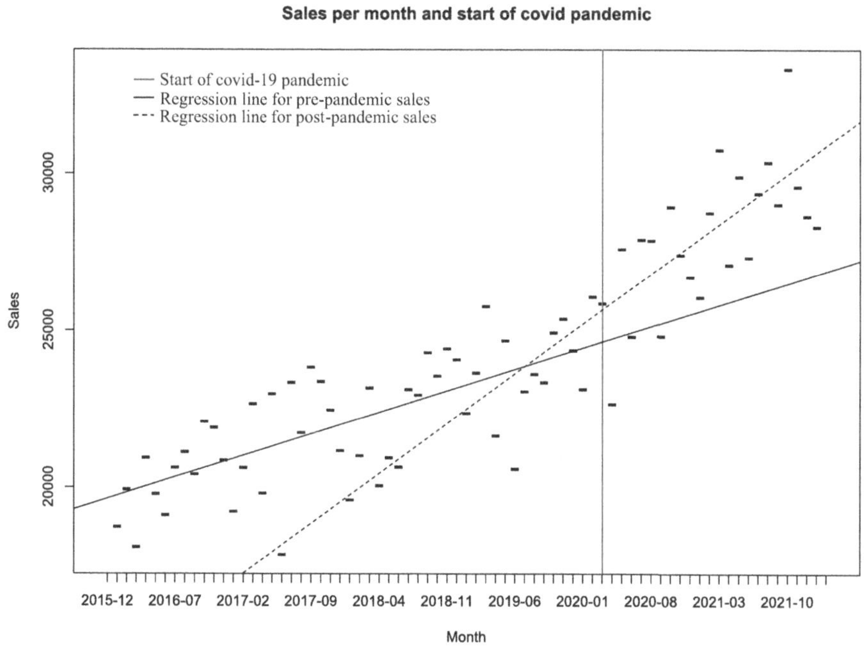

Fig. 1 Monthly sales and regression lines for pre- and post-pandemic sales

Table 1 Chow test for all 15 products and respective p-values

Article name	p-value	Structural break?	Significance level
Bread rolls	2.62E-14	Yes	***
Curd braid	3.02E-12	Yes	***
Butter braid	0	Yes	***
Pretzel croissant	0	Yes	***
Croissant	0	Yes	***
Corn croissant	2.66E-15	Yes	***
Pretzel bun	1.11E-16	Yes	***
Il pollo forte	0	Yes	***
Cream slice	0	Yes	***
Hazelnut croissant	5.69E-13	Yes	***
Roll	0.1562	No	
Bun	0.0180	Yes	*
Raspberry doughnut	0.0003	Yes	***
Sunflower croissant	5.77E-15	Yes	***
Almond croissant	0	Yes	***

*p < .05; **p < .01; ***p < 0.001

2.3 *COVID-19 Stringency Index*

In the context of this study, "crisis" is defined as a pandemic that leads to changes in the sub-indicators listed below. Here, the covid-19 containment measures in Switzerland are quantified using the KOF StringencyPlus Index (KSI+) [25]. The index is calculated based on different sub-indicators and ranges from 0 to 100, with 0 indicating no measures and 100 indicating full lockdown. Concretely, the ten sub-indicators used to derive the KSI+ index are: school closing, workplace closing, cancellation of public events, restrictions on gatherings, closure of public transport, stay-at-home requirements, restrictions on internal movement, international travel controls, public info campaigns, and facial coverings. The sub-indicators are coded based on the Oxford Stringency Index coding methodology [26].

The KSI+ index is not specific to the COVID-19 pandemic, which is a requirement to use it in sales forecasting for a potential next pandemic. The index could hence be derived again and used as an input variable in a forecasting model. Figure 2 depicts the course of the covid pandemic from January 2020 to February 2022. In the course of this paper, the KSI+ index is called "pandemic variable".

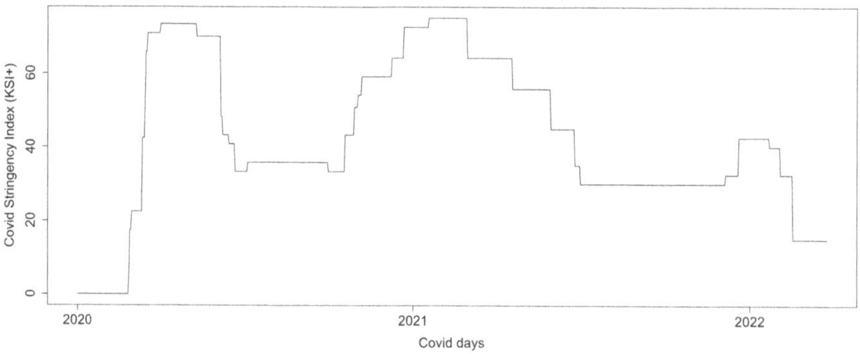

Fig. 2 Progression of covid-19 pandemic over time

3 Methodology

In total, three analysis/experiments are run in this paper. First, the forecast accuracy of two different models is compared. One model uses the pandemic variable as input, the other does not. Apart from that, both models are the same. In this analysis the training set consists of approximately 1500 non-covid and 300 covid days. The test set consists of around 400 covid days. Second, a simulation experiment where 1-day-ahead predictions are made followed by continuous retraining is performed. Here, the training set consists of all non-covid days and the test set of all covid days (~700). This experiment is conducted to simulate a situation in which a pandemic such as the covid pandemic is spreads and ML forecasting models need to adapt. Again, two models are used: One that uses the pandemic variable and one that does not. Third, the simulation is replicated with one change: the regression coefficient corresponding to the pandemic variable is set, not learned. This simulation is performed to test the possibility to transfer learnings from the COVID-19 pandemic to upcoming pandemics. The prediction accuracy of the model that uses the pre-trained pandemic variable is compared against a model that uses the pandemic variable as-is and a model that uses no pandemic variable.

4 Data and Artifact

In the following, the data set and the used algorithm are described in detail.

4.1 Data Set

The data set used in this paper consists of transactional point-of-sale data over 5 years and is provided by a Swiss bakery chain. It covers a total of 901,565 transactions over a timespan starting in December 2015 until February 2022 (2182 selling days). To confirm that the findings of this paper are valid and impactful for a typical bakery, the data set contains the 15 top-selling products. Included variables are a timestamp, the type of product, the sold amount, and the price. Based on the timestamp, the generated features weekday and month are included. External data was used to add weather indicators, specifically daily averages of radiation, rainfall, and temperature, as well as national holidays, (school) vacations and the pandemic variable. Performing extensive autocorrelation analysis, lagged features (1-day-lag, 2-day-lag, and 7-day-lag) as well as a rolling average over 7 days were included. Table 2 shows all products that are included in the analyses and the respective amount of selling (covid) days for each product. The amount of selling days is relevant as 1-day-ahead predictions are made so that the training set size per product is the amount of selling days per product.

4.2 Algorithm: OLS Model

Based on this data and these features, an ML algorithm predicts sales of the next day for each product. Specifically, an Ordinary Least Squares (OLS) regression model makes one-step ahead forecasts, that is, the sales for the next day.

Extensive hyperparameter tuning leads to slightly better predictions for XGBoost [23] compared to OLS regression. However, due to its low computational effort and the interpretability of its parameters, OLS regression is used for the analysis in this paper. In addition, there are no indications that the findings of this paper would not apply in the case of an XGBoost model. On contrary, due to its higher complexity and its ability to find non-linear relationships between the different input variables, it is most likely that the positive influence of the pandemic variable on the prediction accuracy is even higher when a XGBoost model is used.

Table 2 Analyzed products and the respective amount of selling (covid) days

Article name	ID	#Selling days	#Selling covid days
Bread rolls	1	2182	698
Curd braid	2	2027	698
Butter braid	3	1994	697
Pretzel croissant	4	2182	698
Croissant	5	2182	698
Corn croissant	6	2182	698
Pretzel bun	7	2182	698
Il pollo forte	8	1870	600
Cream slice	9	2176	696
Hazelnut croissant	10	2182	698
Roll	11	2182	698
Bun	12	2176	698
Raspberry doughnut	13	1845	604
Sunflower croissant	14	2182	698
Almond croissant	15	2182	698

5 Results

To answer RQ1, the data is split into a training set and a test set by a 75/25% split (no randomization, as the order of data is relevant in time series forecasting). Thus, the training set contains both times of pandemic and times of no pandemic. The test set contains solely times of pandemic, as the pandemic makes up more than a quarter of the total available data. For each product, two models are trained using the training set: One model that uses the pandemic variable (model-1) and one that does not (model-2).

Model-1:

$$\begin{aligned}\text{Sold} \sim \text{weekday} + \text{temperature} + \text{rain} + \text{sun} + \text{lag1} + \text{lag2} + \text{lag\_week} \\ + \text{holiday} + \text{mean\_week} + \text{school} + \text{covid}\end{aligned}$$

Model-2 uses the same input variables but lacks the variable *covid*. In model-1, the variable *covid* is highly significant (p-value < 0.001) for eight products, significant (p-value < 0.01) for three products, and weakly significant (p-value < 0.05) for one product. For one product, the p-value is < 0.1. Subsequently, for both models, forecasts for each product are made based on the test set. The forecast accuracy is measured in terms of RMSE (root mean squared error). Table 3 depicts the results of this

Table 3 Different products and respective prediction accuracy with and without pandemic variable

Article name	Prediction w/ pandemic variable (RMSE)	Prediction w/o pandemic variable (RMSE)	Deviation (RMSE) (%)
Bread rolls	14.63	15.31	+4
Curd braid	7.24	7.20	–1
Butter braid	16.32	19.69	+17
Pretzel croissant	16.20	17.24	+6
Croissant	50.17	52.84	+5
Corn croissant	15.95	16.69	+4
Pretzel bun	12.81	13.63	+6
Il pollo forte	3.53	3.83	+8
Cream slice	24.38	26.19	+7
Hazelnut croissant	12.95	13.24	+2
Roll	10.70	10.85	+1
Bun	11.96	12.07	+1
Raspberry doughnut	26.79	27.19	+1
Sunflower croissant	16.16	16.87	+4
Almond croissant	11.48	11.64	+1
Mean	16.75	17.63	+4.61

experiment. In the third column, the deviation between both models is shown for each product.

Averaged over all products, model-1 outperforms model-2 by 4.61%. The outperformance differs per product, as some products are affected by the pandemic containment measures more strongly than others. In case of curd braid, including the pandemic variable even led to less accurate forecasts on the test set, possibly due to overfitting on the training set.

To further test the beneficial influence of the pandemic variable on the forecast accuracy, a simulation is run to simulate the start of the covid pandemic. During the iterative simulation, similar to a real-world situation, a model is trained based on all available historic data $[t_{-n} : t_0]$, t_0 being the last non-covid day, and provides predictions for each product for the next day (t_1). The training set hence contains all non-pandemic days. In the next iteration (it_2), the previously predicted day becomes part of the training set (now $[t_{-n} : t_1]$) and the next day (t_2) is predicted. These iterations are continued until t_{m-1} is the last day in the training set to predict t_m (left illustration in Fig. 3).

The second simulation represents an attempt to use the information content about the response of sales to changes in the covid index already at the beginning of a pandemic. Since there has not yet been an onset of a new pandemic in which the regression coefficient from the covid-19 pandemic could be used, the second simulation is intended to help provide an estimate of whether the use of the learned regression coefficient from the covid-19 pandemic may be feasible in a next pandemic. To achieve this, the same procedure is used as in the first simulation, but the coefficient of the pandemic variable is determined based on all available data before and after the day to be predicted ($train_1 + train_2$). Subsequently, the pre-trained covid coefficient is cached and the model is retrained based solely on the available historic data $[t_{-n} : t_0]$, t_0 being the last non-covid day ($train_1$). The right illustration in Fig. 3 shows $train_1$ and $train_2$ and the forecasting horizons for each iteration ($it_1, it_2, ..$). However, the covid coefficient of the model is set to the value of the pre-trained cached covid coefficient. Consequently, the forecasting model has no access to future data (after t_0) as it would be the case in a real scenario.

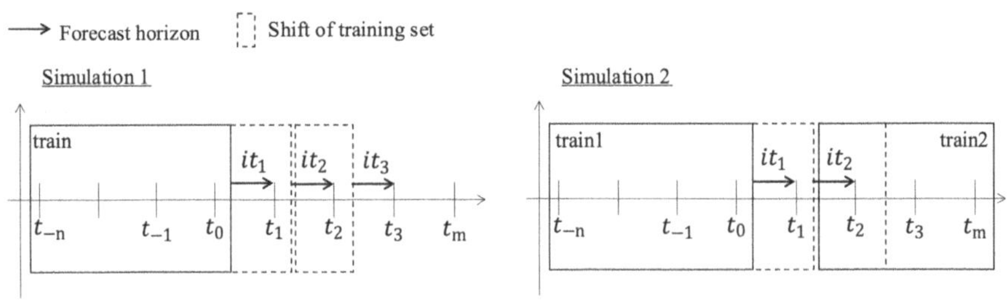

Fig. 3 Sales per month, regression lines for pre- and post-pandemic sales and start of covid pandemic

The results of Simulation 1 and 2 indicate that over all covid-19 pandemic days, including the pandemic variable (model-1) increases the forecast accuracy by 2% (averaged over all products). If the pandemic variable is pre-trained (model-3), the deviation to the model without pandemic variable (model-2) is even higher (2.28%). However, there are differences between different time periods: During the first 100 days of the covid-19 pandemic, model-1 outperforms model-2 only slightly (0.54%). In this period, model-1 and model-3 differ the most, as model-3 outperforms model-2 by 2.4%. After 300 covid days, model-1 and model-3 have almost aligned with each other, as the value of the pandemic variable in both models gradually become similar to each other.

These effects can be exemplarily seen in Fig. 4, which shows two the forecast accuracy in terms of RMSE for model-1 (no pandemic variable) vs. model-2 (with pandemic variable) in the upper illustration and for model-2 (with pandemic variable, but no pre-training) vs. model-3 (with pre-trained pandemic variable) in the lower illustration.

The lower illustration of Fig. 4 depicts the difference between pre-training and no pre-training. After around 300 days of pandemic, both models do not differ much

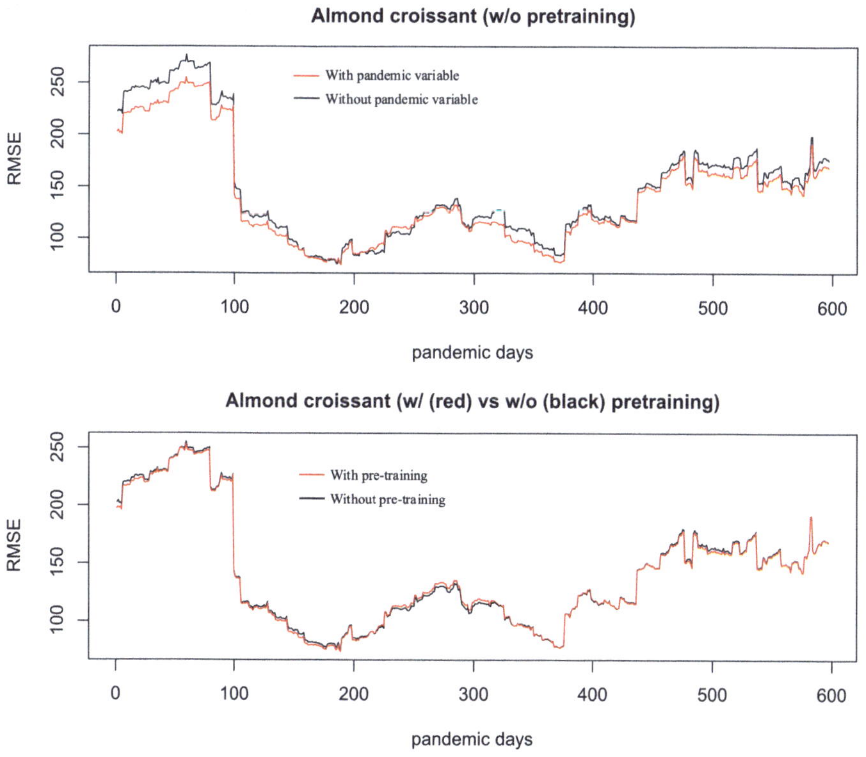

Fig. 4 Comparison between model-1 and model-2 (upper illustration) and model-2 and model-3 (lower illustration) in terms of forecast accuracy (RMSE) during covid-19 pandemic

anymore. Table 5 shows average forecast accuracy in terms of RMSE for the beginning of the covid-19 pandemic (first 200 days) vs. the following 200 days (mid-pandemic). For all three groups (no pandemic variable, covid-variable, pre-trained covid-variable), the forecast accuracy is >10% lower (i.e., higher RMSE) in the beginning of the pandemic compared to mid-pandemic. However, including the pandemic variable into the model decreases the average RMSE in the beginning of the pandemic by 9.3 and including a pre-trained pandemic variable decreases the average RMSE by 15.7.

To summarize, RQ1 can be answered: Including the COVID-19 stringency index (pandemic variable) improves 1-day-ahead forecasts in sales forecasting in the bakery domain. Both the bulk prediction (Table 3) and the iterative predict-retrain-predict process (Tables 4 and 5) show that the pandemic variable is beneficial for the chosen ML forecast model in the bakery domain. RQ2 can be partly answered: In our case, pre-training the pandemic variable based on all available sales data during the covid pandemic has increased forecast accuracy more than using a non-pre-trained pandemic variable. However, there is no data for the same products during another pandemic. Consequently, RQ2 cannot be fully answered as it would require training the pandemic variable based on one pandemic and applying it during the next pandemic.

Table 4 Comparison of forecast accuracy (RMSE) with vs. without pandemic variable for different periods during the covid pandemic for Simulation 1 (without pre-trained pandemic variable) and Simulation 2 (with pre-trained pandemic variable)

Article ID	All days (Sim. 1) (%)	All days (Sim 2) (%)	< 100 days (Sim. 1) (%)	< 100 days (Sim. 2) (%)	> 300 days (Sim. 1) (%)	> 300 days (Sim. 2) (%)
1	0.29	0.56	–1.91	0.80	0.98	0.78
2	0.40	0.08	0.45	4.58	–0.85	0.09
3	9.55	9.81	13.35	14.43	8.06	7.73
4	2.54	2.98	0.95	1.63	2.12	2.10
5	1.15	1.50	–1.89	–1.87	1.55	1.43
6	1.31	1.70	–1.21	0.89	1.80	1.67
7	2.79	3.05	–0.26	–0.60	3.28	3.15
8	1.94	1.71	1.47	2.41	0.75	0.86
9	1.13	1.26	–0.70	0.72	2.11	2.18
10	2.63	3.12	3.82	7.23	1.56	1.86
11	0.76	1.23	–3.52	–1.60	2.15	1.84
12	–0.16	0.16	–4.92	–3.30	1.10	0.41
13	0.98	1.52	–3.01	1.44	1.04	1.01
14	2.12	2.67	–1.36	–0.46	3.10	2.64
15	2.49	2.86	6.81	9.88	1.83	1.99
Mean	**2.00**	**2.28**	**0.54**	**2.41**	**2.04**	**1.99**

Table 5 Forecast accuracy (RMSE) with and without pre-trained and not pre-trained pandemic variable for different periods during the covid pandemic (deviation between first 200 days vs. day 200–400)

Scenario	Mean (RMSE)	Deviation (%)
Days < 200 (pandemic variable, no pre-train)	404.6	
200 > days <400 (pandemic variable, no pre-train)	353	11.80
Days < 200 (no pandemic variable)	413.9	
200 > days < 400 (no pandemic variable)	374.1	14.50
Days < 200 (pre-trained pandemic variable)	398.2	
200 > days < 400 (pre-trained pandemic variable)	353.2	14.20

6 Discussion and Conclusion

In this study, the usefulness of a variable ("pandemic variable") that operationalizes the stringency of covid-19 containment measures in Switzerland for ML-based sales forecasting algorithms was tested. For the operationalization, the KOF StringencyPlus Index (KSI+) [25] was used. It was shown that covid-19 containment measures have a significant impact on the sales of a medium-sized Swiss bakery chain. Thus, including the pandemic variable improves accuracy in ML-based sales forecasting of baked goods.

Three main experiments, for which real data from a medium-sized Swiss bakery was used, were conducted. As a basis, an autoregressive OLS model was used. First, the influence of the pandemic variable on the forecast accuracy in a bulk forecast of ~500 days during the covid-19 pandemic was evaluated. On average, including the pandemic variable increased forecast accuracy by 4.6%. Second, a simulation was run. During this simulation, the algorithm made one-step-ahead sales forecast and was retrained after making the forecasts and comparing it to the actual value. The actual sales are known because the simulation was set in the past. This simulation yielded promising results: the forecast accuracy of the model that uses the pandemic variable was 2% higher over all 15 products and days. Third, the same simulation was run, but the pandemic variable was pre-trained based on the full data set. The pre-trained pandemic variable was used in the iterative setting as described above. In this case, the forecast accuracy was 2.3% higher compared to the model without a pandemic variable.

The containment measures stringency index is generic, meaning that the factors influencing the index value are not specific to the covid-19 pandemic. This way, the stringency index could be determined and applied in ML-based sales forecasting in future pandemics. Findings of related work confirm that the covid-19 pandemic poses a challenge to ML-based forecasting [7, 12]. Several studies deal with the challenge by optimizing the forecasting algorithm itself without including additional feature variables [8–11]. One study [13] aims to increase forecast accuracy by considering expert opinions as additional input variables in the model. Another study [14] adds a feature variable that indicates the different stages of the covid-19 pandemic to increase forecast accuracy. In opposition to the study at hand, a temporal perspective is used, focusing on the phases of the pandemic, rather than a perspective that considers the actual constraints imposed on the population.

An advantage of the chosen methodology is the use of real sales data. Since also the progression of the pandemic variable has not been changed in hindsight, there is no doubt that the pandemic variable would have really improved forecasts. In addition, the pandemic variable is deterministic and can be incorporated without a lag. While other variables like weather or Google Trends Index need to be forecasted themselves (weather) or included with a lag of 1 day (Google Trends Index), the value of the pandemic variable is known around 1 week early.

However, this work does not come without limitations and potential for future research. Decision makers who are responsible for production orders in bakeries have three options in case of future pandemics. First, they can decide to use no pandemic variable at all. In Simulation 1, the test set contains all non-covid days. One-step-ahead forecasts followed by consecutive retraining was done using the pandemic variable. Although the pandemic variable needs some time to adapt, even during the first 200 days of covid-19, the model that uses the pandemic variable outperformed the model that did not. These results indicate that the pandemic variable should be used, which is the second option. Third, decision makers can use the pandemic variable trained based on the covid-19 pandemic and use it their forecasting model in the beginning of the next pandemic. It is difficult to validate the effectiveness of option 3 because the dynamics of a future pandemic are not known yet. It is not certain that the relationship between containment measures and sales remain the same. Customers possibly change their behavior, for example due to accustoming to pandemics in general. To evaluate this, further experiments with data from different pandemics, would need to be done. Although the results in this paper are encouraging, more sophisticated transfer learning methods [27] might be useful to optimize forecasts in the future. In addition, future research could repeat the same experiments using XGBoost or neural networks to compare the findings of this paper with different algorithms.

In summary, the results of this study indicate that a pandemic variable is useful to improve forecasts accuracy in times of pandemics. In this sense, a crisis mode is necessary to enable the algorithm to adapt to changing consumption behavior in times of pandemics.

This study contributes to practice by showing the usefulness of variables that measure the strictness of governments' containment measures as a reaction to pandemics in ML-based sales forecasting algorithms. This study contributes to theory by evaluating the degree to which ML based sales forecasting systems can be relied on in times of great societal change like pandemics. The robustness of such a system is critical for their acceptance and adoption.

References

1. Grove, W. M., Zald, D. H., Lebow, B. S., Snitz, B. E., & Nelson, C. (2000). Clinical versus mechanical prediction: a meta-analysis. *Psychological Assessment, 12*, 19–30.
2. Blohm, I., Antretter, T., Sirén, C., Grichnik, D., & Wincent, J. (2020). It's a peoples game, isn't it?! A comparison between the investment returns of business angels and machine learning algorithms. *Entrepreneurship Theory and Practice, 46*(4).

3. Sun, Z. L., Choi, T. M., Au, K. F., & Yu, Y. (2008). Sales forecasting using extreme learning machine with applications in fashion retailing. *Decision Support Systems, 46*, 411–419.
4. Mentzer, J. T., & Bienstock, C. C. (1998). *Sales forecasting management: Understanding the techniques, systems and management of the sales forecasting process*. SAGE.
5. Beretta, C., & Hellweg, S. (2019). *Lebensmittelverluste in der Schweiz: Mengen und Umweltbelastung. Wissenschaftlicher Schlussbericht*. ETH Zürich.
6. Cam, A., Chui, M., & Hall, B. (2019). *Global AI Survey: AI proves its worth, but few scale impact*. McKinsey Global Institute.
7. Heaven, W. D. Our weird behavior during the pandemic is messing with AI models. Last retrieved August 25, 2022, from https://www.technologyreview.com/2020/05/11/1001563/covid-pandemic-broken-ai-machine-learning-amazon-retail-fraud-humans-in-the-loop/?utm_source=nextdraft&utm_medium=email.
8. Liu, P. (2020). Intermittent demand forecasting for medical consumables with short life cycle using a dynamic neural network during the COVID-19 epidemic. *Health Informatics Journal, 26*, 3106–3122.
9. Lakhal, D. A., Hadj Kacem, S. B., Tagina, M., & Amara, M. A. (2021). Prediction of psychiatric drugs sale during COVID-19. In *2021 IEEE 21st international conference on bioinformatics and bioengineering* (BIBE) (pp. 1–6).
10. Nigam, B., & Shukla, A. C. (2021). Sales forecasting using Box Jenkins method based Arima model considering effect of covid-19 pandemic situation. *International Journal of Engineering Applied Sciences and Technology, 6*(7), 87–97.
11. Nirmala, V. W., Harjadi, D., & Awaluddin, R. (2021). Forecasting by using exponential smoothing method and trend method to optimize product sales in PT. Zamrud Bumi Indonesia During the Covid-19 pandemic. *International Journal of Engineering, Science and Information Technology, 1*(4).
12. Sindihebura, T. T., Pu, X., & Chen, J. (2022). Predictors of sales and the Covid-19 disruption: Evidence from an online marketplace. In *PACIS 2022 proceedings*.
13. Zhang, H., Song, H., Wen, L., & Liu, C. (2021). Forecasting tourism recovery amid COVID-19. *Annals of Tourism Research, 87*, 103149.
14. Leenawong, C., & Chaikajonwat, T. (2022). Event forecasting for Thailand's car sales during the COVID-19 pandemic. *The Brown University Digest of Addiction Theory and Application, 7*, 1–15.
15. Fildes, R., Ma, S., & Kolassa, S. (2019). Retail forecasting: research and practice. *International Journal of Forecasting, 38*(4), 1283–1318.
16. Ramos, P., Santos, N., & Rebelo, R. (2015). Performance of state space and Arima models for consumer retail sales forecasting. *Robotics and Computer-Integrated Manufacturing, 34*, 151–163.
17. Zhang, G. P., & Qi, M. (2005). Neural network forecasting for seasonal and trend time series. *European Journal of Operational Research, 160*(2), 501–514.
18. Veiga, C. P. D., Veiga, C. R. P. D., Puchalski, W., Coelho, L. D. S., & Tortato, U. (2016). Demand forecasting based on natural computing approaches applied to the foodstuff retail segment. *Journal of Retailing and Consumer Services, 31*, 174–181.
19. Chen, F. L., & Ou, T. Y. (2011). Sales forecasting system based on gray extreme learning machine with Taguchi method in retail industry. *Expert Systems with Applications, 38*(3), 1336–1345.
20. Di Pillo, G., Latorre, V., Lucidi, S., & Procacci, E. (2016). An application of support vector machines to sales forecasting under promotions. *Quarterly Journal of Operations Research, 14*(3), 309–325.
21. Ali, Ö. G., Sayın, S., Van Woensel, T., & Fransoo, J. (2009). Sku demand forecasting in the presence of promotions. *Expert Systems with Applications, 36*(10), 12340–12348.
22. Gür Ali, Ö., & Yaman, K. (2013). Selecting rows and columns for training support vector regression models with large retail datasets. *European Journal of Operational Research, 226*(3), 471–480.

23. Chen, T., & Guestrin, C. (2016). XGBoost: A scalable tree boosting system. http://arxiv.org/abs/1603.02754.
24. Chow, G. C. (1960). Tests of equality between sets of coefficients in two linear regressions. *Econometrica: Journal of the Econometric Society, 28*(3), 591–605.
25. Pleninger, R., Streicher, S., & Sturm, J.-E. (2022). Do COVID-19 containment measures work? Evidence from Switzerland. *Swiss Journal of Economics and Statistics, 158*(1), 5.
26. Hale, T., Angrist, N., Cameron-Blake, E., Hallas, L., Kira, B., Majumdar, S., Petherick, A., Phillips, T., Tatlow, H., & Webster, S. (2020). *Variation in government responses to COVID-19* (BSG Working Paper Series). Blavatnik School of Government. University of Oxford.
27. Obst, D., Ghattas, B., Cugliari, J., Oppenheim, G., Claudel, S., & Goude, Y. (2021). Transfer learning for linear regression: A statistical test of gain. arXiv [math.ST].

Artificial Intelligence in Information Systems Research: A Socio-technical Perspective

Dorsa Safaei, Kazem Haki, and Jean-Henry Morin

Abstract While finding its roots in technical disciplines, research on artificial intelligence (AI) has drawn a considerable attention in various disciplines due to AI's broad areas of application. Similarly, information systems (IS) scholars have begun to examine AI-related phenomena given the enormous number of studies published in the last couple of years. Generally, the intellectual core of the IS discipline is to scrutinize novel technologies in their organizational and social contexts from a socio-technical standpoint. Therefore, in this study, we seek to analyze whether and to which extent current AI studies in the IS literature contribute to advancing our socio-technical understanding of AI-related phenomena. To this, we developed a comprehensive analysis framework employing a socio-technical lens and conducted a systematic literature review to analyze AI-related articles in the IS discipline's flagship journals. Demonstrating existing studies' lack of attention to some of the socio-technical components and their interplay, we outline directions for future research.

Keywords Artificial intelligence · Machine learning · Socio-technical perspective · Systematic literature review

D. Safaei (✉)
Geneva School of Business Administration (HES-SO, HEG Genève), Geneva, Switzerland

Institute of Information Service Science—CUI, Geneva School of Social Sciences, University of Geneva, Geneva, Switzerland
e-mail: negin.safaei@hesge.ch

K. Haki
Geneva School of Business Administration (HES-SO, HEG Genève), Geneva, Switzerland

J.-H. Morin
Institute of Information Service Science—CUI, Geneva School of Social Sciences, University of Geneva, Geneva, Switzerland

A. M. Braccini et al. (eds.), *Technologies for Digital Transformation*, Lecture Notes in Information Systems and Organisation 64,
https://doi.org/10.1007/978-3-031-52120-1_5

1 Introduction

Owing to the broad application areas of artificial intelligence (AI), research on AI is gaining traction in information systems (IS) literature [1–3]. While AI has long been studied by IS scholars [4, 5], it has more recently drawn a significant attention in IS research due to advances in machine learning (ML). IS scholars have already given rise to AI's various areas of application for different purposes, such as in human resource management to support the hiring process [6], in pharma firms to reduce the costs and complexities of discovering and developing new drugs [7], at the societal level to find people with emotional distress [8], or in the marketing area to increase sales and predict the effects of different campaigns on sales [9].

Given its wide areas of application, there is no singular, agreed-upon definition of AI [1]. Contingent on the contexts in which AI has been applied, it has been defined differently, highlighting the various types and aspects of AI including the learning ability [10] or the capability of mimicking human skills [11]. In 1956, McCarthy and colleagues, in a workshop that is commonly considered to be a serious starting point to AI, defined AI as "making a machine behave in ways that would be called intelligent if a human were so behaving" [12]. As such, AI reflects the *capability of machines to perform tasks that require human's intelligence and learning capacity* [13, 14]. In turn, ML is a concept that is not the synonym for AI, but can be viewed as a (or the most common) branch of AI. ML is defined as *automation of the learning process* to efficiently and effectively extract meaningful patterns from data [15]. To automate the learning process for AI, ML systems consist of a dataset (a structured collection of data generally associated with labels or features), a model or hypothesis class (a function that maps input to output), and a learning algorithm (the process of converting experience into expertise or knowledge) [15]. Thus, for the sake of simplicity, throughout this paper we mainly use the term AI, which inherently includes ML as its most common branch or technique. We use the term ML when we refer to its pertinent methods or components, or when it is the main focus of the cited references.

In comparison to other disciplines that primarily contribute to the technical or social aspects of AI, IS discipline can contribute to advancing AI studies through a socio-technical lens. In fact, one of the major premises (or even the *raison d'être*) of IS research is to examine the use of technologies in organizational and social contexts from a socio-technical perspective [16, 17]. This is even more decisive for research on AI due to its broad areas of application, and that its technical and social aspects are inextricably intertwined. Against this backdrop and owing to the recent tremendous attention to AI in IS research, it is of great value to investigate whether and how current IS studies contribute to enhancing our socio-technical understanding of AI. Thus, in this study we seek to answer the following research question: *to what extent current AI studies in IS literature account for socio-technical components?*

To answer the research question, we conducted a systematic literature review to analyze current AI publications in the association for information systems (AIS) senior scholars' basket of eight journals. The objective of our review is *not* to analyze how AI can be employed by IS scholars, what is the quality of implemented ML methods, how AI contributes to answering questions that were not possible before, or what is unique about AI compared to traditional techniques. Instead, we seek to analyze whether and to which extent current publications stick to the main premises of the IS discipline, and account for socio-technical components of AI and AI-related phenomena, to eventually outline research alternatives and gaps [18–21]. To this end, our review is guided by an analysis framework that we derived at the outset of our inquiry employing a socio-technical lens. Our review demonstrates the lack of attention to some components of the socio-technical perspective and to the interplay between the socio-technical components. Accordingly, we propose directions for future research in the light of types of IS theories, level of analysis, types of contributions by employing ML, as well as ML constituents such as learning techniques and ML models.

2 Research Background

Because of the considerable attention to ML in recent years, and more broadly to AI, Padmanabhan et al. [22] name the last two decades as a "golden era" for ML. The latter is manifest in the variety of the current AI research in the IS literature: While some IS scholars propose ML methods by combining different ML models or by employing new datasets (e.g., [23]), others focus on exploring AI in interaction with humans to augment intelligence in organizations and society (e.g., [2]). Going beyond AI's applications and underlying methods, some IS scholars give rise to the challenges as well as the negative and unintended consequences entailed in employing AI (e.g., [24, 25]).

Considering the variety of the topics investigated in AI research, it is necessary to discuss particularities of IS phenomena when reviewing current research. In articulating the "intellectual core" of the IS discipline, Sidorova et al. [26] attest that IS research generally intends to include the social context in which technical artifacts are designed and used. Although IS research essentially studies technology-based systems, this analysis requires an understanding of corresponding social systems as well as the interaction between the social and technical systems [27]. Therefore, we opt for a socio-technical lens to guide our analysis of AI research's extant body of knowledge.

A socio-technical perspective to IS [17, 28, 29] considers the social part as equally important as the technical part, as two sides of the same coin. The technical part is concerned with the processes, tasks, and technologies that are needed to transform information to outputs. The social part is concerned with the relationships among people. Therefore, a socio-technical system comprises *actors*, *tasks*, *technology*, and *structure* [17, 29]: *task* describes the goals of the system and the way in which the work gets done to achieve the goals; *technology* includes all technological elements of problem-solving inventions such as computers, design methods, or infrastructure; *actor* includes stakeholders who have an effect on work and any individuals in organizations such as employees, managers, and customers; and *structure* includes systems of communication, authority, and workflow covering both normative and behavioral dimensions such as values, role expectations, and patterns of behavior [17].

These components interact to share a common goal and are embedded in and influenced by an *environment*. Therefore, it is not possible to describe the overall behavior of a socio-technical system based on each isolated aspect, since a diverse set of components that relate to both the social and technical aspects affect the system behavior [17].

3 Research Method

In reviewing the current AI research in the IS literature, we opted for a structured literature review following the suggestions of Webster and Watson [21] and vom Brocke et al. [30]. We applied the method by first selecting the set of articles that fit our research objectives, and then developing a comprehensive analysis framework based on which we systematically coded the retrieved articles.

3.1 Literature Selection

We searched for articles in the AIS senior scholars' basket of eight journals (MISQ, ISR, JMIS, JAIS, EJIS, JIT, ISJ, JSIS) without time limitation. We used two databases including "Web of science" and "Ebsco". We searched for two keywords, namely "machine learning" OR "artificial intelligence" in three parts of the articles including abstract OR title OR keywords. We conducted the literature search in April 2022 and retrieved 116 articles in the first round of literature search. To decide on which articles to include or exclude from the review, we followed Padmanabhan et al. [22] to only include those articles that contribute to ML in either of the following three ways: (1) developed new ML methods or algorithms, or gathered data to improve performance measures (e.g., [31, 32]); (2) implemented ML methods to better understand an IS phenomenon, which includes either measuring causal effects, proposing domain-specific statistical models, or developing structural econometric models (e.g., [33, 34]); or (3) focused on ML contribution as a part of a larger, complex system instead of considering ML alone (e.g., [35, 36]). Furthermore, we included literature reviews and editorials to our overall analysis of the literature.

As such, we excluded ten articles that did not match with the abovementioned criteria. We also further continued our search with the forward and backward search, resulting in eleven additional articles. The latter articles were considered because they had the same contributions as the inclusion criteria. In sum, we concluded our search by 117 articles.

3.2 Analysis Framework

Following the recommendations of Webster and Watson [21], we developed an analysis framework (Table 1) to guide our coding procedure. The analysis framework comprises eight major components and their corresponding sub-components,

Table 1 Analysis framework

Coding components and sub-components	
Research methods in IS [37–39]	• Analytical modeling • Case study • Case survey • Conceptual • Grounded theory • Literature review • Mixed methods • Design science research • Simulation • Survey • Experimental
Theoretical lenses *Open coding*	• Complexity theory • Warranting theory • Focus theory • …
Types of generated IS theories [40]	• Analysis • Explanation • Prediction • Explanation and prediction • Design and action
Socio-technical components [17, 41]	• Tasks • Technology • Actors • Structure • Environment
Phenomena of interest *Open coding*	• Healthcare • Blockchain • Marketing • …
Levels of analysis [14, 42]	• People • Processes • Organization • Inter-organization • Society
Types of contributions by employing ML [22]	• ML methods development • Understanding phenomena using ML • ML in complex systems

(continued)

Table 1 (continued)

Coding components and sub-components	
ML constituents	
Datasets [43–45]	*Primary data:* • Surveys or polls • Transactional tracking • Interviews and focus groups • Social media monitoring • Online tracking • Mobile app/ platform monitoring • Simulation • Experiment • Sensors/GPS monitoring *Secondary data:* Data sources such as social media, websites, sales reports, and multiple data sources
Models [46] *Open coding*	• Decision tree • Neural network • Support vector machine • …
Learning techniques [15, 47]	Supervised learning Unsupervised learning Reinforce learning Deep learning
Validation methods [46] *Open coding*	• Cross-validation • Hold-out • Bootstrapping • …

namely research methods in IS, types of generated IS theories, employed theoretical lenses to inform the generated IS theories, socio-technical components, phenomena of interest, types of contributions by employing ML, levels of analysis, and ML constituents. We derived all the sub-components of the analysis framework using both a priori and axial coding. That is, for some components, all the sub-components were derived from existing research (a priori), whereas for others we derived them after coding a representative portion of articles and then applied them back to all the retrieved articles.

It is noteworthy that, in our analysis framework, research methods in IS differ from the methods, models, and techniques captured in ML constituents. Research methods in IS (e.g., case study, survey, design science) concern the methodological approach employed in each study to rigorously guide the development of IS theories. In turn, ML constituents concern the employed datasets (e.g., sensors, online tracking, social media monitoring), models (e.g., decision tree, neural network), and learning techniques (e.g., supervised learning, unsupervised learning) in the use and application of ML in studying an IS phenomenon. For the ML constituents, we also included validation methods (e.g., cross-validation, bootstrapping) that are used to tune the parameters of a ML model.

4 Results

In this section, building on the analysis framework, we first provide an overview of AI research in the IS literature. We then analyze the retrieved articles from a socio-technical perspective. Finally, we discuss how current studies employed ML constituents.

4.1 Current State of Research

As shown in Fig. 1 (capturing AI-related articles until April 2022), since 1986 researchers in IS started scrutinizing AI, but the number of AI-related articles has significantly increased recently (especially in the last 4 years) due to advances in ML.

Building on the analysis framework components, Table 2 provides an overview of current research on AI. Our results show that IS researchers adopted a variety of research methods. Nonetheless, analytical modeling (30%) to quantitatively (using a mathematical approach) specify parametric relations among different variables is the most common employed research method, followed by conceptual (18%) and design science research (17%) methods. Other research methods, specifically simulation (1%) and survey (1%), are barely employed.

Following Gregor [40], we also coded articles based on the types of generated IS theories. As shown in Table 2, almost half of the articles generated the explanation and prediction type of theories (49%) to offer causal explanations, testable propositions, and eventually provide predictions. A considerable portion of articles also focused on more basic IS theories, specifically analysis theories (24%) to provide analysis and description to the phenomena of interest as well as explanation theories (10%) to purely explain the phenomena of interest. Finally, 17% of articles developed design and action theories with the aim to provide prescriptions and construct artifacts (e.g., [48, 49]).

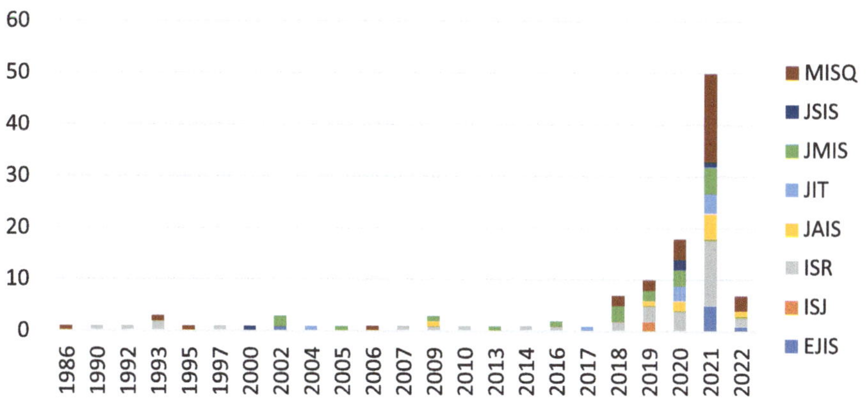

Fig. 1 AI-related articles published in the AIS basket journals over time

Table 2 Overview of the current AI articles based on the analysis framework

Research methods	Share of articles		Types of generated IS theories	Share of articles	
Analytical modeling		30%	Analysis		24%
Case study		7%	Explanation		10%
Case survey		3%	Prediction		0%
Conceptual		18%	Explanation and prediction		49%
Grounded theory		2%	Design and action		17%
Literature		3%	**Level of analysis**	**Share of articles**[a]	
Mixed method		12%	People		34%
Design science research		17%	Process		56%
Simulation		1%	Organization		21%
Survey		1%	Inter-organization		2%
Experiment		6%	Society		6%
Types of contributions by employing ML	**Share of articles**		**Phenomena of interest**	**Share of articles**	
ML methods development		32%	Marketing and sales		16%
Understanding phenomena using ML		32%	Healthcare		10%
ML in complex systems		26%	Social media		7%

[a]For some of the analysis framework's components, the reviewed articles employed more than one sub-component or not all of the sub-components. Therefore, in these cases the accumulation of percentages exceeds or is less than 100%. This holds for some of the components presented in this table as well as in Table 4 and Fig. 2

Our analysis reveals that the process level of analysis in which AI is employed to enhance products and services is the most common level of analysis (56%) in existing research. It is followed by the people level (34%) in which AI is used to solve specific problems by performing tasks better than humans or enhancing human cognition. 21% of articles used AI in the context of organizations and only 2% of articles focused on an inter-organization level of analysis.

In terms of types of contributions by employing ML, our analysis indicates that, interestingly the three types of contributions have drawn almost the same attention by IS scholars. 38 articles (32%) have novelty in ML models, algorithms, or data in comparison to the existing ones and contribute in ML methods development. 37 articles (32%) contribute in understanding IS-related phenomena using ML in either of the following three ways: measuring the effect of a solution or a treatment on an outcome of a new challenging problem; constructing innovative models to accurately describe a phenomenon rather than contributing to the development of a method for a general use; and make statistical models to optimize agent behaviors.

Finally, 31 articles (26%) focus on ML as part of larger and complex systems instead of considering ML alone. It is noteworthy that, some articles such as literature reviews or editorials are not categorized in these types of contributions.

In the reviewed articles, a wide variety of topics are examined, among them topics related to marketing and sales, healthcare, and social media were the most common phenomena of interest. For instance, in the marketing and sales-related articles, there are studies on the effects of online product review on purchases [50], the effectiveness of marketing campaigns for malls [9], or the effectiveness of item recommendations for mobile apps [51].

As for theoretical lenses, our analysis shows that only 21% of the reviewed articles employed a theoretical lens to inform their developed theories. Further, a wide variety of theoretical lenses are employed, such that we cannot indicate commonly employed theories by IS scholars in their AI-related inquiries.

4.2 Socio-technical Analysis of Current Studies

A socio-technical perspective in investigating IS phenomena requires accounting for both the social and technical aspects and their relations [17]. Nevertheless, our analysis of existing studies shows that the majority of the reviewed articles considered less than two socio-technical components in their inquiries (Table 3).

Among the socio-technical components, technology (75%), task (69%), and actor (68%) have drawn the most, and almost the same, attention in existing studies, while less attention is paid to structure (20%) and environment (16%) components (Table 4). In what follows and as summarized in Table 4, we revisit our analysis from Sect. 4.1 on the generated IS theories, types of contributions by employing ML, and the level of analysis from a socio-technical perspective.

In terms of the types of generated IS theories, almost the same pattern as the aforementioned overview, in terms of the attention to specific socio-technical components, can be observed. That is, task, technology, and actor components are omnipresent in different types of generated IS theories. Nevertheless, we detect two distinct points. First, in almost all the articles in the design and action category, technology is considered because they usually design a novel ML method by, for example, combining various ML methods to get better results in a specific problem space. Second, in the analysis category, and to a relatively lower extent in the explanation category, other socio-technical components (e.g., structure and environment) are included. The latter is due to the nature of these IS theory types in giving rise and explaining new phenomena in a comprehensive manner.

Table 3 The number of socio-technical components considered in the existing AI research

Number of socio-technical components	One component		Two components		Three components		Four components		Five components	
Share of articles	◔	15%	◑	42%	◔	29%	◔	9%	◔	5%

Table 4 Analysis of the current AI research from a socio-technical perspective

Socio-technical components	Task	Technology	Actor	Structure	Environment
Share of articles	69%	75%	68%	20%	16%
Types of generated IS theories					
Analysis	86%	86%	61%	21%	32%
Explanation	83%	92%	83%	25%	17%
Explanation and prediction	56%	60%	68%	21%	12%
Design and action	75%	95%	65%	10%	5%
Types of contributions by employing ML					
ML methods development	74%	100%	61%	13%	5%
Understanding phenomena using ML	57%	41%	70%	11%	8%
ML in complex systems	68%	94%	87%	42%	32%
Level of analysis					
People	43%	80%	100%	35%	23%
Process	89%	79%	48%	12%	12%
Organization	88%	68%	84%	36%	28%
Inter-organization	50.0%	50%	100%	50%	100%
Society	57%	86%	100%	71%	29%

When it comes to the types of contributions by employing ML, unsurprisingly it is evident that the technology component is considered in almost all the studies that focus on ML methods development or on ML in complex systems. In the ML methods development type of contribution, all the articles in this category considered technology because the objective of these studies is per se to employ a new method or data to improve intended results. However, in the ML in complex systems type of contribution, similar to the technology component, the actor component is also greatly considered. This is because, in this type of contribution, ML is considered as part of a larger complex system interacting with humans as actors. Further, in the ML in complex systems type of contribution, the structure and environment components are more significantly considered, compared to other contribution types, because ML is not supposed to be seen as a separate part: ML could affect the system around it and the system could affect the ML part. As another insight, the actor component is also dominantly considered in the understanding phenomena using ML type of contribution in which ML is mainly employed to solve human related problems.

As for the level of analysis, in the people level, it is evident that the focus is on the actor and the technology components. Here, scholars aim to suggest a ML model that functions better than humans or scholars analyze the effects of AI on humans. In turn, in the process level of analysis, the focus is on the task and the technology components. In these studies, scholars aim to enhance and improve tasks for generating products or services by using AI. Similar to the people level of analysis, in the society level, the actor and the technology components are focused. But, the difference is the further dominant focus on the structure component in the society level, which covers the systems of communication, authority, or workflow among different actors. In addition, in the society and organization levels of analysis, the environment component is considered more than the other categories. Since only 2% of articles are categorized in the inter-organization level of analysis (Table 2), we refrain to provide analysis for this level.

4.3 Machine Learning Constituents

In total, 62 out of the 117 reviewed articles implemented ML methods in their research, almost half of which (52%) collected primary data, 27% used secondary data, and 21% used both primary and secondary data. This result shows that primary data collection is common in existing AI studies and most of the articles gathered data instead of using existing ones. Researchers employed various data collection methods. As summarized in Fig. 2, the most common primary data collection method is online tracking (23%) in which researchers actively observe users' behavior interacting with different parts of websites or writing reviews. Researchers also commonly used social media monitoring (16%) and experiment (16%) to collect primary data. Regarding secondary data, texts and reviews collected from websites are the most common secondary data employed by researchers.

Regarding learning techniques, as depicted in Fig. 2, the majority of articles (82%) employed supervised learning, which means that they employed labeled datasets. It is important to mention that we categorized semi-supervised in supervised learning group. Among articles that employed supervised learning, 38% implemented deep learning for their analysis. Our analysis also shows that the most common ML models in supervised learning are the different types of neural networks such as convolutional neural networks and recurrent neural networks. Regression and support vector machines are also widely used in supervised learning. Unsupervised learning is employed by 13% of articles, half of which used deep learning for their analysis. Neural networks are also common ML models in unsupervised learning. Only 5% of articles used reinforcement learning as a learning technique and none of them employed deep learning. Reinforcement learning is mainly employed when an agent interacts with the environment and it has to take the best sequence of decisions to maximize a long-term reward [52]. This result shows that the nature of the issues in this field is not of this type. Regarding validation methods, only 52% of articles explicitly mentioned their methods. Our analysis shows that cross-validation is the most common validation method in existing research.

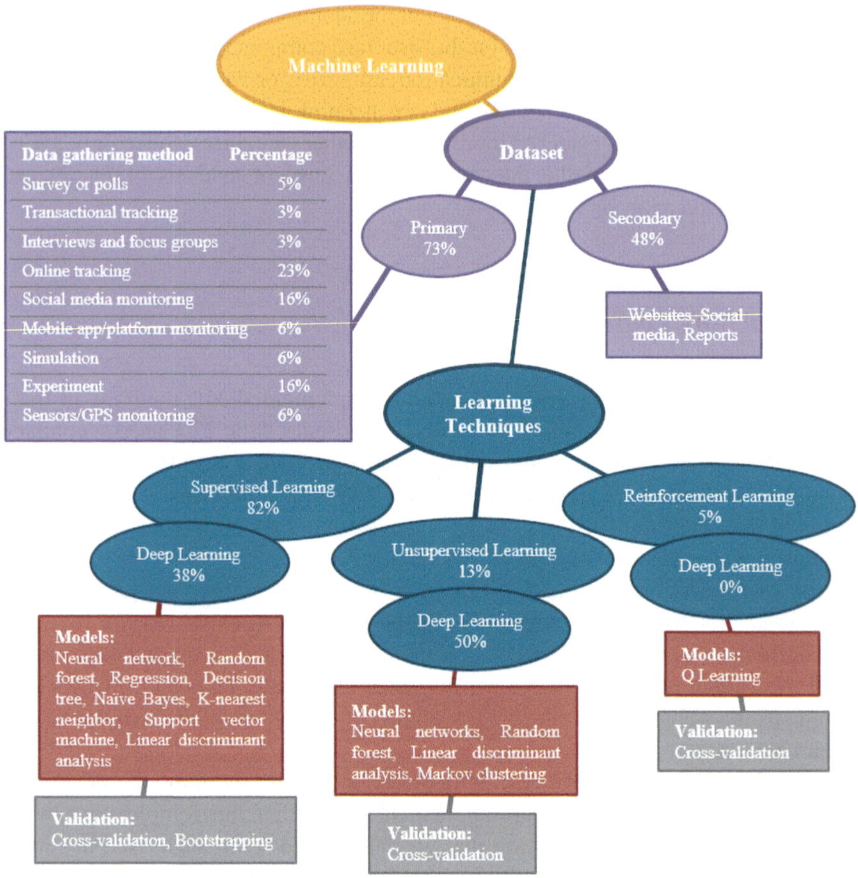

Fig. 2 Overview of ML constituents in the current AI studies

5 Discussion and Conclusion

Although AI has only attracted attention in IS research over the course of last 4 years (Fig. 1), the number of publications is quite significant. This trend is more likely to continue due to the numerous ongoing and upcoming special issues in IS journals and the considerable number of AI-related tracks in IS flagship conferences. Therefore, this seems to be a right time to provide an overview of current AI research, chart new avenues for prospective research, and more importantly, analyze whether and to which extent current studies stick to the IS discipline's premises. We do so from a socio-technical perspective due to the main premise of the IS discipline to examine novel technologies in their organizational and social contexts [26]. Considering both the social and technical aspects is indispensable to develop a balanced and contextual perspective, especially when we encounter complex problems such as human-AI interactions. Our review builds on a comprehensive analysis framework, guiding us to analyze the coverage of both the social and technical aspects in the current AI research. Relying on the presented insights and the analysis of socio-technical components in the preceding section, in what follows we propose some directions for future research.

As the focus of our review indicates, the socio-technical perspective is the central point of gravity in the IS discipline [26]. Nevertheless, our review reveals that, although technology, task, and actor components are to some extent considered in the existing research, there is an evident lack in accounting for the environment and structure components (Table 4), and also in the relations between all the socio-technical components (Table 3). Since the interactions between actors and AI technology in performing tasks are contingent on the structural arrangements and the environment in which interactions occur, we call IS scholars to pay attention to the environment and structure components as well as on the relation between all the socio-technical components. This focus would potentially generate theories that distinguish IS theories from the other disciplines' theories on AI. As such, we encourage future research to take into account the abovementioned theoretical lack in the research directions that we outline in the following.

Starting with the types of generated IS theories, the analysis and explanation are the most basic theory types upon which other types of theories can be developed [40]. Current research pays some attention to these types of theories (Table 2). Nonetheless, owing to criticality of the analysis and explanation theories in further developing a stream of literature, we encourage future research to lay more emphasis on these theory types. The latter calls for more exploratory research on AI. Considering the status of existing research in terms of the employed research methods (Table 2), we specifically encourage future research to conduct case studies and grounded theory-informed inquiries to provide in-depth analyses of AI-related phenomena in their organizational and social contexts. In addition, IS research has recently started recognizing the value of simulation-based experiments in exploratory research for theory development [41, 53, 54]. Considering the low attention to simulations in the current research (Table 2), there is a considerable potential in advancing AI research in the IS discipline by employing this method. Furthermore, using theoretical lenses from the reference disciplines is very common in IS research for informing IS theories specially when we face an uncharted territory or new phenomena. In the current AI-related research, only 21% of articles employed some theoretical lenses to inform their generated theories. Therefore, the prospective research is encouraged to systematically build their AI-related theories on the existing grand theories from, for instance, organization and management sciences literature.

Our analysis also unfolds the focus of current studies on the development of ML methods (Table 2). Therefore, it is not surprising that the existing research primarily focuses on the people and process levels of analysis (Table 2) in the development of ML methods. As previously discussed, there is a lack of focus on the structure and environment components of a socio-technical system (Table 4) as well as on the relation between all the socio-technical components (Table 3). Therefore, in line with the current reviews of AI research [16], and with the socio-technical premises of the IS discipline, we encourage future research to fill the void by examining AI-related phenomena in organization, inter-organization, and society levels of analysis. In addition, by their nature, socio-technical phenomena are multi-level, such that variables at one level can influence variables in another level [17]. Therefore, in line with current studies that seek to bring multi-level inquiries to the forefront of IS research [17, 55], we call for multi-level AI-related inquiries.

As for the types of contributions by employing ML, our review demonstrates a relatively equal attention to all three types of contributions (Table 2). The first type (ML methods development) focuses on the development of new ML methods or algorithms. We thereby foresee the other two types (understanding phenomena using ML and ML in complex systems) to distinguish IS theories from the other disciplines such as computer science that primarily focus on developing ML methods or algorithms. Recently, a considerable attention has been paid to the design and development of AI, and to combining AI with human intelligence, to augment both human and AI in the context of individual work, organizations, or society [2]. When we aim to examine AI in the context of a complex system interacting with humans, the importance of a socio-technical perspective considering all five components becomes even more evident. As expected, our analysis shows that the number of socio-technical components considered in the ML in complex systems type of contribution is more than the other two types of contribution (Table 4); yet the interactions among the different socio-technical components, specifically the effects of the environment, need more attention.

Concerning ML constituents, a considerable number of reviewed articles gathered primary data (Fig. 2). Since the results show that the majority of existing studies applied supervised learning as their technique, it indicates that they get access to labeled datasets. We draw the attention of IS scholars to other, novel techniques that are used in other disciplines such as computer science, but rarely in IS research. For example, sharing data among several organizations (or among several machines) while preserving privacy is an important challenge. There are some techniques such as federated learning that can be applied when multiple decentralized devices or servers commonly train a model by local data samples. The latter technique can help better train models without exchanging data among different organizations or devices.

Moreover, neural networks have been dominantly employed as a ML model in existing research for both supervised and unsupervised learning (Fig. 2). Humans perceive their world with various senses such as vision, tactile, gustatory, auditory, and olfactory. Since in IS research there are several studies that aim to understand human behaviors or help humans with AI-related tools such as smart personal assistants (e.g., [56]), or coordinating humans with AI (e.g., [57]), it is important that machines perceive the world with multiple modalities such as sound, image, or text. Therefore, we encourage the use of multimodal ML [58] to process and relate various data from multiple modalities. The importance of this type of problems is gaining momentum in IS research (e.g., [32]) similar to other disciplines, indicating an extensive potential for the future research.

While extracting novel insights from the existing research, our review has some limitations. First, we only retrieved relevant articles from the AIS senior scholars' basket of eight journals to include high-quality publications. AI is a very rapidly growing topic in IS research and a great deal of work is published in IS conferences over the last years. Therefore, including proceedings of the flagship IS conferences may further develop the discussed insights in our work. Second, although we intended to include all the relevant articles from the selected journals, we limited our search terms to only two keywords (i.e., artificial intelligence, machine learning). Broadening and extending the keywords (e.g., active learning, deep learning) might result to a larger number of articles. Last but not least, our review was limited to the coverage of socio-technical components in the current AI research. Therefore, we did not investigate how AI and its related techniques help IS scholars provide a better understanding of the socio-technical components in IS phenomena.

Acknowledgement This research was funded by RCSO & EM, the University of Applied Sciences of Western Switzerland (HES-SO).

References

1. Berente, N., Gu, B., Recker, J., & Santhanam, R. (2021). Managing artificial intelligence. *MIS Quarterly, 45*, 1433–1450.
2. Jain, H., Padmanabhan, B., Pavlou, P. A., & Raghu, T. (2021). Editorial for the special section on humans, algorithms, and augmented intelligence: The future of work, organizations, and society. *Information Systems Research, 32*, 675–687.
3. Ågerfalk, P. J. (2020). Artificial intelligence as digital agency. *European Journal of Information Systems, 29*, 1–8.
4. Remus, W. E., & Kottemann, J. E. (1986). Toward intelligent decision support systems: An artificially intelligent statistician. *MIS Quarterly, 10*, 403–418.
5. Mookerjee, V. S., & Dos Santos, B. L. (1993). Inductive expert system design: maximizing system value. *Information Systems Research, 4*, 111–140.
6. van den Broek, E., Sergeeva, A., & Huysman, M. (2021). When the machine meets the expert: An ethnography of developing AI for hiring. *MIS Quarterly, 45*, 1557–1580.
7. Lou, B., & Wu, L. (2021). AI on drugs: Can artificial intelligence accelerate drug development? Evidence from a large-scale examination of bio-pharma firms. *MIS Quarterly, 45*, 1451–1482.
8. Chau, M., Li, T. M., Wong, P. W., Xu, J. J., Yip, P. S., & Chen, H. (2020). Finding people with emotional distress in online social media: A design combining machine learning and rule-based classification. *MIS Quarterly, 44*, 933–955.
9. Wang, T., He, C., Jin, F., & Hu, Y. J. (2021). Evaluating the effectiveness of marketing campaigns for malls using a novel interpretable machine learning model. *Information Systems Research, 19*.
10. Castelvecchi, D. (2016). Can we open the black box of AI? *Nature News, 538*, 20–23.
11. Brynjolfsson, E., & Mitchell, T. (2017). What can machine learning do? *Workforce implications. Science, 358*, 1530–1534.
12. McCarthy, J., Minsky, M. L., Rochester, N., & Shannon, C. E. (2006). A proposal for the Dartmouth Summer Research Project on Artificial Intelligence, August 31, 1955. *AI Magazine, 27*, 12.
13. Winston, P. H. (1992). *Artificial intelligence*. Addison-Wesley Longman.
14. Bawack, R. E., Fosso Wamba, S., & Carillo, K. (2019). Artificial intelligence in practice: Implications for IS research. *Americas Conference on Information Systems, 25*.
15. Shalev-Shwartz, S. (2021). *Shai Ben-David: Understanding machine learning: From theory to algorithms*. Cambridge University Press.

16. Niehaus, F., & Wiesche, M. (2021). A socio-technical perspective on organizational interaction with AI: A literature review. *European Journal of Information Systems, 29.*
17. Lyytinen, K., & Newman, M. (2008). Explaining information systems change: A punctuated socio-technical change model. *European Journal of Information Systems, 17*, 589–613.
18. Cooper, H. M. (1988). Organizing knowledge syntheses: A taxonomy of literature reviews. *Knowledge in Society, 1*, 104–126.
19. Paré, G., Trudel, M.-C., Jaana, M., & Kitsiou, S. (2015). Synthesizing information systems knowledge: A typology of literature reviews. *Information & Management, 52*, 183–199.
20. Rowe, F. (2014). What literature review is not: diversity, boundaries and recommendations. *European Journal of Information Systems, 23*, 241–255.
21. Webster, J., & Watson, R. T. (2002). Analyzing the past to prepare for the future: Writing a literature review. *MIS Quarterly, 26*, xiii–xxiii.
22. Padmanabhan, B., Sahoo, N., & Burton-Jones, A. (2022). Machine learning in information systems research. *MIS Quarterly, 46*, iii–xix.
23. Xia Liu, A., Li, Y., & Xu, S. X. (2021). Assessing the unacquainted: inferred reviewer personality and review helpfulness. *MIS Quarterly, 45*, 1113–1148.
24. Teodorescu, M. H., Morse, L., Awwad, Y., & Kane, G. C. (2021). Failures of fairness in automation require a deeper understanding of human-ML augmentation. *MIS Quarterly, 45*, 1483–1499.
25. Mikalef, P., Conboy, K., Lundström, J. E., & Popovič, A. (2022). Thinking responsibly about responsible AI and 'the dark side' of AI. *European Journal of Information Systems, 31*, 1–12.
26. Sidorova, A., Evangelopoulos, N., Valacich, J. S., & Ramakrishnan, T. (2008). Uncovering the intellectual core of the information systems discipline. *MIS Quarterly, 32*, 467–482.
27. Lee, A. S. (2010). Retrospect and prospect: Information systems research in the last and next 25 years. *Journal of Information Technology, 25*, 336–348.
28. Bostrom, R. P., & Heinen, J. S. (1977). MIS problems and failures: A socio-technical perspective. Part I: The causes. *MIS Quarterly, 1*, 17–32.
29. Wu, P. P.-Y., Fookes, C., Pitchforth, J., & Mengersen, K. (2015). A framework for model integration and holistic modeling of socio-technical systems. *Decision Support Systems, 71*, 14–27.
30. Vom Brocke, J., Simons, A., Riemer, K., Niehaves, B., Plattfaut, R., & Cleven, A. (2015). Standing on the shoulders of giants: Challenges and recommendations of literature search in information systems research. *Communications of the Association for Information Systems, 37*, 9.
31. Ebrahimi, M., Nunamaker, J. F., Jr., & Chen, H. (2020). Semi-supervised cyber threat identification in dark net markets: A transductive and deep learning approach. *Journal of Management Information Systems, 37*, 694–722.
32. Zhang, W., & Ram, S. (2020). A comprehensive analysis of triggers and risk factors for asthma based on machine learning and large heterogeneous data sources. *MIS Quarterly, 44*, 305–349.
33. Zhang, N., & Xu, H. (2019). Reconciling the paradoxical findings of choice overload through an analytical lens. *MIS Quarterly, 45*, 1893–1920.
34. Lukyanenko, R. (2019). Expecting the unexpected: Effects of data collection design choices on the quality of crowdsourced user-generated content. *MIS Quarterly, 43*, 623–648.
35. Asatiani, A., Malo, P., Nagbøl, P. R., Penttinen, E., Rinta-Kahila, T., & Salovaara, A. (2021). Socio-technical envelopment of artificial intelligence: An approach to organizational deployment of inscrutable artificial intelligence systems. *Journal of the Association for Information Systems, 22*, 325–352.
36. Diederich, S., Brendel, A. B., Morana, S., & Kolbe, L. (2022). On the design of and interaction with conversational agents: An organizing and assessing review of human-computer interaction research. *Journal of the Association for Information Systems, 23*, 96–138.
37. Saunders, M., Lewis, P., & Thornhill, A. (2009). *Research methods for business students.* Pearson Education.

38. Al Kilani, M. (2016). An overview of research methodology in information system (IS). *Open Access Library Journal, 3*, 1–9.
39. Myers, M. D., & Avison, D. (2002). Qualitative research in information systems: A reader. *Sage*.
40. Gregor, S. (2006). The nature of theory in information systems. *MIS Quarterly, 30*, 611–642.
41. Beese, J., Haki, M. K., Aier, S., & Winter, R. (2019). Simulation-based research in information systems. *Business & Information Systems Engineering, 61*, 503–521.
42. Bariff, M. L., & Ginzberg, M. J. (1982). MIS and the behavioral sciences: Research patterns and prescriptions. *ACM SIGMIS Database: The Database for Advances in Information Systems, 14*, 19–26.
43. Kaplan, B., & Duchon, D. (1988). Combining qualitative and quantitative methods in information systems research: A case study. *MIS Quarterly, 12*, 571–586.
44. Kaplan, B., & Maxwell, J. A. (2005). Qualitative research methods for evaluating computer information systems. In J. G. Anderson & C. E. Aydin (Eds.), *Evaluating the organizational impact of healthcare information systems* (pp. 30–55). Springer.
45. Sapsford, R., & Jupp, V. (1996). Data collection and analysis. *Sage*.
46. Alpaydin, E. (2020). *Introduction to machine learning*. MIT Press.
47. LeCun, Y., Bengio, Y., & Hinton, G. (2015). Deep learning. *Nature, 521*, 436–444.
48. Li, J., Larsen, K., & Abbasi, A. (2020). TheoryOn: A design framework and system for unlocking behavioral knowledge through ontology learning. *MIS Quarterly, 44*, 1733–1772.
49. Zhu, H., Samtani, S., Chen, H., & Nunamaker, J. F., Jr. (2020). Human identification for activities of daily living: A deep transfer learning approach. *Journal of Management Information Systems, 37*, 457–483.
50. Kwark, Y., Lee, G. M., Pavlou, P. A., & Qiu, L. (2021). On the spillover effects of online product reviews on purchases: Evidence from clickstream data. *Information Systems Research, 32*, 895–913.
51. Adamopoulos, P., Ghose, A., & Tuzhilin, A. (2022). Heterogeneous demand effects of recommendation strategies in a mobile application: Evidence from econometric models and machine-learning instruments. *MIS Quarterly, 46*.
52. Sutton, R. S., & Barto, A. G. (2018). *Reinforcement learning: An introduction*. MIT Press.
53. Haki, K., Beese, J., Aier, S., & Winter, R. (2020). The evolution of information systems architecture: An agent-based simulation model. *MIS Quarterly, 44*, 155–184.
54. Dong, J. Q. (2022). Using simulation in information systems research. *Journal of the Association for Information Systems, 23*, 408–417.
55. Markus, M. L., & Robey, D. (1988). Information technology and organizational change: Causal structure in theory and research. *Management Science, 34*, 583–598.
56. Knote, R., Janson, A., Söllner, M., & Leimeister, J. M. (2020). Value co-creation in smart services: a functional affordances perspective on smart personal assistants. *Journal of the Association for Information Systems, 22*, 418–458.
57. Sturm, T., Gerlach, J. P., Pumplun, L., Mesbah, N., Peters, F., Tauchert, C., Nan, N., & Buxmann, P. (2021). Coordinating human and machine learning for effective organizational learning. *MIS Quarterly, 45*, 1581–1602.
58. Baltrušaitis, T., Ahuja, C., & Morency, L.-P. (2018). Multimodal machine learning: A survey and taxonomy. *IEEE Transactions on Pattern Analysis and Machine Intelligence, 41*, 423–443.

Blockchain and Lending Process Efficiency in the Banking Industry

Elena Bruno and Giuseppina Iacoviello

Abstract The Blockchain technology is disrupting the banking industry. It was originally used for cryptocurrency trading, and more recently for smart contracts and peer-to-peer (P2P) and other banking services. There is currently a gap in research about and development of blockchain applications in the banking sector, especially regarding the decentralization of information to mortgage credit processes through ledgers. Following a qualitative research approach, this paper aims to highlight the fact that blockchain technology is both a threat to and an opportunity for banks. The study provides support for the argument that blockchain is a disruptive technology that will create new business opportunities for banks, even though it will also pose new risks. Blockchain technology may improve the efficiency of banking processes, and therefore the products and services that banks offer their customers, in new areas such as lending. From a methodology point of view, we follow common and established guidelines of qualitative research. Starting from a literature review of both the blockchain and the credit process, we discuss the relevant literature within a joint analytical framework. We thus identify paths for future research and discuss the potential of blockchain technology in mortgage lending processes.

Keywords Blockchain · Banking · Mortgage credit process · Process efficiency

E. Bruno · G. Iacoviello (✉)
Department of Economics and Management, University of Pisa, Pisa, Italy
e-mail: giuseppina.iacoviello@unipi.it

A. M. Braccini et al. (eds.), *Technologies for Digital Transformation*, Lecture Notes in Information Systems and Organisation 64,
https://doi.org/10.1007/978-3-031-52120-1_6

1 Introduction

Blockchain is one of the most important and innovative technologies developed in recent years in the banking sector. As such, it has experienced explosive growth and, as many would agree, will have great potential for actual application in the industry [1]. The technology has already changed the dynamics of many industries, and is expected to revolutionize businesses, not only in the banking industry, but across sectors such as healthcare, government, retail, and more.

A blockchain is essentially a digital ledger that provides an unalterable record of transactions between two parties. Computers on a network validate each transaction before it's added to the blockchain, and a transaction cannot be changed or tampered with once completed. These transactions are cryptographically secured to ensure that they remain tamper-proof. Blockchain is therefore a digital platform for disruptive innovation, which means its impact can possibly spread far wider than the revitalizing of financial services [2, 3].

Our analysis of several articles from the literature reveals that banks are progressively embracing the concept of blockchain technology. Current initiatives based on the blockchain are capturing the attention of both practitioners and academics, testifying to the possibility of new application scenarios opening for the recovery of efficiency in the operational processes of banks.

At present, the blockchain finds application in the following main financial categories:

1. Payments and value transfer: the blockchain has been used in this way for the trading of cryptocurrencies and diversification of the sources of collection of venture capital and third parties—Initial Coin Offering-ICO—or for the placement of bond issues [4–8].
2. Asset tokenization: assets can be fungible and interchangeable or non-interchangeable, representing a single property of a specific asset [9–12].
3. Process automation: to support initiatives to recover the efficiency of the entry, for its verification and validation procedures, or to eliminate the use of paper documents and to decrease completion times of the business process [13–15].
4. Notarization: to verify the originality of a digital document and its existence at a certain date and time. This is widely used in the banking sector for bank collateral [16].

Our research focuses on the third topic, with the aim of highlighting the advantage and the possible development of the use of blockchain technologies in lending processes.

A P2P digital lending platform acts as an exchange between shareholders and debtors. An individual with chargeable money can lend it directly to an insolvent actor through a digital platform and earn interest on it [17]. Blockchain-based lending can provide a secure way of offering loans to an inclusive pool of consumers, which can lower costs for all parties.

There are two principal ways of involving blockchain in the lending process. The first is using blockchain-based products as collateral in lending (e.g., crypto assets). The second is developing and using blockchain solutions to streamline the lending process.

The advantage of these new lending models lies in their self-learning ability, their security, and their predictive ability in dynamic conditions. Cloud computing can help to integrate customers' knowledge and needs with data for personalized services in the banking industry [18]. The Italian banking sector is facing serious issues, such as increasing operational costs, an ever-increasing number of fraudulent transactions, and challenges to ensure operational transparency [19]. The system needs to ensure cost efficiency of its operations and transparency for its customers and regulators. To this end, the banking sector has adopted many technology-driven platforms to enhance performance [20]. Blockchain has the potential to eliminate intermediaries, and to improve transparency and traceability of transactions by streamlining, simplifying, and enhancing banks' traditional business processes [21].

Despite its advantages, many sectors are still reluctant to implement blockchain and general Distributed Ledger Technology (DLT). This hesitation may originate from a lack of sufficient knowledge of ways in which to effectively implement a blockchain-enabled application, with reference to consortiums. Indeed, if on the one hand companies and governments demonstrate interest in exploring new uses and assessing their feasibility, on the other hand there is a lack of track records and experience to provide failproof guidelines. Faced with technological, organizational, and social barriers, there is still a need for a general framework that is able to conjugate the technical component with the business and governance layers.

Based on the literature review analysis, we pose the following research questions:

RQ1. "What are the governance practices that banks are leveraging to define their blockchain-enabled credit offer?"

RQ2. "Does the blockchain technology enable banks to achieve new performance objectives in the credit process"?

We carried out the research through pilot interviews, conducted with CEOs/business heads of a large Italian bank (Alpha bank).

The paper is structured as follows: Sect. 2 covers background literature to provide the conceptual context of the problem. Section 3 explains the research design and the methodology we used. In Sect. 4 we discuss the empirical case study; and, finally, in Sect. 5 we explain the findings with the limitations and scope for future research.

2 Literature Review

The term 'blockchain' was introduced with the definition of the Bitcoin protocol, which in 2008 [22] first defined the fundamentals of the technology. Transaction data are stored in blocks that are tightly chained together, completing a Distributed

Ledger (DL) in numerous copies among network nodes. The information is replicated on a high number of independent subjects, and the integrity and robustness of the data is ensured through a consensus algorithm that can be of different types, of which the most common is proof of work (PoW). An alternative to PoW is the Proof of Stake (PoS) protocol that is more cost-effective in terms of time and energy resources, as it ensures a distributed consensus based on participation. In PoS, there is no need for large computational power and resources, because the forgers are selected pseudo randomly (See Table 1).

The security of the system is therefore not devolved onto a central entity considered trustworthy but is rather established by the quality of the protocol used by the participants.

DLT offers numerous applications and can address several of a bank's core process areas: payment services (intra/interbank transfers, peer-to-peer payments, value-added services with cryptocurrency, etc.); finance (trading, post-trading, collateral management, etc.); credit (finalized credit, trade finance, loyalty program, etc.); and Know Your Customer (across all fields) [1].

This list is not exhaustive; there are additional, more vertical areas of operation, such as time stamping and notarization services, as well as the supply chain area, Digital Autonomous Insurance services, and many others.

In recent years, banks have been evolving their operational approach to include this innovative technology through both participation in international consortiums and industry initiatives [1, 23]. Among these, Spunta Banca DLT, promoted by Abi and developed by AbiLab, allows banks to rapidly identify misalignments between intrabank transactions, sharing data in a trustful way because all the exchanges and control activities are managed directly within the application, while processes and communications flow are standardized to minimize delays for fragmentation of procedures [24].

Of the banking and financial industry surveyed, 78% (18 banking groups) have successfully collaborated with the project under the leadership of AbiLab, went live

Table 1 Pow and PoS

Alternative	Who can validate the transactions?	Choosing the node that validates a transaction	Advantages	Limitations
PoW (Proof of Work)	Anyone can become a network node	Randomly, indexed on computing power	+ Security + Trust establishment over a trustless network	– High computing power costs – Data storage costs – Speed limitations
PoS (Proof of Stake)	Anyone can become a network node	Randomly, indexed on economic stake	+ Less computing power costs + Trust establishment over a trustless network	– Favoring the richest nodes – Increased complexity

the 1st of March 2020. The goal was to ensure full visibility of the transactions between banks, rapid management of flows in mutual accounts with daily reconciliations, sharing the rules for symmetrical reconciliation between banks, and integrated management of communication and processes in the event of an imbalance. These institutions therefore implemented a gradual transition from the traditional reconciliation to one based on blockchain DLT technology.

Several components that now characterize the new Spunta Banca DLT application have been designed, starting from CordApp.

There are numerous technical reasons why Corda is ideal for the Spunta procedure. The bank can quickly and easily set up and modify bilateral channels thanks to it. Furthermore, Spunta finds that information exchange on the Corda platform that adheres to the need-to-know principle is appropriate. Since the bank is unable to keep track of every Spunta transaction on the ledgers, having the capacity to archive information is highly helpful. The bank was able to incorporate certain features into the Spunta program, enabling it to comply with GDPR regulations.

Spunta Banca DLT is conceived to create cooperation and synergy at the core level, leaving differentiation and competition at distribution or front-end level. It is operating on Corda, for which AbiLab imposed long term service provision contracts to R3, who committed itself to respect the Service Level Agreement to the extent that ABI Lab and banks declare their willingness to update the application at the pace of the new release.

According to Fedak [25], blockchain contributes by making transactions more secure and valuable; reducing costs through reduced transaction and processing costs; and establishing a positive relationship with a bank's profitability, according to research by Rega [26] which considered 38 European banks. Thus, blockchain technology increases competitiveness with financial technologies, and enables the ability to use the technology to create new business models [24, 27].

While blockchains generally allow participants to store and create a permanent and verifiable record of information (ledgers) necessary for the lending process, private blockchains enhance the security of the network's information through security protocols and access restrictions. Documents and records of transactional interactions stored on the blockchain, or accessible through it, can then be readily accessible to the pool of lender-participants approved to use the network (for instance a syndicate lending group) with more immediacy and less risk of information asymmetry than legacy processes allow.

According to Andoni et al. [28], the most frequently mentioned benefits of blockchain technology include cost efficiency and profits improvement, because banks can reduce their transaction fees and guarantee better record keeping systems with universal online identification systems. Other benefits are enhanced compliance and reduced risk because of a reduction in the possibility for fraud [29]; speedier timelines to update ledgers, because blockchain technology can do it immediately, automatically, and transparently [30]; high levels of data quality to eliminate the risk of errors and duplication [31], and as a result, stored data that is complete, accurate, and reliable [32]; and finally, few regulatory controls. In addition, blockchain technology offers many other opportunities, such as better financial infrastructure and

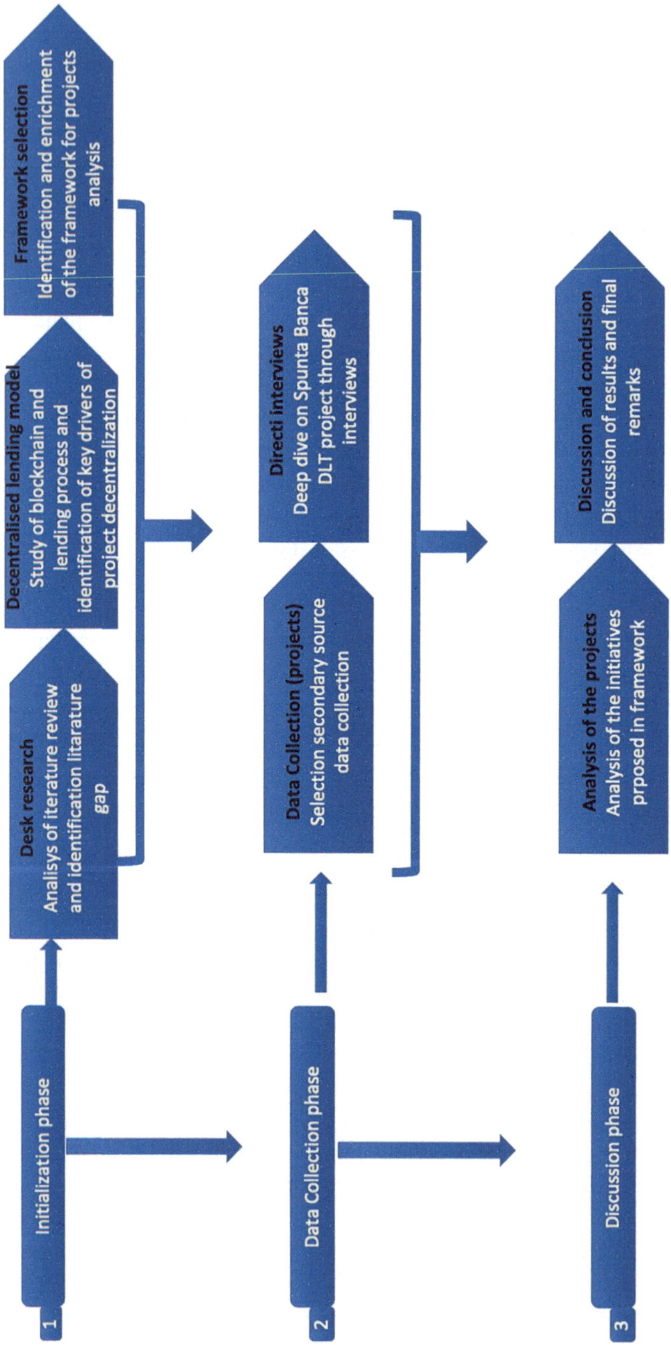

Fig. 1 Research design and methodology

sustainably developed, efficient systems. It also promotes economic growth and develops technology that is sustainable due to its low energy consumption [5, 33–35].

Since its inception, blockchain technology has been closely linked to the financial technology sector. Peters and Panayi [36] argue that blockchain should be characterized as a Fintech 2.0 innovation, focusing on the back-end underlying technology for the financial industry, and not on its application scenarios. The authors consider blockchain as offering a solution to problems like efficiency reduction, transaction lag, fraud, and operational risks. In the area of credit information systems, they note the potential uses of blockchain for information ownership and data sharing. MacDonald et al. [37] argue that blockchain is more than just a new ICT technology that can be applied by banks.

Based on those observations, this paper proposes that blockchain technology constitutes a significant method for business model innovation that enables mitigation of the credit rationing between lenders and borrowers, by generating disintermediation in financial services.

3 Methodology and Research Design

The methodology used in this work is that of the case study [1]. The qualitative approach for collecting information was considered useful in the first step of the research, which was aimed at describing and interpreting the logic of the financing process.

In the following figure we explain the research design and methodology (Fig. 1).

The chosen methodology consists of a qualitative analysis of incumbent projects, which are read through the lens of a literature-based framework. Two approaches were combined: on the one side, information for five out of six selected projects was retrieved from secondary sources, while on the other side we initiated a deep dive into one of these through direct interviews with the project's main stakeholders. We performed a preliminary study of blockchain's technical functioning. Leveraging papers and dedicated books, we investigated how transactions are managed through a network of distributed ledger, which are the main blockchain components, and explored the technology's characteristics and taxonomy. According to Domegan and Fleming [38], qualitative research aims to explore and discover issues about the problem at hand, because very little is known about the problem.

The case identified was considered useful, functional, and instrumental with respect to our intended objective. Alfa Bank, the subject of the investigation, has maintained a marked presence in Italy over time, and has promoted its social and economic development with significant financing operations. The cultural emphasis placed on relations with customers and with the institution's shareholders allows a better understanding of the innovation aspects specifically relevant to the corporate and risk governance structures and the corporate performance objectives.

3.1 Initialization Phase

The research focused on the topic of blockchain projects, highlighting the features and the potential of the technology to create new applications and use cases. The importance of further investigating the relationship between the general topic of blockchain and the choices that an initiator of a blockchain-enabled project must make when designing its governance structure, was identified.

We considered the framework proposed by the Blockchain and Spunta Banca DLT as the main structure for the analysis [39, 40]. This was enriched with additional questions and findings from the literature review.

A comprehensive review of the existing literature was followed by qualitative and semi-structured pilot interviews to facilitate the identification of all relevant domains [41]. A preliminary assumption regarding a distinction between types of stakeholders, according to their level of engagement in the development of the project and decision-making process, was formulated as follows:

- Primary Stakeholders: Vice-President of the Board of Directors, and the other members of the Board of Directors (the project founders, those who are more interested in the success of the solution)
- Secondary Stakeholders: Chief lending officer (CLO) and payment service functions, chief risk manager (CRM), a technical expert in IT functions (the actors partially involved in the projects, those who joined the initiative after the launch or contributed marginally to the development of the project)
- Users: end users of the blockchain-enabled solutions, like consumers and borrowers

After this formulation, we explored the way in which Internet of Value solutions are created, whether on existing or on new platforms.

Then we analyzed the answers to our survey, which was designed specifically for this purpose, and which is the base of the framework we utilized for this research. This is the framework (Table 2).

3.2 Data Collection Phase

We therefore supplemented the literature review with qualitative research as a preliminary step. We identified the experts from Alpha Bank and its IT office, who were closely associated with blockchain application initiatives. We asked the identified experts to participate in a pilot interview. However, only five of the eight experts granted us appointments to share the questionnaire with them. The identified experts on the panel come from a variety of backgrounds, including Vice-President of the board of directors, chief lending officer and payment service functionaries, chief risk manager, and a technical expert from the IT section.

Table 2 The framework of the research

Cluster	Description
Strategy	• Who sets the project goals and assesses the level of integrity of the system? • Who owns the intellectual property right? • Who assigns roles among participants in the network? • What are the membership benefits?
Access	• Who administers access to data? • Who manages the membership process? • How are memberships managed? • Is the network of participants homogeneous in terms of industry? • How are revoking procedures conceived (if any)? • Does the project consider the GNOME Foundation Governance Model (BoD, Executive Director, Advisory Board, GNOME Membership)? • How are interests of earlier and later joiners balanced?
Technology and Conflict Management	• Who is in charge of system updates? • Who is in charge of cybersecurity?
Compliance	• Who oversees community benefits? • Who manages the relation with regulators? • What is the relation with external stakeholders and how it is managed? (Interoperability) • How are responsibilities spread?
Business Model Economic Sustainability	• What are the revenue streams?
Data Upload and Validation	• How are data uploaded and published among participants? • Who owns and controls the data once uploaded?

The pilot interviews were conducted face to face at the experts' convenience at their respective offices, and were further completed by phone. The audio of all the conversations were recorded and analyzed separately for further research. Some of the selected questions were openly linked to the general benefits of implementing blockchain technology, while other questions specifically referenced the benefits of applying blockchain in their traditional banking operations.

3.3 Discussion Phase

For the sake of completeness, the interviews were transcribed verbatim to facilitate the linking of recurring concepts. The output of this activity, being an analysis that considers patterns and drivers of lending strategies, became the backbone for the identification of best practices for utilizing blockchain technologies. First, the responsibilities of each role within the project were highlighted. It seems that all the respondents agree on the central role of a coordinator role created specifically to act as a catalyst for development of the project. Then, other necessary roles related to the application design, the technological infrastructure, architectures integration, and blockchain platform provision were identified.

4 Empirical Research: An Italian Case Study

Alfa Bank is one of the five national systemic banks, and is presently under the supervision of the European Central Banking (ECB). In the last two decades, Alpha has demonstrated a strong interest in technological development and the digitization of financial transactions. More specifically, Alpha has been exploring blockchain technology for almost 10 years. Although the bank does not yet have a structure dedicated to the digitization of operating processes, it created a team of experts from areas of the bank to analyze the possible impacts and benefits of applying blockchain technology to financial business models, as shown in the bank's 2022 business plan. As far as distribution channels are concerned, 2022 figures confirm a growing use of digital services in terms of customers, products, and sales. Multichannel customers number approximately 11.3 million, while 7.5 million clients use the banking app, and the online subsidiary has 62,600 customers. The products available on the multichannel platforms represent approximately 85% of the institution's offering. Sales through remote channels increased to 26.4% of the total number, up from 9.2% in 2019—an effect also of the COVID-19 outbreak. The extension of the bank's target cybersecurity model continued in parallel.

The inherent security of the blockchain network, ensured by both encryption and chaining of blocks, makes it incredibly difficult to manipulate and tamper with the data entered in the ledgers.

The immutable record eliminates the risk of manual errors, increases efficiency, and reduces the possibility of regulatory violations [42].

The mortgage lending process as embedded in blockchain is described in Fig. 2.

Figure 2 shows the changes in the distribution of the activities, resources, and capabilities in blockchain embedded mortgage lending processes mortgage lending process blockchain embedded.

According to Weking et al. [43], the innovative business model implies re-specialization of traditional banking activity, which would result in offering prospective borrowers a tool for efficiently providing both hard and soft information, and offering prospective lenders the tools to soundly assess creditworthiness and risk levels. Figure 2 proposes a new business model, where the green block contains all information about creditworthiness. Bank employees can act as nodes in the network responsible for distributed consensus. Altruistic nodes distributed in the network ensure a fair and trusted system. Identity verification of borrowers happens faster and more efficiently by using smart identity in the blockchain network and verification of financial information, and shared consensus assures efficient governance and transparency in underwriting. Approved loans are cryptographically signed and immutable. Loan restructuring entails approval

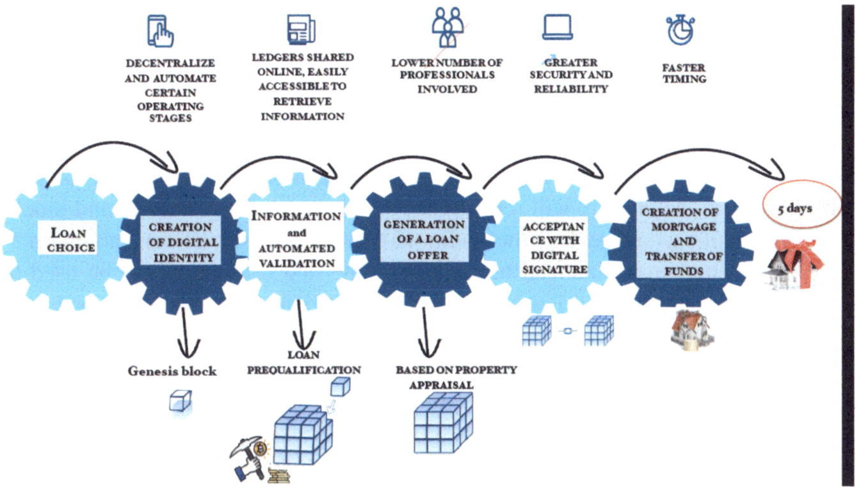

Fig. 2 Blockchain and mortgage lending process (own elaboration)

from the distributed network, providing stringent control of data, classification, and reporting.

However, there are some factors that do not favor the development of blockchain technology; some of these include the trade-off between costs and benefits in the re-engineering of processes in public administration and the creation of judicial archives; the allocation of responsibilities for the implementation of digital platforms and for the definition of rules for access and use of information by users; and the allocation of responsibilities for exercising control over the correct and safe management of information.

5 Discussion and Conclusion

A blockchain system, however, manages an exchange process using a distributed digital ledger, in which data is entered by a geographically distributed network of nodes based on common rules and technology standards (trustless scenario).

So, information is replicated across a high number of independent parties, and data consistency is ensured through a consensus algorithm that can be of different types, the most used being "proof of work". The security of the system is therefore not devolved onto a central entity considered trustworthy, but is rather established by the soundness of the protocol used by the participants.

This technology's major contribution is the creation of a stronger database system in which participants can jointly maintain and edit the information in a decentralized manner, with no individual exercising central control, distinguishing borrowers with different risk classes and maintaining the functionality in a relatively more effective manner, by giving all participants, lenders and borrowers, equal access to the transaction and default records. This innovative system also facilitates faster verification and authentication, reducing uncertainties and improving financing efficiency.

The answer to the first research question ("What are the governance practices that banks are leveraging to define their blockchain-enabled credit offer?"), could be that blockchain technology will reduce the role of bank intermediaries, and blockchain algorithms would replace the traditional role of banks to become an intermediary facilitating smart financial transactions. The first driver that can be used to position case studies is the level of overlapping of primary, secondary, and final users. In simple words, it should be considered whether those who use the blockchain-enabled platforms are also those who make decisions for the whole project. The stronger the engagement of secondary and final users in decision-making processes, the higher the level of effort invested by parties, and the more sound the consensus achieved. The consortium provides basic capabilities—network consensus, transaction distribution and verification, basic smart-contract templates, tokenized assets, or digital documents, among other possibilities—as a kind of utility. Intellectual property rights are retained by initial investors or participants, or the platform's creators. The consortium focuses on establishing second-order benefits unlocked through wider adoption and effective use of the base layer.

In answer to the second research question ("Does the blockchain technology enable the achievement of new performance objectives in the credit process"), we observe that it is expected that the bank systems connected through big data would provide a strong technology platform to offer more cryptographically secure and efficient services around the globe. So, some benefits of blockchain include lower risks and consequently reduced costs.

Among the benefits are:

- Anti-money laundering (AML) and operational risks. Blockchain reduces fraud and fraudulent transactions by using DLT, which uses asymmetric cryptography to encrypt data; while using the workload of each node of the distributed system proves that the powerful algorithm formed by the consensus algorithm can resist external attacks, ensuring that the blockchain data cannot be falsified and are unforgeable, and therefore have high security levels. Once data is stored on the blockchain, that data become tamper-proof and unchangeable, except in accordance with the network's consensus rules. Thus, once debtor information relating to regulatory compliance demands is approved by the lender-participants for inclusion on a block, it becomes immutable, and any future iterations of that information can be compared to an as-agreed accurate baseline that cannot have been altered without the blockchain participants' agreement and recording of such change. Therefore, any new data layered on a block can be more easily reviewed and confirmed as accurate by participants through comparison to a previously confirmed iteration of that information, in accordance with the relevant consensus requirements. This iterative trail of information on the blockchain, along with ease of comparability, streamlines data requests and reviews, and helps to combat fraud.

- Reputational risk, by reinforcing trust and granting high levels of data quality through adequate protection, accuracy, and control. Blockchain systems also eliminate the risk of errors and duplication and, consequently, the risk of borrower complaints by responding with the principles of banking transparency law.
- Credit risk. Blockchain improves the credit worthiness process, the transparency and immutability of data, and transaction speed, and results in significantly reduced transaction costs. It also improves the collateral traceability in the form of initial and variation margins; it allows the sharing of information for better evaluating changes of value in the borrowers' financial positions and for better auditability and transparency; and it eliminates 'double data,' so that each transaction added to the blockchain ensures that the inputs for that transaction were not use previously.

The blockchain also increases access to finance for these main reasons:

- It creates a connected banking system, in which large and small banks ae both present. Private blockchains, like their public counterparts, still require consensus agreement mechanisms, and their implementation would also pave the way for information standardization, so data requests can often vary for the same or similar information. This increases the cumulative effort on the part of the lender to retrieve and process such information. As information added to a blockchain first requires authentication by the parties to it, advance agreement between the participants about what information is required and how it is to be presented for addition to the chain, can reduce effort duplication across institutions and reduce the demands on debtors and the lending system as a whole [44].
- It increases transparency in the banking sector. The ledger characteristic of blockchains can be used by lending parties to track every interaction between lender and debtor. Future interactions with a debtor (e.g., new loans or new disbursements) can also be recorded on the blockchain to keep a running ledger of transactions with that party. The complete information regarding that debtor's current borrowing activities can be made available to prior lenders simultaneous engaging in new transactions. This continuous feed of transactional information increases transparency in the lending space, while reducing reporting burdens on borrowers to notify lenders, under existing agreements, of new transactions. Blockchain technology enhances the accuracy of record keeping, increases transparency, reduces fraud, and provides superior security by keeping data in a database in a way that protects the central database from attacks [45]. Transparency is supported, since the transactions are shared across all nodes, which fosters confidence in a community of users [46].
- It enhances efficiency of financial services, because the system depends on less physical infrastructure for the transfer of goods and services. According to Wamba et al. [47], blockchain technology's transparency strongly predicts behavioral intent to utilize blockchain technology.

However, some practical challenges remain. The implementation of blockchain calls for a thorough technological and regulatory evaluation, increased societal awareness, immense collaboration and insight, stringent planning, and sound technical expertise.

Italian banks are guided by the Bank of Italy and BCE guidelines on data protection and governance. Information security awareness levels are still low in the domestic banking system, a feature that exposes banks to data security threats and cybercrimes. Traditionally, banks are not culturally oriented to use distributed and decentralized data storage and processing. The regulatory framework for information security and cybercrime must be enforced more stringently.

Although this is not the first academic research linking blockchain technology to the mortgage lending process, it is the first research proposing an application of blockchain technology to mortgage lending from the perspective of reshaping traditional banking activity.

Our research is limited in that it covers only the origination stage of the mortgage value chain; the servicing of mortgage lending generated loans is not covered by our analysis. We also do not explore the dynamics of a secondary market for the mortgage-backed security shares.

As one of the few papers analyzing the application of blockchain technology reshaping the traditional credit system, we can leave interesting topics to future research. For example, we do not consider the cost of obtaining corporate information in the blockchain platform, or the possibility of feeders of collateral information from the offline world. Hence, further research about these topics is needed.

References

1. AbiLab. (2020). Rapporto AbiLab 2020. Principali trend di evoluzione e priorità di investimento e ricerca ICT delle banche italiane.
2. Doshi, R. (2021). *Blockchain adoption journey and impact on financial services industry*. InfoSys.
3. Zhang, L., Xie, Y., Zheng, Y., Xue, W., Zheng, X., & Xu, X. (2020). The challenges and countermeasures of blockchain in finance and economics. *Systems Research and Behavioral Science, 37*(3), 691–698. https://doi.org/10.1002/sres.2710
4. Bates, A. W. (2015). *Teaching in a digital age: Guidelines for designing teaching and learning*. BCcampus.
5. Cocco, L., Pinna, A., & Marchesi, M. (2017). Banking on blockchain: Costs savings thanks to the blockchain technology. *Future Internet, 9*(3), 25. https://doi.org/10.3390/fi9030025
6. Gupta, A., & Gupta, S. (2018). Blockchain technology: Application in Indian banking sector. *Delhi Business Review, 19*(2), 89–94. https://doi.org/10.51768/dbr.v19i2.192201807
7. Bates, D., & Migliore, P. (2018). Innovate or stagnate: Digitalisation in investment management. *Journal of Securities Operations & Custody, 10*(4), 296–304.
8. Karim, S., Rabbani, M. R., & Bawazir, H. (2022). Applications of blockchain technology in the finance and banking industry beyond digital currencies. In S. Khan, M. Haider, M. H. Syed, R. Hammad, & A. F. Bushager (Eds.), *Blockchain technology and computational excellence for society 5.0* (pp. 216–238). IGI Global. https://doi.org/10.4018/978-1-7998-8382-1.ch011

9. Degener, S. M. (2018). *How blockchain affects business models in international banking*. Bachelor's thesis, University of Twente.
10. Popova, N. A., & Butakova, N. G. (2019). Research of a possibility of using blockchain technology without tokens to protect banking transactions. In *2019 IEEE conference of Russian young researchers in electrical and electronic engineering (EIConRus)* (pp. 1764–1768). https://doi.org/10.1109/EIConRus.2019.8657279
11. Belitski, M., & Boreiko, D. (2022). Success factors of initial coin offerings. *The Journal of Technology Transfer, 47*(6), 1690–1706. https://doi.org/10.1007/s10961-021-09894-x
12. Campino, J., Brochado, A., & Rosa, Á. (2021). Initial coin offerings (ICOs): The importance of human capital. *Research Square*. https://doi.org/10.21203/rs.3.rs-171187/v1
13. Ittay, E. (2017). Blockchain technology: Transforming libertarian cryptocurrency dreams to finance and banking realities. *The IEEE Computer Society, 50*(9). https://doi.org/10.1109/MC.2017.3571042
14. Seretakis, A. (2017). Blockchain, securities markets and central banking. *Journal of Financial Economics, 1*, 425–435. https://doi.org/10.2139/ssrn.3007402
15. Oh, J. S., & Shong, I. (2017). A case study on business model innovations using blockchain: Focusing on financial institutions. *Asia Pacific Journal of Innovation and Entrepreneurship, 11*(3), 335–344. https://doi.org/10.1108/APJIE-12-2017-038
16. Mohite, V. (2018). Reducing uncertainty in trade and deciphering future challenges in banking industry through application of blockchain technology. *International Bulletin of Management and Economics, 9*(special issue), 49–55.
17. Ozili, P. K. (2018). Impact of digital finance on financial inclusion and stability. *Borsa Istanbul Review,* 329–340. Available online at https://doi.org/10.1016/j.bir.2017.12.003
18. Larson, D., & Chang, V. A. (2016). A review and future direction of agile, business intelligence, analytic s and data science. *International Journal of Information Management, 36*(5), 700–710. https://doi.org/10.1016/j.ijinfomgt.2016.04.013
19. Kumar, K., & Prakash, A. (2018). Developing a framework for assessing sustainable banking performance of the Indian banking sector. *Social Responsibility Journal, 15*(5), 689–709. https://doi.org/10.1108/SRJ-07-2018-0162
20. Palmié, M., Wincent, J., Parida, V., & Caglar, U. (2020). The evolution of the financial technology ecosystem: An introduction and agenda for future research on disruptive innovations in ecosystems. *Technological Forecasting and Social Change, 151*, 119779. https://doi.org/10.1016/j.techfore.2019.119779
21. Frizzo-Barker, J., Chow-White, P. A., Adams, P. R., Mentanko, J., Ha, S., & Green, S. (2020). Blockchain as a disruptive technology for business: A systematic review. *International Journal of Information Management, 51*, 102029. https://doi.org/10.1016/j.ijinfomgt.2019.10.014
22. Nakamoto, S. (2008, August 21). Bitcoin: A peer-to-peer electronic cash system. Available at https://doi.org/10.2139/ssrn.3440802
23. Guo, Y., & Liang, C. (2016). Blockchain application and outlook in the banking industry. *Financial Innovation, 2*, 24. https://doi.org/10.1186/s40854-016-0034-9
24. Cucari, N., Lagasio, V., Lia, G., & Torriero, C. (2022). The impact of blockchain in banking processes: The Interbank Spunta case study. *Technology Analysis & Strategic Management, 34*(2), 138–150. https://doi.org/10.1080/09537325.2021.1891217
25. Fedak, V. (2018) Blockchain and Big Data: The match made in heavens. Available via https://towardsdatascience.com/blockchain-and-big-data-the-match-made-in-heavens-337887a0ce73
26. Rega, F. G., & Riccardi, N. (2018). Blockchain in the banking industry: An overview. White Paper. https://www.researchgate.net/profile/FedericoRega/publication/327601993_Blockchain_in_the_banking_industry_an_Overview/links/5bfefaeaa6fdcc1b8d49f252/Blockchain-in-the-banking-industry-an-Overview.pdf
27. Kocianski, S. (2018). The blockchain in banking report: The future of blockchain solutions and technologies. Available via http://uk.businessinsider.com/blockchain-in-banking-2018-5
28. Andoni, M., Robu, V., Flynn, D., Abram, S., Geach, D., Jenkins, D., & Peacock, A. (2019). Blockchain technology in the energy sector: A systematic review of challenges and opportu-

nities. *Renewable and Sustainable Energy Reviews, 100*, 143–174. https://doi.org/10.1016/j.rser.2018.10.014
29. Umalkar, M., MacNeil, A., & Light, D. (2016). *What every CEO should know about blockchain*. Academic Press.
30. Hughes, L., Dwivedi, Y. K., Misra, S. K., Rana, N. P., Raghavan, V., & Akella, V. (2019). Blockchain research, practice, and policy: Applications, benefits, limitations, emerging research themes and research agenda. *International Journal of Information Management, 49*, 114–129. https://doi.org/10.1016/j.ijinfomgt.2019.02.005
31. Martin-Bariteau, F. (2018). *Blockchain and the European Union General Data Protection Regulation: The CNIL's perspective* (Blockchain. Working Paper Series 1). https://doi.org/10.2139/ssrn.3275783.
32. Reyna, A., Martín, C., Chen, J., Soler, E., & Díaz, M. (2018). On blockchain and its integration with IoT. Challenges and opportunities. *Future Generation Computer Systems, 88*, 173–190. https://doi.org/10.1016/j.future.2018.05.046
33. Accenture. (2018). *Building the future-ready bank*. Banking Technology Vision. Retrieved June 16, 2019. https://www.readkong.com/page/building-the-future-ready-bank-banking-technology-vision-4973963
34. Kouzinopoulos, C. S., Spathoulas, G., Giannoutakis, K. M., Votis, K., Pandey, P., Tzovaras, D., & Nijdam, N. A. (2018). Using blockchains to strengthen the security of internet of things. In *International ISCIS security workshop* (pp. 90–100). Springer.
35. Chen, R. R., Chen, K., & Ou, C. X. (2023). Facilitating interorganizational trust in strategic alliances by leveraging blockchain-based systems: Case studies of two eastern banks. *International Journal of Information Management, 68*, 102521. https://doi.org/10.1016/j.ijinfomgt.2022.102521
36. Peters, G. W., & Panayi, E. (2016). Understanding modern banking ledgers through blockchain technologies: Future of transaction processing and smart contracts on the internet of money. In P. Tasca, T. Aste, L. Pelizzon, & N. Perony (Eds.), *Banking beyond banks and money* (pp. 239–278). Springer. https://doi.org/10.1007/978-3-319-42448-4_13
37. MacDonald, T. J., Allen, D. W., & Potts, J. (2016). Blockchains and the boundaries of self-organized economies: Predictions for the future of banking. In P. Tasca, T. Aste, L. Pelizzon, & N. Perony (Eds.), *Banking beyond banks and money* (pp. 279–296). Springer. https://doi.org/10.2139/ssrn.2749514
38. Domegan, C., & Fleming, D. (2007). *Marketing research in Ireland: Theory and practice*. Gill & Macmillan.
39. Glaser, F. (2017). Pervasive decentralisation of digital infrastructures: A framework for blockchain enabled system and use case analysis (January 2017). In *Proceedings of the 50th Hawaii international conference on system sciences (HICSS-50), Waikoloa Village, Hawaii, January 4–7*. Available at SSRN: https://ssrn.com/abstract=3052165
40. Shah, T., & Jani, S. (2018). *Applications of blockchain technology in banking & finance*. Parul University. https://doi.org/10.13140/RG.2.2.35237.96489
41. Zomorodi, M., & Lynn, M. R. (2010). Instrument development measuring critical care nurses' attitudes and behaviors with end-of-life care. *Nursing Research, 59*(4), 234. Available at http://hdl.handle.net/10822/1022504
42. Shah, T., Jani, S., & Priyan, P. K. (2018). *Applications of blockchain technology in banking & finance: A conceptual approach*. GH Patel Postgraduate Institute of Business Management, 12.
43. Weking, J., Mandalenakis, M., Hein, A., Hermes, S., Böhm, M., & Krcmar, H. (2020). The impact of blockchain technology on business models—A taxonomy and archetypal patterns. *Electronic Markets, 30*(2), 285–305. https://doi.org/10.1007/s12525-019-00386-3
44. Raddatz, N., Coyne, J., Menard, P., & Crossler, R. E. (2023). Becoming a blockchain user: Understanding consumers' benefits realisation to use blockchain-based applications. *European Journal of Information System, 32*(2), 287–314. https://doi.org/10.1080/0960085X.2021.1944823

45. Park, J. H., & Park, J. H. (2017). Blockchain security in cloud computing: Use cases, challenges, and solutions. *Symmetry, 9*(8), 164. https://doi.org/10.3390/sym9080164
46. Osmani, M., El-Haddadeh, R., Hindi, N., Janssen, M., & Weerakkody, V. (2021). Blockchain for next generation services in banking and finance: Cost, benefit, risk and opportunity analysis. *Journal of Enterprise Information Management, 34*(3), 884–899. https://doi.org/10.1108/JEIM-02-2020-0044
47. Wamba, S. F., Jean Robert, K. K., Ransome, E. B., & John, G. K. (2019). Bitcoin, blockchain and fintech: A systematic review and case studies in the supply chain. *Production Planning & Control, 31*(2–3), 115–142. https://doi.org/10.1080/09537287.2019.1631460

Under Pressure: Strategic Choices and Contextual Trade-Offs of SMEs Facing Industry 4.0 Implementation

Anastassiya Zabudkina, Olivier Lisein, and François Pichault

Abstract Besides sharing similar characteristics of staff headcount, turnover, and balance sheet total, each small and medium entreprise (SME) has its unique context that may influence their intention to implement Industry 4.0. The contextual factors encouraging or preventing SMEs from implementing Industry 4.0 receive an increasing attention by the research community. However, there is still a scarcity of studies that go beyond simple inventorying of contextual enablers and barriers and that try to assess their influence on SMEs' strategic choices regarding Industry 4.0 implementation. The authors of this study decided to tackle these gaps by conducting a narrative literature review focused on the following research question: *How contextual enablers and barriers influence SMEs' strategic choices regarding Industry 4.0 implementation?* Analysed through the lens of institutional approach, the results allow the authors to generate a global framework composed of 35 contextual triggers potentially leading SMEs to trade-offs regarding 5 dimensions of strategic choices for Industry 4.0 implementation.

Keywords Industry 4.0 · SMEs' context · Strategies

1 Introduction

While traditional industry already has its issues, the emerging paradigm of the fourth industrial revolution, also known as Industry 4.0 or Industry of the Future, couples them with numerous challenges. The concept of Industry 4.0 aims to reunite the industrial players in the scope of a far-reaching network that interconnects data, people, processes, services, and systems inside and among the companies [1, 2]. In doing so, companies can improve production efficiency and quality, reduce natural

A. Zabudkina (✉) · O. Lisein · F. Pichault
HEC Liège – Management School, University of Liège, Liège, Belgium
e-mail: a.zabudkina@uliege.be

A. M. Braccini et al. (eds.), *Technologies for Digital Transformation*, Lecture Notes in Information Systems and Organisation 64,
https://doi.org/10.1007/978-3-031-52120-1_7

resources usage and waste as well as optimize working and safety conditions of their employees [3, 4]. As new technologies and capacities to integrate and manipulate them represent basic requirements for Industry 4.0, academic research on the topic is dominated by techno-centric approaches [5–7]. Nevertheless, by focusing only on technology adoption-related problems, industrial firms overlook their transformation on human and managerial levels and risk increasing organizational barriers [8, 9].

Considering its requirements and opportunities, the concept of Industry 4.0 was practically conceived in favour of large enterprises and often neglects the particularities of small and medium-sized enterprises (SMEs) [10–12]. However, the growing body of academic literature highlights that SMEs often act in the same industrial value chain with large companies, the changing standards of which can influence their positioning towards Industry 4.0 [12, 13]. Therefore, both profiles should be considered equally, thanks to distinct approaches, while studying the implementation of Industry 4.0.

Recently, the academic investigation into Industry 4.0 implementation among SMEs has received increasing attention. On one hand, several studies focus on the elaboration of strategic roadmaps and guidelines for SMEs implementing Industry 4.0. These studies reflect on the appropriate ways of implementing Industry 4.0 through the analysis of SMEs' characteristics [14], their obstacles [15], success factors [16] and outcomes [17] regarding Industry 4.0. However, little attention has been paid to inventorying the *strategic choices* that SMEs favour in practice regarding Industry 4.0 implementation. On the other hand, numerous studies inventory the most common contextual *enablers* and *barriers* SMEs face while considering Industry 4.0 implementation. Generally, scholars identify and classify various factors that encourage or impede SMEs to implement Industry 4.0: resources constraints, flexible organizational structure, lack of conscious planning, etc. [10, 18, 19]. Such classifications are often mobilized to explore the influence of the enablers and barriers on SMEs' intention to implement Industry 4.0 technologies [13, 20]. However, there is a lack of studies exploring the potential influence of these contextual factors on SMEs' *strategic choices* regarding Industry 4.0 implementation.

To address the above-mentioned gaps, this study focuses on the following research question:

How contextual enablers and barriers influence SMEs' strategic choices regarding Industry 4.0 implementation?

The study mobilizes the institutional approach according to which the organizations are influenced by pressures arising from external sources (such as government and regulatory agencies) and from within the organization itself [21–23]. Several studies established that companies, including SMEs, can be encouraged to implement Industry 4.0 due to the pressures deriving from the regulatory bodies, accreditation agencies and peer associations [24–26]. By going one step further, this study aims to explore the influence of pressures emerging from the outer but also inner context on SMEs' *strategic choices* regarding Industry 4.0. To identify the key contextual *enablers* and *barriers* as well as the *strategic choices* of SMEs in the scope of Industry 4.0 implementation, a narrative literature review is conducted [27, 28]. This method is privileged because of its greater possibilities to explore the novel conceptualization of *enablers* and *barriers* related to Industry 4.0 implementation by SMEs [27–29]. It also allows characterizing SMEs' *strategic choices* by capturing the orientation of their goals towards desired outcomes of Industry 4.0 implementation. The study results in an analytical framework composed of 35 contextual triggers, potentially leading SMEs to *trade-offs* regarding 5 dimensions of *strategic choices* for Industry 4.0 implementation.

The paper is structured as follows. First, the theoretical background covers the key concepts of the research question. Second, the research methods and data analysis are described. Then, the findings are presented and followed by their discussion. The paper closes with the overview of major contributions and limits of this literature review and suggestions for future research.

2 Theoretical Background

2.1 Industry 4.0

In the scope of progressive globalization, new technological possibilities and increased competition, the concept of Industry 4.0 marks the beginning of the new industry by amalgamating complex industrial processes with innovative technologies [5, 30, 31]. By going one step further than digitalization and computer-integrated processes, Industry 4.0 stands for a far-reaching network of industrial players supported by cyber-physical systems (CPS), based on heterogeneous data and knowledge integration [31, 32]. The interpretation of Industry 4.0 often relies on several design principles and technological trends mutually interconnected [33, 34]. The technological trends refer to the implementation of new technologies. The basic technologies refer to technologies that help to generate data (i.e., sensors, actuators) and transmit it (i.e., Internet of Things) [35]. The advanced technologies refer to technologies that process data (i.e., big data, cloud computing) and apply it (i.e., smart machines, autonomous robotics) [35]. The vertical and horizontal integration of these technologies requires designing new processes based on interoperability, virtualization, decentralization, and real-time capability [31, 34]. Industry 4.0 is expected to encourage industrial companies to address sustainability issues in terms of economic, social, and environmental impacts [4, 6]. Based on the concept of Triple Bottom Line of sustainability, the three dimensions should be faced simultaneously by focusing on the balance among making profit, accounting environmental issues, and contributing into human capital [4, 6]. The latter aspect represents an important preoccupation for companies as Industry 4.0 implementation is based on the human-machine interaction [7, 33, 34]. As a matter of fact, human operators are expected to become *Operators 4.0* as their physical and cognitive capacities can be enhanced thanks to new technologies [7, 33]. Due to the crucial for Industry 4.0 soft skills such as creativity, entrepreneurial thinking, conflict solving and problem-solving, the human role remains fundamental for companies facing such transformation [36–38].

Since the concept of Industry 4.0 assimilates across countries with different institutional characteristics which can lead to distinct meanings [25], there is still no generally accepted definition for Industry 4.0 [32]. Thus, this study summarizes the common characteristics of Industry 4.0 as follows: *a horizontally and vertically integrated sociotechnical system that relies on an interconnected spectrum of physical, digital, and human elements, interacting in a network structure, and contributing to the system as a complete entity.* The idea of *complete entity* represents a key element for Industry 4.0, as for its successful implementation companies should be ready to undergo the changes not only on technological level, but, above all, on organizational and human levels [5, 8, 39].

2.2 SMEs and Their Specific Features

According to the European Commission [40], to be defined as a SME, an enterprise must employ "fewer than 250 persons and which have an annual turnover not exceeding EUR 50 million, and/or an annual balance sheet total not exceeding EUR 43 million". Within this category, small enterprises employ fewer than 50 persons and micro enterprises—fewer than 10 persons. Besides the number of employees, the key characteristics of SMEs can be captured via their structure, resources, and culture [41]. Generally, SMEs experience the resource constraints in terms of financial resources and time availability for strategic decisions [41]. The studies often present SMEs as ill-equipped to perform important changes on digital or technological level [10, 34]. Because of their environmental vulnerability, SMEs are often "under pressure to respond to structural and market-orientation instability" ([41], p. 3178). It is often conditioned by their lack of strategic planning to anticipate and respond effectively to changing market environments [3, 6, 10]. Whereas continuous improvement is often left out from SMEs' priorities, they remain reactive to supply chain-driven innovations leading to cost reduction or increase in productivity [6, 42]. In this case, SMEs are used to cooperate with industry-based actors rather than with external ones, such as universities or research centres [42, 43]. The hierarchy system of SMEs often relies on a vertical, short-lined organization with a centralized decision-making power in the hands of the manager deeply involved in the daily life of the enterprise [10, 44]. Thus, the decision about change or innovation is often based on 'gut feeling' of the manager rather than on research and development process, generally undeveloped within SMEs [11]. Due to SMEs' informality of working practices, they often benefit from flexible organizational structure and proximity of relations between managers and employees, due to which the latter benefit from straight line of view of business issues and customer experiences [41]. The functioning of SMEs is mainly geared towards operational activities that lead to highly specialized products [11, 44, 45]. It often implies the inclination toward niche markets that allows SMEs to be highly reactive towards customers' needs [10, 34, 45]. By tending to maintain their expertise and keep customers satisfied, SMEs focus on fulfilling the existing orders rather than on improving their generally low degree of process standardization [6, 11, 45].

2.3 SMEs in the Context of Industry 4.0

The state of Industry 4.0 implementation among industrial SMEs is generally characterized by their struggling to understand this concept and, therefore, the fact of being lagged behind large companies [38, 46]. Considering the series of factors studied and suggested for Industry 4.0, the concept is globally conceived in favour of large enterprises and often outlooks the particularities of SMEs [6, 11, 44]. For instance, to embrace Industry 4.0 as a continuous process based on changes, adaptations, and improvements [9], a strategic long-term vision developed on multiple levels appears to be key for industrial companies [32, 47–49]. However, focused on day-to-day operations and short-term strategies, SMEs often lack a continuous improvement strategy in the scope of Industry 4.0 implementation [10, 12, 20]. One of the most cited requirements of Industry 4.0—simultaneous integration of Industry 4.0 technologies on vertical and horizontal level—is particularly challenging for SMEs [12, 38, 50]. Besides the difficulty of imposing such transformation to their value-chain, SMEs should deal with their low digitalization level exposed to the variety and complexity of technological requirements of Industry 4.0 [3, 43, 46, 51, 52]. Together with lack of financial and organizational resources, these challenges tend to push SMEs to report Industry 4.0 implementation or limit it to the adoption of basic technologies [10, 53–55].

To address the above-mentioned challenges, the research community conducted several studies. For instance, some studies demonstrate the importance to analyse and mobilize the existing driving forces within SMEs [3, 6, 10]. One of the most cited elements driving SMEs to implement Industry 4.0 lays in their flexible organizational structure, which allows responding to changes triggered by Industry 4.0 [6]. SMEs can achieve significant Industry 4.0 outcomes by combining the CEO's dedication to innovation, and employees' participation in innovative activities [10, 48]. Moreover, proactive SMEs are aware of the importance of the committed workforce that goes from shop-floor employees to managers [55]. Other studies focus on elaborating strategic roadmaps [18] and frameworks assessing SMEs' Industry 4.0 maturity [15]. The strategic roadmaps provide the guidelines targeting various areas of transformation that SMEs can apply for a successful transition towards Industry 4.0 [16]. The maturity models establish several stages that define the state of SMEs' readiness or evolution towards Industry 4.0 implementation regarding their resources, skills, and environment [11, 13]. The authors stress the importance of nurturing a willingness to change, reinforced by sufficient readiness across employees, technologies, management, external support, and value chain, as critical in enabling Industry 4.0 implementation in SMEs [18]. The researchers also highlight the importance to align the requirements of SMEs with the requirements of Industry

4.0 that should be articulated into a strategy for a "progressive, potentially multistep process" of implementation ([13], p. 2). As SMEs often tend to implement Industry 4.0 without considering required conditions and establishing appropriate foundation and purpose, the strategic roadmaps allow avoiding additional organizational barriers or creating a strategic misalignment [9].

From institutional perspective, Industry 4.0 can be considered as a trigger for creating of "new sets of logics and arrangements that would compete with those already existing" ([56], p. 4). Therefore, a more in-depth analysis of the contextual opportunities and constraints the SMEs face during Industry 4.0 implementation can help to better understand the *trade-offs* they can be led to make regarding their *strategic choices*.

3 Methodology

Based on a narrative literature review [27, 28], the study explores the influence of SMEs' contextual *enablers* and *barriers* on their *strategic choices* regarding Industry 4.0 implementation. This method is privileged because of its greater possibilities to explore the studies that combine the elements of both concepts—the strategic choices and their link to the context of SMEs—by focusing on patterns and connections among findings [27]. To preserve the transparency and reflexivity of the entire process of narrative literature review [29], a two-step research protocol has been established (see Fig. 1), as detailed in the following sections.

3.1 Data Identification and Selection

The aim of the first step was to identify and select relevant scientific literature on three main concepts—SMEs' context composed of *enablers* and *barriers* and SMEs' *strategic choices* to implement Industry 4.0. As narrative literature review traditionally begins with "a small number of articles and books, which are then used to identify key authors and other articles that are related to the particular topic" ([57], p. 257), the snowballing procedure was conducted in three steps [29, 58].

First, the search for the start set of sources was conducted. It was based on several identification principles (see Fig. 1). To facilitate the identification of relevant sources, the key notions were conceptualized (see Table 1). To conduct the search, Scopus database was privileged for its broad coverage of disciplines and publishers [58]. One of the main characteristics of narrative literature review—the inclusive and flexible organization of various sources and types of evidence [29, 59]—was used as another identification principle. To enhance this heterogeneity, the study cross-fertilized different kinds of literature and topics regarding SMEs implementing Industry 4.0. Out of 127 document results, only 10 sources were included in the start set due to the in-depth analysis via selection principles (see Fig. 1). Second, the

Resource Identification Principles	- Conceptualization of key notions. - Search in Scopus data base via key words: "industry 4.0" OR "industry of the future" OR "fourth industrial revolution" AND "implementation" OR "adoption" AND "SMEs" OR "small medium enterprises" AND "enablers" OR "barriers" OR "challenges" OR "strategy" - Consideration of all methodological approaches. - Cross-fertilization of different kinds of literature: finance, management, production.	
Number of unique documents identified: **N = 127**		
Resource Selection Principles	**Exclusion 1**: The notions in the identified documents do not correspond to the conceptualized key notions of enablers, barriers, and context. **Exclusion 2:** The elements referring to strategic decision-making of SMEs in the identified documents are absent or not sufficient to identify the strategic choices of SMEs. **Exclusion 3:** The use of data, words, and text is absent or not sufficient to establish the influence of SMEs' context shaped by enablers and barriers on their strategic choices.	
Screening of Resources	1) Documents removed due to exclusion criterion #1: **n= 64** 2) Documents removed due to exclusion criterion #2: **n = 31** 3) Documents removed due to exclusion criterion #3: **n = 22** The pool of eligible documents for start set: **N= 10**	
Snowballing technic	Backward snowballing - Consultation of the references of 10 eligible documents using the resource identification and selection principles. **N = 13**	Forward snowballing - Citation analysis of 10 eligible documents in Scopus database using the resource identification and selection principles. **N = 11**
Scopus Alerts	- Weekly alerts set in Scopus data base via keywords from Resources Identification Principles - January – April 2022 **N = 5**	
Final pool of eligible resources: **N= 39**		
Data coding and analysis	Coding of contextual enablers and barriers **Cycle 1** - Search for trends of Industry 4.0 via keywords: "enablers", "drivers", and "barriers", "challenges" - In-depth analysis of the findings of each study to develop the identified trends. - Use of attributive codes 'B' and 'E'. **Cycle 2** - Categorization of identified trends by thematic groups. - 6 thematic categories for inner context. - 2 thematic categories for outer context of SMEs. **Cycle 3** - Sub-categorization of trends in each thematic group. - 26 triggers leading to contextual pressure in inner context. - 9 triggers leading to contextual pressure in outer context.	Coding of strategic choices **Cycle 1** - Search for trends related to conceptualized notion of strategic choices via keywords: "strategy", "aim", "purpose", "result", "benefit", "outcome", "change", "choose", "improve". - In-depth analysis of the findings of each study to develop the identified trends. - Use of the attributive code 'SC'. **Cycle 2** - Categorization of identified trends by groups. - 5 thematic groups corresponding to strategies with two strategic choices.
	Data analysis: Institutional approach [78, 90]	

Fig. 1 Research protocol

Table 1 Conceptualized key notions of the study (authors' own)

Key notions	Conceptualization	Authors
Strategic Choices	Orientation of SMEs' goals and actions towards desired outcomes regarding Industry 4.0 implementation	[60, 61]
SMEs' Context	Inner factors and outer factors shaping the environment of SMEs	[23, 62]
Enablers	Factors that function as vehicles to mobilize SMEs' efforts to implement Industry 4.0	[63]
Barriers	Factors that might reduce SMEs' ability and hinder their decision to implement Industry 4.0	[64]

iteration of new selection of sources was conducted following backward and forward snowballing [58]. The backward snowballing allowed to add 13 new scientific sources. The forward snowballing allowed to add 11 new scientific sources (see Fig. 1). Finally, weekly alerts were set up on Scopus (see Fig. 1). This third step was added to complement the snowballing and identify additional recent papers [58]. This procedure allowed to add five new scientific sources. Overall, 39 studies were mobilized for the literature review (see Appendix).

3.2 Data Coding and Analysis

The coding process of the data was conducted in two times: first, for the notions related to SMEs' contextual *enablers* and *barriers* and then for the elements related to SMEs' *strategic choices* (see Fig. 1). During each round, the data from analysed studies was systematically extracted and evaluated in several cycles [65].

First, the coding was conducted for the notions related to the contextual *enablers* and *barriers* affecting SMEs' implementation of Industry 4.0 (see Fig. 1). In the scope of the first-cycle coding, each source was monitored for the factors or trends identified as encouraging or preventing Industry 4.0 implementation within SMEs. The second-cycle coding focused on establishing SMEs' context via categorization of identified barriers and enablers by thematic groups. To do so, the existing classifications of enablers and barriers were mobilized [10, 18, 38, 45, 66]. The validity and coherence of chosen categories was revised in several rounds of discussion together with the authors of this study. Overall, eight thematic categories—six for inner context and two for outer context—were formed. Since each of these categories counted multiple trends with sufficiently distinctive features, the third-step coding focused on isolating and gathering these trends into subcategories. For each distinctive feature identified in a respective category of *enablers* and *barriers*, the encouraging and obstructing trends were regrouped according to the common characteristics. Through multiple rounds of discussion, the authors achieved a consensus upon 26 triggers leading to contextual pressures in SMEs' inner context and 9 triggers leading to contextual pressures in SMEs' outer context.

Second, the coding was conducted for the notions related to SMEs' *strategic choices* regarding Industry 4.0 (see Fig. 1). The inductive approach [67] was mobilized during this part of coding to capture the diversity of the data related to SMEs' orientation of goals and actions towards desired outcomes of Industry 4.0 implementation. In the scope of the first-cycle coding, each source was monitored for the factors or trends that reflect SMEs' *strategic choices*. Guided by the key-words, the authors conducted an in-depth analysis of the findings of each study to capture the trends that can be referred to as *strategic choices*. The second-cycle coding focused on the categorization of identified strategic choices by thematic group. The logic behind this process was based on putting together trends related to SMEs' goals and actions regarding Industry 4.0 that have a common strategic dimension. Through multiple rounds of discussion, the authors achieved a consensus upon five thematic groups, each one corresponding to a dimension with two potential *strategic choices* for SMEs facing Industry 4.0 implementation.

Parallelly to this coding process, the authors analysed the data by referring to the institutional approach [22, 23]. Institutional theory helped the authors in understanding the external and internal pressures[1] that encourage or impede SMEs in their strategic decision-making regarding Industry 4.0 implementation [21, 68]. The authors also analysed the contextual *enablers* and *barriers* that can lead to *trade-offs* when SMEs make their strategic choices. These *trade-offs* refer to the situations formed by opposite factors—*enablers* and *barriers*—when SMEs choose their priorities regarding Industry 4.0 [69], as presented in the next section.

4 Results

This section presents the results of the narrative literature review in the following order. First, the pressures triggered by the *enablers* and *barriers* in the inner context of SMEs facing Industry 4.0 are illustrated with several examples. Then, some examples are given to depict the pressures that SMEs might experience from the *enablers* and *barriers* in their outer context. The section concludes with the illustration of several dimensions within which SMEs have two *strategic choices* regarding Industry 4.0 implementation.

4.1 Pressures in the Inner Context of SMEs

The inner context refers to a complex system of SMEs' structure, resources, culture, and strategy that can be captured between the factors encouraging and impeding Industry 4.0 implementation (see Table 2). According to the current state of the inner context that can tend to be either an *enabler* or a *barrier*, these factors can put

[1] The concept of pressure refers here to "the contextual dynamics that precipitate the need for organizational adaptation" ([21], p. 1023).

Table 2 Pressures in the inner context of SMEs facing Industry 4.0 (authors' own)

Triggers		Enablers			Barriers	
Organizational Structure	1	Decentralized control with little hierarchical levels	[6, 10, 36, 70]	→ ←	Organizational complexity with centralized power	[13, 38, 44, 71]
	2	Higher digital adequacy in larger size SMEs	[18, 48, 54, 72]	→ ←	Less reasons for digital optimization in small family businesses	[1, 10, 38, 50, 73]
	3	Structure compatible for digitalization	[74, 75]	→ ←	Hardly digitizable operational systems	[11, 12, 45]
Technological Resources	4	Regular use of company data in decision-making	[3, 10, 44, 46]	→ ←	Lack of awareness of the potential impact of data analytics	[9, 12, 44, 76, 77]
	5	Perceived value and ease of use of new technologies	[12, 74, 78]	→ ←	Lack of knowledge of new technologies and their potentialities	[20, 38, 45, 66, 72, 79]
	6	Digital maturity	[70, 75, 80]	→ ←	Immature IT infrastructure	[1, 12, 45, 66, 73, 78, 79]
	7	Mastering of cybersecurity	[78]	→ ←	Cybersecurity issues	[3, 38, 46, 77]
	8	Smart modular workstation	[70]	→ ←	Space constraints	[46, 66]
Financial Resources	9	Capacity to anticipate the financial advantages of innovation	[76, 78, 80]	→ ←	Lack of experience in budgeting the adoption of innovation	[10, 36, 45, 46, 54, 66]
	10	Financial resource availability	[13, 16, 80]	→ ←	Limited financial resources and low investments in research and development	[9, 10, 36, 46, 54, 66, 77–79]

(continued)

Table 2 (continued)

Triggers		Enablers			Barriers	
Human Resources	11	Information and digital technology expertise	[8, 16, 36, 48, 74]	→ ←	Lack of technical and support expertise	[3, 18, 44, 77, 79]
	12	Valorisation of soft skills	[36, 50, 70]	→ ←	Lack of appropriate soft skills	[10, 38, 44, 46, 66, 78, 79]
	13	Employee involvement and empowerment practices	[3, 10, 13, 18, 81]	→ ←	Lack of consideration of workers' autonomy and motivation	[39]
	14	Regular employee training	[36, 39, 44, 80]	→ ←	Lack of regular employee training	[10, 13, 39, 45, 46, 54, 79]
Managerial and Organizational Culture	15	Open-minded for change and adaptation leaders	[10, 50, 54]	→ ←	Leaders with a 'conservative' profile to change	[3, 10, 44]
	16	Management competency for digital transformation	[16, 44]	→ ←	Lack of digital vision by the top management	[10, 12, 38, 78]
	17	Managers' will to risk	[13, 19]	→ ←	Lack of risk management tools	[20, 46]
	18	Multidisciplinary knowledge and a good understanding of the operational professions	[44]	→ ←	Lack of appropriate skills, competencies, and experience	[10, 18]
	19	Change management competency	[16, 70]	→ ←	Lack of experience in change management	[44, 46]
	20	Culture based on experimentation and improvement	[3, 6, 19, 46]	→ ←	Lack of robust culture of adaptation and openness	[9, 11, 45, 73]
	21	Culture based on cooperation and sharing	[13, 19, 36, 46, 50]	→ ←	Lack of cooperation and resistance	[20, 38, 46, 66, 79]
	22	Effective knowledge-based communication	[3, 44]	→ ←	Lack of communication and transparency	[13, 38, 46, 66]

(continued)

Table 2 (continued)

Triggers		Enablers			Barriers	
Business strategy	23	Continuous improvement strategy on global scale	[36, 44, 48]	→ ←	Focus on short-term operational strategies	[6, 10, 20, 44, 66]
	24	Open innovation for new opportunities	[8, 43, 73, 82]	→ ←	Lack of access to shared knowledge	[11, 48, 73]
	25	Long-term collaboration with other SMEs	[8, 18, 43, 48, 50]	→ ←	Lack of trust and cooperation with other SMEs	[11, 46, 71]
	26	Customer-orientated strategy	[10, 45, 46, 80]	→ ←	Uncertainty about actual and potential customer needs	[45, 71, 80]

SMEs under pressure to adapt their organization in the scope of Industry 4.0 implementation [21].

On the level of the organizational structure, SMEs can consider the *enablers* and *barriers* related to the organizational complexity of SMEs (*trigger 1*). The suggestion to decentralize the organizational functions and to reduce the number of hierarchical levels [6, 36, 70] can encourage the SMEs with a rigid and bureaucratic organizational structure to adjust it [13, 71]. However, the distributed control and simplified internal processes suggested as a favourable precondition for Industry 4.0 implementation [6, 70] can be difficult to introduce into complex organizational structure with centralized decision-making and non-cooperative leadership [13, 38, 44]. On the level of human resources, SMEs can face the *enablers* and *barriers* related to their capacity to empower the employees (*trigger 13*). The involvement of employees in decision-making processes [3, 13, 81] and the commitment to their concerns [18] are among enabling factors for SMEs facing Industry 4.0 implementation. Nevertheless, such practices can be challenging within certain SMEs, where the employees' well-being and involvement in everyday life of the company are not among their priorities [39]. As for managerial and organizational culture, the *trigger 20* can be illustrated by the *enablers* and *barriers* regarding SMEs' capacity to innovate. An organizational culture nurtured by continual internal innovations [3, 19] can develop a greater ability to respond to changing environment, thus, driving towards Industry 4.0 implementation [6]. However, the mindset of "if it ain't broke, don't fix it" within some SMEs can prevent them from investing in Industry 4.0, sticking to old practices ([45], p. 12). Finally, on the level of business strategy, the SMEs' might face *enablers* and *barriers* regarding their capacity to collaborate with other SMEs (*trigger 25*). In fact, the ability to share and exchange tacit knowledge and innovation strategy with other SMEs can encourage Industry 4.0 implementation [18, 43, 48]. However, this attitude can represent a real challenge within certain

SMEs who privilege an individualistic functioning [71] or lack trust to cooperate with their peers [11, 46].

4.2 Pressures in the Outer Context of SMEs

According to the results of the literature review, the outer context of SMEs facing Industry 4.0 can be captured between the *enablers* and *barriers* related to their market conditions and key stakeholders (see Table 3). The presence of these driving and hindering triggers is generally out of the control of SMEs and can put them under pressure to implement or not Industry 4.0 [78].

For instance, SMEs might face the *enablers* and *barriers* related to their labour market (*trigger 29*). The difficulty of finding employees with required expertise can impede [79] or encourage SMEs to accelerate the automatization of certain processes [10, 12]. The government and its programs supporting SMEs in digitalization and innovation can also present some *enablers* and *barriers* (*trigger 30*). The countries where the government develop constantly such programs can encourage SMEs

Table 3 Pressures in the outer context of SMEs facing Industry 4.0 (authors' own)

Triggers		Enablers			Barriers	
Market Conditions	27	Market uncertainty driving the innovation	[71, 78]	→ ←	Market uncertainty hindering the innovation	[3, 20, 44, 73, 78]
	28	Supportive legislation	[20, 71]	→ ←	Restrictive legislation	[3, 66]
	29	Boosting effect of labour shortage	[10, 12, 78]	→ ←	Retarding effect of labour shortage	[78, 79]
Stakeholders	30	Governmental supporting programs	[3, 70, 71, 80]	→ ←	Lack of awareness campaigns about existing programs	[16, 48, 73]
	31	Financial support from the government	[16, 73, 80]	→ ←	Problematic tendering systems	[10, 66]
	32	Pressure from customers and professional network	[1, 12, 13, 20, 45, 74, 80]	→ ←	Resistance from customers and professional network	[10, 45, 50, 66]
	33	Competitive pressure	[10, 12, 13, 18–20, 74]	→ ←	Low level/awareness of concurrency	[45, 66, 79, 80]
	34	Industry 4.0 solutions tailored to SMEs' needs	[12, 18, 20, 44]	→ ←	Difficulty to reach technical providers	[13, 39, 66, 79]
	35	Sharing of success stories of bigger firms	[11, 80]	→ ←	Lack of inspiring examples of Industry 4.0 implementation	[45]

to implement Industry 4.0 [3, 70, 80]. However, the supporting programs can be difficult to benefit from if they are not sufficiently promoted among SMEs [16, 73] or their instructions are not clear [48]. The position of SMEs' professional networks towards innovation can be experienced as an *enabler* or a *barrier* regarding Industry 4.0 implementation (*trigger 32*). The pressure to implement new technologies that comes from customers [20, 74, 80] and firms from the same value chain [1, 13] often encourages SMEs to implement Industry 4.0. The opposite effect can be triggered by SMEs' subcontractors or customers who are not used to seizing the potential of new technologies [45, 50] and refuse to collaborate [10, 66]. The *trigger 34* is illustrated by the *enablers* and *barriers* regarding the availability of Industry 4.0 solutions adapted to SMEs' needs. Advanced in Industry 4.0 SMEs or technical providers who create the technological solutions adapted to the profile of SMEs can encourage them to implement new technologies [12, 18, 44]. However, because of a low-technology industrial sector in which they might operate [13, 79], SMEs can be disconnected from industries providing such solutions [39] and, therefore, struggle to benefit from such firm-specific solutions.

4.3 Strategic Choices of SMEs

Our review of the literature shows that *strategic choices* made by SMEs regarding Industry 4.0 implementation can take different forms, depending on the orientations they intend to favour (see Table 4). The characterization of *strategic choices* is

Table 4 Strategic choices of SMEs facing Industry 4.0 (authors' own)

Dimensions		Strategic choice 1			Strategic choice 2	
Profitability	36	Reactive and short-term ROI	[1, 6, 12, 19, 20, 38, 43–45, 54, 66, 71, 74–79]	→ ←	Proactive and medium or long-term ROI	[17, 36, 38, 48]
Purpose	37	Financial and operational excellence	[1, 9, 13, 20, 38, 44, 48, 50, 54, 71, 74, 77–79]	→ ←	Triple Bottom Line	[6, 8, 10, 12, 17, 36, 39, 43, 46, 73, 76]
Focus	38	Technological capital	[9, 10, 12, 13, 18, 20, 36, 39, 73, 74, 76, 77]	→ ←	Human capital	[8, 10, 12, 13, 36, 38, 46, 50, 81]
Technology	39	Basic technologies	[1, 9, 13, 20, 38, 44, 48, 50, 54, 71, 74, 77–79]	→ ←	Advanced technologies	[1, 9, 10, 18, 20, 36, 38, 43, 45, 48, 50, 54, 71, 73, 74, 77, 81, 83]
Solution	40	Standard	[43, 54, 74]	→ ←	Customized	[43, 71, 81]

achieved through five dimensions, each of which encompasses two extreme options between which several alternatives remain possible.

The profitability that SMEs aim by implementing Industry 4.0 (*dimension 36*) can be distinguished in terms of short-term and long-term ROI. SMEs can be attracted by the trend of extending the payback and pursue a long-term generation of benefits and performance improvements [38, 48]. However, SMEs can go for more straightforward and low-risk ROI, driven by the concerns about the lack of guarantee of payback and the financial value of the project [1, 45, 71]. The purpose followed by SMEs while implementing Industry 4.0 (*dimension 37*) is conceptualized in terms of main desired improvements. By focusing on costs reduction and operational efficiency, they easily implement new solutions that allow to improve productivity, lead times and corporate flexibility [38, 76, 77]. By balancing economic benefits, environmental actions and social capital development, they can mobilize the Triple Bottom Line perspective and expand their goals towards improving energy and resource consumption and working conditions [6, 39]. The area of transformation that SMEs focus on by implementing Industry 4.0 is illustrated through two *strategic choices* in the *dimension 38*. SMEs can focus on the improvement of their technological solutions to achieve higher product quality and improved time-to-market of products [9, 18]. By privileging the organizational acceptance, new job profiles and designs, new competencies, and clear objectives, SMEs can orient the change towards the empowerment of their human resources [13, 36, 76]. On the level of solutions allowing to implement Industry 4.0, the *dimension 40* refers to standard or customized solutions. By focusing on the outcomes that a specific technology can offer, SMEs tend to implement off-the-shelf solutions that generally developed by suppliers in response to the needs of large companies [43, 74]. By prioritizing customized solutions, they focus on the development of a new smart business model that goes beyond simple implementation of new technologies [71].

5 Discussion

This study joins the ongoing research discussion about Industry 4.0 implementation within SMEs by elaborating an analytical framework of how SMEs' context can affect their *strategic choices* (see Fig. 2). Even if SMEs generally struggle to implement Industry 4.0 through a conscious planning and methodological approach [10, 66], they make specific *strategic choices* by orienting their actions and goals towards desired outcomes and established norms of Industry 4.0. Such choices can be

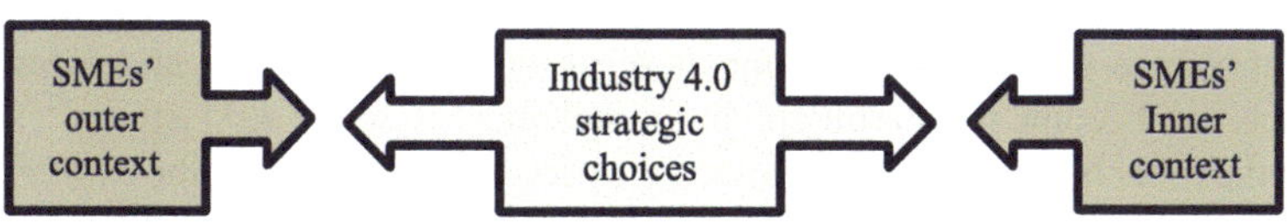

Fig. 2 Analytical framework of SMEs facing Industry 4.0 implementation

influenced by the *enablers* and *barriers* identified in SMEs' inner and outer context. From institutional perspective [22, 23, 61], the *enablers* and the *barriers* that mobilize and hamper SMEs' efforts to implement Industry 4.0 can be interpreted as institutional pressures arising from SMEs' inner and outer context. Such pressures can lead SMEs to contextual *trade-offs* regarding their *strategic choices*.

On one hand, this study analyses the pressures triggered by the *enablers* and *barriers* of SMEs' outer context to illustrate their influence on SMEs' *strategic choices* regarding Industry 4.0. Such pressures can arise from SMEs' organization field [68, 84]. Industry, professional associations, and inter-organizational networks can be the source of normative pressure pushing SMEs to adhere to norms and to embrace methods considered to be reasonable [85]. Government agencies, parent firms, dominant suppliers and customers can be the source of coercive pressure shaping the behaviour of SMEs through regulations or frameworks to apply [86]. Best practices, competitors, and peers can be the source of mimetic pressure, stimulating SMEs to adopt similar procedures and attitudes [87]. Following this logic, the present study puts together the *enablers* and *barriers* deriving from the same source of external pressure and emphasizes their mutually exclusive nature that can lead SMEs to different *trade-offs*. These *trade-offs* can push SMEs to prioritize an *enabler* or a *barrier* when making their *strategic choices* regarding Industry 4.0 implementation. Whereas both, enabling and impeding external pressures, can lead to one of *strategic choices*, the papers analysed in the scope of our literature review usually tend to highlight the *enablers* for such matter. For instance, the source of mimetic pressure leading to the *strategic choice* oriented towards long-term ROI could be the sharing of the success stories of Industry 4.0 implementation [11, 80]. Generally hesitating about the benefits of long run strategies and their possibilities in terms of covering the initial costs [71, 74], SMEs can acquire and replicate the competencies and methodologies that are readily accessible in their field [88]. Another potential source of mimetic pressure—successful competitors—can lead to the implementation of advanced technologies [12, 74]. The fact that SMEs' technologically more advanced competitors are positively perceived by peers within the same industry [26] can convince SMEs to overcome their prejudice about technologies with uncertain results [12]. The normative pressure represented by customers' requirements to use specific Industry 4.0 technologies can push SMEs to implement standard solutions as a potential *strategic choice* [20, 74]. In case SMEs are the suppliers of large companies who constantly innovate in terms of automation and connectivity, the latter "call the shots" by establishing the standards for technological solutions that might be implemented by the first ([12], p. 11). Regulatory standards or customers' requirements might exert the coercive pressure pushing SMEs to embrace the *strategic choice* oriented to Triple Bottom Line [20, 80]. Just like SMEs adopting new technologies to reduce carbon footprint across their supply chain [26], the compliance with legal requirements regarding the traceability and security of products can become the starting point to implement Industry 4.0 [20].

On the other hand, our study analyses the pressures triggered by the *enablers* and *barriers* of SMEs' inner context to illustrate their influence on SMEs' *strategic choices*. The internal source of pressure might derive from the internal dynamics and complexity of SMEs' organization [23]. Considering that every organization represents a "mosaic of groups structured by functional tasks and employment status", the potential source of pressure can be the divergence of groups' interests regarding SMEs' objectives, organizational structure, and performance evaluation ([21], p. 1033). The way the groups are committed to the current model of organizational functioning—loyal, indifferent, competitive, opposed—can also be the origin of internal pressures [21]. Building upon this reasoning, our study explores the *enablers* and *barriers* related to the similar source of internal pressure and highlights their conflicting nature. Such conflicting nature may lead SMEs to contextual *trade-offs* when making their strategic choices regarding Industry 4.0. Although both supportive and obstructive internal pressures can influence SMEs' strategic decision-making, the reviewed literature usually tends to focus on the *barriers* in this regard. For instance, SMEs may opt for the *strategic choice* with short-term ROI because of their resource constraints [75] and short-term strategic vision [48]. Indeed, avoiding long-term investments can be explained by SMEs' "business model innovation aspirations" that are "often not conscious and not handled as an opportunity but rather as a compulsion" ([10], p. 128). From institutional perspective, such an attitude refers to the status quo value commitment according to which SMEs' actors adhere to the established and commonly used institutional template [21]. The same value commitment can prevent SMEs from embracing the *strategic choice* focused on human capital. As the implementation of Industry 4.0 technologies may require new competencies, new processes and new testing methods, SMEs can consider such learning curve "too expensive and time consuming" ([45], p. 12). This attitude can be explained by SMEs' lack of technical and support expertise of workers [3, 18], lack of regular employee training [13, 46] and the lack of a robust culture of adaptation and openness [11, 73]. Generally, SMEs tend to begin with the implementation of basic technologies considered as easily programmable for their environment [10, 36, 74]. Frequently mentioned reluctance of SMEs towards data analysis and lack of perception of its use [52, 74, 78] often slows down the integration of more advanced technologies. However, according to the study conducted by Cimini et al. [36], once SMEs acquire the necessary basic technologies, they can step further toward more advanced solutions.

Finally, with respect to institutional theory, this study suggests an interesting assumption regarding the contextual *trade-offs* that SMEs may realize by making certain *strategic choices*. From institutional perspective, SMEs, confronted with institutional pressures, seek to respond strategically to gain legitimacy and ensure their survival [61, 89]. Through the tactics of acquiescence strategy, they might decide to conform to the pressures for self-serving reasons [61]. The tactics of compromise strategy allow propelling SMEs' own interests [61]. The strategy of avoidance refers to the tactics of bypassing the necessity of conforming to pressures [61]. The tactics of defiance strategy can lead SMEs to the rejection of the institutional norms [61]. The tactics of manipulation strategy can be applied to co-opt, influence, or control an institutional pressure [61]. Following this logic, the contextual *trade-offs* can become intentional when SMEs must decide which *strategic choice* to make regarding Industry 4.0 implementation. Some *strategic choices*, such as long-term ROI, Triple Bottom Line, or human-oriented change, may refer to acquiescence strategies, whereby SMEs conform to the requirements of Industry 4.0 for reasons that serve their own interests [61]. In this case, SMEs might lean more towards the *enablers* of their context since such transformations help them to embrace Industry 4.0 as promoted by the institutions behind these enablers [26, 88, 90]. The *strategic choices* related to Industry 4.0 technologies where SMEs start by implementing basic technologies to continue with the advanced ones [36] might be explained by compromise strategies where SMEs might pursue their own interests through tactics of balancing [61]. Here, SMEs might be placed between the *enablers* and *barriers* of their context as they seek to strike a balance between the conflicting external pressures or conflicting internal pressures. The *strategic choices* with short-term ROI or technological orientation of change might be partly explained by SMEs' attempt to bypass the need to conform to pressures—the avoidance strategy [61]. For instance, SMEs can implement new technology requiring few processual changes and hire experts to handle this technology to avoid changing the organizational culture, upskilling the workers, or causing workers' resistance [76].

6 Conclusion

The aim of this theoretical study was to identify and analyse the influence of contextual *enablers* and *barriers* on SMEs' *strategic choices* regarding Industry 4.0 implementation. Through narrative literature review [27, 28], the study mobilized previous studies focused on SMEs implementing Industry 4.0 and addressed their findings from a novel and original perspective.

The obtained framework goes beyond such common characteristics as size, sector of activity, limited financial resources or flexible organizational structure used by existing studies to describe SMEs facing Industry 4.0 implementation [6, 10]. The framework captures the uniqueness of SMEs' strategic decision-making by highlighting 35 contextual triggers leading SMEs to potential *trade-offs* regarding 5 dimensions of *strategic choices* in the scope of Industry 4.0 implementation. The authors plan to test empirically the analytical framework with managers and other key actors of SMEs facing Industry 4.0 implementation. The outcomes of this future study are expected to help to adjust several aspects of the framework according to the evolving reality of SMEs. These outcomes are expected also to achieve a better understanding and empirical-based explanation of SMEs' *trade-offs* between contextual elements and *strategic choices* regarding Industry 4.0 implementation.

This study suggests several managerial implications. First, the framework obtained in the scope of this study can be further transformed into a methodological tool for SMEs planning to implement Industry 4.0. The analysis of their specific inner and external contexts may help SMEs to tailor their *strategic choices* for Industry 4.0 implementation according to their needs and specificities. Second, the framework can be transformed into an analytical tool for SMEs already involved in the process of Industry 4.0 implementation. The panoramic analysis of contextual factors likely to influence *strategic choices* may help SMEs to take a step back and assess their current situation related to Industry 4.0 implementation.

This study has several limitations that can be addressed by future research. The identified *strategic choices* do not cover all examples of the orientation of SMEs' goals towards desired outcomes of Industry 4.0. Therefore, the future research is invited to enrich by a more fine-grained categorization the proposition of SMEs' *strategic choices* regarding Industry 4.0 implementation covered by this study. Since the concept of Industry 4.0 is adopted by countries with distinct institutional characteristics, it gives rise to divergent interpretations [25]. Moreover, the requirements and particularities of Industry 4.0 implementation vary across industrial sectors [18]. Therefore, future research may refine the proposed framework by considering the institutional particularities of specific regions or activity sectors, allowing a more tailored tool to assess the influence of SMEs' context on their *strategic choices* regarding Industry 4.0.

Acknowledgments This study has been initiated by the Digital Lab and co-financed by its partners, Wallonie Entreprendre, Equans, John Cockerill, and AGC.

The research has been supported by donations of the Caterpillar Foundation, US in the context of the Chair Industry 4.h (human).

Appendix

Articles included in the literature review.

Ref.	Year	Country	Method	Publication
[8]	2019	Italy	Questionnaire and in-depth interviews	European Journal of Innovation Management
[50]	2020	Italy, Poland, Germany, Austria, Hungary	Survey	Management Decision
[71]	2020	Brazil	Case study	International Journal of Production Economics
[1]	2019	USA	Survey	Journal of Manufacturing Technology Management
[72]	2020	Italy	Survey	Procedia CIRP
[36]	2020	Italy	Case studies	Journal of Manufacturing Technology Management
[73]	2021	Italy	Semi-structured in-depth interviews, multiple case studies	Technological Forecasting and Social Change
[13]	2021	Spain	Interviews and survey	European Management Journal
[74]	2019	Iran Malaysia	Questionnaire	Journal of Industrial Information Integration

Ref.	Year	Country	Method	Publication
[16]	2021	Italy, Netherlands, France, Spain, Sweden, Germany, Denmark	Literature review and in-depth interviews	Journal of Manufacturing Technology Management
[18]	2022	–	Systematic literature review	Journal of Manufacturing Technology Management
[10]	2019	Hungary	In-depth interviews	Technological Forecasting and Social Change
[39]	2021	Italy	Multiple case study	IEEE Transactions on Engineering Management
[79]	2020	Poland	Quantitative and semi-directive interviews	Sustainability [Switzerland]
[80]	2022	Malaysia	Survey	International Journal of Computer Integrated Manufacturing
[3]	2021	Brazil	Interviews and focus groups	Sustainability [Switzerland]
[9]	2021	Sweden	Case studies	Journal of Manufacturing Technology Management
[45]	2018	Finland	Interviews and focus groups	Journal of Manufacturing Technology Management
[54]	2020	UK	Survey	Computers in Industry
[76]	2020	India	Case studies	International Journal of Production Research
[11]	2018	–	In-depth literature review	Journal of Manufacturing Systems
[44]	2020	France	Questionnaires	International Journal of Production Research
[77]	2018	–	Literature review	International Journal of Production Research
[12]	2018	Germany	Case studies	Technological Forecasting and Social Change
[6]	2018	Germany	Survey	Sustainability
[82]	2022	Thailand	Survey	International Journal of Technology
[75]	2020	Czech Republic	Survey	Business: Theory and Practice
[66]	2020	Italy, Austria, USA, Thailand	Workshops	Palgrave Macmillan
[83]	2020	Czech Republic	Questionnaire	Applied Sciences
[38]	2020	Austria, France, Germany, Italy, Slovenia	Survey and interviews	Journal of Manufacturing Technology Management
[78]	2019	Japan	Survey	Sustainability
[46]	2019	Italy, Austria, USA, Thailand	Workshops	Palgrave Macmillan
[43]	2021	Italia	Survey	International Journal of Production Economics
[70]	2022	India	Case studies	Computers and Industrial Engineering

Ref.	Year	Country	Method	Publication
[48]	2022	Spain	Questionnaire	Journal of Small Business Management
[20]	2022	Denmark	Survey and semi-structured interviews	Production Planning and Control
[81]	2021	EU27	Quantitative analysis of EU survey	Journal of Manufacturing Technology Management
[17]	2021	Norway	Pilot cases	IFIP Advances in Information and Communication Technology book series
[19]	2019	Czech Republic	Survey and case studies	Social Sciences

References

1. Bosman, L., Hartman, N., & Sutherland, J. (2019). How manufacturing firm characteristics can influence decision making for investing in Industry 4.0 technologies. *Journal of Manufacturing Technology Management, 31*(5), 1117–1141. https://doi.org/10.1108/JMTM-09-2018-0283
2. Kohler, D., & Weisz, J. (2021). Industry 4.0: the 4th Industrial revolution. Volume 2—Organizational and societal challenges. *Les Cahiers du Digital, 2*, 7–44.
3. Machado, E., Scavarda, L. F., Caiado, R. G. G., & Thomé, A. M. T. (2021). Barriers and enablers for the integration of Industry 4.0 and sustainability in supply chains of MSMEs. *Sustainability (Switzerland), 13*(21). https://doi.org/10.3390/su132111664
4. Margherita, E. G., & Braccini, A. M. (2020). Industry 4.0 technologies in flexible manufacturing for sustainable organizational value: Reflections from a multiple case study of Italian manufacturers. *Information Systems Frontiers*. https://doi.org/10.1007/s10796-020-10047-y
5. Margherita, E. G., & Braccini, A. M. (2021). Examining the development of a digital ecosystem in an Industry 4.0 context: a sociotechnical perspective. *SN Business and Economics, 1*(89), 1–18. https://doi.org/10.1007/s43546-021-00096-z
6. Müller, J. M., Kiel, D., & Voigt, K.-I. (2018). What drives the implementation of Industry 4.0? The role of opportunities and challenges in the context of sustainability. *Sustainability, 10*(1), 247. https://doi.org/10.3390/su10010247
7. Sony, M., & Naik, S. (2020). Industry 4.0 integration with socio-technical systems theory: a systematic review and proposed theoretical model. *Technology in Society, 61*. https://doi.org/10.1016/j.techsoc.2020.101248
8. Agostini, L., & Filippini, R. (2019). Organizational and managerial challenges in the path towards Industry 4.0. *European Journal of Innovation Management, 22*(3), 406–421. https://doi.org/10.1108/EJIM-02-2018-0030
9. Machado, C. G., Winroth, M., Almström, P., Ericson Öberg, A., Kurdve, M., & AlMashalah, S. (2021). Digital organisational readiness: experiences from manufacturing companies. *Journal of Manufacturing Technology Management, 32*(9), 167–182. https://doi.org/10.1108/JMTM-05-2019-0188
10. Horváth, D., & Szabó, R. Z. S. (2019). Driving forces and barriers of Industry 4.0: Do multinational and small and medium-sized companies have equal opportunities? *Technological Forecasting and Social Change, 146*, 119–132. https://doi.org/10.1016/j.techfore.2019.05.021
11. Mittal, S., Khan, M. A., Romero, D., & Wuest, T. (2018). A critical review of smart manufacturing and Industry 4.0 maturity models: Implications for small and medium-sized enterprises (SMEs). *Journal of Manufacturing Systems, 49*, 194–214. https://doi.org/10.1016/j.jmsy.2018.10.005

12. Müller, J. M., Buliga, O., & Voigt, K.-I. (2018). Fortune favors the prepared: How SMEs approach business model innovations in Industry 4.0. *Technological Forecasting and Social Change, 132*, 2–17. https://doi.org/10.1016/j.techfore.2017.12.019
13. Estensoro, M., Larrea, M., Müller, J. M., & Sisti, E. (2021). A resource-based view on SMEs regarding the transition to more sophisticated stages of Industry 4.0. *European Management Journal, 40*(5), 778–792. https://doi.org/10.1016/j.emj.2021.10.001
14. Müller, J., Kazantsev, N., Romanello, R., Adamczuk, G., Ghobakhlo, M., Hamzeh, R., Das, D., Tabane, E., Drogovoz, P., & Michna, A. (2020). Integration model for Industry 4.0 from multiple SMEs worldwide. In *21st international working seminar on production economics, Innsbruck, Austria.*
15. Amaral, A., & Peças, P. (2021). SMEs and Industry 4.0: Two case studies of digitalization for a smoother integration. *Computers in Industry, 125*. https://doi.org/10.1016/j.compind.2020.103333
16. Ghobakhloo, M., & Iranmanesh, M. (2021). Digital transformation success under Industry 4.0: A strategic guideline for manufacturing SMEs. *Journal of Manufacturing Technology Management, 32*(8), 1533–1556. https://doi.org/10.1108/JMTM-11-2020-0455
17. Verhulst, E., & Brenden, S. F. (2021). Strategic roadmapping towards Industry 4.0 for manufacturing SMEs. In A. Dolgui, A. Bernard, D. Lemoine, G. von Cieminski, & D. Romero (Eds.), *Advances in production management systems. Artificial intelligence for sustainable and resilient production systems. APMS 2021. IFIP advances in information and communication technology* (Vol. 631). Springer. https://doi.org/10.1007/978-3-030-85902-2_1
18. Ghobakhloo, M., Iranmanesh, M., Vilkas, M., Grybauskas, A., & Amran, A. (2022). Drivers and barriers of Industry 4.0 technology adoption among manufacturing SMEs: A systematic review and transformation roadmap. *Journal of Manufacturing Technology Management, 33*(6), 1029–1058. https://doi.org/10.1108/JMTM-12-2021-0505
19. Vrchota, J., Volek, T., & Novotná, M. (2019). Factors introducing Industry 4.0 to SMES. *Social Sciences, 8*(5), 130. https://doi.org/10.3390/socsci8050130
20. Stentoft, J., Adsbøll Wickstrøm, K., Philipsen, K., & Haug, A. (2021). Drivers and barriers for Industry 4.0 readiness and practice: Empirical evidence from small and medium-sized manufacturers. *Production Planning and Control, 32*(10), 811–828. https://doi.org/10.1080/09537287.2020.1768318
21. Greenwood, R., & Hinings, C. R. (1996). Understanding radical organizational change: Bringing together the old and the new institutionalism. *The Academy of Management Review, 21*(4), 1022–1054. https://doi.org/10.2307/259163
22. Scott, W. R. (2014). *Institutions and organizations: ideas, interests, and identities* (4th ed.). Sage.
23. Zucker, L. G. (1987). Institutional theories of organization. *Annual Review of Sociology, 13*, 443–464.
24. Bag, S., Pretorius, J. H. C., Gupta, S., & Dwivedi, Y. K. (2021). Role of institutional pressures and resources in the adoption of big data analytics powered artificial intelligence, sustainable manufacturing practices and circular economy capabilities. *Technological Forecasting and Social Change, 163*. https://doi.org/10.1016/j.techfore.2020.120420
25. Fogaça, D., Grijalvo, M., & Sacomano Neto, M. (2022). An institutional perspective in the Industry 4.0 scenario: A systematic literature review. *Journal of Industrial Engineering and Management, 15*(2), 309. https://doi.org/10.3926/jiem.3724
26. Gupta, S., Modgil, S., Gunasekaran, A., & Bag, S. (2020). Dynamic capabilities and institutional theories for Industry 4.0 and digital supply chain. *Supply Chain Forum: An International Journal, 21*(3), 139–157. https://doi.org/10.1080/16258312.2020.1757369
27. Baumeister, R. F., & Leary, M. R. (1997). Writing narrative literature reviews. *Review of General Psychology, 1*(3), 311–320.
28. Hammersley, M. (2001). On "systematic" reviews of research literatures: A "narrative" response to Evans and Benefield. *British Educational Research Journal, 27*(5), 543–554. https://doi.org/10.1080/01411920120095726

29. Fan, D., Breslin, D., Callahan, J. L., & Iszatt-White, M. (2022). Advancing literature review methodology through rigour, generativity, scope and transparency. *International Journal of Management Reviews, 24*(2), 171–180. https://doi.org/10.1111/ijmr.12291
30. Kamble, S. S., Gunasekaran, A., & Gawankar, S. A. (2018). Sustainable Industry 4.0 framework: A systematic literature review identifying the current trends and future perspectives. *Process Safety and Environmental Protection, 117*, 408–425. https://doi.org/10.1016/j.psep.2018.05.009
31. Zheng, T., Ardolino, M., Bacchetti, A., & Perona, M. (2021). The applications of Industry 4.0 technologies in manufacturing context: a systematic literature review. *International Journal of Production Research, 59*(6), 1922–1954. https://doi.org/10.1080/00207543.2020.1824085
32. Schneider, P. (2018). Managerial challenges of Industry 4.0: an empirically backed research agenda for a nascent field. *Review Managerial Science, 12*, 803–848. https://doi.org/10.1007/s11846-018-0283-2
33. Da Silva, V. L., Kovaleski, J. L., Pagani, R. N., De Matos Silva, J., & Corsi, A. (2020). Implementation of Industry 4.0 concept in companies: empirical evidences. *International Journal of Computer Integrated Manufacturing, 33*(4), 325–342. https://doi.org/10.1080/0951192X.2019.1699258
34. Ghobakhloo, M. (2018). The future of manufacturing industry: a strategic roadmap toward Industry 4.0. *Journal of Manufacturing Technology Management, 29*(6), 910–936. https://doi.org/10.1108/JMTM-02-2018-0057
35. Klingenberg, C. O., Borges, M. A. V., & Antunes, J. A. V., Jr. (2019). Industry 4.0 as a data-driven paradigm: A systematic literature review on technologies. *Journal of Manufacturing Technology Management, 32*(3), 570–592. https://doi.org/10.1108/JMTM-09-2018-0325
36. Cimini, C., Boffelli, A., Lagorio, A., Kalchschmidt, M. G. M., & Pinto, R. (2020). How do Industry 4.0 technologies influence organisational change? An empirical analysis of Italian SMEs. *Journal of Manufacturing Technology Management, 32*(3), 695–721. https://doi.org/10.1108/jmtm-04-2019-0135
37. Hernandez-de-Menendez, M., Morales-Menendez, R., Escobar, C. A., & McGovern, M. (2020). Competencies for Industry 4.0. *International Journal on Interactive Design and Manufacturing, 14*(4), 1511–1524. https://doi.org/10.1007/s12008-020-00716-2
38. Pessot, E., Zangiacomi, A., Battistella, C., Rocchi, V., Sala, A., & Sacco, M. (2020). What matters in implementing the factory of the future: Insights from a survey in European manufacturing regions. *Journal of Manufacturing Technology Management, 32*(3), 795–819. https://doi.org/10.1108/JMTM-05-2019-0169
39. Ietto, B., Ancillai, C., Sabatini, A., Carayannis, E., & Gregori, G. L. (2022). The role of external actors in SMEs' human-centered Industry 4.0 adoption: An empirical perspective on Italian competence centers. *IEEE Transactions on Engineering Management*, 1–16. https://doi.org/10.1109/TEM.2022.3144881
40. European Commission. Document 32003H0361. Commission Recommendation of 6 May 2003 concerning the definition of micro, small and medium-sized enterprises. European Commission. https://eur-lex.europa.eu/legal-content/EN/ALL/?uri=CELEX:32003H0361
41. Harney, B., Gilman, M., Mayson, S., & Raby, S. (2022). Advancing understanding of HRM in small and medium-sized enterprises (SMEs): Critical questions and future prospects. *The International Journal of Human Resource Management, 33*(16), 3175–3196. https://doi.org/10.1080/09585192.2022.2109375
42. Hervas-Oliver, J.-L., Sempere-Ripoll, F., Boronat-Moll, C., & Estelles-Miguel, S. (2020). SME open innovation for process development: Understanding process-dedicated external knowledge sourcing. *Journal of Small Business Management, 58*(2), 409–445. https://doi.org/10.1080/00472778.2019.1680072
43. Ricci, R., Battaglia, D., & Neirotti, P. (2021). External knowledge search, opportunity recognition and Industry 4.0 adoption in SMEs. *International Journal of Production Economics, 240*. https://doi.org/10.1016/j.ijpe.2021.108234

44. Moeuf, A., Lamouri, S., Pellerin, R., Tamayo-Giraldo, S., Tobon-Valencia, E., & Eburdy, R. (2020). Identification of critical success factors, risks and opportunities of Industry 4.0 in SMEs. *International Journal of Production Research, 58*(5), 1384–1400. https://doi.org/10.1080/00207543.2019.1636323
45. Martinsuo, M., & Luomaranta, T. (2018). Adopting additive manufacturing in SMEs: Exploring the challenges and solutions. *Journal of Manufacturing Technology Management, 29*(6), 937–957. https://doi.org/10.1108/JMTM-02-2018-0030
46. Rauch, E., Vickery, A. R., Brown, C. A., & Matt, D. T. (2020). SME requirements and guidelines for the design of smart and highly adaptable manufacturing systems. In D. T. Matt, V. Modrák, & H. Zsifkovits (Eds.), *Industry 4.0 for SMEs: Challenges, opportunities, and requirements* (pp. 39–72). Palgrave Macmillan. https://doi.org/10.1007/978-3-030-25425-4
47. Müller, J. M. (2019). Assessing the barriers to Industry 4.0 implementation from a workers' perspective. In D. Ivanov, A. Dolgui, & F. Yalaoui (Eds.), *IFAC-Papers OnLine* (Vol. 52, Issue 13, pp. 2189–2194). https://doi.org/10.1016/j.ifacol.2019.11.530
48. Somohano-Rodríguez, F. M., Madrid-Guijarro, A., & López-Fernández, J. M. (2022). Does Industry 4.0 really matter for SME innovation? *Journal of Small Business Management, 60*(4), 1001–1028. https://doi.org/10.1080/00472778.2020.1780728
49. Veile, J. W., Kiel, D., Müller, J. M., & Voigt, K.-I. (2019). Lessons learned from Industry 4.0 implementation in the German manufacturing industry. *Journal of Manufacturing Technology Management, 31*(5), 977–997. https://doi.org/10.1108/JMTM-08-2018-0270
50. Agostini, L., & Nosella, A. (2020). The adoption of Industry 4.0 technologies in SMEs: Results of an international study. *Management Decision, 58*(4), 625–664. https://doi.org/10.1108/MD-09-2018-0973
51. Ludwig, T., Kotthaus, C., Stein, M., Pipek, V., & Wulf, V. (2018). Revive old discussions! Socio-technical challenges for small and medium enterprises within Industry 4.0. In: *Proceedings of 16th European conference on computer-supported cooperative work-exploratory papers*. European Society for Socially Embedded Technologies (EUSSET). https://dl.eusset.eu/handle/20.500.12015/3116.
52. Wong, L.-W., Leong, L.-Y., Hew, J.-J., Tan, G. W.-H., & Ooi, K.-B. (2020). Time to seize the digital evolution: Adoption of blockchain in operations and supply chain management among Malaysian SMEs. *International Journal of Information Management, 52*. https://doi.org/10.1016/j.ijinfomgt.2019.08.005
53. Hobscheidt, D., Kühn, A., & Dumitrescu, R. (2021). Derivation of socio-technical solution patterns for Industry 4.0 problem classes. *Procedia CIRP, 100*, 301–306. https://doi.org/10.1016/j.procir.2021.05.070
54. Masood, T., & Sonntag, P. (2020). Industry 4.0: Adoption challenges and benefits for SMEs. *Computers in Industry, 121*. https://doi.org/10.1016/j.compind.2020.103261
55. Santos, B., Dieste, M., Orzes, G., & Charrua-Santos, F. (2022). Resources and capabilities for Industry 4.0 implementation: Evidence from proactive Portuguese SMEs. *Journal of Manufacturing Technology Management, 34*(1), 25–43. https://doi.org/10.1108/JMTM-02-2022-0074
56. Oti-Sarpong, K., Pärn, E. A., Burgess, G., & Zaki, M. (2022). Transforming the construction sector: An institutional complexity perspective. *Construction Innovation, 22*(2), 361–387. https://doi.org/10.1108/CI-04-2021-0071
57. Jones, O., & Gatrell, C. (2014). Editorial: The future of writing and reviewing for IJMR: Editorial. *International Journal of Management Reviews, 16*(3), 249–264. https://doi.org/10.1111/ijmr.12038
58. Wohlin, C. (2014). Guidelines for snowballing in systematic literature studies and a replication in software engineering. In *Proceedings of the 18th international conference on evaluation and assessment in software engineering* (pp. 1–10).
59. Madden, A., Bailey, C., Alfes, K., & Fletcher, L. (2018). Using narrative evidence synthesis in HRM research: An overview of the method, its application, and the lessons learned. *Human Resource Management, 57*(2), 641–657. https://doi.org/10.1002/hrm.21858

60. Child, J. (1972). Organizational structure, environment and performance: The role of strategic choice. *Sociology, 6*(1), 1–22.
61. Oliver, C. (1991). Strategic responses to institutional processes. *The Academy of Management Review, 16*(1), 145–179.
62. Pettigrew, A. M. (1987). Context and action in the transformation of the firm. *Journal of Management Studies, 24*(6), 649–670. https://doi.org/10.1111/j.1467-6486.1987.tb00467.x
63. Ozorhon, B., Abbott, C., & Aouad, G. (2014). Integration and leadership as enablers of innovation in construction: Case study. *Journal of Management in Engineering, 30*(2), 256–263. https://doi.org/10.1061/(ASCE)ME.1943-5479.0000204
64. Coad, A., Pellegrino, G., & Savona, M. (2016). Barriers to innovation and firm productivity. *Economics of Innovation and New Technology, 25*(3), 321–334. https://doi.org/10.1080/10438599.2015.1076193
65. Saldaña, J. (2013). *The coding manual for qualitative researchers* (2nd ed.). SAGE.
66. Orzes, G., Poklemba, R., & Towner, W. T. (2020). Implementing Industry 4.0 in SMEs: A focus group study on organizational requirements. In D. T. Matt, V. Modrák, & H. Zsifkovits (Eds.), *Industry 4.0 for SMEs: Challenges, opportunities, and requirements* (pp. 251–277). Palgrave Macmillan. https://doi.org/10.1007/978-3-030-25425-4
67. Linneberg, S. M., & Korsgaard, S. (2019). Coding qualitative data: A synthesis guiding the novice. *Qualitative Research Journal, 19*(3), 259–270. https://doi.org/10.1108/QRJ-12-2018-0012
68. Dimaggio, P. J., & Powell, W. W. (1983). The Iron Cage Revisited: Institutional isomorphism and collective rationality. *American Sociological Review, 48*(2), 147–160. https://www.jstor.org/stable/2095101
69. Cennamo, C., & Santalo, J. (2013). Platform competition strategic trade-offs in platform markets. *Strategic Management Journal, 34*(11), 1331–1350. https://doi.org/10.1002/smj.2066
70. Shukla, M., & Shankar, R. (2022). An extended technology-organization-environment framework to investigate smart manufacturing system implementation in small and medium enterprises. *Computers and Industrial Engineering, 163*. https://doi.org/10.1016/j.cie.2021.107865
71. Benitez, G. B., Ayala, N. F., & Frank, A. G. (2020). Industry 4.0 innovation ecosystems: An evolutionary perspective on value cocreation. *International Journal of Production Economics, 228*. https://doi.org/10.1016/j.ijpe.2020.107735
72. Brozzi, R., Riedl, M., & Matt, D. (2020). Key readiness indicators to assess the digital level of manufacturing SMEs. *Procedia CIRP, 96*, 201–206. https://doi.org/10.1016/j.procir.2021.01.075
73. Cugno, M., Castagnoli, R., & Büchi, G. (2021). Openness to Industry 4.0 and performance: The impact of barriers and incentives. *Technological Forecasting and Social Change, 168*. https://doi.org/10.1016/j.techfore.2021.120756
74. Ghobakhloo, M., & Ching, N. T. (2019). Adoption of digital technologies of smart manufacturing in SMEs. *Journal of Industrial Information Integration, 16*. https://doi.org/10.1016/j.jii.2019.100107
75. Nwaiwu, F., Duduci, M., Chromjakova, F., & Otekhile, C.-A. F. (2020). Industry 4.0 concepts within the Czech SME manufacturing sector: An empirical assessment of critical success factors. *Business: Theory and Practice, 21*(1), 58–70. https://doi.org/10.3846/btp.2020.10712
76. Mittal, S., Khan, M. A., Purohit, J. K., Menon, K., Romero, D., & Wuest, T. (2020). A smart manufacturing adoption framework for SMEs. *International Journal of Production Research, 58*(5), 1555–1573. https://doi.org/10.1080/00207543.2019.1661540
77. Moeuf, A., Pellerin, R., Lamouri, S., Tamayo-Giraldo, S., & Barbaray, R. (2018). The industrial management of SMEs in the era of Industry 4.0. *International Journal of Production Research, 56*(3), 1118–1136. https://doi.org/10.1080/00207543.2017.1372647
78. Prause, M. (2019). Challenges of Industry 4.0 technology adoption for SMEs: The case of Japan. *Sustainability, 11*(20). https://doi.org/10.3390/su11205807
79. Ingaldi, M., & Ulewicz, R. (2020). Problems with the implementation of Industry 4.0 in enterprises from the SME sector. *Sustainability (Switzerland), 12*(1). https://doi.org/10.3390/SU12010217

80. Khin, S., & Hung Kee, D. M. (2022). Identifying the driving and moderating factors of Malaysian SMEs' readiness for Industry 4.0. *International Journal of Computer Integrated Manufacturing, 35*(27), 761–779. https://doi.org/10.1080/0951192X.2022.2025619
81. Vereycken, Y., Ramioul, M., Desiere, S., & Bal, M. (2021). Human resource practices accompanying Industry 4.0 in European manufacturing industry. *Journal of Manufacturing Technology Management, 32*(5), 1016–1036. https://doi.org/10.1108/JMTM-08-2020-0331
82. Naruetharadhol, P., Srisathan, W. A., Gebsombut, N., Wongthahan, P., & Ketkaew, C. (2022). Industry 4.0 for Thai SMEs: implementing open innovation as innovation capability management. *International Journal of Technology, 13*(1), 48–57. https://doi.org/10.14716/ijtech.v13i1.4746
83. Pech, M., & Vrchota, J. (2020). Classification of small- and medium-sized enterprises based on the level of Industry 4.0 implementation. *Applied Sciences, 10*(15). https://doi.org/10.3390/app10155150
84. Mignerat, M., & Rivard, S. (2009). Positioning the institutional perspective in information systems research. *Journal of Information Technology, 24*(4), 369–391. https://doi.org/10.1057/jit.2009.13
85. Mizruchi, M. S., & Fein, L. C. (1999). The social construction of organizational knowledge: A study of the uses of coercive, mimetic, and normative isomorphism. *Administrative Science Quarterly, 44*(4), 653–683. https://doi.org/10.2307/2667051
86. Heugens, P. P. M. A. R., & Lander, M. W. (2009). Structure! agency! (and other quarrels): A meta-analysis of institutional theories of organization. *Academy of Management Journal, 52*(1), 61–85. https://doi.org/10.5465/amj.2009.36461835
87. Barreto, I., & Baden-Fuller, C. (2006). To conform or to perform? Mimetic behaviour, legitimacy-based groups and performance consequences. *Journal of Management Studies, 43*(7), 1559–1581. https://doi.org/10.1111/j.1467-6486.2006.00620.x
88. Caldera, H. T. S., Desha, C., & Dawes, L. (2019). Evaluating the enablers and barriers for successful implementation of sustainable business practice in 'lean' SMEs. *Journal of Cleaner Production, 218*, 575–590. https://doi.org/10.1016/j.jclepro.2019.01.239
89. Suchman, M. C. (1995). Managing legitimacy: Strategic and institutional approaches. *Academy of Management Review, 20*(3), 571–611. http://www.jstor.com/stable/258788
90. Shibin, K. T., Dubey, R., Gunasekaran, A., Hazen, B., Roubaud, D., Gupta, S., & Foropon, C. (2020). Examining sustainable supply chain management of SMEs using resource based view and institutional theory. *Annals of Operations Research, 290*(1–2), 301–326. https://doi.org/10.1007/s10479-017-2706-x

Part II
Exploring Implications of Emerging Technologies

The Context Sets the Tone: A Literature Review on Emotion Recognition from Speech Using AI

Fabian Thaler, Maximilian Haug, Heiko Gewald, and Philipp Brune

Abstract Customers' emotions play a crucial role in the service industry. The better the staff understands the customer, the better their service. Human emotions elicit measurable speech markers, such as increased speech rate or higher pitch, and AI can interpret these signals. In recent years, significant progress has been made in automatically recognizing basic emotions such as joy, anger, etc. However, there is a lot of disagreement regarding evaluating the crucial feature types and the feature dimensions to be analyzed. By utilizing a systematic literature review of 81 articles, this article analyses the specification of context and DSR implications for feature types and emotion dimensions for emotional speech analysis. The results show that these are generally insufficiently specified. Accordingly, this paper aims to optimize the potential for generalization of DSR results and thereby improves theory building in this discipline.

Keywords Design science research · Emotion recognition · Artificial intelligence

1 Introduction

In recent years, companies and organizations have been facing the constant challenge of digital transformation [1, 2]. Digital products and services are therefore becoming increasingly important in this transformation process with the aim of not only achieving but also maintaining competitive advantages [3]. Companies need to identify cutting-edge technologies in order to leverage their operations to the next level. Especially artificial intelligence (AI) seems to provide promising use cases in the future. In this context, the ability to align artificial intelligence with existing or new products or services will be relevant to designing a sustainable and

F. Thaler (✉) · M. Haug · H. Gewald · P. Brune
Neu-Ulm University of Applied Sciences, Neu-Ulm, Germany
e-mail: fabian.thaler@hnu.de

A. M. Braccini et al. (eds.), *Technologies for Digital Transformation*, Lecture Notes in Information Systems and Organisation 64,
https://doi.org/10.1007/978-3-031-52120-1_8

future-oriented business strategy, as it will also impact the future strategic positioning of these companies or organizations [4–6].

In order for companies to generate revenue through the digital alignment of their product and service portfolios and to remain competitive in the long term, they must be able to adapt both their internal processes and structures as well as their external products and services to the constantly changing, complex environment of digitalization [7, 8].

The service industry is utilizing a variety of forms of AI to serve its customers along the entire value chain, ranging from direct contact with the customer to back-office analysis of customer behavior [9]. The application of AI offers companies in the service sector great scope for increasing revenue as customer relationships become more valuable. Companies already use various aspects of AI in this regard. Primarily, to provide a better experience for their customers, which results in more sold products and the reduction in operational cost e.g., in terms of support hotlines. Amazon uses AI very efficiently in their recommendation system, which increases engagement revenue and spills over to other areas of the internet [10]. Similarly, YouTube algorithms can be seen through that lens. Another relatively prominent operational area of AI are call centers. Customers are generally not willing to wait in a queue for the next available agent and therefore rather talk to a chatbot. Natural language processing (NLP) helps in that regard to provide an environment in which customers can truly interact with a system that does not only hold pre-defined answers, which can be quite annoying.

The next logical step in this human-machine interaction is the recognition of customer emotion as well as mimicry of emotions to react adequately towards for example, an angry customer [11, 12]. Based on emotion recognition it would also be feasible to redirect customers either faster or slower to actual human agents to handle the situation. This way human resources can be allocated more efficiently and build stronger ties to customers.

The voice interface is very prevalent in today's digital world. Hotlines operate on voice, and even internet searches, on Google for example, use voice. It is assumed that already 50% of internet searches are voice searches [13]. This opens up a high potential to process speech for increased support of customers and companies. Smart-speakers are also on the rise and a forecast states that nearly 90% of smartphone users will actively use voice assistants by 2023 [14, 15].

Given this growing interest in the interface of voice and speech processing, we take the perspective of Design Science Research (DSR) to understand how research has been conducted in the past and what we can learn in programming artifacts that can be used in the service industry. We use this lens to focus on actual contexts in which AI is used and tested in the real world to provide actual value for companies. DSR research has the big benefit that it is deeply rooted in a specific context and provides the opportunity to evaluate and further develop an artifact. It furthermore provides the opportunity to evaluate the artifact for applicability and further refinement to achieve better results for a given context. We understand that this may come at the price of generalizability. However, we argue that especially in the service industry context-tailored solutions provide a competitive advantage for companies, which we would address with a DSR approach. Here, we focus on the emotional part of voice recognition since it seems the next promising step in this area [11, 12]. Due to the importance of voice in the future, we ask the simple question:

RQ: *How can research in emotion recognition through speech gain value through a DSR approach?*

To answer this question, we conducted a systematic literature review [16] using the database Web of Science to identify relevant literature in emotion recognition through speech using artificial intelligence. The goal for the literature review and also to answer the proposed research question is the presentation of guidelines that we derive from the literature on how DSR can make a difference in this area and how, especially DSR, still has great potential that is currently untouched.

The remainder of this paper is structured as follows. First, we will review related work to lay the groundwork for the concept of emotion and how AI deals with human emotion. Afterwards, we provide a concise summary of the basic nature of DSR, why the methodology applies, along with the main process steps.

Subsequently, we provide the methodology for our literature review, followed by the results section. In the discussion section, we provide guidelines for further research in the area of emotion recognition through speech. Finally, the article ends with a conclusion.

2 Background and Related Work

2.1 The Concept of Emotions

The term "emotion" is still a relatively vague concept in research. Researchers could not yet find a conclusive and satisfactory definition. As an example, Mulligan and Scherer [17] state: "There is no commonly agreed-upon definition of emotion in any of the disciplines that study this phenomenon." However, there were attempts to incorporate various emotional states into a broad definition. A concept that includes affective, cognitive, behavioral, expressive and physiological changes [18]. This broad definition already shows the complexity of the concept of emotion, which has ramifications towards psychological reactions to internal and external stimuli [19].

In research, we often find "basic emotions", which consistently exist across cultures. These are namely joy, love, sadness, fear, anger, and surprise [20–22]. But still, there is discussion about extensions of these emotions and facets that can be found across the basic emotions [23]. Thereby, complex emotions are composed of different basic emotions [21]. Even though the clear definition of emotion and basic emotions remains disputed, what is undisputed is the fact that emotions play an important role in comprehending human behavior [24]. Therefore, research has a key interest in understanding and detecting human emotions to comprehend decision-making processes as well as general human behavior.

2.2 Recognizing Emotions Using Artificial Intelligence

Due to emotions inducing human behavior, research showed great interest in detecting emotions, even though the concept is still not clearly defined. As a proxy to measure emotions, body reactions were investigated. Among them there are, increased heart rate, sweating, pupillary response, or constriction of blood vessels [19, 25]. Using such proxies showed to be very practical simply due to the fact that they were measurable, and for the most part, people were not able to willingly manipulate such body reactions [23]. Therefore, artificial intelligence seemed to be an adequate tool to investigate and classify different body reactions since understanding an individual's emotional state would provide several applications in service or marketing.

There have been several approaches to incorporate machine learning into recognizing basic human emotions by investigating body reactions, may they be visual or auditory [19]. In the visual section, plenty of research investigated facial expressions and micro-expressions, which are hardly noticeable with the human eye [26]. Basing the research on the basic human emotions, machine learning techniques already provide satisfactory results in detecting them [27].

A very different approach towards detecting emotions is the application of electroencephalograms (EEG), which directly measure the brain's electric activity [28]. Such approaches, of course, provide very satisfactory results since researchers can reach close to the very essence of human thought [19]. However, this form of research has its limitations, especially in the field, since individuals need to wear special devices and their acceptance or even cost stand in no relation to the benefit they would provide. EEGs in a real-life service or marketing scenario, therefore, are unrealistic.

This problem of practicability opens up new ways of emotion recognition through speech. Speech is easily accessible, and even in the last century, researchers have already suggested that speech analysis leads to the identification of emotions [29]. Classification algorithms to detect emotions in the speech were constructed in a very basic form without the support of what we today would classify as artificial intelligence or neural networks [30]. These attempts lacked the technological possibilities that we have today. Over the last decade, research in artificial intelligence and the improvement of technological capabilities made it easier to investigate different features and configurations of speech.

2.3 Emotion Recognition Through Speech Analysis

Research on emotion recognition through speech utilizes several aspects of speech. Frequently, rather than *what* was said, it is *how* something was said of interest for the recognition of different emotions. Therefore, acoustic features such as amplitude, formants, or pitch determine how emotions are classified [31, 32]. A relatively widespread methodology incorporates the usage of Mel-frequency cepstral coefficients (MFCCs), which are so-called spectral features but still in an acoustic manner. Past research showed that MFCCs are promising in identifying patterns in speech [33–36]. These patterns can also involve emotions. Therefore, MFCCs also found usage in the theme of speech emotion recognition [37–39].

To make use of MFCCs, research provides several approaches to identify emotions through speech. Hidden Markov Models (HMM) have been used for more than two decades to identify emotions in speech. An examples for HMM can be found in the approach of Schuller and Rigoll [40], who identified seven emotional states with an accuracy of 78%. However, the techniques we have access to today are more sophisticated, and research turns towards deep learning (DL) or machine learning (ML). Such approaches involve recurrent neural networks (RNN) [41] and a mix of convolutional neural networks (CNN) and RNN [25, 42–44]. These novel approaches yield an accuracy up to almost 97% for seven emotional states [42].

Specifically, in [44], based on the fusion of a total of seven acoustic features, such as MFCCs, Mel Spectrograms, Spectral Contrast, Tonnetz, Chromagram, as well as the Δ MFCC and $\Delta\Delta$ MFCC, a 1D CNN model for the detection of seven emotional states is presented. The model consists of three convolutional layers, two max-pooling layers, a flattening layer, and a dense layer. The authors have achieved accuracy in discriminating seven emotions of about 96.7%.

Besides acoustic features, some research also used contextual features, for example, what is said with more focus on the wording to improve accuracy [41, 45]. However, such approaches only yielded relatively low accuracy as seen in the work of Fayek and Lech [45] who distinguished five emotional states with an accuracy of 65%.

2.4 The DSR Framework

DSR is a design-oriented research methodology for solving a specific problem [46]. The main focus is on the appropriate design and evaluation of a value-added artifact. Thus, the DSR approach ensures that research concerning the creation of an artifact takes place within a solid methodological framework. In this regard, the methodology is frequently used in information systems and computer science research and service design and service research [47, 48]. As DSR deals with constantly evolving technologies and increasingly complex environments, the approach is particularly well suited for developing new types of service solutions [48]. Therefore, we see great value in focusing on DSR in the context of AI to ensure that services can have a real benefit.

In general, the DSR process consists of six steps [46, 48]. The first step involves **defining the specific research problem** and the underlying **motivation** for solving it. Doing so enhances the researcher's understanding of the reasoning behind the problem. It motivates both the researcher and the research audience to pursue the solution at hand and accept its results [46]. The second step is to set the **objective of**

a solution. The objectives of a solution should be derived rationally from the problem specification. Therefore, it is necessary to gain knowledge about the current state of research regarding the problem and existing solution approaches, including their effectiveness. The third step ensues the **design and the development** of the artifactual solution. Within this activity, the desired functionality, architecture, and artifact creation are determined. An extensive understanding of the underlying theory underlying the problem is required to implement this step successfully. The **demonstration** of the effectiveness of an artifact in solving the problem is addressed in the fourth step. Here, experiments, simulations, or other appropriate activities are employed. Adequate knowledge about how the artifact is applied to solve the problem is a prerequisite. During the fifth step, the **evaluation**, observations concerning the artifact's performance are conducted and evaluated. The evaluation step includes comparisons of the objectives of a solution with the actual observed results from the previous step, the demonstration. Upon completion of this step, researchers may return to step three, targeting improvements in the effectiveness of the artifact, or proceed into step six, the **communication** and address further improvements in future projects. Communicating the problem, the justification explaining the importance of a solution, the artifact itself, its utility and novelty, the rigor of its design, and its effectiveness proceeds wherever appropriate. In scientific research publications, researchers may use the sequential flow of the DSR process to structure their work and thus increase its accessibility to researchers and other relevant stakeholders (e.g., practitioners). An awareness of the disciplinary culture is crucial in this last step [46].

3 Methodology

Until now, no literature review to our knowledge that analyzes emotion recognition in speech, and associated lies and deception detection, through the lens of DSR exists. The lens of DSR is valuable since it always keeps the specific context insight and provides opportunities to validate artifacts in a real-world scenario. We want to extend research in design science and give impulses and guidelines for further research to achieve better outcomes.

For our literature review, we followed the suggestions of Webster and Watson [16] to ensure a rigorous procedure in how we conducted the review. We also checked for past literature reviews in the field of DSR and tailored our procedure accordingly (see e.g., zur Heiden [49]). Since emotion recognition through speech and generally the emergence of machine learning is a relatively new field in IS, we conducted a literature review on the database "Web of Science". We chose this approach to incorporate well-known journals and try to get an overview of the current research landscape with the topic of emotions and speech.

In the first step, we used a relatively wide approach by searching with the terms "Artificial Intelligence" OR "Machine learning", "Emotions", and "Speech". This keyword search yielded 246 hits in the Web of Science database. Since we wanted to get an overview of the research, we excluded all papers that were not peer-reviewed or published through a journal or conference. This exclusion yielded 138 articles that were open for a deeper investigation.

In the second step, we checked the publications concerning their publication year and relevancy for the literature review. For the publication year, we excluded all publications prior to 2010. This happened since we want to make sure to give an up-to-date overview of the research to provide state-of-the-art insights into how to conduct research in the area of emotion recognition through speech.

In the third step, we investigated the papers and checked them for relevancy. An article was relevant when the focus was the recognition of emotions using a certain form of artificial intelligence approach. This resulted in 65 relevant articles. Thereafter, a forward search has been conducted resulting in the identification of a further 16 recent and relevant articles addressing the subject matter. Thus, a total of 81 relevant scientific publications were retrieved, see Fig. 1.

Lastly, we defined several categories to structure the literature review with Webster and Watson [16]. In line with suggestions from zur Heiden [49], we set a

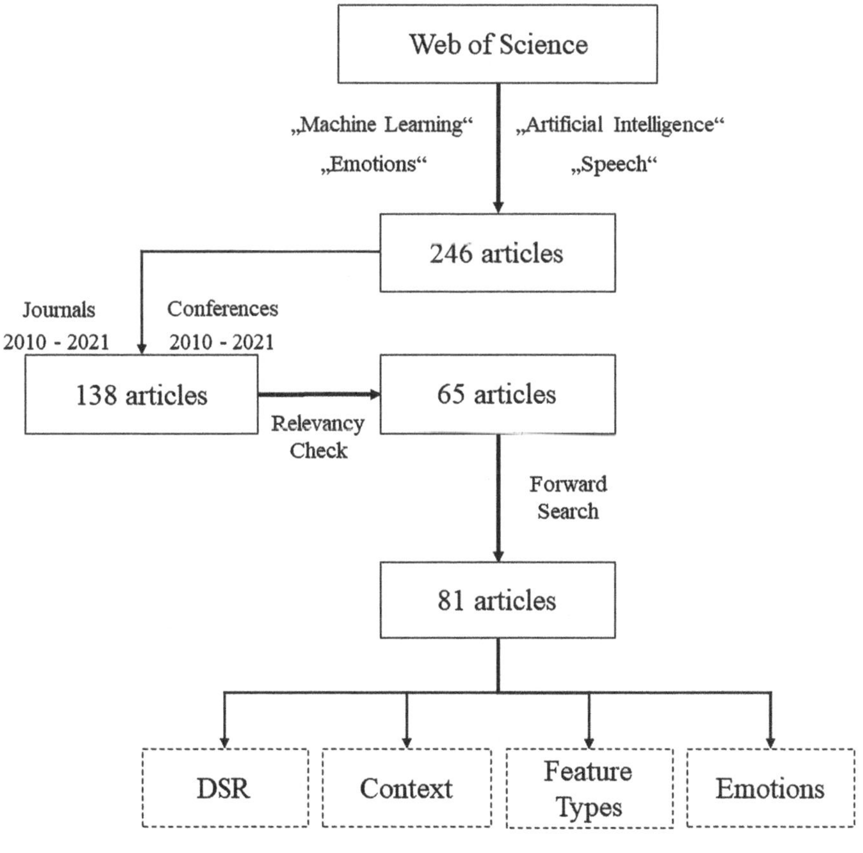

Fig. 1 Literature review methodology showing 81 relevant articles

focus on the research context to determine which practical implications the proposed solutions have. We then also analyzed whether the approaches followed a DSR methodology. This was done because DSR methodology provides a solid framework that incorporates a clear context as well as further development and evaluation of artifacts. Then, we focused on the feature types that were used to classify speech. Lastly, we checked for the basic emotions the approaches wanted to identify based on the extracted speech features. The results will present insights into the different categories and provide metrics about their quantity. We then go ahead and derive guidelines from the insights in the discussion.

4 Results

The analysis of all 81 relevant papers shows that nine papers serve a human-computer interaction-related context, two a marketing-related context, 23 a medical context, one article a political context, one article an E-learning context, and 31 a technological context. Furthermore, 14 papers do not address any context at all.

In 52 of the analyzed 81 relevant papers, a purely acoustic approach to emotion recognition is used. Another 17 use an additional modality besides acoustics, such as demographic, linguistic, or visual features. Four papers omit the acoustic component entirely and base their approaches on demographic, linguistic, visual, spatio-temporal or a combination of these modalities. The remaining six articles do not precisely indicate the feature types.

The analyzed emotions vary from 2 [50–52] to 22 [53]—only 27 papers specified which emotions were analyzed. The remaining 54 articles did not identify the emotions to be explored.

Also of interest is that none of the documents in the technological context has a clear use case. Furthermore, none of the papers analyzed employs a DSR approach.

The results of the respected articles in terms of context, feature types, and analyzed emotions are shown in Table 1.

When design implications of a presented IT artifact are pointed out, these design decisions must be justified on the basis of contextual or decision-based factors [49]. Therefore, the context used must at least be described beforehand. None of the articles analyzed demonstrated the design implications of their respective contexts in this regard. In addition, of the total 81 relevant articles, a full 14 did not describe any contextual dimensions at all. Although theoretically possible, no paper showed the design implications of a contextual size without providing a description. The medical contextual dimension is the most frequently described dimension, while its design implications are again not shown. None of the papers mention the influence of context on the design of the IT artifact, which shows that none of the documents had an interest in a DSR approach.

Table 1 Analyzed articles with their context dimension, feature types and the analyzed emotions in comparison

Context	Number of articles with context	Feature types utilized in the articles	Employed emotions
Human-Computer-Interaction	9	5× Acoustic 2× Acoustic, Demographic 1× Spatiotemporal 1× Not specified	2× 4 Emotions 7× Not specified
Marketing	2	1× Acoustic 1× Acoustic, Lexical	2× Not specified
Medical	23	12× Acoustic 4× Acoustic, Lexical 4× Acoustic, Visual 1× Demographic, Visual 2× Lexical	3× 2 Emotions 2× 6 Emotions 1× 8 Emotions 17× Not specified
No context	14	8× Acoustic 2× Acoustic, Demographic 2× Acoustic, Lexical 1× Acoustic, Visual 1× Not Specified	1× 5 Emotions 1× 7 Emotions 1× 11 Emotions 1× 15 Emotions 10× Not specified
Political	1	1× Acoustic	1× Not specified
Technological	31	25× Acoustic 2× Acoustic, Lexical 4× Not Specified	4× 5 Emotions 9× 7 Emotions 1× 8 Emotions 1× 22 Emotions 17× Not Specified
E-Learning	1	1× Lexical	1× 3 Emotions

5 Discussion

Based on the results of the systematic literature review of the 81 articles classified as relevant, we propose three guidelines in the following, from which researchers may benefit when conducting speech analysis with AI while considering a DSR approach.

These guidelines serve as recommendations for context-aware DSR studies. The existing emotion analysis approaches using spoken language could be improved by using these guidelines, and new approaches considering these would be more substantively underpinned from the outset. There are already many different approaches to DSR projects [49].

Many of the studies reviewed are either medical or technology-oriented. Mainly the latter introduce technological innovations [54]. The one-time transfer of technological innovations to medical fields, for example, supports depression detection [52]. Others use a human-to-machine approach or establish a marketing [55], policy

[56], or an e-learning-context [57]. However, some authors entirely refrain from describing a context and its relevant dimensions as drivers, which is contraproductive as the underlying context cannot be specified on its own [49].

For example, Anagnostopoulos and Khoruzhnicov [58] developed a model for recognizing 15 different emotions from acoustic features. Still, they failed to explicitly mention roles or indicators as examples of person-specific features of a context.

Since context consists of a potentially endless list of requirements that researchers cannot fully describe, context and IT artifacts are mutually dependent [59].

Therefore, we recommend that the particular characteristics of the specific context shall be defined upfront of a DSR project and that the design implications arising from the context specific features should be included, as their omission compromises the scientific validity of the results [49].

The context description is often placed in an introductory section or a specific problem description when analyzing all articles. In contrast, the design implications derived from the context features are usually entirely omitted from the design section of the IT artifact. Researchers should place the context description and design implications in these research sections and not add new context-specific or even context dimension-specific sections because the context and its dimensions are an essential part of DSR-oriented research [46]. We, therefore, suggest the following guideline:

Guideline 1. *Authors are encouraged to consider DSR approaches when conducting research projects on emotion recognition using speech with the involvement of AI.*

In this way, it is possible to implement a context-related IT artifact in a clear framework, and thus ensure that the artifact can also satisfy this appropriate context [48].

Another aspect discovered in analyzing the 81 relevant articles from IS journals is the practical relationship between the IT artifact and its context. Only 67 publications even consider the context when developing their IT artifacts. This is not beneficial since the context influences the design of the IT artifact, but conversely, the IT artifact's design exploits the context. None of the analyzed works relate the expected shifts in the different context dimensions as seen in similar studies [60]. Considering the proposed guideline, it would therefore also be beneficial to specify the expected changes in context resulting from the IT artifact and its corresponding design within the project.

Furthermore, it is striking that the analyzed works differ enormously in the features used for analysis. There is no consensus about the types of components to be examined to analyze emotions. Some papers, for instance, Hansen and Zhang [51] or Alvarez and Sierra [61] use exclusively acoustic features. Others use only lexical features, Berger and Branco [62], and further use a mixture of feature types, Duville and Alonso-Valerdi [63], for their emotion analyses. Some of the analyzed papers do not specify the feature types used, such as Chen and Zhang [64]. Given the emergence of such disagreement or even uncertainty among researchers within the same field, the notion for a second Guideline arises:

Guideline 2. *When analyzing emotions based on spoken language, it should be taken into account to define and justify the features to be considered as precisely as possible before the analysis.*

However, an even more significant disagreement occurs when it comes down to analyzing the emotions. Depending on which of the numerous existing approaches is applied regarding the characterization of emotions, fundamental deviations occur as to their principles and, naturally, to the number of emotional states involved.

Although such a discrepancy presupposes an adequate explanation of which, how many emotional states were included in the analysis, according to which concept, and on which grounds, only 27 of the 81 articles analyzed provide sufficient information in this regard. However, even in these articles, the emotions under investigation are of such a diverse nature that the individual approaches cannot be readily compared. Thus, the analyzed emotion dimensions by themselves range from 2, Weidman and Sun [50], to 22 different dimensions, Kamiloglu and Boateng [53]. Moreover, it may not be possible to adequately evaluate the effectiveness of the individual emotion dimensions in relation to the respective context, which leads to our third guideline:

Guideline 3. *When analyzing emotions based on spoken language, it is advantageous to define and justify the emotion dimensions that will be analyzed clearly in advance and embed them in the corresponding context of the IT artifact.*

These guidelines are intended to lay the groundwork for future DSR projects in the course of automatic speech-based emotion recognition that takes into account both universalism and particularism as such solution approaches become increasingly important [49]. The guidelines require a further description of the context in which researchers must pre-initiate their IT artifact. The approach to a project in the DSR context covers both an idiographic and a nomothetic knowledge domain [65]. Researchers should nevertheless follow accepted guidelines and frameworks for DSR. This mainly concerns the work of Hevner and March [66], Peffers and Tuunanen [46], and Gregor and Jones [67] [49].

5.1 Practical Implications

This research has practical implications especially for service industry as motivated in the introduction. First, with the encouragement to tap into DSR and leverage its benefits, research provides results that are in line with solutions of real-world problems. Even though DSR is not considered as product development tool, we argue that due to adherence to a certain context, the step from the DSR artifact to a working software in business is easier to do. Of course, this comes at the prize of generalizability. However, since AI is heavily dependent on a reliable database which provides real-world data, we see great benefits for practitioners to build on DSR results in order to further develop the respective artifacts towards are working product.

6 Limitations and Further Research

This literature review also has limitations. It is possible that we did not incorporate all relevant literature concerning emotion and machine learning with the presented methodology. This is also possible because the literature review focused on the Web of Science database. Furthermore, it is possible that some publications indeed followed a DSR approach. However, in that case, it would be surprising that not a single research paper explicitly mentioned a DSR approach.

Further research should validate the proposed guidelines by applying them to DSR studies. In addition, the research conducted in this paper could be extended to other disciplines and more practice-oriented publications or applications to test the applicability of the suggested guidelines and integrate the procedures with existing DSR principles.

7 Conclusion

The context is an essential concept in the IS, especially in DSR. If research in artificial intelligence wants to make a difference, we are in urgent need to research close to the context. It is not sufficient to increase the accuracy to detect certain concepts, but the testing in a real world scenario. Analysis of studies regarding emotion recognition using language shows that context is highly neglected, and no research approaches have DSR methodologies. The contribution of this article is to communicate clear guidelines to improve future DSR or related research in IS and associated disciplines.

The study presents the current state of DSR in the field of automated emotion recognition based on speech and the accompanying consideration of context, the feature being analyzed, and emotional dimensions. We also present guidelines for context-aware DSR that complement current DSR frameworks and models. Researchers and practitioners can use the guidelines to conduct DSR studies and broaden their focus on the context of their research subjects.

References

1. Vial, G. (2019). Understanding digital transformation: A review and a research agenda. *The Journal of Strategic Information Systems, 28*(2), 118–144.
2. Wessel, L., Baiyere, A., Ologeanu-Taddei, R., Cha, J., & Blegind Jensen, T. (2021). Unpacking the difference between digital transformation and IT-enabled organizational transformation. *Journal of the Association for Information Systems, 22*(1), 102–129.
3. Weking, J., Stocker, M., Kowalkiewicz, M., Bohm, M., & Krcmar, H. (2018). Archetypes for industry 4.0 business model innovations. In *Proceedings of the 24th Americas conference on information systems (AMCIS)*. Association for Information Systems (AIS).

4. Hentschel, R., Bley, K., & Schön, H. (2021). Shifting micro-enterprises into the cloud: Guidelines for cloud service providers. In *Proceedings of the 54th Hawaii international conference on system sciences*.
5. Pappas, I. O., Mikalef, P., Giannakos, M. N., Krogstie, J., & Lekakos, G. (2018). Big data and business analytics ecosystems: paving the way towards digital transformation and sustainable societies. *Information Systems and e-Business Management, 16*, 479–491. Springer.
6. Wiener, M., Saunders, C., & Marabelli, M. (2020). Big-data business models: A critical literature review and multiperspective research framework. *Journal of Information Technology, 35*(1), 66–91.
7. Bley, K., Pappas, I. O., & Strahringer, S. (2021). *Innovation capability in small industrial companies—A set theoretic approach to maturity models*. ECIS 2021 Research Papers, 69.
8. Opland, L. E., Pappas, I. O., Engesmo, J., & Jaccheri, L. (2022). Employee-driven digital innovation: A systematic review and a research agenda. *Journal of Business Research, 143*, 255–271.
9. Huang, M.-H., & Rust, R. T. (2018). Artificial intelligence in service. *Journal of Service Research, 21*(2), 155–172.
10. Smith, B., & Linden, G. (2017). Two decades of recommender systems at Amazon. com. *IEEE Internet Computing, 21*(3), 12–18.
11. Sudarsan, V., & Kumar, G. (2019). Voice call analytics using natural language processing. *International Journal of Statistics and Applied Mathematics, 4*, 133–136.
12. Ponomareff, L. (2017). How AI is disrupting the role of call centres and call centre staff. *ComputerWeekly.com*.
13. DBS Interactive. (2020). Voice search statistics and emerging trends [18-May-2021]. Available from https://www.dbswebsite.com/blog/trends-in-voice-search/.
14. Perrin, N. (2020). *How consumer search behavior is adapting to mobile, voice and visual channels*. eMarketer (Ed.).
15. Griffin, J. (2021). Voice search statistics for 2020 [07.04.2021]. Available from https://www.thesearchreview.com/google-voice-searches-doubled-past-year-17111/.
16. Webster, J., & Watson, R. T. (2002). Analyzing the past to prepare for the future: Writing a literature review. *MIS Quarterly, 26*(2), xiii–xxiii.
17. Mulligan, K., & Scherer, K. R. (2012). Toward a working definition of emotion. *Emotion Review, 4*(4), 345–357.
18. Tyng, C. M., et al. (2017). The influences of emotion on learning and memory. *Frontiers in Psychology, 8*(1454), 1–22.
19. Zhang, J., Yin, Z., Chen, P., & Nichele, S. (2020). Emotion recognition using multi-modal data and machine learning techniques: A tutorial and review. *Information Fusion, 59*, 103–126.
20. Plutchik, R. (2001). The nature of emotions: Human emotions have deep evolutionary roots, a fact that may explain their complexity and provide tools for clinical practice. *American Scientist, 89*(4), 344–350.
21. Russell, J. A. (1980). A circumplex model of affect. *Journal of Personality and Social Psychology, 39*(6), 1161–1178.
22. Shaver, P., Schwartz, J., Kirson, D., & O'Connor, C. (1987). Emotion knowledge: further exploration of a prototype approach. *Journal of Personality and Social Psychology, 52*(6), 1061–1086.
23. Shu, L., Xie, J., Yang, M., Li, Z., Li, Z., Liao, D., Xu, X., & Yang, X. (2018). A review of emotion recognition using physiological signals. *Sensors, 18*(7).
24. Elster, J. (2009). *Strong feelings: Emotion, addiction, and human behavior*. MIT Press.
25. Soleymani, M., Asghari-Esfeden, S., Fu, Y., & Pantic, M. (2015). Analysis of EEG signals and facial expressions for continuous emotion detection. *IEEE Transactions on Affective Computing, 7*(1), 17–28.
26. Matsumoto, D., & Hwang, H. C. (2018). Microexpressions differentiate truths from lies about future malicious intent. *Frontiers in Psychology, 9*(December), 1–11.

27. Tivatansakul, S., Ohkura, M., Puangpontip, S., & Achalakul, T. (2014). Emotional healthcare system: Emotion detection by facial expressions using Japanese database. In *2014 6th computer science and electronic engineering conference (CEEC)*. IEEE.
28. Proverbio, A. M., Vanutelli, M. E., & Adorni, R. (2013). Can you catch a liar? How negative emotions affect brain responses when lying or telling the truth. *PLoS One, 8*(3), 1–12.
29. Scherer, K. R. (1995). Expression of emotion in voice and music. *Journal of Voice, 9*(3), 235–248.
30. Amir, N., & Ron, S. (1998). Towards an automatic classification of emotions in speech. In *Fifth international conference on spoken language processing*.
31. Demircan, S., & Kahramanlı, H. (2014). Feature extraction from speech data for emotion recognition. *Journal of Advances in Computer Networks, 2*(1), 28–30.
32. Slimi, A., Hamroun, M., Zrigui, M., & Nicolas, H. (2020). Emotion recognition from speech using spectrograms and shallow neural networks. In *18th international conference on advances in mobile computing and multimedia* (pp. 35–39). Association for Computing Machinery.
33. Logan, B. (2000). Mel frequency cepstral coefficients for music modeling. In *International symposium on music information retrieval, Plymouth, MA, USA*.
34. Fraser, K. C., Meltzer, J. A., & Rudzicz, F. (2016). Linguistic features identify Alzheimer's disease in narrative speech. *Journal of Alzheimer's Disease, 49*(2), 407–422.
35. Dave, N. (2013). Feature extraction methods LPC, PLP and MFCC in speech recognition. *International Journal for Advance Research in Engineering and Technology, 1*(6), 1–4.
36. Gupta, D., Bansal, P., & Choudhary, K. (2018). The state of the art of feature extraction techniques in speech recognition. In S. S. Agrawal et al. (Eds.), *Speech and language processing for human-machine communications* (pp. 195–207). Springer.
37. Pakyurek, M., Atmis, M., Kulac, S., & Uludag, U. (2020). Extraction of novel features based on histograms of MFCCs used in emotion classification from generated original speech dataset. *Elektronika ir Elektrotechnika, 26*(1), 46–51.
38. Lalitha, S., Geyasruti, D., Narayanan, R., & Shravani, M. (2015). Emotion detection using MFCC and cepstrum features. *Procedia Computer Science, 70*, 29–35.
39. Kishore, K. K., & Satish, P. K. (2013). Emotion recognition in speech using MFCC and wavelet features. In *3rd IEEE international advance computing conference (IACC)*. IEEE.
40. Schuller, B., Rigoll, G., & Lang, M. (2003). Hidden Markov model-based speech emotion recognition. In *IEEE international conference on acoustics, speech, and signal processing*. IEEE.
41. Trigeorgis, G., Ringeval, F., Brueckner, R., Marchi, E., Nicolaou, M. A., Schuller, B., & Zafeiriou, S. (2016). Adieu features? end-to-end speech emotion recognition using a deep convolutional recurrent network. In *2016 IEEE international conference on acoustics, speech and signal processing (ICASSP)*. IEEE.
42. Zhao, J., Mao, X., & Chen, L. (2019). Speech emotion recognition using deep 1D & 2D CNN LSTM networks. *Biomedical Signal Processing and Control, 47*, 312–323.
43. Nam, Y., & Lee, C. (2021). Cascaded convolutional neural network architecture for speech emotion recognition in noisy conditions. *Sensors, 21*(13), 4399.
44. Jahangir, R., Teh, Y. W., Mujtaba, G., Alroobaea, R., Shaikh, Z. H., & Ali, I. (2022). Convolutional neural network-based cross-corpus speech emotion recognition with data augmentation and features fusion. *Machine Vision and Applications, 33*(3), 1–16.
45. Fayek, H. M., Lech, M., & Cavedon, L. (2017). Evaluating deep learning architectures for speech emotion recognition. *Neural Networks, 92*, 60–68.
46. Peffers, K., Tuunanen, T., Rothenberger, M., & Chatterjee, S. (2007). A design science research methodology for information systems research. *Journal of Management Information Systems, 24*(3), 45–77.
47. Sudbury-Riley, L., Hunter-Jones, P., Al-Abdin, A., Lewin, D., & Naraine, M. V. (2020). The trajectory touchpoint technique: A deep dive methodology for service innovation. *Journal of Service Research, 23*(2), 229–251.
48. Teixeira, J. G., Patrício, L., & Tuunanen, T. (2019). Advancing service design research with design science research. *Journal of Service Management, 30*(5), 577–592.

49. zur Heiden, P. (2020). Considering context in design science research: A systematic literature review. In *International conference on design science research in information systems and technology*. Springer.
50. Weidman, A. C., Sun, J., Vazire, S., Quoidbach, J., Ungar, L. H., & Dunn, E. W. (2020). (Not) hearing happiness: Predicting fluctuations in happy mood from acoustic cues using machine learning. *Emotion (Washington, D.C.), 20*(4), 642–658.
51. Hansen, L., Zhang, Y. P., Wolf, D., Sechidis, K., Ladegaard, N., & Fusaroli, R. (2022). A generalizable speech emotion recognition model reveals depression and remission. *Acta Psychiatrica Scandinavica, 145*(2), 186–199.
52. Lu, X., Shi, D., Liu, Y., & Yuan, J. (2021). Speech depression recognition based on attentional residual network. *Frontiers in Bioscience (Landmark Edition), 26*(12), 1746–1759.
53. Kamiloglu, R. G., Boateng, G., Balabanova, A., Cao, C., & Sauter, D. A. (2021). Superior communication of positive emotions through nonverbal vocalisations compared to speech prosody. *Journal of Nonverbal Behavior, 45*(4), 419–454.
54. Anvarjon, T., Mustaqeem, & Kwon, S. (2020). Deep-net: A lightweight CNN-based speech emotion recognition system using deep frequency features. *Sensors (Basel, Switzerland), 20*(18).
55. Govindaraj, S., & Gopalakrishnan, K. (2016). Intensified sentiment analysis of customer product reviews using acoustic and textual features. *ETRI Journal, 38*(3), 494–501.
56. Franzoni, V., Biondi, G., & Milani, A. (2020). Emotional sounds of crowds: spectrogram-based analysis using deep learning. *Multimedia Tools and Applications, 79*, 1–13.
57. Bekmanova, G., Yergesh, B., Sharipbay, A., & Mukanova, A. (2022). Emotional speech recognition method based on word transcription. *Sensors, 22*(5), 1937.
58. Anagnostopoulos, T., Khoruzhnikov, S. E., Grudinin, V. A., & Skourlas, C. (2014). РАСПОЗНАВАНИЕ И ПРОГНОЗИРОВАНИЕ ДЛИТЕЛЬНЫХ ЭМОЦИЙ В РЕЧИ (Extended speech emotion recognition and prediction). *Scientific and Technical Journal of Information Technologies Mechanics and Optics, 14*(6), 137–145.
59. Alexander, C. (1964). *Notes on the synthesis of form* (Vol. 5). Harvard University Press.
60. Schuster, R., Wagner, G., & Schryen, G. (2018). Information systems design science research and cumulative knowledge development: an exploratory study. In *International conference on information systems (ICIS)*.
61. Alvarez, A., Sierra, B., Arruti, A., López-Gil, J. M., & Garay-Vitoria, N. (2015). Classifier subset selection for the stacked generalization method applied to emotion recognition in speech. *Sensors (Basel, Switzerland), 16*(1).
62. Berger, S. E., Branco, P., Vachon-Presseau, E., Abdullah, T. B., Cecchi, G., & Apkarian, A. V. (2021). Quantitative language features identify placebo responders in chronic back pain. *Pain, 162*(6), 1692–1704.
63. Duville, M. M., Alonso-Valerdi, L.M., & Ibarra-Zarate, D. I. (2021). The Mexican Emotional Speech Database (MESD): Elaboration and assessment based on machine learning. In *Annual international conference of the IEEE Engineering in Medicine and Biology Society* (pp. 1644–1647). IEEE Engineering in Medicine and Biology Society.
64. Chen, S., Zhang, M., Yang, X., Zhao, Z., Zou, T., & Sun, X. (2021). The impact of attention mechanisms on speech emotion recognition. *Sensors (Basel, Switzerland), 21*(22).
65. Baskerville, R. L., Kaul, M., & Storey, V. C. (2015). Genres of inquiry in design-science research. *MIS Quarterly, 39*(3), 541–564.
66. Hevner, A. R., March, S. T., & Park, J. (2004). Design science in information systems research. *MIS Quarterly, 28*, 75–105.
67. Gregor, S., & Jones, D. (2007). *The anatomy of a design theory*. Association for Information Systems.

Understanding the Links Between Neuroscience, Physiological Tools and Stress, with the Eventual Neuroscientific Impact of Culture, in Organizational, Managerial and Information Systems (IS) Fields Through a Social Network Analysis

Raffaele Silvestre and Mauro Romanelli

Abstract This study aims to understand the links between neuroscience, physiological tools and stress, with the eventual neuroscientific impact of culture on the stress, in organizational, managerial and Information Systems (IS) fields through a social network analysis. It was conducted a systematic literature review and a bibliometric analysis by using one online database, such as Scopus. A dataset of 173 publications was analyzed through citation and co-citation analysis. Results of co-citation analysis shown the existence of a network of the 15 most cited sources and 2 topic clusters: the cluster of stress, work stress, of the effects of stressors, of the possible consequent physiological, cognitive and neurobiological responses with a consequent evaluation of a stress management training program in an organizational setting and the cluster of the study of events and conditions that influence decision-making processes to verify whether they are stressors, analyzed also from a neurobiological point of view, with particular emphasis, in some contributions, on events that can generate technostress. This paper contributes to the literature by presenting a comprehensive overview on the link between neuroscience, physiological tools and stress in organizational, managerial and IS fields and leads to further reflections on the use of information and communication technologies to obtain even more sophisticated and more predictive neuroscientific information of stress and, consequently, of individuals' behaviors and on the possible neuroscientific impact of culture on the stress.

R. Silvestre (✉) · M. Romanelli
Department of Business and Economics, University of Naples "Parthenope", Naples, Italy
e-mail: raffaele.silvestre@studenti.uniparthenope.it; mauro.romanelli@uniparthenope.it

A. M. Braccini et al. (eds.), *Technologies for Digital Transformation*, Lecture Notes in Information Systems and Organisation 64,
https://doi.org/10.1007/978-3-031-52120-1_9

Keywords Neuroscience · Cognitive neuroscience · Stress · Event stress · Cultural stress · Physiological tools · Systematic literature review · Bibliometric analysis · Citation analysis · Co-citation analysis

1 Introduction

Neuroscience, and in particular cognitive neuroscience, the use of physiological tools in the cognitive neuroscience field and the different forms of stress, such as cultural, event, physical and mental stress, and burnout, represent three topics much discussed in the managerial, organizational and Information Systems (IS) literature.

According to Oliverio [1], "Neuroscience is a hybrid discipline, which ranges from molecular neurobiology studies to those on structure and function of neurons of the nervous system, up to psychobiology, and neuropsychology, which extends into the clinical field" (p. 3). It can be defined as a set of scientifically conducted studies on the nervous system able to reveal, among other more technical information, interesting details on how neural mechanisms can translate into certain behaviors of individuals [1].

In the neuroscience field, "cognitive neuroscience has the ambitious theoretical objective of identifying, understanding, explaining, and possibly modifying the neurobiological mechanisms of the mind that regulate human cognition and mental processes" ([2], p. 2).

Then, "in recent years there was an interesting evolution in neuroscience which increasingly makes it a science of Big Data thanks to the use of modern information and communication technologies (ICTs) for the collection and analysis of neuroscientific data. It is certain that the use of these new technologies will allow us to know, in a more in-depth way, the brain and the neural mechanisms that inform our decision-making processes, our attitudes and our behaviors, but at the same time it is raising strong ethical concerns" ([2], p. 2).

Furthermore, many scholars stressed the links between Neuroscience and Management, giving rise to Neuromanagement. According to Cocco [3]: "It is time for management to update itself and embark on a path to innovate the behavioral part and the "managerial mind" by linking these elements to the developments of recent revolutionary studies and research on the human brain and on the processes of choice and decision" (p. 18).

It is interesting, also to note how, in the neuroscience and cognitive neuroscience field, different and varied tools are used to understand and to describe the neural and cerebral mechanisms that inform individuals' choices and behaviors in various contexts. With specific reference to consumer neuroscience, interesting is the classification reported in the work of Alvino, L., Pavone, L., Abhishta, A., Robben, H. [4] where consumer neuroscience tools are divided in three categories: behavioral tools; physiological tools and neurophysiological tools. With reference to the physiological measures, Butmee, T., Lansdown, T.C., Walker, G.H. [5], in their work, also recalling Miller, S. [6], according to whom "physiological measurement of workload is a factually based concept that relies on evidence that increased mental demands lead to increased physical response from the body" (p. 5), qualified them as measures "based on the concept that increased mental demands can lead to increased physical response from human body" (p. 290) and summarized them, after reviewed of several studies, with reference to the assessment of driver's mental workloads, in five categories: (1) eye behavior measurement (e.g., blink rate and blink duration); (2) measures of cardiac functions (e.g. Heart Rate (HR) and Heart Rate Variability (HRV)); (3) measures of brain functions (e.g., electroencephalogram (EEG)); (4) measures of muscle functions (e.g. electromyogram (EMG)); and (5) other (e.g. electrodermal Activity (EDA) and Hormone Levels). Finally, Rehmann, A. J. [7], considering some reviews of physiological measures, listed a variety of different tools that can be used to assess variations in workload. Precisely, the Authors classified the various tools into three major categories, or physiological subsystems: (1) eye related measures (e.g. Blink Duration and Eye Movement Analysis); (2) brain related measures (e.g. Electroencephalographic Activity (EEG), Event Related Potentials (ERP) and Magnetoencephalographic Activity (MEG)); and (3) heart related measures (e.g. Electrocardiogram (EKG, ECG) and Heart Rate Variability (HRV)). The Authors considered also other measures, such as skin and muscle activity, that have also been used (e.g. Blood Pressure, Blood Volume, Electrodermal Activity (EDA) and Galvanic Skin Response).

Also stress turns out to be a very hot topic in the scientific literature in general and in the organizational, managerial and Information Systems literature in particular.

Suggestive is the definition of Bruce S. McEwen [8] because linked the concept of stress to the brain and qualified it as "a state of the mind, involving both brain and body as well as their interactions; it differs among individuals and reflects not only major life events but also the conflicts and pressures of daily life that alter physiological systems to produce a chronic stress burden that, in turn, is a factor in the expression of disease" (p. 17180).

At this point, considering the literature on the topic of neuroscience, cognitive neuroscience, the use of physiological tools and stress, with the eventual neuroscientific impact of culture on the stress, in the organizational, managerial and Information Systems fields, it starting from afar, even from 1970 considering our research on Scopus, and covering various forms of stress such as physical, mental, cultural or event-related stress. Umer, W., Yu, Y., Antwi Afari, M.F. [9], referring, in the abstract, to the physical and mental stress experienced by workers on construction sites, assessed the effect of mental stress, driven by cognitive task, on physical stress using both subjective measures, such as ratings of perceived exertion, and objective measures, such as heart rate, skin temperature and skin conductance noting how this mental stress determines "a significant increase in subjective ratings of perceived exertion accompanied by an increase in skin temperature and skin conductance, while heart rate remains unaffected". Interesting is, also, the contribution of Kazar, G., Comu, S. [10] because they examined the relationship between construction sites accidents and physiological variables indicative of physical fatigue and mental stress using physiological tools such as blood sugar level (BSL), electrodermal activity (EDA), heart rate (HR) and skin temperature (ST). Chase, M.A. [11] sought to explain how the results of neuroscience can translate into useful tools to stem the growing wave of stress in the workforce. The Author introduced "the concept of aligning workplace practices with biological processes" (p. 16) with hope "to open a debate around shifting cultural perceptions of what constitutes the real well-being of work forces" (p. 16). Again, Dhiman, S. [12] stressed the importance of mindfulness for the stress exploring how Theravada Buddhism understands mindfulness and presented a critical review of the existing mindfulness literature in healthcare and in cognitive and clinical psychology considering that research has shown that mindfulness improves markers of health [13], it reduces physiological markers of stress [14] and it can literally change our brain [15]. While, Frimanson, L., Hornbach, J., Hartmann, F.G.H. [16] argued how "the prolonged anticipatory threat of being held accountable adds to stress buildup over time" (p. 1) observing an increase in the levels of stress hormone (cortisol and thyrotropin) in the participants.

Moving on to analyze the particular manifestation of technostress, Weinert, C., Maier, C., Laumer, S., Weitzel, T. [17] and Zhang, Z., Teo, H.-H. [18] recognized and analyzed how frequent interruptions and malfunctions of information and communication technologies and information systems can generate technological stress in the user which takes the name of technostress. The Authors analyzed this form of stress using neuroscientific tools, such as the skin conductance, the functional magnetic resonance imaging (fMRI) and the electroencephalography (EEG), to detect the degree of physiological arousal and neural activation associated with mental stress, with the aim of understanding how instrumental and emotional support reduces the consequences of techno-stressors, such as reduced end-user performance, techno-exhaustion, and physiological arousal. While Riedl, R. [19] considered the stress resulting from prolonged and inappropriate use of videoconferencing, especially today as a consequence of lockdowns due to the coronavirus disease (COVID-19) and the resulting restricted social mobility writing a paper that develop "a definition for Zoom fatigue and presents a conceptual framework that explores the major root causes of videoconferencing fatigue and stress" (p. 153). Tuulik, V. [20] calculated "correlations among the clinical, psychological/psychometric, and quantitative electropsychological (QEEG) variables of the functional changes of the CNS in chemical stress" (p. 107). While Seitz, S.R., Smith, S.A. [21] highlighted, in the context of forced language-switching in the workplace, how "bilingual employees forced to use a home language in a work setting experience discomfort, stress, and anxiety" (p. 6).

Regarding the study of stress in combination with neuroscience in the field of Information Systems, interesting is the contribution of Baumgartner, D., Fischer, T., Riedl, R., Dreiseitl, S. [22] because the Authors considered technostress an important topic particularly in Information Systems research (IS) and NeuroIS where the Heart rate variability (HRV) is considered "as a measure of (techno)stress and is widely used in scientific investigations" (p. 221). While, Fischer, T., Halmerbauer, G., Meyr, E., Riedl, R. [23] presented, as an additional data collection method for technostress research, the method of blood pressure measurement and stated that, "considering that blood pressure is an important stress indicator and that, to the best of our knowledge, no prior Information Systems (IS) paper had an explicit focus on blood pressure measurement, the present paper is urgently needed, in particular from a technostress measurement perspective" (p. 25).

Based on these considerations, it emerges that neuroscience, cognitive neuroscience, the use of physiological tools and stress are assuming increasing importance in the managerial, organizational and Information Systems (IS) fields. However, it is important to emphasize, above all, the growing use of new neuroscientific technologies and, particularly the physiological tools, to study the different manifestations of stress, both in its negative sense of distress and in its positive sense of eustress, to support business management decisions in an increasingly complex and dynamic context, characterized by increasingly complex technologies and events such as Covid 19 and the political, social and military instability that is characterizing our society today and that are increasingly exposing people, and in particular workers, to incredible sources of stress to be managed in an optimal way to try to draw energy and positive results from it.

Despite this, from a careful analysis of the literature, few studies still emerge that use of neuroscientific tools, including physiological tools, to directly analyze and understand the impact of stress, in particular of cultural stress and technostress, on neural and cerebral mechanisms and, therefore, on behaviors in the company or, even, to study stress starting from the analysis of neural and cerebral mechanisms in particular circumstances that can cause stressful situations, also considering the possible impact of existing cultural differences on these neural and cerebral mechanisms, differences interpreted in neuroscientific terms, so as to be able to understand the intrinsic mechanisms that, if existing and continuously fed, can generate stress with consequent external manifestations that are often detected only subsequently and, often, delayed with respect to the ensuing consequences. It is evident how, this new interpretation, can allow manager to promptly detect potential manifestations of stress in the company and to develop new recruits, internal and not only external, on which to act to optimize the consequences, negative in the case of distress and positive in the case of eustress, of potential stressful situations.

For this reason, the purpose of this research is to highlight the developments on the topic of "neuroscience, cognitive neuroscience, the use of physiological tools and stress, with the eventual neuroscientific impact of culture on the stress, in organizational (field of organization of business activities and field of human resource management to obtain better performance by manager and workers), managerial (field of business management, through the definition of strategies, company objectives and all the management actions aimed at their pursuit) and IS (field of arrangement of people, data, procedures, and information technology that interact to collect, process, store, and provide as output the information needed to support an organization) fields", and to guide academics in identifying possible insights. A Systematic Literature Review and a Bibliometric Analysis was conducted by employing a quantitative approach that involves citation analysis and co-citation analysis (Social Network Analysis). Social Network Analysis is a process of investigating social structures using networks and graph theory where the relationships, which can be represented through the connections, also called arcs, between individuals, or nodes, are represented through graphs [24]. In the neuroscientific field, the integration between the studies of social neuroscience and the analysis tools of networks is interesting to understand how the brain influences and is influenced by the social environment by integrating the knowledge developed by neuroscience which, still today, is limited to studying the brain especially in isolation. The Firstly, it was conducted a systematic search of the literature by using one online database, such as Scopus. This enabled us to obtain a final dataset of 173 publications, that it was then performed through bibliometric techniques of citation and co-citation analysis to explore the foundations and topical connections, in terms of citation structure and cluster formation, of research into Neuroscience, physiological tools and stress in organizational, managerial and IS fields.

This research seeks to answer the following research questions:

- RQ1. What is the state of the art of research on the link between neuroscience, physiological tools and stress, with the possible neuroscientific impact and influence of culture on the stress, in the organizational, managerial and Information Systems (IS) fields?
- RQ2. What are the most relevant contributions and topical connections among the cited references?

The structure of this paper is as follows. First, the paper highlights a Systematic Literature Review and a Bibliometric Analysis employing a quantitative approach that involves citation analysis and co-citation analysis (Research Methodology). Finally, it discusses the results of the Systematic Literature Review and bibliometric analysis (Sects. 4 and 5).

2 Research Methodology

In order to understand academic contributions to the topic of neuroscience, cognitive neuroscience, the use of physiological tools and stress, with the eventual neuroscientific impact of culture on the stress, in organizational, managerial and IS fields, we performed a systematic search of the literature. This approach is particularly suitable for collecting, handling and analyzing quantitative bibliographic data derived from academic contributions on a topic. Consistent with prior literature [25–28], this research involved applying a Systematic Literature review method through a quantitative approach that involves citation and co-citation analysis. They are two forms of bibliometrics or quantitative bibliography that involve counting citations to other publications in a body of literature and using these counts to develop statistical distribution [25]. In particular, citation analysis is a bibliometric technique that allows academics to investigate the evolution of knowledge production in a specific context, as well as the relationships between Authors, journals, and the sources therein [27]. Co-citation analysis, instead, is a form of document coupling which measures the number of documents that have cited any given pair of documents [25].

As Gundolf and Filser [26] stated, data was performed using the following approach: (1) data collection: papers were added to the dataset by searching and screening one of most important online databases for scientific research; (2) data analysis: the final dataset was descriptively analyzed (dataset analysis) and then performed through bibliometric techniques of citation analysis and co-citation analysis.

The flow chart that reports the different phases of this Systematic Literature review and citation and co-citation network analysis is shown in Fig. 1.

2.1 Data Collection

The first step, data collection, involves a suitable source for a systematic search of the literature. We selected one online database, such as Scopus.

Scopus is one of the most powerful and widely used research engines for the academic literature search and selection, on account of their coverage of scientific journals, books, and conference proceedings of peer-reviewed literature. To obtain a comprehensive dataset, we generated a search string by using some subject terms, related to Neuroscience and Stress, in title, abstract or among keywords. These subject terms were chosen based on the literature about Neuroscience, Cognitive Neuroscience, physiological tools and stress and, in particular, based on Parthasarathi and Kable [29] and based on Vogel, J., Auinger, A., Riedl, R. [30].

This allowed us to identify a total of 331 results in the area of Business, Management and Accounting (the generic subject area considered by Scopus to classify papers that address issues related to one of the three areas of Business, Management and Accounting, areas closest to those we consider in this study, i.e. organizational, managerial and information systems fields), corresponding to as many contributions published from the starting date of Scopus' coverage to June 2022 and considering all the countries of origin of the papers considered in Scopus. Consistent with the literature on bibliometric methods [31], keywords were stemmed and used in combination with wild cards to include both singular and plural expressions. We then performed the screening and eligibility processes to remove duplicates, to exclude papers that do not properly match with Business, Management and Accounting subject areas, to exclude papers that were not written in English language and letters. After the screening and eligibility processes, the final dataset for the subsequent analysis consisted of 173 publications. We considered, for the analysis: Journal Articles, Books, Book Chapters, Editorials, Conference Papers, Notes, Conference Reviews, Reviews and Short Surveys. Scopus inserts these contributions in the area of Business, Management and Accounting. It was this set of 173 publications that citation analysis and co-citation analysis (citation structure and cluster formation) was carried out on. The literature inclusion/exclusion criteria are shown in Table 1.

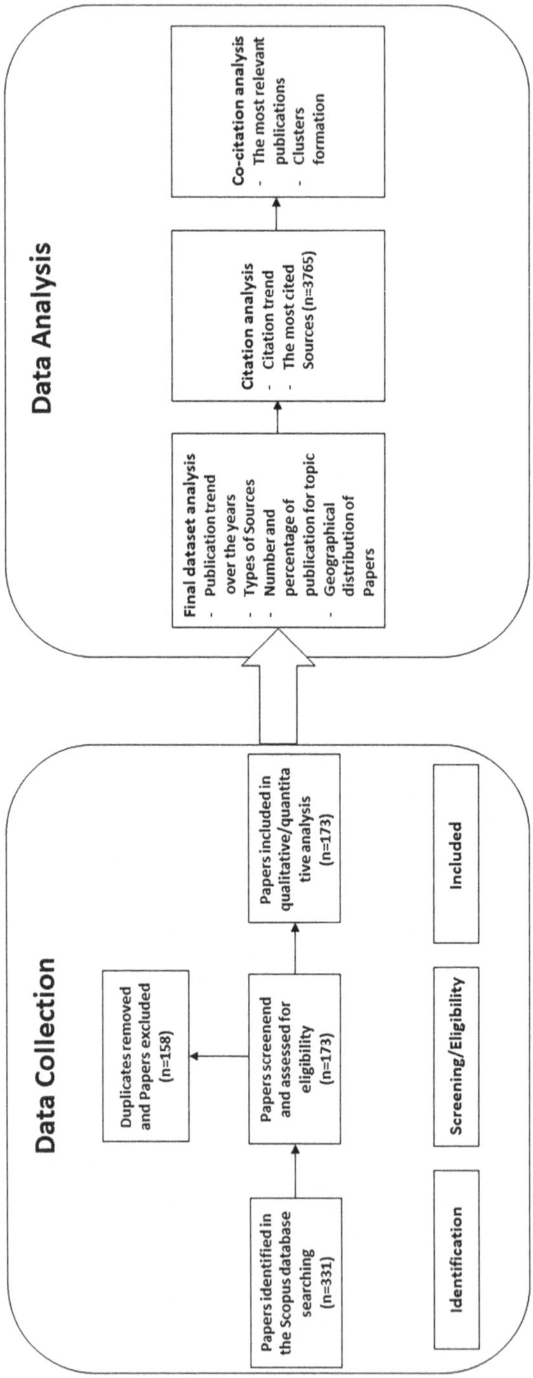

Fig. 1 The research methodology flow chart

Table 1 Literature inclusion/exclusion criteria

Literature inclusion/ exclusion criteria	Literature included	Literature excluded
Subject areas	Contributions classified, in Scopus, in Business, Management and Accounting subject areas	Contributions classified, in Scopus, in different subject areas than the Business, Management and Accounting subject areas
Language	Contributions that were written in English language	Contributions that were not written in English language
Document types	Journals Articles, Books, Book Chapters, Editorials, Conference Papers, Notes, Conference Reviews, Reviews and Shorts Surveys	Letters
Duplication	One publication, in Scopus, of the contributions considered	Duplicate, in Scopus, of the contributions considered

3 Results

We examined the final dataset in three steps: (1) we descriptively analyzed the sample of 173 publications to obtain information on publication trend over the years, on the types of sources and on the geographical distribution of papers; (2) we descriptively analyzed the sample to obtain information on citation trends over the years, on the most frequently cited sources and on the number and on the percentage of publication for topic (citation analysis); and (3) we used SNA tools to reveal the citation network and the topic clusters (co-citation analysis). In what follows, we present the results of final dataset analysis (Sect. 3.1), citation analysis (Sect. 3.2), and co-citation analysis (Sect. 3.3).

3.1 Dataset Analysis

After data collected, the final dataset of 173 publications was analyzed to obtain descriptive data on publication trend over the years, on the types of sources and on the geographical distribution of papers.

Figure 2 shows a substantially increasing trend since 1970 in the research field of neuroscience, cognitive neuroscience, the use of physiological tools and stress in organizational, managerial and IS fields with different peaks. In particular, there is a slight peak in 1996 with 4 publications, new peaks in 2010, 2012, 2013, 2014 and 2015 with, respectively, 6-6-5-6-6 publications and an important growing trend since 2016 with 23 publications in 2019, 20 publications in 2020, 14 publications in 2021 and 8 publications to 2022 from January to June.

While Fig. 3 shows the types of sources in the original dataset. In particular, these are mainly Journal articles, 115 (66%), followed by Book Chapters, 20 (12%), Conference Papers, 17 (10%), Reviews, 14 (8%), Books, 3 (2%) and the other

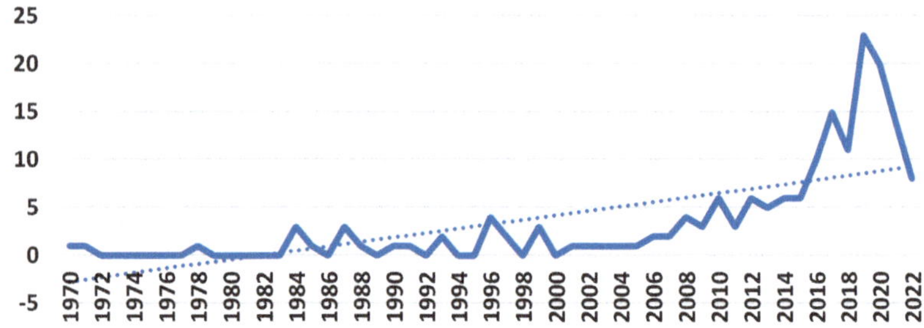

Fig. 2 Publication trend over the years (n = 173)

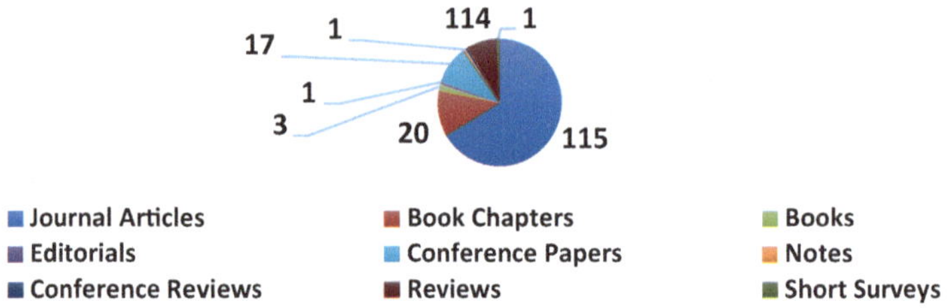

Fig. 3 Types of sources (n = 173)

sources with negligible percentages (Editorials, Notes, Conference Reviews and Short Surveys).

Finally, Fig. 4 shows the geographical distribution of papers in Scopus and considered for this research. In particular, based on the data presented in Scopus, the graph shows a dominance of papers placed in the United States (41) followed by United Kingdom (17), Austria, India and Germany (10), Australia (7), Japan, Canada, Sweden, and Italy (5), Malaysia, China and Singapore (3), Spain, South Korea, Ireland, Portugal, Switzerland, Finland, Poland and South Africa (2), Saudi Arabia, Turkey, Vietnam, Netherlands, Lithuania, Romania, Taiwan, Iran, Sri Lanka, Hong Kong, Indonesia, Estonia, the Russian Federation and France (1) and, finally, 19 results whose geographical location is undefined.

3.2 *Citation Analysis*

Citation analysis is the second part of our data analysis and deals with the yearly trend in citations (Fig. 5), the most active Sources (Fig. 6) and the number and the percentage of publication for topic (Fig. 7).

Consistent with our research aim, we built upon the publications within our original database to create a basis for cluster development. Our dataset consists of 173 sources in Scopus. The number of citations, in the citation range from 0 to 414 in the period range from 1970 to 2022 (considering 1970 first year with a publication in Scopus in this research Topic) is 3765, while the average number of citations per document is 21.76.

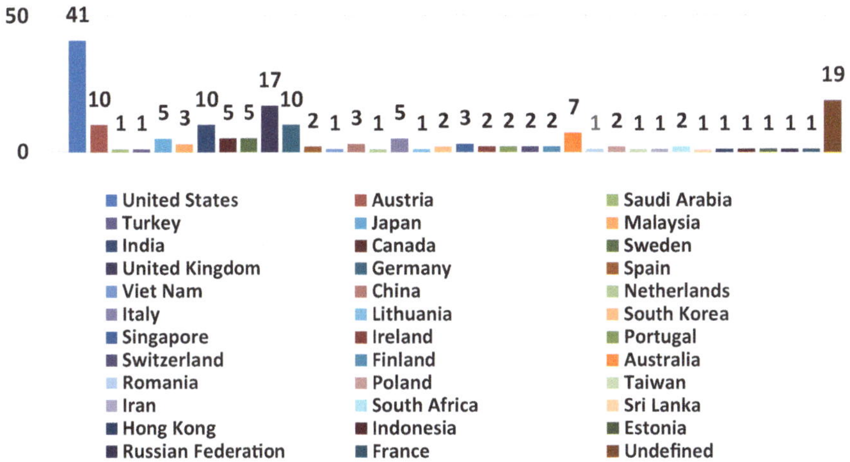

Fig. 4 Geographical distribution of papers (n = 173)

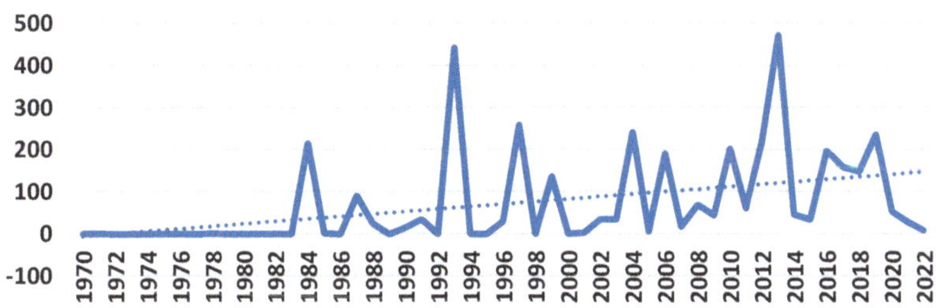

Fig. 5 Citation trend, in Scopus, over the years (n = 3765)

Fig. 6 The most frequently cited sources (n = 3765)

As shown by Fig. 5 the citations trend is a non-linear trend with 216 citations in 1984, a tendency to decline until 1993, when we have a record, with 444 citations. After a new decline, citations start to rise again and record, between increases and decreases, two new peaks in 1997, with 260 citations, and in 2004 with 243 citations. But the most important peak is reached in 2013 that shows 472 citations.

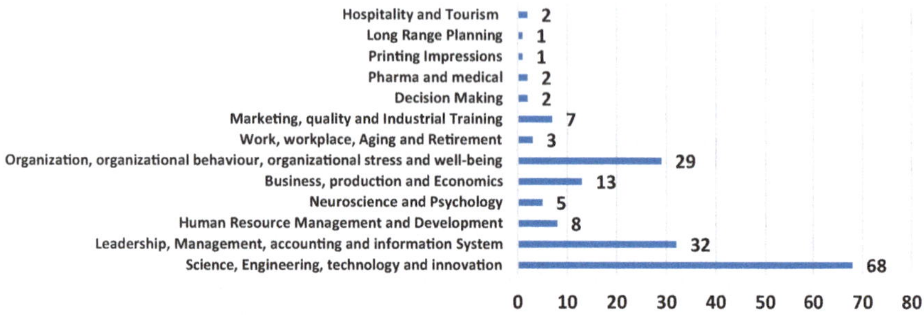

Fig. 7 Number of publications for topic

We, further, identified the most frequently cited sources (Fig. 6). As shown by Fig. 6, the most active sources were: Academy of Management Journal (832), followed by Journal of Management (550), Journal of Organizational Behavior (435), Personnel Psychology (250), Academy of Management Learning and Education (190), Data Base for Advances in Information Systems (136) and International Journal of Stress Management (121).

Figure 6 also shows the relevance of research on "neuroscience, cognitive neuroscience, the use of physiological tools and stress, with the eventual neuroscientific impact of culture on the stress, in organizational, managerial and IS fields" published by sources dealing with Business, Management and stress Management (such as International Journal of Stress Management (121) and Journal of Business Venturing (62)), with the Information Systems (such as Lecture Notes in Information Systems and Organization (61) and Information Systems Research (62)), with Psychology (such as Personnel Psychology (250)) and with Organizational Research and Leadership (such as Organizational Research Methods (64) and Leadership Quarterly (61).

Considering the heterogeneity of the journals, books and proceedings that make up the sample considered in this analysis, it is interesting, at this point, to aggregate the data relating to the published papers and the topic analyzed by each of them, to understand the prevailing context in which Neuroscience, the physiological tools and stress are used in business environment.

On the basis of the data collected, it emerged that the journals, books and proceedings considered are mainly concerned with Science, Engineering, technology and innovation with stress with 68 publications and a percentage of the total of 39%; Leadership, Management, Accounting and Information Systems together with stress with 32 publications and a percentage of the total of 18%; Organization, Organizational behavior, Organizational stress and well-being with 29 publications and a percentage of 17%, as can be seen in Fig. 7 that indicates the frequency with which the journals, books and proceedings of the sample published papers relating to the different ways in which Neuroscience, physiological tools and stress, considering also the possible neuroscientific impact of culture on the stress, has been considered in combination in the specific managerial and business context.

3.3 Co-citation Analysis

The third part of our research concerns analysis of co-citations and topical connections. We conducted a co-citation analysis, using the software VoSviewer, by considering a total of 173 publications on the topic of "neuroscience, physiological tools and stress, with the possible neuroscientific impact of culture on the stress, in organizational, managerial and Information Systems fields".

Consistent with Abrahamson and Rosenkopf [32], Agrifoglio and colleagues [33] and Silvestre and Agrifoglio [2], we used a network density, the ratio of the actual to the maximum number of links between actors in a network, as a measure for verifying network health and effectiveness. Data analysis shown that our network is composed by 15 nodes and 53 edges, while the density ratio, calculated using the software Gephi, is 0.505 ($p \geq 0.50$ is considered as high).

Further information on the influence of different sources is shown by network analysis of the co-citations, the results of which are shown in Fig. 8 (the nodes refer to the cited papers and the arcs indicate a co-citation between two papers).

Figure 8 shows that the relationships between the most cited 15 sources can be explained as 2 clusters with 53 links and a total link strength of 66. The first cluster (in red) is composed of 9 Items while the second cluster (in green) is composed of 6 Items.

4 Discussion

This study analyzed citations and publication trends in order to come to a better understanding of the topic of "neuroscience, the use of physiological tools and stress, with the possible neuroscientific impact of culture on the stress, in organizational, managerial and Information Systems fields".

An initial result is that the number of contributions in this stream of research has tended to increase since 1970, reaching different peaks in different years.

Moreover, analysis of the citations and publication trends indicates that this is a current topic, and one that is especially relevant to researchers in the fields of Business, Management and stress Management, Information Systems and in the fields of Organizational Research and Leadership.

Furthermore, after the co-citation analysis, carried out using VoSviewer and the data extracted from Scopus and downloaded in the cvs/excel format, including references, our contribution offers a broad overview of the relevant literature, analyzing the most influential sources, emerging in VoSviewer after the co-citation analysis, and classifying them in two Clusters: (1) cluster of stress, especially work stress, of the effects of stressors, of the possible consequent physiological, cognitive and neurobiological responses and of the evaluation of a stress management training program in an organizational setting and (2) cluster of the study of the conditions that influence decision-making processes and the study of certain events, to verify whether they are stressors, also with the contextual development of tools and models, to evaluate if specific life events are

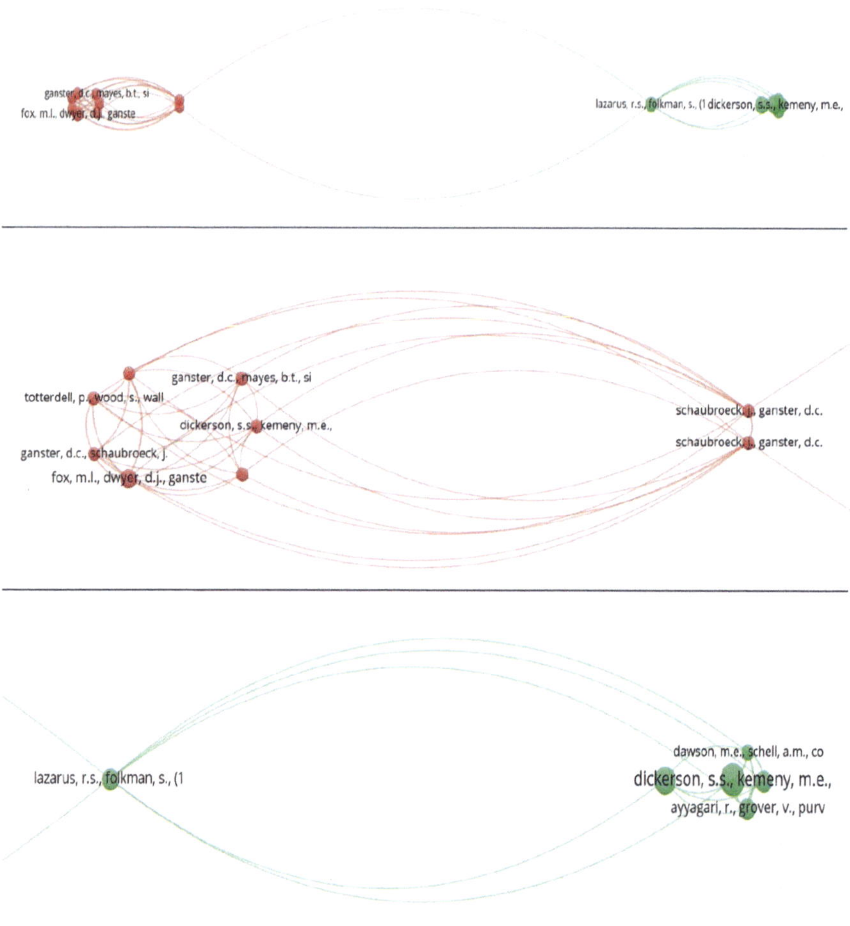

Fig. 8 Co-citation graphs

perceived as stressful, also from a neurobiological point of view and, in some contributions, with particular emphasis on events that can generate technostress.

Cluster 1 contains contributions that studied the stress and, in particular, work stress considering, in some cases, the effects of different stressors on people's health and the possible physiological, cognitive and neurobiological responses with the evaluation, in some works, of a stress management training program in an organizational setting. In particular, Dickerson, S.S., Kemeny, M.E. [34] analyzed acute psychological stressors through a meta-analysis of 208 laboratory studies and tested a theoretical model delineating conditions capable of eliciting cortisol responses noting how psychological stressors increased cortisol levels but with effects that varied widely across tasks. Some Authors analyzed the physiological responses to work-related stress with particular attention to the effects on blood pressure, cardiovascular responsiveness and skin temperature as well as, in some contributions, the consideration of the effects generated by stress on cortisol and catecholamine levels and on neurotransmitters in general [35–37]. Again, Ganster, D.C., Schaubroeck J. [38] reviewed and summarized "the literature on work stress with particular emphasis on those studies that examined the effects of work characteristics on employees' health" (p. 235). While, Jia Lin Xie and Gary Johns [39] incorporated, in their study, "the multiple effects of jobs to explore a curvilinear relationship between job scope and stress" (p. 1302) and explored "the relationship between specific job characteristics and stress to probe the reasons for the curves" (p. 1303). Interesting is, also, the work of Meurs, J.A., Perrewé, P.L. [40] because they considered that the "organizational stress research could benefit from an integrative approach that seeks to incorporate both the positive aspects and the more traditional negative aspects of the stress experience" (p. 1043). Finally, Ganster, D.C., Mayes, B.T., Sime, W.E., Tharp, G.D. [41] reported the evaluation of a stress management training program in an organizational setting.

Cluster 2 contains articles that studied particular events that can generate technostress. In particular, Ayyagari, R., Grover, V., Purvis, R. [42] drawn from IS and stress research to build and to test a specific model of technostress with the aim of investigating the role of the characteristics of technology in inducing stress in individuals. While, Riedl, R., Kindermann, H., Auinger, A., Javor, A. [43], as part of the study of technostress from a neurobiological perspective, analyzed, through a laboratory experiment, "the effects of system breakdown on changes in users' levels of cortisol, which is a major stress hormone in humans" (p. 61), showing how "cortisol levels increase significantly as a consequence of system breakdown in a human-computer interaction task" (p. 61). Other papers considered developing and using new tools and models to analyze and understand which life situations can be classified as stressful. Interesting are: the contribution of Dickerson, S.S., Kemeny, M.E. [34] because they tested "a theoretical model delineating conditions capable of eliciting cortisol responses" (p. 355) and the work of Cohen, S., Kamarck, T., Mermelstein, R. [44] because they presented the evidence "for the reliability and validity of a 14-item instrument, the Perceived Stress Scale (PSS), designed to measure the degree to which situations in one's life are appraised as stressful" (p. 385). Finally, interesting is also the contribution of Dawson, M.E., Schell, A.M., Courtney, C.G. [45] with the consideration of the skin conductance response in studies involving decision-making identifying the cortical and subcortical mechanisms involved in relation to decision-making and related cognitive processes.

It is interesting to note the book of Lazarus, R.S., Folkman, S. [46] that act as a sort bridge between the two clusters. It presents elements that connect the first cluster, of the effects of different stressors on people's health and the possible physiological, cognitive and neurobiological responses, with the second cluster, of certain events as stressors, underlining the importance of stress as stressor and as a response to different events and the necessity to study it using different tools depending on the meaning used, also physiological and neurobiological tools, in various contexts for a better stress appraisal and coping. Curious is also the article of Dickerson, S.S., Kemeny, M.E. [34] because it is present in both clusters. Probably, this characteristic is linked to the fact that the paper carries out a meta-analysis to examined acute psychological stressors and, at the same time, analyzed the responses to cortisol generated by the stressors themselves.

5 Research Implications

This study focused on an interesting trend, that of neuroscience, physiological tools and stress, with the possible neuroscientific impact of culture on the stress, in organizational, managerial and IS fields, which offers more and more new and challenging insights for scholars and manager, pushing forward the need for the next research agenda on this topic. In particular, this analysis, conducted using the database online Scopus, identified several clusters of research domains, and each can represent a possible locus for further integrations and cross fertilization.

The first cluster contains studies that talked about physical and mental stress experienced by workers in manual work using both subjective measures, such as ratings of perceived exertion, and objective measures, such as heart rate, skin temperature and skin conductance, to understand how stress manifests itself in physiological and neurological terms to optimize it.

The second cluster contains specific studies that analyzed the possibility and opportunity of understanding stress, in contexts such as the corporate one, using neurobiological tools, as well as physiological and neuroscientific in general, also with reference to non-manual work contexts. Also in this case the aim is to manage stress in the best possible way to produce positive effects for all the actors involved.

The third cluster contains contributes that analyzed the stress that arises from the continuous evaluation of one's own performance and the prolonged threat of being held accountable for the results, using neurobiological tools such as the levels of stress hormone (cortisol and thyrotropin) and physiological tools.

The fourth cluster contains studies that focused on technostress, deriving from the use of more and more new information and communication technologies, analyzed through physiological and neuroscientific tools in general.

The fifth cluster collects publications that stressed the importance of mindfulness to reduce stress in the workplace, to reduce physiological markers of stress and thus provide a new tool for understanding and managing stressful situations.

The sixth cluster contains studies which, considering the culture expressed in terms of the language used in a country, analyzed the stress deriving from the need, for many workers, to change the language in the relationships with other stakeholders from different cultural backgrounds. The contributions present in this cluster appear to be scarce, underlining the need for further studies to investigate neuroscientific aspects of the stress deriving from cultural shocks in companies that are increasingly internationalizing in an increasingly globalized and, therefore, increasingly connected world.

The seventh and last cluster reports publications that exalted stress in combination with neuroscience in the Information Systems field and, therefore, in the NeuroIS field. These contributions underlined an important revolution which already sees in place a growing application of the Neuroscience tools and theories in the context of Information Systems.

With reference to each field considered in this study, organizational, managerial and information systems, it is interesting to note, from the analysis of the papers reported in Scopus, that there is some interest, albeit to be developed further, in the study of stress through neuroscience and related physiological tools.

Specifically, in the organizational field it is necessary to recall the work of Umer, W., Yu, Y., Antwi Afari, M.F. [9] in which the Authors considered the importance of using both subjective (assessments of perceived exertion) and objective (heart rate, skin temperature and skin conductance) measures to assess the effect of cognitive task-led mental stress, on physical stress in carrying out labor-intensive and physically demanding tasks, revealing inter-individual differences between participants and, consequently, the importance of examining each worker separately to develop better mitigation strategies and individualized training programs. Interesting is, also, the contribution of Mani, S., Mishra, M. [47] in which they tried to provide a new neuroscientific perspective to improve employee engagement in companies identifying four neurochemical substances, the DOSE (dopamine, oxytocin , serotonin and endorphins) capable of stimulating employee motivation and the well-being. Finally, Evans, G.W., Johansson, G., Rydstedt, L. [48] realized a study capable of providing "methodological contributions to the stress and health literature" (p. 199). The Authors discussed, also, the possibility of using work redesign studies to better investigate stress and health.

In the managerial field, an important contribution is the work of Lee, E.-J., Yun, J.H. [49] where "using functional near-infrared spectroscopy (fNIRS), hemodynamic responses in the dorsolateral prefrontal cortex (DLPFC) were recorded while subjects were deliberating over choices under the situations of business moral dilemma" (p. 438) showing that "severe time constraint can overburden the activities of moral brain and elevate decision stress" (p. 438). While, Wichary, S., Mata, R., Rieskamp, J. [50] assessed emotional stress using subjective measures (state anxiety, arousal, and pleasantness ratings) and objective measures (skin conductance), demonstrating how "emotional stress impacts decision making" (p. 525).

With reference to the information systems field, however, the results highlighted the need and the usefulness of integrating traditional tools with innovative technologies related to neuroscience and physiological aspects for the collection and processing of information, also relating to stress, to support of an organization. Expressive, in this sense, the work of Salma, N., Mai, B., Namuduri, K., (...), Parde, N., Nielsen, R. [51] that tried to demonstrate "how electroencephalograph (EEG) signals can be used to analyze people's mental states while engaging in cognitive processes during IS decision-making" (p. 211). Finally, important is the contribution of Baumgartner, D., Fischer, T., Riedl, R., Dreiseitl, S. [22] which provided evidence to support the idea that "NeuroIS scholars have to deliberately make methodological decisions such as those related to preprocessing of physiological data" (p. 221).

It is evident that, in the literature, emerges the usefulness of neuroscientific and, in general, physiological tools for the study of different forms of stress in order to obtain more and more significant informations. In particular, among the most commonly used and most cited tools and indicators transversally in almost all clusters of papers that emerged in Scopus, it is possible to detect: the heart rate variability (HRV); the cheek-skin-temperature; the skin conductance; the electrodermal activity; the brain signals; the electroencephalogram (EEG); the blood-pressure levels; the body-temperature (BT); the functional magnetic resonance imaging (fMRI); the functional near-infrared spectroscopy (fNIRS) based hyperscanning technique; the electrocardiogram (ECG); the dopamine, oxytocin, serotonin and endorphins; the eye tracking; the salivary biomarkers cortisol and alpha amylase; the cognitive abilities and markers of neurocognitive efficiency; the catecholamines; the pupil diameter; the excretion of adrenaline and noradrenaline; the epinephrine and norepinephrine; the respiration rate (RR) and the gastrointestinal disorders.

Evidently, this study provides interesting implications and insights for scholars and manager. In terms of theoretical implications, it provides a synoptic picture of the current diffusion of knowledge on the topic of "neuroscience, physiological tools and stress, with the possible neuroscientific impact of culture on the stress, in organizational, managerial and IS fields" that can to use scholars to start their in-depth research by focusing on issues that deserve further development, such as the stress that can arise from culture shocks and how culture, considered in neuroscientific terms, impacts on the development and management of different forms of stress.

In terms of managerial implications, the study highlights the most relevant research domains on which manager can focus in facing the question of stress management increasing the practical use of physiological and neurobiological tools to better understand the brain mechanisms underlying stress and the role and the impact on stress of cultural differences, analyzed in neuroscientific terms, so as to develop rapid and effective interventions capable of optimizing stress helping to improve well-being and health of manager and employees in a company and the health of the entire Organization.

6 Future Research and Limitations

Our findings suggest that there are fruitful opportunities for future development. In particular, a possible future study could be directed towards a greater deepening of the study and understanding the stress in organizational and managerial fields using neuroscience tools to understand the neural mechanism of this phenomenon. Particular attention and development should be devoted to cultural stress and its neural and, therefore, neuroscientific determinants as well as to cultural differences, analyzed in neuroscientific terms and their impact on the development and management of different forms of stress, for a better understanding of the state of health of managers and employees in the company. Furthermore, greater attention should be paid to the stress deriving from particular events which, by modifying the environmental conditions, can generate stress, as happened with the pandemic Covid 19.

The findings also suggest the link between ICT and neuroscience contributing to the NeuroIS research. Some contributions underline the possibility of studying stress in the context of Information Systems (IS) research using neuroscience tools. So, we believe that further IS research could be aimed at a greater understanding of stress to obtain even more sophisticated and more predictive neuroscientific information of individuals' behaviors and decisions under stress using neuroscientific.

Of course, this research is not free from limitations. The first limitation is linked to the use of a single online database; therefore, it is necessary to extend the research using other online databases. The second limitation is related to the nature of the topic in this study because it is in continuous evolution and, so, the contribution will require to be constantly updated. More in general, this study can nonetheless serve as an advantageous starting point for scholars, who can move with their research along the lines proposed above. Future research should certainly focus on enriching the framework.

So, our analysis represents a starting point in the ongoing debate on the topic of "neuroscience, physiological tools and stress, with the eventual neuroscientific impact of culture on the stress, in organizational, managerial and IS fields" and, also with its limitations, we believe that this contribution can serve as a reference point, offering a guide to scholars interested in approaching this research stream.

References

1. Oliverio, A. (2011). *Prima lezione di Neuroscienze*. Editori Laterza.
2. Silvestre, R., & Agrifoglio, R. (2021). Understanding the links between neuroscience and culture through a social network analysis: insights for IS research. In *ItAIS 2021 Proceedings—XVIII conference of the Italian Chapter of AIS, Digital resilience and sustainability: people, organizations, and society*. AIS eLibrary, University of Trento.
3. Cocco, G. C. (2016). *Neuromanagement. Per una nuova scienza del management* (1st ed.). FrancoAngeli Edizioni.
4. Alvino, L., Pavone, L., Abhishta, A., & Robben, H. (2020). Picking your brains: Where and how neuroscience tools can enhance marketing research. *Frontiers in Neuroscience, 14*, 577666. https://doi.org/10.3389/fnins.2020.577666
5. Butmee, T., Lansdown, T. C., & Walker, G. H. (2019). Mental workload and performance measurements in driving task: A review literature. In S. Bagnara, R. Tartaglia, S. Albolino, T. Alexander, & Y. Fujita (Eds.), *Volume VI: Transport ergonomics and human factors (TEHF), aerospace human factors and ergonomics (2019), Proceedings of the 20th congress of the International Ergonomics Association (IEA 2018)* (Vol. 823, pp. 286–294). Springer. https://doi.org/10.1007/978-3-319-96074-6_31
6. Miller, S. (2001). *Workload measures*. National Advanced Driving Simulator.
7. Rehmann, A. J. (1995). *Handbook of human performance measures and crew requirements for flightdeck research*. Repository & Open Science Access Portal.
8. McEwen, B. S. (2012). Brain on stress: How the social environment gets under the skin. *Proceedings of the National Academy of Sciences of the United States of America, 109*(suppl. 2), 17180–17185. https://doi.org/10.1073/pnas.1121254109
9. Umer, W., Yu, Y., & Antwi Afari, M. F. (2022). Quantifying the effect of mental stress on physical stress for construction tasks. *Journal of Construction Engineering and Management, 148*(3), 04021204. https://doi.org/10.1061/(ASCE)CO.1943-7862.0002243

10. Kazar, G., & Comu, S. (2022). Exploring the relations between the physiological factors and the likelihood of accidents on construction sites. *Engineering, Construction and Architectural Management, 29*(1), 456–475. https://doi.org/10.1108/ECAM-11-2020-0958
11. Chase, M. A. (2019). Stemming the tide of work-related stress: it's not rocket science, it's neuroscience. *Development and Learning in Organizations, 33*(4), 16–19. https://doi.org/10.1108/DLO-09-2018-0123
12. Dhiman, S. (2018). Mindfulness in the workplace: Meaning, role, and applications. In S. Dhiman, G. E. Roberts, & J. E. Crossman (Eds.), *The Palgrave handbook of workplace spirituality and fulfillment* (Book, 1–2) (pp. 177–210). Springer. https://doi.org/10.1007/978-3-319-62163-0_56
13. Creswell, J. D., Taren, A. A., Lindsay, E. K., Greco, C. M., Gianaros, P. J., Fairgrieve, A., Marsland, A. L., Brown, K. W., Way, B. M., Rosen, R. K., & Ferris, J. L. (2016). Alterations in resting-state functional connectivity link mindfulness meditation with reduced interleukin-6: A randomized controlled trial. *Biological Psychiatry, 80*(1), 53–61. https://doi.org/10.1016/j.biopsych.2016.01.008
14. Pascoe, M. C., Thompson, D. R., Jenkins, Z. M., & Ski, C. F. (2017). Mindfulness mediates the physiological markers of stress: Systematic review and meta-analysis. *Journal of Psychiatric Research, 95*, 156–178. https://doi.org/10.1016/j.jpsychires.2017.08.004
15. Congleton, C., Britta, K., Hölzel, B. K., & Lazar, S. W. (2015). Mindfulness can literally change your brain. *Harvard Business Review, Psychology.*
16. Frimanson, L., Hornbach, J., & Hartmann, F. G. H. (2021). Performance evaluations and stress: Field evidence of the hormonal effects of evaluation frequency. *Accounting, Organizations and Society, 95*, 101279. https://doi.org/10.1016/j.aos.2021.101279
17. Weinert, C., Maier, C., Laumer, S., & Weitzel, T. (2020). Technostress mitigation: an experimental study of social support during a computer freeze. *Journal of Business Economics, 90*(8), 1199–1249. https://doi.org/10.1007/s11573-020-00986-y
18. Zhang, Z., & Teo, H.-H. (2020). A neuroimaging study of how ICT-enabled interruptions induce mental stress. In F. D. Davis, R. Riedl, J. vom Brocke, P.-M. Léger, A. Randolph, & T. Fischer (Eds.), *Information systems and neuroscience, NeuroIS Retreat 2019 (2020), LNISO* (Vol. 32, pp. 31–39). Springer. https://doi.org/10.1007/978-3-030-28144-1_4
19. Riedl, R. (2022). On the stress potential of videoconferencing: definition and root causes of Zoom fatigue. *Electronic Markets, 32*(1), 153–177. https://doi.org/10.1007/s12525-021-00501-3
20. Tuulik, V. (1996). The functional state of the central nervous system in chemical stress. *International Journal of Stress Management, 3*(2), 107–115. https://doi.org/10.1007/BF01857719
21. Seitz, S. R., & Smith, S. A. (2022). Talking the talk: Considering forced language-switching in the workplace. *Human Resource Management Review, 32*(2), 100833. https://doi.org/10.1016/j.hrmr.2021.100833
22. Baumgartner, D., Fischer, T., Riedl, R., & Dreiseitl, S. (2019). Analysis of heart rate variability (HRV) feature robustness for measuring technostress. In F. D. Davis, R. Riedl, J. vom Brocke, P.-M. Léger, & A. B. Randolph (Eds.), *Information systems and neuroscience: NeuroIS Retreat 2018 (2019), LNISO* (Vol. 29, pp. 221–228). Springer. https://doi.org/10.1007/978-3-030-01087-4_27
23. Fischer, T., Halmerbauer, G., Meyr, E., & Riedl, R. (2017). Blood pressure measurement: A classic of stress measurement and its role in technostress research. In F. D. Davis, R. Riedl, J. vom Brocke, P.-M. Léger, & A. B. Randolph (Eds.), *Information systems and neuroscience Gmunden Retreat on NeuroIS 2017 (2017), LNISO* (Vol. 25, pp. 25–35). Springer. https://doi.org/10.1007/978-3-319-67431-5_4
24. Goldenberg, D. (2019). Social network analysis: From graph theory to applications with python. In *PyCon 2019—3rd Israeli National Python Conference, Israel, 2019.*
25. Culnan, M. J. (1987). Mapping the intellectual structure of MIS, 1980-1985: A co-citation analysis. *MIS Quarterly: Management Information Systems, 11*(3), 341–350. https://doi.org/10.2307/248680

26. Gundolf, K., & Filser, M. (2013). Management research and religion: A citation analysis. *Journal of Business Ethics, 112*(1), 177–185. https://doi.org/10.1007/s10551-012-1240-7
27. Kraus, S., Filser, M., O'Dwyer, M., & Shaw, E. (2014). Social entrepreneurship: An exploratory citation analysis. *Review of Managerial Science, 8*(2), 275–292. https://doi.org/10.1007/s11846-013-0104-6
28. Liao, Y., Deschamps, F., Loures, E. D. F. R., & Ramos, L. F. (2017). P.: Past, present and future of industry 4.0-a systematic literature review and research agenda proposal. *International Journal of Production Research, 55*(12), 3609–3629. https://doi.org/10.1080/00207543.2017.1308576
29. Parthasarathi, T., & Kable, J. W. (2017). Cognitive neuroscience methods: An introductory overview for social scientists. In P. M. Nichols & D. C. Robertson (Eds.), *Thinking about bribery. Neuroscience, moral cognition and the psychology of bribery 2017, Book* (pp. 33–66). Cambridge University Press. https://doi.org/10.1017/9781316450765.002
30. Vogel, J., Auinger, A., & Riedl, R. (2019). Cardiovascular, neurophysiological, and biochemical stress indicators: A short review for information systems researchers: NeuroIS Retreat 2018. In F. D. Davis, R. Riedl, J. vom Brocke, P.-M. Léger, & A. B. Randolph (Eds.), *Information systems and neuroscience: NeuroIS Retreat 2018 (2019), LNISO* (Vol. 29, pp. 259–273). Springer. https://doi.org/10.1007/978-3-030-01087-4_31
31. Zupic, I., & Čater, T. (2015). Bibliometric methods in management and organization. *Organizational Research Methods, 18*(3), 429–472. https://doi.org/10.1177/1094428114562629
32. Abrahamson, E., & Rosenkopf, L. (1997). Social network effects on the extent of innovation diffusion: A computer simulation. *Organization Science, 8*(3), 289–309. https://doi.org/10.1287/orsc.8.3.289
33. Agrifoglio, R., Metallo, C., & di Nauta, P. (2021). Understanding knowledge management in public organizations through the organizational knowing perspective: A systematic literature review and bibliometric analysis. *Public Organization Review, 21*(1), 137–156. https://doi.org/10.1007/s11115-020-00480-7
34. Dickerson, S. S., & Kemeny, M. E. (2004). Acute stressors and cortisol responses: A theoretical integration and synthesis of laboratory research. *Psychological Bulletin, 130*(3), 355–391. https://doi.org/10.1037/0033-2909.130.3.355
35. Fox, M. L., Dwyer, D. J., & Ganster, D. C. (1993). Effects of stressful job demands and control on physiological and attitudinal outcomes in a hospital setting. *Academy of Management Journal, 36*(2), 289–318. https://doi.org/10.2307/256524
36. Schaubroeck, J., & Ganster, D. C. (1993). chronic demands and responsivity to challenge. *Journal of Applied Psychology, 78*(1), 73–85. https://doi.org/10.1037/0021-9010.78.1.73
37. Schaubroeck, J., Ganster, D. C., Sime, W. E., & Ditman, D. (1993). A field experiment testing supervisory role clarification. *Personnel Psychology, 46*(1), 1–25. https://doi.org/10.1111/j.1744-6570.1993.tb00865.x
38. Ganster, D. C., & Schaubroeck, J. (1991). Work stress and employee health. *Journal of Management, 17*(2), 235–271. https://doi.org/10.1177/014920639101700202
39. Xie, J. L., & Johns, G. (1995). Job scope and stress: Can job scope be too high? *The Academy of Management Journal, 38)5*, 1288–1309.
40. Meurs, J. A., & Perrewé, P. L. (2011). Cognitive activation theory of stress: An integrative theoretical approach to work stress. *Journal of Management, 37*(4), 1043–1068. https://doi.org/10.1177/0149206310387303
41. Ganster, D. C., Mayes, B. T., Sime, W. E., & Tharp, G. D. (1982). Managing organizational stress: A field experiment. *Journal of Applied Psychology, 67*(5), 533–542. https://doi.org/10.1037/0021-9010.67.5.533
42. Ayyagari, R., Grover, V., & Purvis, R. (2011). Technostress: Technological antecedents and implications. *MIS Quarterly: Management Information Systems, 35*(4), 831–858. https://doi.org/10.2307/41409963

43. Riedl, R., Kindermann, H., Auinger, A., & Javor, A. (2012). Technostress from a neurobiological perspective: System breakdown increases the stress hormone cortisol in computer users. *Business and Information Systems Engineering, 4*(2), 61–69. https://doi.org/10.1007/s12599-012-0207-7
44. Cohen, S., Kamarck, T., & Mermelstein, R. (1983). A global measure of perceived stress. *Journal of Health and Social Behavior, 24*(4), 385–396. https://doi.org/10.2307/2136404
45. Dawson, M. E., Schell, A. M., & Courtney, C. G. (2011). The skin conductance response, anticipation, and decision-making. *Journal of Neuroscience, Psychology, and Economics, 4*(2), 111–116. https://doi.org/10.1037/a0022619
46. Lazarus, R. S., & Folkman, S. (1984). *Stress: Appraisal and coping* (p. 456). Springer.
47. Mani, S., & Mishra, M. (2020). Are your employees getting their daily dose of DOSE?—A neuroscience perspective to enhance employee engagement. *Development and Learning in Organizations, 35*(5), 11–14. https://doi.org/10.1108/DLO-08-2020-0179
48. Evans, G. W., Johansson, G., & Rydstedt, L. (1999). Hassles on the job: A study of a job intervention with urban bus drivers. *Journal of Organizational Behavior, 20*(2), 199–208. https://doi.org/10.1002/(SICI)1099-1379(199903)20:2<199::AID-JOB939>3.0.CO;2-I
49. Lee, E.-J., & Yun, J. H. (2019). Moral incompetency under time constraint. *Journal of Business Research, 99*, 438–445. https://doi.org/10.1016/j.jbusres.2017.10.043
50. Wichary, S., Mata, R., & Rieskamp, J. (2016). Probabilistic inferences under emotional stress: how arousal affects decision processes. *Journal of Behavioral Decision Making, 29*(5), 525–538. https://doi.org/10.1002/bdm.1896
51. Salma, N., Mai, B., Namuduri, K., Mamun, R., Hashem, Y., Takabi, H., Parde, N., & Nielsen, R. (2017). Using EEG signal to analyze is decision making cognitive processes. In F. D. Davis, R. Riedl, J. vom Brocke, P.-M. Léger, & A. B. Randolph (Eds.), *Information systems and neuroscience Gmunden Retreat on NeuroIS 2017 (2017), LNISO* (Vol. 25, pp. 211–218). Springer. https://doi.org/10.1007/978-3-319-67431-5_24

Digitalize Thy Place: Benefits and Challenges in the Development of Smart Destinations

Sara Nicoletti, Francesca Capo, and Lorena Maria D'Agostino

Abstract Digital transformation is affecting companies worldwide, with effects on different industries. In this paper we focus on the tourism sector, and investigate how firms and related territories may leverage digital transformation and which challenges they may face in adopting digital solutions. To do so, we rely on a qualitative approach and performed ten interviews to different actors in the field to examine the adoption of an innovative online hospitality data intelligence platform, called HBenchmark, and how it can promote the development of the tourist destination of Livigno and its territory Valtellina. Our findings point to two main dimensions, related to both the benefits and challenges in the development of smart destinations, and offer contributions to literature about digital transformation and smart destinations while providing implications for public actors and managers.

Keywords Digital transformation · Smart destinations · Qualitative methods

1 Introduction

Nowadays, companies that want to keep up with the times, and therefore digitize, must necessarily implement strategies that take into account the potential that new digital technologies and Big Data offer [1]. Digital transformation is affecting different fields, changing the activities, processes and capability requirements of businesses and other stakeholders [2]. In particular, digital transformation becomes key for businesses and stakeholders operating in the tourism sector, which need to seize

S. Nicoletti · F. Capo (✉) · L. M. D'Agostino
Department of Economics, Management and Statistics, University of Milano-Bicocca, Milan, Italy
e-mail: francesca.capo@unimib.it

A. M. Braccini et al. (eds.), *Technologies for Digital Transformation*, Lecture Notes in Information Systems and Organisation 64,
https://doi.org/10.1007/978-3-031-52120-1_10

the opportunities deriving from the use and sharing of data and availability of innovative digital tools. The incredible evolution of digital technologies and high-speed Internet services are totally changing the digital landscape for the urban development and attractiveness of the territories [2]. However, some territories struggle in leveraging digital tools and embodying the characteristics of smart destinations [3]. In this sense, while literature has extensively explored the concept of digital transformation and its relationship with cities and touristic destinations [1, 4–6], we know less about how different stakeholders in the territory perceive digital tools and adopt them in their touristic business [7, 8].

This chapter addresses this issue and outlines the reasons why firms and actors operating in the tourism sector (i.e., businesses, hotels and destinations) decide whether to adopt digital tools to formulate and implement their strategies. Specifically, we ask the following research question: *how firms and related territories leverage digital transformation and which challenges they face in adopting digital solutions?* In particular, this chapter examines the use of an innovative online hospitality data intelligence platform, called HBenchmark, in promoting the development of the tourist destination of Livigno and the territory where it is located, Valtellina.

The choice of these territories was driven by the fact that Valtellina is a large and fragmented area made up of very heterogeneous tourist realities, different targets and offers. Also, the tourist phenomenon in this territory is not evenly distributed, but tends to be concentrated mostly in Livigno, which is the leading destination of the territory and accommodates half of the total incoming tourists. For these reasons, these territories are suitable for the exploration of HBenchmark platform to answer the research question and investigate how different stakeholders leverage digital transformation.

We address this question by means of a qualitative approach [9–11]. Specifically, we conducted ten interviews with managers, entrepreneurs and hoteliers to examine the use of HBenchmark.

Our findings reveal that firms can benefit from using digital transformation tools (e.g., platforms) as they provide: greater awareness for decision makers, through the monitoring of marketing actions and the possibility to measure the economic growth of a destination; accurate future predictions, anticipating bookings' future trends; more appropriate management of resources and improvement in relations and partnerships with various actors. Also, our analysis points to some challenges experienced by these actors in trying to leverage digital transformation: lack of trust in sharing private data, the lack of basic digital infrastructures, and the lack of partnership and interest in comparing with competitors.

This chapter contributes to literature about digital transformation and smart destinations and territories [12, 13], and provides implications and solutions for public actors and managers, both in terms of suggesting the key performance indicators (KPIs) worth monitoring for digital development of urban areas and territories and by offering insights into how actors operating in the tourism sector can renew their business models to adapt to continual digital changes.

2 Theoretical Background

2.1 Digital Tourism and Smart Destinations

The incredible evolution of digital technologies together with the spread of high-speed Internet services have triggered a process of digital transformation worldwide, with important consequences on the tourism sector. In particular, digital transformation has opened up opportunities for the creation of customized tourism experiences and hospitality services [14, 15]. Organizations in this sector have undertaken a major re-engineering of structures, processes and strategies to take advantage of the full potential offered by emerging ICTs [15].The Internet, smartphones, social media and User Generated Contents have transformed the mechanisms of supply and demand: emerged mobile solutions, such as location-based services and augmented reality applications, have been increasingly implemented to assist tourists with navigating, finding locations and making bookings and reservations. Travellers' experience has completely transformed, becoming more and more smart and innovative [16].

This change in the tourism experience due to the emergence of new technologies has led to the development of digital tourism, a new way of perceiving destinations. Digital tourism [5] calls for a shifting focus from the territory to the tourist him/herself, who seeks an experience by discovering the chosen destination in a completely customized way. This shift, made possible by technological development, calls organizations to adopt a new way of interpreting the tourist experience by leveraging smart mobile devices and Big Data to understand the rationales behind touristic choices and needs. Indeed, the enormous growth of mobile devices and applications is changing travel habits, and the data collected through them become key for firms to develop a "location awareness" (https://digitalinnovationgazette.com/) which, together with real-time and forward-looking data, could be used to improve their marketing practices and eventually their value creation processes.

Alongside digital tourism, innovative technologies have triggered the emergence of the concept of smart cities and smart destinations [12, 17]. Extant research [4, 18] has referred to smartness as the combination of three aspects: effectiveness, environmental consideration, and innovation. As such, a smart city is a city able to provide effective public and private services to different stakeholders, to ensure an adequate quality of the environment, and to leverage innovative technologies to improve quality of life and services for citizens and other stakeholders [18]. Relatedly, smart destinations refer to broader and peculiar cases of smart cities [12]. In particular, the focus of smart destinations is on technologies which can substantially improve, alongside citizens' quality of life, tourists' experience during their visits in a specific location [19, 20], and on spaces such as rural areas which, although extending beyond the traditional boundaries of the city, can also benefit from the adoption and development of smart tools [8].

A smart destination is a destination where organizations, tourists and local administrations constantly work together to carry out three main activities: (a) collect destination data from all possible sources; (b) analyse the collected data by elaborating specific processes to determine tourists' behaviour in the destination; (c) implement measures through economic, financial and territorial interventions to improve the destination, making it more sustainable and adaptable to the needs and tastes of tourists.

However, smart destinations have to deal with some important challenges in order to create long-term value for their territories and for the tourists and residents visiting or inhabiting them [21]. First, they need to manage personal privacy, which affects companies, governments and privates [21]. Second, they need to limit the risk of unreliable information and fake data [21]. Third, they need to consider that the use of connected digital devices, such as smartphones, can have both positive and negative sides [22]. On the one hand, having a lot of information that can always be consulted on mobile devices ensures that the tourist does not feel lost, experiencing greater tourist satisfaction. On the other hand, a continuous attachment to smartphones does not let the tourist disconnect from his/her everyday life and deprives him/her to enjoy the sense of adventure [22].

The provision of innovative technologies and digital tools can upgrade the service quality of tourism organizations, increasing the positive image of a destination and improving the visitation and recommendation intentions of tourists [23]. Also, it can trigger a more sustainable approach to the development and offering of tourism products and services [5]. However, in light of the different challenges that digital tools may entail, stakeholders operating in the territory may not be willing to adopt them, leading to the emergence of barriers in the development of smart destinations. In the following section, we build on a case-study to articulate, alongside the benefits, the challenges perceived by several stakeholders in leveraging digital tools to innovate their territories.

3 Methodology

3.1 Data Collection

We answer our research question by developing a qualitative approach [9, 11]. In order to obtain in-depth qualitative data, the primary sources were interviews with informants dealing with the adoption and development of the HBenchmark project in Livigno and in Valtellina (Italy). HBenchmark is a Hospitality Data Intelligence online platform developed by Group Develon S.r.l., an Italian digital company headquartered in Altavilla Vicentina (VI) which designs, develops and offers digital products and services to the market. The choice to analyse HBenchmark was guided by the main goal for which this platform was created, that is the possibility of using aggregated performance data to monitor tourists' flows and outline more effectively commercial, marketing and investment strategies.

Therefore, in this paper we focus on the partnership between HBenchmark platform and the tourism destination Livigno, which is a famous alpine destination located in the upper Valtellina, situated in the province of Sondrio (North of Italy). The province of Sondrio is a fragmented area divided into five Mountain Communities: Valchiavenna, Valtellina of Morbegno, Valtellina of Sondrio, Valtellina of Tirano and Alta Valtellina. Livigno is part of the Alta-Valtellina Mountain community and its status of duty-free zone has favoured tourism development since the end of the 1950s. The tourist phenomenon in Valtellina is not evenly distributed, but tends to be concentrated mostly in Livigno (46.8%), which accommodates almost half of the total incoming tourists, followed by Bormio, which collects 15.2% of the movement [24].

The interviewees were selected by combining "purposive and snowball sampling techniques" [25]. This means that, at first, we chose few interviewees who could greatly inform us about the issue at the centre of our investigation, i.e. how firms and related territories leverage digital transformation and which challenges they face in adopting digital solutions. Then, we proceeded by interviewing other informants who the first interviewees recommended as relevant for our analysis (i.e. through snowballing sampling), until we reached the level of "theoretical saturation" [26], meaning that further interviews did not seemed to provide any new significant theoretical insights.

The interviews conducted had the main goal of identifying the dynamics and processes occurring between the different managers, entrepreneurs and hoteliers involved in the project. All interviewees were contacted prior to the interviews via e-mail or phone call for the presentation of the study goal and, later, face-to-face meetings and video calls were organized. All respondents gave permission to be registered during the interviews and to publish their name in this study. Each interview lasted from 9 to 59 min and the entire data collection was carried out from March 2021 to July 2021. As recommended for exploratory research, open-ended interviews were guided by few closed questions.

In the initial phase of the interviews, the goal was to explore the context, understand the functioning of HBenchmark platform and obtain general insights into the rationales of why hoteliers used or not of the platform. In later stages, more in-depth interviews were conducted to understand more in detail the themes emerged during our first interviews and situate them in the context of the theoretical categories emerged [27]. In the last phase of the interviews, which took place in July 2021, some interviewees were asked if there were any news on the adoption of the platform in the territory compared to past months. Once the interviews were done, the recordings were listened to and then transcribed. Table 1 summarizes the interviews conducted for this study.

3.2 Data Analysis

We analysed our data collected by means of Gioia methodology [10], which enables researchers to inductively transform the initial empirical themes (close to the nature of informants) into theoretically sound categories (close to the nature of researchers). Specifically, in the first phase, the focus was on the terms used by the

Table 1 Overview of interviewees

Interview no.	Position	Date	Duration
No. 1	Entrepreneur and hotelier in Livigno and President of Federalberghi in the province of Sondrio	10/03/2021	39 min
No. 2	Commercial and business development Manager from HBenchmark	10/03/2021	59 min
No. 3	Booking manager Agency of Tourism Promotion (APT) of Livigno	12/03/2021	21 min
No. 4	Project manager of Valtellina Tourism	22/03/2021	36 min
No. 5	Director of the Tourist Observatory of the province of Sondrio	23/03/2021	17 min
No. 6	Commercial and business development Manager from HBenchmark	21/04/2021	20 min
No. 7	Marketing Director of BivioLife Livigno	21/04/2021	26 min
No. 8	Entrepreneur and hotelier in Livigno & President of Federalberghi in the province of Sondrio	15/07/2021	9 min
No.9	Booking manager APT Livigno	20/07/2021	11 min
No. 10	Marketing Director of BivioLife Livigno	22/07/2021	16 min

informants. Therefore, the transcripts of the interviews were examined in detail to identify first-order concepts regarding the adoption of HBenchmark platform in Livigno and Valtellina.

In the second phase, the focus was on identifying similarities between the various categories, theoretically answering the question "what is happening here?" and determining more theoretical themes—called second order themes. In the third phase, the second order themes were grouped into aggregate dimensions—in this case "benefits" and "challenges" of the digital transformation—to form a theoretical model.

Therefore, once we identified first order concepts, the second order themes and the aggregate dimensions, it was possible to construct a data structure. The data structure, depicted in Fig. 1, visually shows the process that starts from raw data and then reaches sound theoretical conclusions.

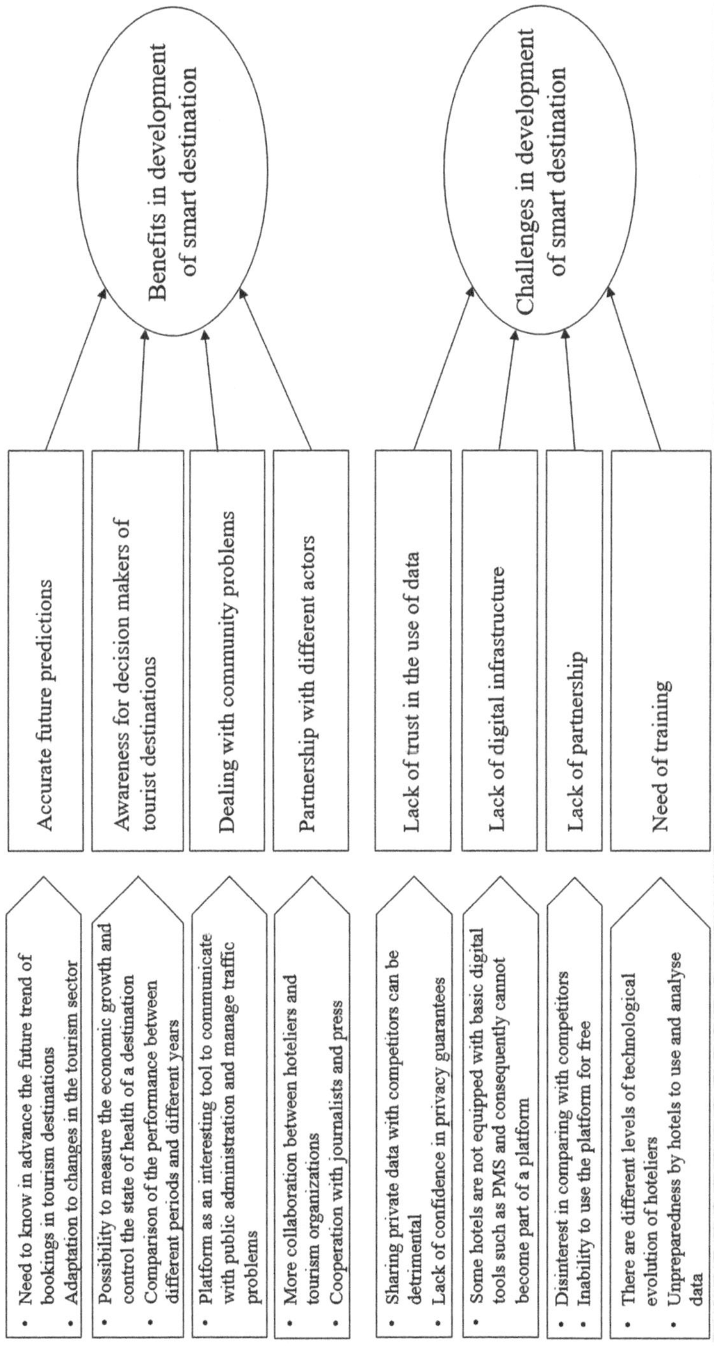

Fig. 1 Data structure

4 Findings

HBenchmark platform owes its name to the main service it offers to hoteliers, namely benchmarking, which can be defined as "a continuing and systematic process which involves confronting the effectiveness measured by productivity, quality and experience with the results of those companies and organizations which can be seen as a model of perfection" ([28]: 498]). HBenchmark allows the acquisition, aggregation and comparative analysis of a series of performance indicators, with the aim of having both an analysis of the state of health of the hotel/structure and the relative forecasts, obtained through consolidated data. In addition to this, the platform allows the comparison with competitors present in the territory.

The tourism sector is changing. Hoteliers have to manage more and more aspects, because, for example, setting the right price requires in-depth analysis, complex and expensive evaluations and projections. So, while the market changes, tools which analyse it, as HBenchmark, are being developed as well (Interview no. 2, Commercial and Business Development Manager from Hbenchmark).

The platform is present in over 25 destinations in Italy and abroad and is fully integrated with over 90% of the Property Management System (PMS) present on the market, which is used by hoteliers to manage their bookings. The platform has been designed to address three types of users: tourism public administration, hotels, and camping.

For tourism public administration, the platform aggregates the anonymous data of all the hotels which use the service and provides data on tourism trends in real time as well as forecasts and strategic information to promote the destination. With the software, it is possible to understand how tourists' demand grows, when it is appropriate to organize an event or how the tourists behave when the weather is adverse. For example, the platform allows to compare the performance of different periods during the same year or the same period in different years with respect to the weather, to understand the rationales of certain occupancies, prices, and markets.

Decision makers can verify that one weekend may have gone well or badly compared to another based on the good/adverse weather, rather than merely based, for example, on inappropriate marketing actions (Interview no. 6, Commercial and Business Development Manager from HBenchmark).

HBenchmark allows hotels' decision makers to operate with a more holistic awareness of the complex hotel market as they know in real time the tourist flows as well as current and future (up to 12 months) market prices. Thanks to performance and comparison indicators, it is possible to understand whether and how tourist demand grows in one location, which prices work best on certain dates and to position them as a function of the demand pressures on the territory in specific seasons. In this way, if structures and hotels are able to equip themselves with technological tools that provide objective data, they can promptly redirect their strategic choices in terms of revenues and promotion, but also seize opportunities emerged in the market.

HBenchmark in Livigno and Valtellina The partnership between HBenchmark and Livigno has been promoted by Agency of Tourist Promotion (APT) Livigno in collaboration with Tourism and Commerce Association (ATC) and with hotel managers. The pilot project started in September 2019 and involved 11 hotels of the area during the winter season, while the launch of the official project started in October 2020 with an initial 3-year partnership.

In Livigno, the partnership signed between HBenchmark and APT and ATC makes sure that hotels linked to these latter do not pay any costs for the adoption of the platform, as they are covered by APT and ATC. The only requirement to use HBenchmark is the disposal of a PMS. PMS is the administration system used by an individual hotel to manage different activities in-house, such as bookings, occupancy rate, check-in/check-out, guest profiles. Livigno is an excellence from the point of view of the use of PMS by the hotels (about the 90% of the hotels are provided with PMS), even if the use of PMS by apartments is still far from its potential.

The data we get are partial because only about 30% of hotels of the area participate in at the project. However, achieving full coverage is challenging not only because of the absence of many hotels, but also because the majority of apartments are excluded a priori as they are not equipped with PMS. This is a relevant problem, as APT Livigno is linked with more than 1500 apartments which cannot use the platform and therefore cannot share important information. That is why the partnership between HBenchmark and Livigno could be the opportunity for apartments to adopt a PMS or to find a similar solution. In addition, the partnership would be effective if everyone joins the project to get full data as much close to reality (Interview no. 3, Booking manager APT Livigno).

According to privacy guarantees, APT Livigno cannot see data coming from individual hotels, but only aggregated data of the whole location. In this way, APT Livigno can get and share data that are important to understand the demand trends of the destination as a whole and to study accurate investment strategies over the years while maintaining the hotels' privacy. Another important aspect related to the platform is that, by delivering real-time data, it is possible to monitor if marketing actions have some effect on bookings. With HBenchmark, it is possible to understand right from the first day of an advertising launch if it is getting positive or negative results in terms of conversion rate.

Another aspect that can be gathered by the use of the platform and the elaboration of its data is the identification of weak periods during the year to invest in communication or create an event. These two aspects and many others would be impossible to be caught day by day without the use of an innovative platform as HBenchmark.

Even regarding the use of HBenchmark by the hotels, it is possible to gain several benefits in terms of individual performance improvement, as shown in the quotes below.

An active hotelier who wants to keep up with the times and to invest and improve its business should use an innovative software as HBenchmark (Interview no. 1,

Entrepreneur and hotelier in Livigno & President of Federalberghi in the province of Sondrio).

With a frequent use of the platform, if I see that my prices are higher compared to those of my set of competitors (or compared to those of my category), but I also see that the occupation in Livigno is going to be high, I can promptly lower my prices. Another information I can get from the platform is that, by analysing the demand trends in Livigno, I can better organize the flow of hotel staff (especially in the Covid-19 period) and in this way I can optimize my resources (Interview no. 8, Entrepreneur and hotelier in Livigno & President of Federalberghi in the province of Sondrio).

Also, the use of digital devices such as HBenchmark platform can trigger beneficial effects for societal well-being (e.g. environmental issues).

The communication and promotion activities, both at a territorial level and in contexts such as fairs, is no longer based on paper material but on digital devices, through apps, websites and social network. This change has a considerable effect on the waste of material resources and consequently on pollution. Also, it has spurred an effect on consumers and their requests: nowadays tourists go to info points less and less because they have all the information just a click away much faster than in the past (Interview no. 3, Booking manager APT Livigno).

Despite the benefits for both the tourism public administration and the hoteliers, in the years 2020–2021 there were some problems and interruptions in the implementation of the project in Livigno. Indeed, right after the launch of the project in October 2019, there was a first slowdown in December 2019 for two reasons: first, there was the need to understand if other actors from the province of Sondrio wanted to participate in the project; second, there was the need to explain them the use of the data and the return they could get by sharing their own data. Then, due to COVID-19 pandemic, the project was completely stopped from March 2020 until October 2020, when the official partnership started. The main problem caused by the pandemic is that the stop affecting the tourism sector and all tourists' restraints have cleared data of 2020 and in part of 2021: in particular, data for these 2 years are not stabilized and not comparable with those of the previous years during which structures experienced full capacity.

Unfortunately, the platform is to be explored more as it has not been used as it should have been and as we wanted to (Interview no. 9, Booking manager APT Livigno).

Other problems that hinder the development of the project and the effectiveness of HBenchmark (for those who use it) are linked to resistance from hoteliers for various reasons. In particular, in Livigno, the main resistances in using HBenchmark have to do with privacy, as there is probably a lack of trust in sharing private data. A concern shared by hoteliers is that their competitors could see and exploit their own data, as they do not trust the privacy guarantees provided by HBenchmark itself.

A limit to the use of HBenchmark for BivioLife, which is not currently participating in the project, has to deal with the lack of confidence in privacy guarantees:

BivioLife is a group of four hotels made up of rather large structures (in particular one of the hotels is oversized compared to the Livigno average). The problem would be to deal with much smaller structures. Consequently, if BivioLife participates in the HBenchmark project, the other hoteliers could create a competitive set with themselves and the four structures of BivioLife and go back to the BivioLife data, or at least get an idea of them (Interview no. 7, Marketing Director of BivioLife Livigno).

However, another relevant aspect regarding the privacy of customer data in this era of digital transformation regards the lack of trust in sharing private data:

To respect customers' privacy more and more, and therefore the use of their data, our hotels have been equipped with digital devices, such as document scanners, which automatically save customer personal data in our databases. In this way there is no longer the risk of losing or sending around photocopies or paper documents with their data. Moreover, we have adopted ethical and moral rules within the company according to which, for example, our staff signs a non-disclosure document regarding customer data or make sure to turn off the computers when they finish their work shift so that no external person can access customer data. Other effective ways to pay attention to privacy are the use of multiple passwords to access the data and the saving in servers protected from external attacks (Interview no. 10, Marketing Director of BivioLife Livigno).

Another reason that slows the development of the project in Livigno is the lack of digital devices and software in those few hotels that do not feel the need to equip themselves with tools such as PMS and, consequently, with more developed software such as HBenchmark. However, as stated before, about 90% of hotels in the area use PMS and therefore this problem only minimally affects the success of HBenchmark in Livigno.

A further reason that hinders the complete coverage of the project is the lack of partnership between APT, ATC and hotels. Indeed, about 30 hotels in Livigno are not associated with APT Livigno and therefore cannot take advantage of the free use of the platform.

Livigno is the only destination in the whole Valtellina territory to use HBenchmark platform. There have been attempts to spread its use in other places of the valley, but so far without success. From a tourist point of view, the landscape in Valtellina is very fragmented with different realities, with the province of Sondrio that deals with tourism promotion and communication for the territory as a whole. In the Alta Valtellina Mountain Community, there are three different tourist organizations that manage their own territories: APT Livigno, Bormio Marketing and the Valfurva tourist consortium. The other four Mountain Communities are managed by their respective tourist consortia: Media Valle/Tirano, Sondrio/Valmalenco, Bassa Valle/Morbegno, Valchiavenna. All the data regarding tourist flows in the province of Sondrio are collected by a platform called the Tourist Observatory of the province of Sondrio. This web platform was created to respond to a regulatory need.

In the past years, ISTAT has instructed the Italian regions to collect statistical data relating to annual arrivals and presences on their territory. The Lombardy region, in turn, has entrusted the provinces with the collection and management of data. In the province of Sondrio, there already existed a system (i.e., the platform of the Provincial Tourist Observatory) to collect all the provincial tourist data (Interview no. 5, Director of the Tourist Observatory of the province of Sondrio).

Therefore, the main purpose of the Tourist Observatory of the province of Sondrio is to collect data on hotel and extra-hotel attendance and deal with both public and private entities.

Through the Tourist Observatory platform, it is possible to interact with public administrations, such as the municipalities that want to manage and collect the tourist tax. Also, the platform acts as a bidirectional channel between the province and all the 2600 hotels and non-hotel structures to communicate information such as price lists or changes to the structures (Interview no. 5, Director of the Tourist Observatory of the province of Sondrio).

Tourist Observatory is also used for functions related to tourist flows in the province (for example attendance at events or ski passes), even if there is a specific entity that deals with the communication and promotion of the whole Valtellina in a more customized way. This entity is Valtellina Turismo, a cooperative consortium with a tourism governance model typical of private Destination Management Organizations (DMOs). Valtellina Turismo mainly carries out promotion and communication functions and, to a lesser extent, commercialization at the provincial level. For this reason, HBenchmark platform can be an advanced data analysis tool that, in line with the purposes of Valtellina Turismo, can help the entire Valtellina territory to become a smart destination.

Since the end of 2019, R.G., an entrepreneur in Livigno and president of Federalberghi Sondrio, tried to spread HBenchmark from Livigno throughout the province, without success up to now. This process has been brought forward by training meetings with various entities in the province of Sondrio to spread knowledge about the software and present its functionalities.

The platform HBenchmark would help a reality like Valtellina Turismo to carry out specific marketing actions and to appropriately invest resources. With this software, it would be possible to immediately understand some aspects related to the launch of a communication or marketing campaign: for example, how much it converts in terms of bookings, how much it performs, how certain markets behave in terms of reservation timing (e.g., foreign markets move earlier).

Another aspect for which Valtellina Turismo considers HBenchmark a valid tool is that it allows to understand how many bookings are generated by events.

With the collection of ex-post statistical data, bookings are not clearly attributable to the event itself. That is why a software like HBenchmark can be very useful for our analysis and to predict future trends (Interview no. 4, Project manager of Valtellina Tourism).

A further aspect concerns the relationship with the press:

We often receive requests during the year from journalists who want to know how many tourist presences have been in the various locations or even the expected arrivals for a certain future period. This often happens before or after certain high season periods, for example during Christmas time. To this day, the statistical data—which are collected through direct communications from the hoteliers from the Tourist Observatory—are delayed by a couple of months. With HBenchmark we could know in real time the flows of both past and future bookings (Interview no. 4, Project manager of Valtellina Tourism).

Moreover, HBenchmark would also be an interesting tool for communicating with public administrations and therefore for managing, for example, traffic problems in Valtellina. If the platform was adopted at the provincial level, the police could access the data to better organize resources and increase controls in certain periods and places.

Even if today Valtellina Turismo is not part of the project with HBenchmark, the adoption of the software in the next years has not been excluded. However, the project requires territorial participation:

It would make sense to adopt the platform only with the operational support of all territorial partners, or at least of most of them, to have significant data, otherwise data are not usable (Interview no. 4, Project manager of Valtellina Tourism).

In fact, even though HBenchmark was appreciated by the partners in the presentation phase, several problems, both similar and different from those emerged in Livigno, appeared. Specifically, one of the reasons why HBenchmark cannot be implemented in Valtellina is the lack of digital technologies and software, such as PMS, without which HBenchmark cannot function.

There are different levels of technological evolution of hoteliers. There are some realities like Valmalenco where PMS use is not at all spread, others where PMS is spread a little more but with percentages of 50/60%. One of the first steps to undertake is to deal with the digitalization of hotels and make sure that everyone is equipped with PMS otherwise it doesn't even make sense to adopt a more developed software such as HBenchmark (Interview no. 4, Project manager of Valtellina Tourism).

A further reason that hinders the adoption of the platform is that some very small territories (for example Madesimo) have shown that in their areas there are very few hotels, therefore the use of the platform does not seem to provide, in the short term, useful data for an internal comparison. However, as described in the quote below, these small realities have a chance with HBenchmark to get insights that could be helpful to plan future strategies.

These small territories should have a broader vision and think at the level of Valtellina. In addition to this, smaller territories such as Madesimo could compare itself with other small destinations, such as Aprica or Valmalenco, to understand their pricing policies and their markets, by making comparisons that can still be useful for individual strategies (Interview no. 4, Project manager of Valtellina Tourism).

Also, the development of the platform is challenged by the fact that hotels in various Valtellina destinations, unlike hotels in Livigno for which the costs of platform adoption are sustained by the APT, should bear these costs by themselves (i.e., around to 1000 euros per year, in absence of concessions).

Finally, our findings point to two other challenges that emerged with regards to the adoption of HBenchmark platform, which are similar to the ones emerged in the area of Livigno. First, the concern of hoteliers about data privacy: although HBenchmark ensures data privacy for hotels, many of them still believe that their individual bookings can be traced. Second, some hotels in the territory seem to lack interest in the HBenchmark or are not able to appropriately use and analyse data provided by the platform.

5 Conclusion

5.1 Discussion

The goal of this paper was to understand how firms and related territories leverage digital transformation and which challenges they face in adopting digital solutions. Our findings extend research related to digital transformation, smart cities and smart tourism [4, 5, 15], and provide innovative insights in terms of the benefits and challenges of digital tools as perceived by different stakeholders in the territory [7, 8].

In particular, our exploration of HBenchmark platform in Livigno and Valtellina enabled us to outline the following benefits and barriers to adoption of digital tools. Although Livigno and Valtellina represent different territories (e.g., Valtellina is a large area made up of very heterogeneous tourist realities, different targets and offers, where tourism is not evenly distributed, while Livigno is the leading destination of the territory, accommodating almost half of the total incoming tourists), our findings point to some common benefits that digital tools can provide to their areas. First, they can enable greater awareness for decision makers, through immediate monitoring of marketing actions, quick price adjustment based on occupancy rates, comparison of the performances between different periods and different years, possibility to measure the economic growth and monitor the state of the art of diverse destinations. Second, digital tools may allow to create accurate future predictions, knowing in advance the future booking trends and identifying the best periods for the organization of events. Third, by leveraging digital transformation territories may more appropriately manage their resources, whether monetary in terms of marketing campaign or human in terms of staff management. Finally, digital tools can help destinations to improve relationships and partnerships with various actors, which may be competitors, DMOs, public administrations, journalists and the press.

On the other hand, our investigation also underlines some challenges territories experience in the adoption and development of digital tools. First, we can identify the lack of basic digital infrastructures such as PMS which represents a requirement in order to use the platform. In Livigno about 90% of the hotels are equipped with PMS, while almost all the apartments—which are about 1500—are excluded a priori from the project and therefore from sharing their data. In Valtellina, on the other hand, the technological situation is completely different. Indeed in this territory, there are destinations that do not even use PMS and others where PMS is used, but only up to 50/60%, which is still not enough to exploit the potential of platforms such as HBenchmark. Second, we can consider the lack of trust in sharing private data. Specifically hoteliers, both from Livigno and from Valtellina, are concerned that their individual data can be traced by competitors and by the destination and do not trust the privacy guarantees provided by HBenchmark. Third, some concerns pertain to the lack of partnership and interest in comparing with competitors. In fact, in Livigno, the 30 hotels that are not linked with APT or ATC, the organizations promoting the project, are not interested in having relations with competitors and compare themselves with them. In Valtellina, instead, there are some destinations with very few hotels and for them the use of the platform would not provide useful data for internal comparison. Also, these destinations are probably too small to be interested in comparing themselves with the larger ones. Finally, we can identify the lack of preparation by hotels and destinations in analysing the data they derive from using the platform. Indeed from our interviews it emerged how hoteliers and tourist organizations show different levels of technological evolution, which in turn suggests that, for destinations to become smart, it may be key in the future to engage into ad hoc training activities.

5.2 Potential Solutions and Implications for Policy Makers and Managers

This chapter provides implications and solutions for public actors and managers, both in terms of suggesting the key performance indicators (KPIs) worth monitoring for the digital development of urban areas and territories and of offering insights into how tourism businesses can renew their business models to adapt to continual digital changes.

As the tourism sector is changing, public actors and hotels' decision makers need to be aware of the importance of digitals tools and the use of consolidated data to know in real time the tourist flows as well as current and future market prices. KPIs are more and more essential to analyse the state of health of tourism businesses: they allow the comparison of tourist demand with competitors operating in the territory and the forecast of marketing dimensions (e.g., price) as a function of the demand pressures in specific periods. Therefore, one solution to seize emerging opportunities entails the adoption of technological tools that provide objective data and the implementation of ad hoc training activities to analyse KPIs appropriately to promptly redirect strategic choices.

On the other hand, as a response to the digital revolution and the change in consumer behaviour, public actors and managers have to adapt to these changes by reviewing their business models with a multi-stakeholder perspective. The solution to adapt to continual digital changes can be the implementation of new digital business models, which require the collaboration of multiple functional areas within a firm. The joint work by multiple functional areas leads to more aggregate and optimized results. This allows not only to create synergies, but also to undertake more informed decisions regarding strategic trade-offs related to the use of new technologies, elaboration of Big Data and the collaboration with new partners. Also in the tourism sector, the introduction of digital business models based on platforms allow the integration of different stakeholders' needs and facilitate information exchanges and value co-creation. For this reason, the analysis of how businesses create value for and with their stakeholders is essential for the renewal of business models.

Our paper highlights also that firms have heterogenous approaches to digital transformation according to firm size. This has important policy implications. Indeed, small firms have troubles to embrace digital technologies because of the lack of internal resources, and they may need more external support and collaboration; on the other hand, larger firms—with significant higher internal resources—are more resistant to use external sources of information (such as an external platform like HBenchmark) or collaborate. The implication for policy makers is that such heterogenous approaches may produce a failure in the development of smart destinations because it renders cooperation between stakeholders more difficult, hence specific attention should be devoted in promoting the mutual benefits of collaboration and support between larger and smaller players. For example, large hotels could share their internal data at given conditions (e.g. at more aggregated levels) and support smaller businesses (e.g. by taking charge of a greater part of the cost of HBenchmark), so that overall the smart destination becomes more attractive for a wide array of tourists, with possible spillover effects for different types of accommodation (e.g. good reputation of the location, attraction of hybrid customers). Such heterogeneity in terms of size has important implication for managers. Small hotels' managers should be aware of the need to invest in digital technologies, but also of the need to search for external support and collaboration. Larger firms' managers should be more open to support other firms, especially smaller businesses, as their successful involvement in digital technologies would benefit the whole smart destination and, eventually, also the performance of larger hotels.

5.3 Contributions and Limitations

This study contributes to the broad literature on digital transformation by highlighting how the change is not merely driven by the adoption of digital technologies, but it requires changes for the actors involved [29], both in terms of internal processes and attitude towards new technologies (e.g. how privacy issues are viewed and managed). We contribute specifically to the literature on digital tourism and smart destinations by highlighting the role of different actors [12]. We have provided evidence of the necessity to introduce digital technologies with the support of institutional actors (e.g. tourist promotion agencies), as well as with the leading role of some key private actors (e.g. larger hoteliers). In this sense, our findings confirm that smart tourism development demands the mobilization of a diverse array of stakeholders [30].

In addition, we specifically contribute to smart tourism literature [4, 18]. Extant research has referred to smartness as the combination of effectiveness, environmental consideration, and innovation. In particular, smart destinations are based on technologies which improve tourists' experience [19, 20]. To this literature, this chapter firstly contributes by highlighting the peculiarity of innovation in tourism, that requires the "capacity for heterogeneous organizations and people to interact, to share mutually advantageous objectives, and thus, to exchange information and knowledge using common communication codes" ([31]: 460). In this sense, our research provides evidence of smart tourism being based on "mutually advantageous objectives" related to a wide range of sustainability issues, among which we have emphasised the role of the protection of people's privacy. Secondly, we provide evidence of how digital tools can impact positively on different stakeholders of smart destinations (i.e., hoteliers, destinations), contributing to empirical studies on how smart destinations are backed up by ICT technologies [19].

It is important to acknowledge that, in its current stage, this research presents some limitations. First, it focuses on the specific contexts of Livigno and the territory to which it belongs, Valtellina, without comparing them with other similar territories. Future studies could thus explore different tourist destinations, with other peculiar characteristics—sea, mountain, lake or city—in order to conduct analyses that take into account multiple aspects deriving from diverse environments that may enjoy different levels of technological development. The second limitation has to do with the fact that our investigation focuses on a specific digital tool (i.e., HBenchmark platform) to analyse the development of smart destinations. However, it is possible that some hotels or actors that do not currently adopt HBenchmark, may use other software with similar or different functions. Hence future research may take into account not only multiple destinations but also different digital tools for more in-depth analyses and comparisons.

References

1. Vial, G. (2019). Understanding digital transformation: A review and a research agenda. *The Journal of Strategic Information Systems, 22*, 118–144.
2. Correani, A., De Massis, A., Frattini, F., Petruzzelli, A. M., & Natalicchio, A. (2020). Implementing a digital strategy: Learning from the experience of three digital transformation projects. *California Management Review, 62*(4), 37–56.
3. OECD. (2019). Enhancing the contribution of digitalisation to the smart cities of the future. From https://www.oecd.org/regional/urban-development.htm
4. Dameri, R. P., & Rosenthal-Sabroux, C. (Eds.). (2014). *Smart city: How to create public and economic value with high technology in urban space*. Springer.
5. Li, Y., Hu, C., Huang, C., & Duan, L. (2017). The concept of smart tourism in the context of tourism information services. *Tourism Management, 58*, 293–300.
6. Wang, D., Fesenmaier, D. R., Werthner, H., & Wöber, K. (2010). The journal of information technology & tourism: A content analysis of the past 10 years. *Information Technology & Tourism, 12*(1), 3–16.
7. Baggio, R., Micera, R., & Del Chiappa, G. (2020). Smart tourism destinations: a critical reflection. *Journal of Hospitality and Tourism Technology, 11*(3), 407–423.
8. Sorokina, E., Wang, Y., Fyall, A., Lugosi, P., Torres, E., & Jung, T. (2022). Constructing a smart destination framework: A destination marketing organization perspective. *Journal of Destination Marketing & Management, 23*, 100688.
9. Flick, U. (2004). Triangulation in qualitative research. *A Companion to Qualitative Research, 3*, 178–183.
10. Gioia, D. A., Corley, K. G., & Hamilton, A. L. (2013). Seeking qualitative rigor in inductive research: Notes on the Gioia methodology. *Organizational Research Methods, 16*(1), 15–31.
11. Strauss, A., & Corbin, J. (1998). *Basics of qualitative research techniques*. Sage.

12. Gretzel, U., & de Mendonça, M. C. (2019). Smart destination brands: semiotic analysis of visual and verbal signs. *International Journal of Tourism Cities, 5*, 560–580.
13. Broekhuizen, T. L., Broekhuis, M., Gijsenberg, M. J., & Wieringa, J. E. (2021). Introduction to the special issue—Digital business models: A multi-disciplinary and multi-stakeholder perspective. *Journal of Business Research, 122*, 847–852.
14. Tussyadiah, I. P., & Fesenmaier, D. R. (2009). Mediating tourist experiences: Access to places via shared videos. *Annals of Tourism Research, 36*(1), 24–40.
15. Wang, D., Park, S., & Fesenmaier, D. R. (2012). The role of smartphones in mediating the touristic experience. *Journal of Travel Research, 51*(4), 371–387.
16. Bagnoli, C. (2021). Smart destination. Il nuovo turismo passa dagli algoritmi. From https://www.econopoly.ilsole24ore.com/2021/06/15/turismo-smart-algoritmi/
17. Albino, V., Berardi, U., & Dangelico, R. M. (2015). Smart cities: Definitions, dimensions, performance, and initiatives. *Journal of Urban Technology, 22*(1), 3–21.
18. Buhalis, D., & Amaranggana, A. (2013). Smart tourism destinations. In *Information and communication technologies in tourism 2014* (pp. 553–564). Springer.
19. Femenia-Serra, F., Perles-Ribes, J. F., & Ivars-Baidal, J. A. (2019). Smart destinations and tech-savvy millennial tourists: hype versus reality. *Tourism Review, 74*(1), 63–81.
20. Romao, J., Kourtit, K., Neuts, B., & Nijkamp, P. (2018). The smart city as a common place for tourists and residents: A structural analysis of the determinants of urban attractiveness. *Cities, 78*, 67–75.
21. Gahr, D., Rodríguez, Y., & Hernández-Martín, R. (2014). Smart destinations. The optimisation of tourism destination management. In *Seminario de Economí a Canaria*.
22. Wang, D., & Fesenmaier, D. R. (2013). Transforming the travel experience: The use of smartphones for travel. In *Information and communication technologies in tourism 2013* (pp. 58–69). Springer.
23. Kock, F., Josiassen, A., & Assaf, A. G. (2016). Advancing destination image: The destination content model. *Annals of Tourism Research, 61*, 28–44.
24. Tourist Observatory of the province of Sondrio, Turismo in provincia di Sondrio (2018). Report from https://abit.so.it/.
25. Patton, M. Q. (2002). Two decades of developments in qualitative inquiry: A personal, experiential perspective. *Qualitative Social Work, 1*(3), 261–283.
26. Glaser, B., & Strauss, A. (1967). Grounded theory: The discovery of grounded theory. *Sociology the Journal of the British Sociological Association, 12*(1), 27–49.
27. Grodal, S., Anteby, M., & Holm, A. L. (2020). Achieving rigor in qualitative analysis: The role of active categorization in theory building. *Academy of Management Review, 46*(3), 591–612.
28. Nazarko, J., Anna Kuźmicz, K., Szubzda-Prutis, E., & Urban, J. (2009). The general concept of benchmarking and its application in higher education in Europe. *Higher Education in Europe, 34*(3–4), 497–510.
29. Verhoef, P. C., Broekhuizen, T., Bart, Y., Bhattacharya, A., Dong, J. Q., Fabian, N., & Haenlein, M. (2021). Digital transformation: A multidisciplinary reflection and research agenda. *Journal of Business Research, 122*, 889–901.
30. Presenza, A., Micera, R., Splendiani, S., & Del Chiappa, G. (2014). Stakeholder e-involvement and participatory tourism planning: analysis of an Italian case study. *International Journal of Knowledge-Based Development, 5*(3), 311–328.
31. Pencarelli, T. (2020). The digital revolution in the travel and tourism industry. *Information Technology & Tourism, 22*(3), 455–476.

Digital Transformation and Dysfunctions: Case Study of a Japanese Leading Technology Company, Analysis from Socio-Technical Approach

Soen Hayashi

Abstract The implementation of digital transformation often fails due to organizational issues. This paper aims to analyze the organizational issues of OMRON Corporation (OMRON) in Japan. The theories are Socio-Economic Approach to Management (SEAM) and Socio-Technical Approach (STA). The digital transformation of OMRON was summarized from a socio-technological perspective. The interview was analyzed with the framework of SEAM's "dysfunctions." OMRON has predicted social needs and developed technologies for growing significantly. The findings of interview include bellows dysfunctions and effects. The teammate's work in the department is too fragmented, and there is little communication and coordination between teammates. This may cause a delay in new product development and quality problems later; In introducing new materials, problems often occur among the R&D department, materials procurement department, and quality department. The problems outside organization and supply chain management will occur when quality problems and responsibilities of delivery on suppliers of materials. The social factors of these dysfunctions are the organization is too vertically divided, and sectionalism is strong. In addition, there are few active communication and challenges because no one takes responsibility. The technical factors are the tremendous success of the company's past technological developments, and it isn't very objective toward product development that emphasizes product technology and functions.

Keywords Digital transformation · Socio-economic approach to management · Socio-technical approach

S. Hayashi (✉)
University of Montpellier, Montpellier, France

A. M. Braccini et al. (eds.), *Technologies for Digital Transformation*, Lecture Notes in Information Systems and Organisation 64,
https://doi.org/10.1007/978-3-031-52120-1_11

1 Introduction

Digital transformation has become an essential strategy for companies to achieve sustainable growth. The same is true for start-up companies such as IT and traditional companies such as the manufacturing industry. On the other hand, the success rate of digital transformation is only about 30% [1, 2]. This paper aims to identify what kinds of organizational problems exist, analysis what is the factors and effects in the implementation. The theories are Socio-Economic Approach to Management (SEAM) and Socio-Technical Approach (STA). The research method is a case study of OMRON Corporation (OMRON), a leading technology company in Japan. The history of digital transformation in OMRON was summarized from a socio-technical perspective, and the content of the interview was analyzed with the framework of SEAM's "dysfunctions". From a technical perspective, OMRON develops products and that meets the needs of society and provides solutions that contribute to social development. Focusing on the core technology of sensing and control, the company worked on system development using industrial automation and cybernation technology for the information-oriented society and digitizing products. From a social perspective, OMRON advocates the ideal form of a proper corporate organization, such as the eradication of the 'Big Company Diseases' for organization changing. On the other hand, there are many dysfunctions problems among departments and outside of organizations infield practice [3].

Previous research includes the corporate reform of OMRON [4], organizational reform and global strategy [5]. But no research had done about the organization problem or Socio-Technical Approach.

2 Theories

2.1 SEAM Theory

The theory of Socio-Economic Approach to Management (SEAM) is a research approach from the perspective of socio-economic to organizational development. Since it was first proposed in France in the 1973, it became one of the important management approaches in Europe and USA by accumulating practices in the development of many companies and sectors [6]. The development of corporate organizations centered on North America and organizational reforms through digital transformation were mainly analyzed from a financial perspective, but human factors were rarely considered. SEAM, on the other hand, is a management tool that can be evaluated more comprehensively with an approach from both financial and human aspects [7, 8]. SEAM was mainly applied practically in the healthcare and nursing sector at the beginning, then it has also been also applied to general companies in commercial fields. SEAM is an important research tool because digital transformation requires multifaceted evaluation on its implementation. Using SEAM's framework of "dysfunctions", it causes "hidden costs" which do not appear directly in accounting or books but ultimately affect the company's financial outcomes [6].

2.2 STA Theory

The "Socio-Technical Approach to System Information" (STA) is an approach perspective that requires consideration of social and technical aspects in the implementation of IT and system information [9]. STA suggests that human and technical behavior is oriented in a coherent and interactive manner. It also proposes that any change in technological behavior will also affect work-related social relationships, feelings, and attitudes along with its effects on the success or failure of new technological behavior. Technological interventions and development in the already existing organizational system is one of the most difficult tasks due to the fact that organizations are profoundly affected by technological advancements and require a flexible customized change model which aligns with a social network of the organization.

3 Research Method

The research method is a case study, which includes interviews representatives from each department of OMRON, analyzes the content using SEAM's dysfunction framework and finds problems within and between organizations. Interviewees: 15 representatives from 9 departments. Table 1 shows the subjects' departments, positions, and interview items. The interviewees were selected from those who frequently interact with other departments and organizations. From a social point of view, status and class are not restricted. People within the organization are independent of rank or position, and all personnel are considered "actors" representing different departments [3].

4 Case Study: Digital Transformation and Business Reforms of OMRON

OMRON is a Hi-tech company founded in Japan in 1933 and has grown with sensing and control as its core technology. Currently, there are four Business Companies: Industrial Automation Business, Electronic and Mechanical Components (EMC), and Healthcare Business, and Social Solutions and Service Business. Before the words such as IT, IoT, and digital transformation came out, the company had already provided products and solutions that meet the needs of society through

Table 1 The department and position of interviewees and the questions list (edited by author)

No.	Department	Position	Interview questions:
1	R&D	Director	(1) What's the relation between corporate digital transformation and your department and daily works. (2) What are the good points and bad points of the implement of digital transformation? (3) What are the issues in communication between organizations and departments? (4) What are the issues for promoting project or daily communication? (5) What's your requests for improvement in digital transformation
2	R&D	Manager	
3	R&D	Group Leader	
4	R&D	Technical Engineer	
5	Product management	Manager	
6	Product management	PIC	
7	Procurement	Group Leader	
8	SCM	Group Leader	
9	Quality control	Assistant Manager	
10	Quality control	Assistant Manager	
11	Production technology	Manager	
12	Production technology	Group Leader	
13	Product sales	Senior Leader	
14	Package design	Senior Leader	
15	Cloud platform	Adviser	

commercialization strategies such as automation and cybernation and by digitizing in each of these fields. In addition to these core technologies, OMRON is also a company that has contributed significantly to the ideal organizational development. Those will be summarized as follows.

4.1 SINIC Theory: The Compass for Corporate Development

SINIC Theory (Seed-Innovation to Need-impetus Cyclic Evolution) is a compass for OMRON to predict the future developing. OMRON first announced this predictive theory to the world at the International Future Research World Congress in 1970 by the founder, Kazuma Tateishi. It was believed that solving social issues through business to create a better society, based on the cycle of interrelationships among Science, Technology and Society. Taking the Cybernation Society as an example, OMRON predicted the rise of cybernetics, computer science, and the other automation technologies in 1940s. Those became the seeds of electronic control technologies, sensing/programming and automation machine. Core business and product of OMRON were developed by the prediction of social needs based on SINIC Theory.

4.2 The Concept of 'Big Company Diseases'

OMRON also made a significant contribution on organizational issue is known as 'Big Company Diseases' or 'Big Business Syndrome' (BCD in this paper). The founder on OMRON, Kazuma Tateishi, recognized this syndrome in 1983. He found the company was in a decline state during the process of expanding its organization and growing into a large company with the success of its business. The communication and distance between top management and frontline become far away that causes the delay of understanding the situation and decision making. And the workers avoid challenges for fear of risk, which causes the lack of venture spirit and entrepreneur spirit. The BCD is not only problem in Japanese company. It's an international problem as IBM, GM also warned as those companies grow to be big.

4.3 OMRON's Business Reform

OMRON implemented three business structures reform in 1998 to recover profits [4]. The first is the reform of the management structure, which introduced a Business Company System and an executive officer system. The second is the business structure reform, which sold four unprofitable businesses. The third is carrying out structural reforms of fixed costs and reduced the number of employees of group companies. Through these reforms, the organizational functions were reconstructed, and all business units accelerated the spin-off of strategic management units. In addition, at the individual level, it aimed a shift from "manufacturing human resources" in the mass production era to "creative human resources" that provide high value-added products and services.

4.4 The Implementing Digital Transformation of OMRON

OMRON has introduced SAP, a platform that all employees can share all information of company operation; PLUS (Parts Library for strategic Use), a parts information system for material purchasing; and ELITE system, in which VMI can be shared with suppliers; G-HRMS (Global human resource management system) can visualize the human resources registration, skills, and work history of the entire group company and can play an active role in job rotation.

5 Analysis of the Interviews

Socio-Economic Institute of Firms and Organizations Research (ISEOR) has good model to classify the dysfunctions. The classification framework of dysfunctions has been modified as bellow for this research (Table 2).

The current issues of organizational dysfunctions from the interviews can be summarized as follows in the order of the above categories.

5.1 Problems of Communication and Teamwork Within the Department

When developing a new product, a team is formed such as product manager, team leader, in charge of hardware in product structural design, in charge of software and IT. The work role of each team is too fragmented, and there is little coordination between teammates. Due to the lack of information sharing and communication, the development schedule of new products may be delayed. It takes time when involving other members and departments in some problems happen. So people may not want to launch the problem in early stage. It may miss the time to solve the problem and later develop into a bigger problem. If the upper management does not launch the subordinates' problems, the progress status cannot be known, and the final decision cannot be made. For example, in the production management department adjusts the production schedule, respond to increased production. They may put pressure on the supplier's factory to respond. If there is no report or consultation on the problem with the boss, the supplier cannot meet the expected delivery date. As

Table 2 Modified by author based on ISEOR model of dysfunctions

Dysfunctions	Sub-categories
Communication/Coordination/Cooperation	1. Cross-department 2. With third parties/outside of organization 3. Vertical communication/coordination 4. Horizontal communication/coordination
Time management	1. Deadline compliance 2. Activity scheduling 3. Task achievement improvement
Work condition	1. Work hours and schedule 2. Physical work conditions
Work organization	1. Distributions of tasks, missions 2. Work motivation 3. Job autonomy
Strategy implementation	1. Corporate strategy linkages 2. Information systems improvement 3. HR management improvement

a result, it is necessary to pursue who is responsible and in what process the problem occurred as the beginning.

5.2 *Problems of Coordination and Cooperation Between Departments*

In the process of introducing new materials and components, problems often occur between R&D department, production management department, and materials procurement departments. The incentive for introduction new material emphasize on cost advantages. In many cases, the R&D department is involved in the initial development of new materials. Then the purchasing department comes into play in evaluating the probability and cost advantages. In addition, the quality department will appear in the final quality audit and assessment. In the long process, every department needs to cooperate, but oversight and communication do not go well sometimes. It becomes a significant quality problem after using. If that becomes a big issue, there will be an argument about which department is responsible for approval and how to deal with the loss. Many departments gather or hold meetings and discussions. In many cases, a massive amount of materials and time are spent for meeting. Especially in the Hanko (seal) culture of Japanese companies, the approval of each department manager is required. Then explanation is required in advance, and it often takes time.

5.3 *Outside of Organization Issues and Supply Chain Management*

OMRON, which makes finished products, has many suppliers in supply chain. Omron has its own factories, but there are also cases using OEM contractors for outsourcing. It will take a long process from new product development to mass production. In the case of using own factory, there are design review meetings and approval work in the process. These processes are cumbersome and require extensive explanation and evidence submission. These processes are often a major stumbling block in the cry for digital transformation. For development engineers, they sometimes prefer to outsource to an OEM because it simplifies the process and responds flexibly. At the mass production stage, the production control department and quality control department will be added into the new project. But if there is a possibility or responsibility for any problems in manufacturing or delivery, it may be imposed on the supplier or OEM contractor. Besides, the quest of QCD (quality, cost, delivery) is required too much, and the demand for shortening delivery lead time and cost down is very strict. Especially when delivery problems or quality problems occur, PICs are often pushed to suppliers and OEMs. On the other hand, even if the task content can be outsourced, but the contract cost will be high if it is outsourced, so the task will be kept in internal staff in many cases. As a result, the overtime work of internal staff increases, sticking to non-value-added task. It may be inefficient.

5.4 Many New Product Developments Are Carried Out Every Year, but Often There Are Too Much Emphasized on Technologies and Functions

As a result, the products developed may not have significant features change or may be too expensive for getting much market share. It can be said that the technology and products have been recognized and grown because the products have been developed and grown into a large company over a long period of time. Pulled by the success dilemma of the past, there are few new challenges in technology and products. Also, if someone makes a mistake or failure, the person may be transferred to another department or demoted. Therefore valuable lessons of failure will not be applied to the following product or next team members. No department takes responsibility or risk, so the new product will be without any breakthroughs or innovative. It may become a bottleneck in new fields and business growth in the future.

5.5 In Terms of Organizational Structure, There Are Many Middle Management Layers in Each Department

They are strongly stable-minded and choose safe ideas. When deciding something, the concept of group action and team thinking is deep-rooted. Many meetings are held, but there is usually no decision-maker. Many people are reluctant to stay in middle management because they make more decisions and become more responsible when they are promoted to a higher position. As a result, the organization is filled with many middle management positions. This will form an atmosphere in which everyone does not want to cause many problems in the surrounding mood.

6 Discussion

With its SINIC theory, OMRON has developed the company with innovative technology and product development by identifying the fundamental needs of society and significant development directions. With the core technology of Sensing & Control +Thinking, the company is releasing products that contribute to social solutions and the digitization for other companies. It is truly a leading global technology company expanding in four business domains. OMRON also actively engaged in structural reforms and digital transformations for the company's growth. Furthermore, the company identified the "Big Company Disease," and clarified the relationship that a company is a public nature of society. Those leaved a significant benchmark for organization development. On the other hand, as analyzed the interview contents with the framework of 'dysfunctions', there are many problems on cross-department communication and vertical hierarchical reporting within the department. Barriers to communication between departments are also a manifestation of sectionalism. As the organization grows to be big, the division and working role for each person in charge, and communication barriers are likely to be created. In addition, there is no information sharing or reporting to superiors within the department, and it lacks the agility of decision-making. Or the problem is often postponed without being resolved. If the situation gets worse and you try to get it back, it will take longer, increasing the loss. The social factors of these dysfunctions are that the company is structurally too stable, the vertical division of labor progresses, and it tends to become sectionalism. In addition, there are many middle managers, and they tend to seek stability in their thinking and actions. Even if there is a problem, there is a strong tendency not to make it an issue. These also affect employee behavior patterns. In order not to take risks and not seek change, the group orientation becomes more vital than the individual as an individual action pattern. Even if there is any meeting, many members will gather, and the responsibility will be unknown, or the solution will be postponed. Regarding these social factors, it is necessary to regain the venture spirit and entrepreneurial spirit from the stability consciousness, remove the stability consciousness in large companies, and regain the venture spirit and entrepreneurial spirit by company and business division. There is. Rather than settling in a large company or stable organization, it is necessary to continue transforming the organization in line with the ever-developing society of IT and digital transformation. Regarding technical factors, the success of the company's past technological developments is excellent, and it isn't very objective toward product development that emphasizes product technology and functions, and these opinions become stronger. Regarding the technical elements, it is necessary to involve the development and technology thoughts and the marketing department, etc., to shift to solution thinking for the needs and problems in the market. The product hardware of the past has developed it. Still, with the penetration of digital transformation in the future, the development of this software will make it more and more essential to propose solutions that solve the needs of further customers. There is a movement to co-create with others, a technology company that identifies these actual needs and provides solutions to society using digital transformation. Still, it is necessary to take measures against significant corporate diseases due to social factors.

7 Result

The above discussion results can summarize the problem of organizational dysfunction in the implementation of digital transformation at OMRON into the following social and technical factors.

7.1 Social Factors

The social factors of these dysfunctions are the organization is too vertically divided, and sectionalism is strong. In addition, there are few active communication and challenges because no one takes responsibility and fears failure. There is a tendency for everyone to seek safety because the company is too stable and relies on it, and structurally there are too many middle management layers. Proposals for improving these problems require that social factors remove the stability consciousness of large companies and regain the venture spirit and entrepreneurial spirit of each company and business division.

7.2 Technical Factors

The technical factors are the tremendous success of the company's past technological developments, and it isn't very objective toward product development that emphasizes product technology and functions. As a result, the product cost becomes too high, the product cannot be sold, and the sales share is reduced. Regarding technical elements, it is necessary to involve development and technology thoughts and marketing departments, and shift to solution thinking for market needs and problems. The above analysis and findings can be summarized in Table 3.

8 Conclusion

This paper aims to analyze organizational issues of OMRON in digital transformation. The Theory of Socio-Economic Approach to Management and Socio-Technical Approach are used for analysis. The interview was analyzed with the framework of SEAM's dysfunction. The findings of this research identify many problems within and between organizations and departments as follows.

1. Teamwork and communication problems within the department: The teammate's work is too fragmented, and there is little communication and coordination between them. This causes a delay in new product development and quality problems later. Also, delays in reporting to superiors in the production

Table 3 The factors and effects of dysfunctions in this research (edited by author)

	Factors	Dysfunctions	Effect/Hidden costs
Social	– Big organization – No drastic changing – Obvious job role – Too stable in the organization – Too many middle management – Focus on humanity	– Less communication/ coordination among departments – Sectionalism – No much on problem report/ discussing – No will to take risk or responsibility – No eager for promotion	– Delay of new project – Problems extended to be solved – Loss by problems unsolved – Waste of time for long meeting and large members – Over time working
Technical	– Hi-technology – Strong experience on success in the past – Huge organization and many business division – Long supply chain – Too many IoT, IT department	– Unclear responsibility of quality and delivery problem with supplier and OEMs – Poor supply chain management – No will to take risks	– Damages on relationship with suppliers – Externalization of disadvantages – No breakthrough on new technology – Less innovation

management department will significantly develop issues such as delivery delay problems.

2. Problems of coordination and cooperation between departments: In the process of introducing new materials, problems often occur between the development department, production management department, and materials procurement department. The responsibility is always unclear when a quality problem occurs, and the loss is enormous. No department wants to take the risk or responsibility, so the meeting members always become large, and the approval process becomes long. But problems remain unsolved.
3. Out-of-organization problems and supply chain management: Department may impose quality problems and responsibilities to suppliers and OEMs. For example, OMRON requests a strict demand for shortening the lead time and reduces cost. Especially when delivery problems or quality problems occur, they are often pushed to suppliers and OEMs, too.

The social factors of dysfunctions can be found that the organization is too vertically divided, and sectionalism is strong. Everyone tend to seek in safety way because no one want to take responsibility and fears failure. There are too many middle management layers in company structure. The technical factors are the tremendous success of the company's technological developments in the past, and it was not very objective toward product development that emphasizes product technology and function. Proposals for improving these problems require that social factors remove the stability consciousness of large companies and regain the venture spirit and entrepreneurial spirit of each business division. Regarding technical factors, it is necessary to involve development and technology thoughts with marketing department, and shift to solution thinking for market needs.

The limitation of this study is necessary to deepen the analysis of relevant between dysfunctions and hidden costs. The further research will be more interviews with the front line of every department, and make clearer if the organizational problems are caused by the Big Company Diseases or by dysfunctions of digital transformation.

The contribution to theory is applying SEAM and STA theories to clarify the organizational problem in this research. The contribution to practice is analyzing the factor of dysfunction and impact of implementing IT and data technologies.

References

1. BCG. (2020). *A digital strategy roadmap to drive transformation.* https://www.bcg.com/capabilities/digital-technology-data/digital-strategy-roadmap#collapsible%2D%2D1
2. IDC Japan. (2017). Japan IT market 2018 top 10 predictions: The transformation of digital native company. https://www.idcjapan.co.jp/Report/Top10_Predictions/jpj43163817.html
3. Ikeda, K., & Numada, Y. (2021). A study on digital transformation and organizational communication. Tokaigakuen University Repository, 26, 2021.
4. Imaguchi, T., Ri, S., Shin,M., & Nozaka, M. 2005. Restructuring of Business and Organization, Personel and Procurment(II), Mita Business Research, 48(4): 47-69
5. Ri, S. (2020). Reconstruct the Process of Organization Functions in Multi-National Enterprises. *Modern Management and Economy Study*,110-140.
6. Savall, H., & Zardet, V. (2008). Mastering hidden costs and socio-economic performance. Information Age Publishing.
7. Conbere, J., & Heorihiadi, A. (2011). Socio-economic approach to management. Organization Development Practitioner, 43(1), 6–10.
8. Conbere, J., Heorihiadi, A., & Cristallini, V. (2012). The key to SEAM's effectiveness, the ISEOR-AOM conference, *Lyon, France June*, 10 2012.
9. Kling, B., & Lamb, R., (1999). IT and Organizational Change in Digital Economies: A Social-Technical Aprroach. *Computers and Society*, 17–25.

Digitalization, Online Services, and Entrepreneurial Environment in the Italian Smart Cities' Transition

Filippo Marchesani and Federica Ceci

Abstract Cities are facing increased dynamism due to rapid technological development, digitalization, and citizens' requirements, creating novel opportunities for smart city transformation. If, until a few years ago, the city's development from a smart perspective was an opportunity, today, it has assumed a predominant character on a social and economic level. This study investigates the evolution of the online service implementation in cities over the years and its impact on the entrepreneurial environment. Using panel data based on 20 Italian cities for 11 years period ranging from 2011 to January 2022, this paper evaluates the online services' evolution and implementation using cluster analysis to identify two clusters (cities in transition and developed). Moreover, we performed a predictive validity analysis to identify the relationship between the clusters and the entrepreneurial environment. The results show that, at the emergent stage of the digitalization process, the development of the city's smartness was important to have an advantage over other cities; today, the implementation of smart city services is essential to create a favourable local environment for the development of entrepreneurial opportunities.

Keywords Smart City · Digitalization · Online services

1 Introduction

The current relationship between a city and its citizens is considered central to the essence of smart cities. Smart cities' implementation seeks to digitally interconnect and combine services within a city to provide efficient services by increasing efficiency and sustainability of the city [1]. In the transition toward smart cities, cities will be more user-friendly as the functions are improved through digitalization [2].

F. Marchesani (✉) · F. Ceci
University of "G. d'Annunzio" Chieti – Pescara, Pescara, Italy
e-mail: filippo.marchesani@unich.it; f.ceci@unich.it

A. M. Braccini et al. (eds.), *Technologies for Digital Transformation*, Lecture Notes in Information Systems and Organisation 64,
https://doi.org/10.1007/978-3-031-52120-1_12

In implementing this transformation, cities make use of digital technologies such as information communication and technologies (ICTs), Internet of Things (IoT) and Artificial Intelligence (AI) to build platforms and information infrastructure and to collect (and share) data with internal and external stakeholder [3–5]. Given the pervasive diffusion of digital technologies, the digitalization process of cities has become mandatory on the public agenda in the coming years.

The digital approach to smart city implementation focuses mainly on implementing and developing services for the cities' users, such as citizens and firms [6]. This connection generates a linkage between the development trajectories of cities and the local environment. Furthermore, the development of cities from a smart perspective, combined with the cities' worldwide competition in terms of human and financial capital, innovation and tourism [7, 8], has led the development of these practices to be considered fundamental in the cities' development at the local and global level [9].

Considering the Italian context, cities' digital transformation and digitalization have enhanced their impact in the recent decade [10]. However, this recent trend makes it difficult to produce a comprehensive analysis. Furthermore, although there is a large body of theoretical contributions focusing on the smart implementation in cities [9, 11], there is still no common framework to assess the smart implementation in cities and its influence on the local economic and environmental context. Thus, this paper will analyze the digital advancement in Italy (a country fully committed to smart urban policies) by considering a sample of 20 cities clustered into 2 groups: cities "in transition" and cities "advanced". To assess the digital advancement over the years in cities, we construct a dataset that includes a sample of 10 cities. For each city, we consider the number of online services offered by the municipality to the different city actors, i.e., tourists, firms and citizens.

Our level of analysis is city-level; this allows us to systematically analyze this phenomenon and consider differences in the implementation of the smart city model according to different cities' sizes and geographical areas. Building on an original dataset described above, we aim to answer the following research questions: "How is the smart cities transition taking place in Italy over the last decade" and "what is the relation between the smart city transition and the entrepreneurial environment?"

In order to do so, we will investigate the evolution of online services offered by municipalities over the years and how this evolution has impacted Italian cities by changing their scenarios and trajectories. Furthermore, we will explore the relationship between the development of smart city services and the city's business environment.

The paper is organized as follows. The second section provides a brief literature review by considering the influence of digital advancement in cities and its relationship with the economic environment and smart city implementation; in the third section, we describe our research methodology. In the four-section, we discuss our results and their significance. Finally, in the last section, we present the conclusions of the study, limitations, and future avenues.

2 Literature Review

The smart city's implementation and advancement attracted relevant attention over the past decades [10, 12, 13]. To understand this concept is important to understand the role played by the cities in society and consider them as an influent element for the future. Today, cities play a key role in the social and economic aspects worldwide and have a huge impact on the environment as they are able to attract a large flow of people [14], companies [15] and tourists [16] by offering an ad-hoc scenario based on their needs and objectives.

At the same time, the existing scenario requires cities to reshape their trajectories to manage new challenges properly [10]. Thus, throughout the "smart" cities implementation, cities have started to advance solutions which influence users and stakeholders, aiming to have long-term positive effects on the economy and urban landscape [13]. For instance, technological advancement in cities and citizens-centric policies respond to cities' development needs and linking digital advancement with its users is considered a key element for city growth [17, 18]. Therefore, ICT, IoT and AI are a (non-mandatory) part of cities' transformation process and directly impact cities' development trajectories [19].

2.1 Smart City and Digital Advance

Today, cities are changing their relationship with stakeholders by offering an increasingly dynamic and competitive environment capable of responding quickly to the needs of society [20]. This transformation takes advantage of the preponderant impact of technological advancement and digitalization that reshapes services and offers new development models.

Following the definition proposed by Bakici [21], smart cities are considered high-tech intensive and advanced cities that connect people, information and city elements using new technologies to create a sustainable, greener city, competitive and innovative commerce, and increased life quality. The implementation of technology and technological advancement has made it possible to reorganize urban architecture to become efficient, sustainable and perform in the urban context. This evolution allows you to interact in time with your users and stakeholders, obtaining the necessary information and creating a user-friendly environment. Furthermore, this transformation has allowed cities to become a container capable of supporting entrepreneurs, citizens and tourists by placing them at the centre of the city's development trajectories [19, 22]. Specifically, based on a user-centric approach, digitalization in cities aims to enhance the engagement of citizens and communities [23].

Specifically, numerous cities made important investments to provide extensive and proactive online services, and interest began to be identified in the factors determining the users' reactions to and the use of smart services in the urban area [24, 25]. However, these investments modify the relationship between users and cities.

Consequently, the online services propose a more user-oriented approach, where the citizen must be positioned at the centre of the development and the transformation of electronic public services [4].

The cities' digitalization focuses on developing online services for different city actors, including institutions, firms, and citizens, on providing services to improve citizens' quality of life and the city's competitiveness [26]. Although today the role of technology is predominant in our society, online services, ICT applications, implementation of the IoT in cities and innovative technologies have been often underutilized [27]. This topic has grown in importance in light of recent developments in the quality of information, services and systems using digital technologies [9]. This need has led cities to reorganize and modify their services to respond quickly and efficiently. For example, Barcelona is acknowledged as successfully developing an ecosystem where urban development, digital services and quality of life pursue policies that benefit the local dynamics of innovation [28, p. 269].

At the same time, smart city discourses in Italy support the construction of a new urban identity, functioning as a discipline mechanism that can be defined as a 'Smartmentality [10]'. In those scenarios, smart cities consider a specific model of a technologically advanced, sustainable and economically attractive city, while 'diverse' cities, those following different development paths, are implicitly reframed as smart-deviant [10, p. 889]. The difference between being a smart city or not being smart leads to obvious local influence. In Italy, the smart city implementation faced cut-throat competition in creative solutions to people's problems and obtaining national and European funding [29–31]. This transformation has created the need to modify one's practices to adapt to an increasingly competitive context [32].

In this transformation, Italy represents an interesting case in the relationship between technological development and the geographical environment [9, 10]. Although, to date, there are still regional disparities between north and south, the development of smart cities over the years appears to play a normalizing role. Specifically, the development of the smart city project in Italy has started and coincided with the transformation taking place in the north's main cities [10, 33]; the south has been reducing this gap over the years by developing projects aimed at elevating the urban context in a smart perspective [34, 35].

For example, cities like Naples and Caserta represent metropolitan areas that implement smartness and smart services as an urban policy paradigm. Those online services and smart actions have targeted young people across Naples. While the initial project focuses on the economic development around users and firms, the long-term objectives involve nurturing a "local information society" by creating and promoting digital knowledge in its users [34, p. 216].

Thus, since digitalization in cities bears the potential to help cities to move into a new competitive and technological advanced scenario useful to embrace sustainable and efficient practices [19, 36], in this study, we explore how the evolution of smart cities' services offerings is taking place in Italy in the last decade.

2.2 Digitalization and Entrepreneurial Environment

Digital development in cities has always influenced the social and business environment. Today, through the use of ICT, AI, and IoT, governments aim to consider the information they collect from citizens, firms, entrepreneurs, and startups to provide public and private services more efficiently and sustainably [7, 26, 37]. This evolution aims to promote the development of a local system of innovation and entrepreneurship through the collaboration of various local programs, where different actors in the ecosystem, such as citizens, entrepreneurs, startups and universities, interact to generate synergies and urban advancement [38, p. 144].

This synergy increased the relationship between the city's urban and economic development. Specifically, recent trends in urban literature have demonstrated that certain features of city policies in terms of innovation and technological advancements influence the supply and demand for entrepreneurship, thus shifting the equilibrium level of local entrepreneurship [39, p. 3]. This influence led to important determinants of local entrepreneurship. For example, large cities or urban clusters often influence developing economic activities and create a more advanced economic environment [40, 41]. At the same time, the development and digitization of cities reduce the gap between small/medium and large cities by offering a technological environment suitable for developing entrepreneurial activities and innovative firms, as well as promoting and attracting knowledge in the city [42].

Therefore, the development and implementation of online services increasingly customized to the needs of stakeholders will play a fundamental role in the urban landscape of cities. However, the entrepreneurial geography highlight that the clustering of entrepreneurial tech startups tends to be across a relatively small set of global cities and metro areas [43]. Previously, considering the geographical level, only a limited sample of cities could provide more of the key inputs, like online services, technological advancement, innovative policy and a smart environment useful to offer a diverse array of services to end-user such as entrepreneurs and companies that are strongly connected for their innovative and entrepreneurial activities [4, 9, 44].

This gap has been reduced over the years; cities are evolving into a smart perspective over the years. This evolution is mainly present in cities that have started their digitalization process, and technological advancement affects the entrepreneurial environment [45]. Transforming cities is not only a consequence of the demographic shifts associated with the mass urban migration but also of the ability of cities to adapt by exploiting opportunities and available resources, adapting them to an increasingly competitive context [21, 34, 46]. Today, cities are becoming a container for innovation and entrepreneurial opportunities. The change of recent years, combined with the reorganization of cities in the last decade, allows us to raise the smart city vision in a much broader and more efficient context than the cities, metropolises, and megalopolises considering the business environment. Following this process, digitalization in cities works as a "driver of innovation". The technological advancements in cities are converging paradigms helping to drive entrepreneurship and innovation in urban areas worldwide [47, p. 5].

Despite this growing trend about the relationship between entrepreneurship, innovation and smart cities concerning the role of digitalization, there is still a gap in the scientific relevance of the matter. The literature on that relationship is still embryonic, and the current research results are mainly theoretical.

3 Methodology

3.1 Sample and Variable Description

Cities are increasingly providing smart services for their users, and this caused a proliferation of technological implementation. This led to profound structural change in cities, modifying at the same time the provision of services and the relationship with users. However, the technological transition toward a smarter city follows different paths and routes according to the plethora of indicators and tools useful to advance this comprehensive phenomenon. To evaluate the smart services advancement in cities, we collected data on a sample of 20 Italian cities over 11 years (2011–January 2022). Italy represents an ideal context to study the development of smart cities as it is widely treated in academic literature in terms of technological development [48] and smart city implementation [10].

The choice of this sample is motivated by the following two reasons. Firstly, the sample of Italian cities is equally distributed on the Italian territory. Therefore, to statistically assess the sample's representativeness and guarantee the sample's heterogeneity, we applied probability-proportional-to-size sampling [49]. Moreover, to consider the economic development of each stratum, we based on the European Commission distinction. This distinction considers the GDP as an economic measure in each city by assessing less-economic developed (<20,000 € per capita), medium development (20,000 € to 40,000) and high development cities (<40,000 €). Secondly, it relates to the homogeneity of the identified variables within each city, reducing the risk of inferences or distortions of the data.

Based on these criteria, we identified 20 Italian cities for analysis. We constructed an original database as follows: data has been collected using the "*Wayback Machine*" website (https://archive.org), which allowed us to collect and record backwards online services offered by the municipalities from 2011 to 1 January 2022 throughout the following procedure. Based on the official website of the cities, we (1) identified the online services proposed by the cities, (2) considered and computed the total number of online services proposed by thematic areas each year (3) carried out the same procedure backwards in previous years using the previously indicated website.

The variables construction is based on the number of services each city offers in the various categories (i.e. online tourism considers services related to public events, tourist information requests, renting public spaces for events …) proposed by the city in the specific section of its website. Therefore, most of the services were naturally grouped on the site of each city. However, when this grouping was not present on the website, we distributed the services present in proportion to the sample analyzed.

This data evaluation and retrieval process led to the creation of 10 variables used in the city evaluation process (see Table 1).

Today, scholars and practitioners highlight the role of digitalization and technological advancement in cities [9], as well as the prominent role of digital technologies in the relationship between cities and stakeholders [4]; however, there is still no well-accepted definition of the variables in literature to explain this phenomenon, given the multidisciplinary and the still embryonic development of the phenomenon [13]. Thus, in this study, we focus on the relationship between the digital development of cities and stakeholders by considering specific cities' online services, such as Taxes, School, Electoral, Tourism, Urbanistic, House, Innovation, Firms, Culture, and Sports.

As shown in Fig. 1, the implementation of those online services has been spread over the last decades. Today, a large set of online services are concentrated into the *Online Schools, Online Taxes, Online Urban Environment* and *Online Electoral*, which aim to simplify the bureaucracy for citizens, offer intuitive services and respond promptly to citizens' needs. Those constant evolutions over the years had an impact on the relationship between the city and citizens by improving not only the service offered but also reducing waiting times [17] by producing services more efficient and in line with the current technological development [46].

Table 1 Variables description

Variable	Description
Online taxes	Taxes and duties (Fines, Tari, Catering, IMU, Tasi etc.
Online school	Educational services (Scholarships, schools, books, Conventions etc.
Online electoral	Certification, declarations, corrections, certifications etc.
Online tourism	Accommodation, events, public spaces, tourist activities etc.
Online urban environment	Work in progress, traffic, public land, special services etc.
Online house	Social housing, rental support, requests, certifications, amnesty, SUE, GEBAC etc.
Online innovation	Wi-Fi, innovation calls, Smart city, IT equipment sale, call for digitalization etc.
Online culture	Cinema, Libraries, Events, Updated program calendar, cultural events etc.
Online firms	SUAP, Calls, Funds, Youth Entrepreneurship etc.
Online sport	Sports events, tickets, charity marathons, renting, Baby Camps etc.

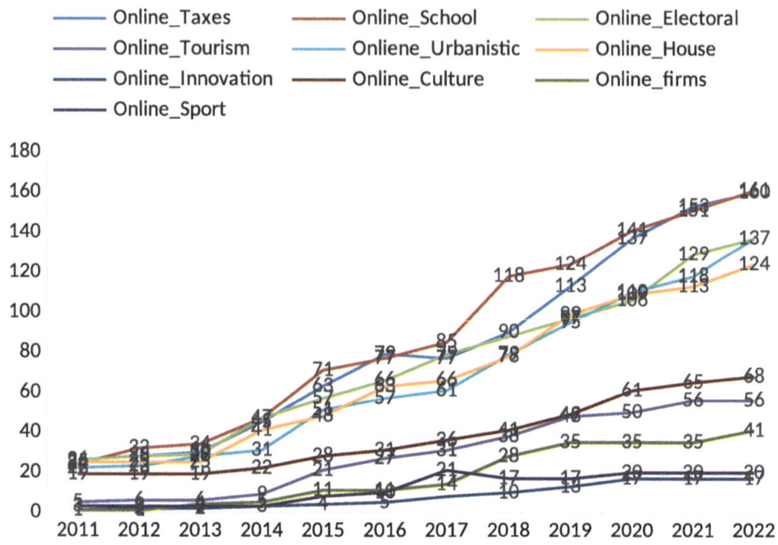

Fig. 1 Variables description

3.2 *Analytical Approach*

To assess the development of smart city online services and to investigate how cities introduced and implemented online services over the years, we performed cluster analysis, which aims to cluster cities according to the online services development in two different stages: initial stage (2012) and current situation (2022). Using cluster analysis, we aim to identify groups of cities similar to one another in relation to a large set of online services over the years. Furthermore, this process aims to integrate heterogeneous units in several levels of clusters that tend to be both homogeneous in terms of internal characteristics and mutually comprehensive. In other words, we divided our sample into a limited number of clusters according to the level of "similarity" based on the implementation and development of online services over the years.

Thus, we performed a hierarchical cluster analysis to highlight the evolution in Italy in the last decade, the characteristics of the cities, and how they have changed their trajectories according to different development strategies and policies. In addition, cluster analysis provides a tool to visualize the data structure through a dendrogram (see Figs. 2 and 3), highlighting two different clusters expressing two distinct levels of development in 2012 and 2022.

To assess this analytical approach's robustness and validity, we test the statistical significance of the configurations by performing a series of one-way comparisons. Moreover, using the Kruskal-Wallis equality-of-populations rank, we test the configuration among clusters using the discriminating variables.

Finally, to assess the external validity of the proposed configurations, we associate the clusters with four economic indicators that act as a proxy for the

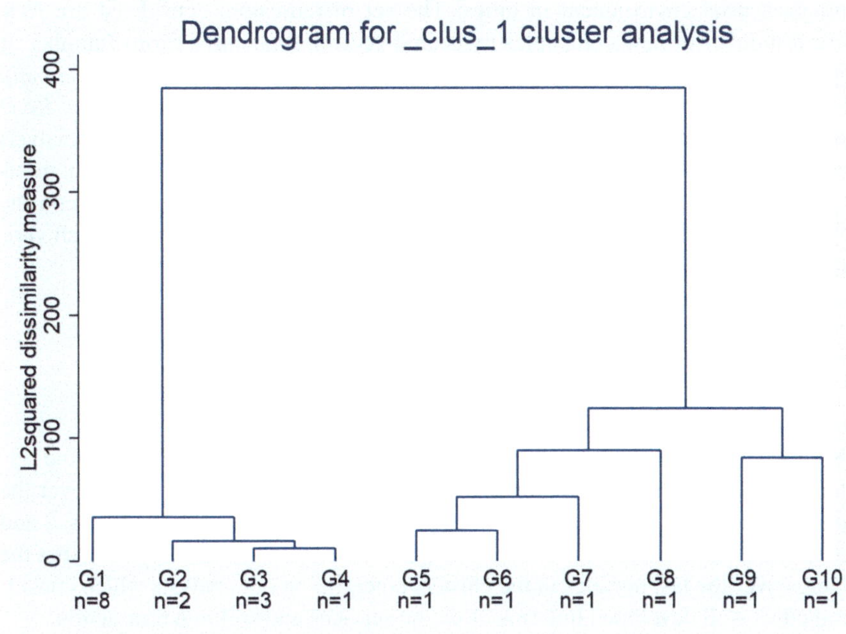

Fig. 2 Dendrogram for the cluster analysis 2011

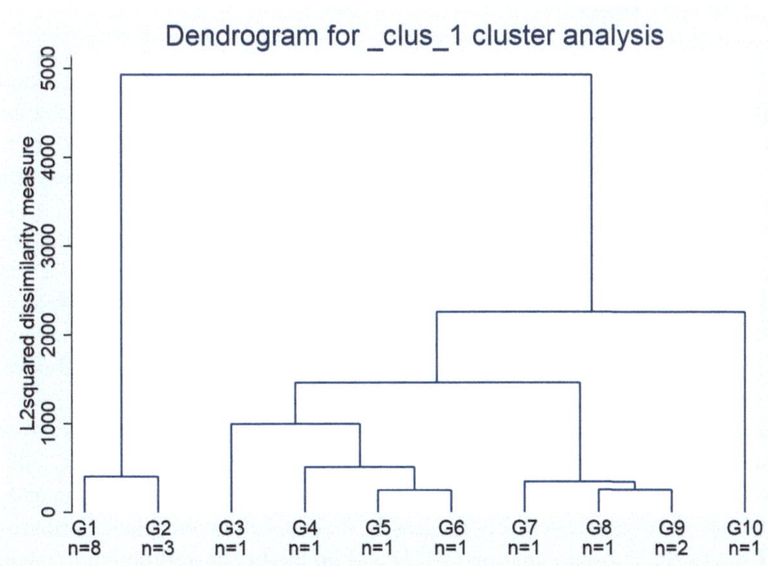

Fig. 3 Dendrogram for the cluster analysis 2022

entrepreneurial environment in cities. The set of indicators considered are *New Firms* (number of new companies registered yearly), *Innovative Firms* (number of high-tech startups and spin-offs registered in the city yearly), *Youth Entrepreneurship* (Enterprises founded yearly by entrepreneurs under 30 years) and *Investment R&D* (yearly companies' investments in R&D). These indicators are based on the analysis proposed by the Italian National Statistical Institute (ISTAT) in the annual monitoring. The variables were operationalized on the population of each city and on the total number of companies present in each city to weigh the strength of each variable on our sample's characteristics and ensure the rigour of our results.

4 Results

Using the cluster analysis, we capture the evolution of cities in terms of online services by showing that the implementation of these practices has changed over the years. Specifically, Table 2 shows the characteristics of the Clusters and Figs. 2 and 3 show the clustering in 2011 and 2022. Specifically, Table 2 explicitly describes the change over the last decades in the clusters emerging in our analysis which considered cities well developed in terms of online services and still in a transaction.

4.1 Cluster Analysis

The clusters display significant differences in both development and timeline. Specifically, they were highlighted as the most prominent services in cluster analysis in 2011 were the *Online Electoral* ($F = 37.22$, with $p < 0.000$) and *Online House* ($F = 22.23$, with p 0.000), respectively. Services that in 2022 took on less importance to the benefit of customized services for citizens, such as *Online Taxes* ($F = 19.42$, with $p < 0.000$), *Online Tourism* ($F = 33.63$, with $p < 0.001$), *Online School* ($F = 24.32$, with $p < 0.001$) and *Online Firms* ($F = 23.62$, with $p < 0.000$). This highlights how the constant evolution is in line with the current development trends of smart cities moving into a stakeholder-centric perspective, where cities modify and evolve their architecture based on national and international development needs and opportunities [9, 23].

Focusing on the cluster representation of our sample, Fig. 2 highlights the situation in 2011, which displays a low level of development of online services, with few cities (mainly located in the north) advanced in the online implementation and others that have not yet started this process in their development plan. Furthermore, Fig. 3 shows the current situation (2022) and highlights how although many cities are still behind in this process, other cities have taken this path by eliminating the main gap due to geographical position (see Caserta, Rome and Naples).

Figure 2 shows that the first cluster groups 14 and the second 6 cities. The cities in the first cluster are those in transition to digitization and online services

Table 2 Characteristics of the clusters

	2011			2022		
	Cluster 1 (n = 14)	Cluster 2 (n = 6)	F-value *or* chi-squared[2] (probability)	Cluster 1 (n = 11)	Cluster 2 (n = 9)	F-value *or* chi-squared[2] (probability)
Taxonomic variables						
Online taxes						
Cluster mean	0.987	2.411	7.91	3.221	9.752	19.42
Std. Deviation	0.631	1.631	0.008	2.891	5.342	0.000
Online school						
Cluster mean	0.528	3.454	9.22	3.768	13.325	24.32
Std. Deviation	0.652	1.976	0.002	2.231	6.112	0.002
Online electoral						
Cluster mean	0.842	3.125	37.22	3.665	9.753	3.11
Std. Deviation	0.771	2.443	0.000	3.113	8.212	0.076
Online tourism						
Cluster mean	0.121	0.756	2.65	0.918	4.242	33.65
Std. Deviation	0.198	0.881	0.082	1.764	4.535	0.000
Online urbanistic						
Cluster mean	0.699	2.371	6.12	4.019	10.231	11.34
Std. Deviation	0.845	2.198	0.139	2.003	7.432	0.001
Online house						
Cluster mean	0.177	4.122	22.23	1.652	12.454	14.23
Std. Deviation	0.334	2.454	0.000	2.719	6.219	0.002
Online innovation						
Cluster mean	0.000	0.191	2.324	0.716	1.442	0.77
Std. Deviation	0.000	0.388	0.177	1.088	1.064	0.347
Online culture						
Cluster mean	0.214	2.833	9.22	2.090	5.112	2.03
Std. Deviation	0.425	2.224	0.019	2.221	4.255	0.162
Online firms						

(continued)

Table 2 (continued)

	2011			2022		
	Cluster 1 (n = 14)	Cluster 2 (n = 6)	F-value *or* chi-squared² (probability)	Cluster 1 (n = 11)	Cluster 2 (n = 9)	F-value *or* chi-squared² (probability)
Cluster mean	0.000	0.166	2.27	0.636	3.778	23.62
Std. Deviation	0.000	0.408	0.134	0.924	5.459	0.000
Online sport						
Cluster mean	0.000	0.641	2.27	0.909	2.275	2.75
Std. Deviation	0.000	0.545	0.134	0.301	3.248	0.092
Predictive variables						
New firms						
Cluster mean	8.762	9.161	1.331	8.223	9.243	3.713
Std. Deviation	0.628	0.570	0.099	0.465	0.707	0.0001
Innovative firms						
Cluster mean	7.248	7.974	2.029	7.192	8.309	4.777
Std. Deviation	0.791	0.552	0.029	0.354	0.671	0.001
Youth entrepreneurship						
Cluster mean	11.039	11.254	1.164	10.911	11.268	2.132
Std. Deviation	0.419	0.245	0.001	0.439	0.218	0.041
Investment R&D						
Cluster mean	12.085	14.445	3.567	12.516	15.032	5.352
Std. Deviation	1.544	0.646	0.003	0.867	0.753	0.001

Cluster means considering the average values of the taxonomic variables for the clusters. F-values represent the continuous variables, and Chi-squared values report the categorical variables

development. Specifically, G1 highlights the less developed cities in terms of online services (i.e., Cosenza, Palermo, Salerno, Reggio Calabria, Messina, Lecce, Verona, Bari) and the groups G2 (Genoa and Verona), G3 (Naples, Foggia and Catania) and G4 (Rome) has begun the implementation of online services. Meanwhile, the second cluster highlights how only some cities (i.e., Bergamo, Brescia, Milan, Turin, Florence and Bologna) have started providing online services to their citizens and how these cities are mainly located in northern Italy.

Figure 3 shows the current state of the art, highlighting the cities' evolution in terms of online services as well as the cities' trajectories over the last decade.

Specifically, the cluster analysis highlights how the distribution of cities has changed and how, over the years, the geographic influence on the implementation of online services in Italian cities has been reduced. Specifically, although there has been a generalized increase in service implementation, there are still two very distinct clusters. In the first cluster, we highlight the cities further back in the G1 (i.e. Cosenza, Salerno, Palermo, Reggio Calabria, Messina, Verona, Bari and Foggia) and those that are even less developed but are beginning a transformation process in the G2 (Genoa, Catania and Lecce). Meanwhile, the second cluster highlight two clear divisions. The group of cities that initiated this process (i.e., Bergamo, Brescia, Bologna, Turin, Caserta, Florence, Rome and Naples) and the city with the greatest development in the area G10 (Milan). This progress highpoints that southern cities such as Caserta and Naples have taken an important step forward in the implementation of these services and that Milan, currently at the centre of innovative, commercial and financial development in Italy, is the most developed city in terms of online services offered to its users.

4.2 *Predictive Validity*

Table 2 explicitly describes the two clusters that group cities "in transition" and the cities "developed" in terms of online services implementation in two distinct moments, 2011 and January 2022. Moreover, in the second section, it reports the results of the predictive validity of the clusters for the variables youth entrepreneurship, new firms, innovative firms and Investment in R&D to determine which cluster has more potential to channel the local entrepreneurial environment and foster innovation shedding light on the impact of the two clusters over the years on the entrepreneurial environment in cities.

The results provide evidence of predictive validity, as we found significant differences among the two configurations in the set of variables used to validate clusters and highlight how clusters configuration have changed their relationship with the local ecosystem over the years (2011–2022).

Whilst the two clusters display significant differences in the *New Firms* ($F = 3.713$, with $p < 0.001$) and in *Innovative Firms* ($F = 4.777$, with $p < 0.001$), they display marginal differences in the firm's *R&D Investment* ($F = 2.132$, with $p > 0.041$) and display not equally large differences in the promotion of *Youth Entrepreneurship* in the city over the years ($F = 5.352$, with $p > 0.001$). This leads us to consider three possible directions.

First, the positive value for *New firms* ($F = 3.713$ with $p < 0.001$) and *Innovative Firms* ($F = 4.777$ with $p < 0.001$) in 2021 compared to 2012 (*New firms*, $F = 1.331$ with $p < 0.099$, and *Innovative Firms*, $F = 20.29$ with $p < 0.029$) suggested that over the years the evolution of smart cities is having an impact on the system local entrepreneurial and innovative drive. This result is in line with the theoretical development of smart cities, which increasingly represent a centre of economic, technological and innovative development [50].

Second, we highlight how the impact of smart city development is marginally reduced compared to the drive towards *Youth Entrepreneurship*, reducing the positive difference from 2012 (F = 1.164, with $p < 0.001$) to 2022 (F = 2.132, with $p < 0.041$). This result highlights that, over the years, the most advanced cities in the implementation of the smart city had an impact on youth entrepreneurship development. However, this value has decreased over the years with the overall growth and development of cities in this perspective.

Third, we highlight how there is a partial difference between the development and implementation of online services and the *R&D Investments* of firms in the city with an increasing trend from 2012 (F = 5.467, with $p < 0.003$) to 2022 (F = 5.352, with $p < 0.001$). This result is in line whit the current literature [51] and displays how both cities and firms are currently anchored to the digital revolution that is taking place globally [26].

5 Conclusion and Discussion

Although the smart cities' implementation is still ongoing and its development is highly debated, in recent years, it has undoubtedly recorded a remarkable interest for academics, urban planners and policymakers [5, 9, 52] and has progressively become crucial in designing urban policies [8].

For this reason, issues in city evolution from city to smart city have gained attention, and scholars and practitioners have dealt with the influence of the smart transition in relation to users such as citizens and tourists and entrepreneurial environment in terms of firms and innovation [7, 37]. The study explores the evolution over the years of the smart transition in the Italian context, showing how the approach to the smart city has changed in the last decade. Specifically, if at the beginning of this process (2011), being smart was an advantage for cities in terms of urban development and economic environment, today, a smart city assumes a fundamental role in urban dynamics by becoming a central part of policymakers and governments.

Considering a sample of 20 Italian cities, we identified 2 clusters (cities in transition and developed) in 2011 and 2022. The two clusters have been tested to assess their predictive validity related to the entrepreneurial environment and determine which clusters have better performance. The results suggest that cities in a cluster whit a high development of online services are more sensitive to the business environment showing a positive value in the creation of new firms and influencing the development and promotion of innovative firms in the city compared to the first cluster. At the same time, no distinct differences related to youth entrepreneurship and the local firms' R&D investments in the past decades are highlighted.

These results provide two interesting insights. Firstly, the results show how digital development and online services influence the entrepreneurial environment by promoting new business activities and attracting others based on the services and the technological environment offered. Secondly, it shows that the implementation of smart cities is becoming predominant in the development strategies of cities. As a result, many cities have reshaped their policy over the years to reduce the gap with the more advanced smart cities. Specifically, to date, this smart transition of cities is assuming a central role in the internal dynamics of development. If, in 2011, being smart was an advantage over other cities in terms of planning and services offered, now do not follow this smart transition can be a problem in long-term scenarios. Therefore, it has become imperative to support the local economic context.

Based on these results, this manuscript contributes to the current academic debate about smart city development and the "smart" transition. Specifically, our findings enrich the current debate on the role of digitization in urban architecture and the relationship between users and cities. Furthermore, we contribute to the debate on the relationship between smart cities and the economic environment, highlighting how the "smart" transformation of cities relates to the local economic context to create a favourable local environment for the development of entrepreneurial opportunities.

This research has some limitations. First, due to the nature of the open data and the sources, we focus on 20 Italian cities. Future studies could enrich our analysis using a larger sample of analysis. Second, we focus on one country (Italy), and we are unable to catch country differences, urban development plans and local policies. Third, our analysis is based on online services proposed by the cities as a proxy for the digitalization process. Although online services represent a representative variable of this process, future studies could enrich this dataset by investing in R&D and technological services (Public Wi-Fi, Mobility, App ...) to test our proposed taxonomy. Despite these limitations, which open up new directions for future studies, we believe this research presents important findings that will be useful to policymakers and academics interested in smart city development, digital transformation, online services, and technological advancement in the city.

References

1. Krishnan, B., Arumugam, S., & Maddulety, K. (2020). Critical success factors for the digitalization of smart cities. *International Journal of Technology Management and Sustainable Development, 19*(1), 69–86.
2. Linde, L., Sjödin, D., Parida, V., & Wincent, J. (2021). Dynamic capabilities for ecosystem orchestration a capability-based framework for smart city innovation initiatives. *Technological Forecasting and Social Change, 166*, 120614.
3. Rahman, M. A., Rashid, M. M., Shamim Hossain, M., Hassanain, E., Alhamid, M. F., & Guizani, M. (2019). Blockchain and IoT-based cognitive edge framework for sharing economy services in a Smart City. *IEEE Access, 7*, 18611–18621.
4. Gagliardi, D., Schina, L., Sarcinella, M. L., Mangialardi, G., Niglia, F., & Corallo, A. (2017). Information and communication technologies and public participation: Interactive maps and value added for citizens. *Government Information Quarterly, 34*(1), 153–166.
5. Yigitcanlar, T., Kankanamge, N., & Vella, K. (2020). How are Smart City concepts and technologies perceived and utilized? A systematic geo-Twitter analysis of smart cities in Australia. *Journal of Urban Technology*.

6. Paskaleva, K., & Cooper, I. (2018). Open innovation and the evaluation of internet-enabled public services in smart cities. *Technovation, 78*(July), 4–14.
7. Taylor Buck, N., & While, A. (2017). Competitive urbanism and the limits to smart city innovation: The UK future cities initiative. *Urban Studies, 54*(2), 501–519.
8. Marchesani, F., Iaia, L., Masciarelli, F., & Christofi, M. (2022). *Smart City's internationalization and international management strategies in the digital era: A systematic literature review.*
9. Christofi, M., Iaia, L., Marchesani, F., & Masciarelli, F. (2021). Marketing innovation and internationalization in smart city development: A systematic review, framework and research agenda. *International Marketing Review, 38*(5), 948–984.
10. Vanolo, A. (2014). Smartmentality: The Smart City as disciplinary strategy. *Urban Studies, 51*(5), 883–898.
11. Martin, C. J., Evans, J., & Karvonen, A. (2018). Smart and sustainable? Five tensions in the visions and practices of the smart-sustainable city in Europe and North America. *Technological Forecasting and Social Change, 133*, 269–278.
12. Ismagilova, E., Hughes, L., Dwivedi, Y. K., & Raman, K. R. (2019). Smart cities: Advances in research—An information systems perspective. *International Journal of Information Management., 47*, 88–100.
13. Albino, V., Berardi, U., & Dangelico, R. M. (2015). Smart cities: Definitions, dimensions, performance, and initiatives. *Journal of Urban Technology, 22*, 3–21.
14. Romão, J., Kourtit, K., Neuts, B., & Nijkamp, P. (2018). The smart city as a common place for tourists and residents: A structural analysis of the determinants of urban attractiveness. *Cities, 78*, 67–75.
15. Hollands, R. G. (2015). Critical interventions into the corporate smart city. *Cambridge Journal of Regions, Economy and Society, 8*(1), 61–77.
16. Shafiee, S., Rajabzadeh Ghatari, A., Hasanzadeh, A., & Jahanyan, S. (2021). Smart tourism destinations: A systematic review. *Tourism Review, 76*(3), 505–528.
17. Nikki Han, M. J., & Kim, M. J. (2021). A critical review of the smart city in relation to citizen adoption towards sustainable smart living. *Habitat International, 108*, 102312.
18. Paskaleva, K. A. (2011). The smart city: A nexus for open innovation? *Intelligent Buildings International., 3*, 153–171.
19. Silva, B. N., Khan, M., & Han, K. (2018). Towards sustainable smart cities: A review of trends, architectures, components, and open challenges in smart cities. *Sustainable Cities and Society, 38*, 697–713.
20. Ooms, W., Caniëls, M. C. J., Roijakkers, N., & Cobben, D. (2020). Ecosystems for smart cities: Tracing the evolution of governance structures in a Dutch smart city initiative. *The International Entrepreneurship and Management Journal, 16*(4), 1225–1258.
21. Bakici, T., Almirall, E., & Wareham, J. (2013). A Smart City initiative: The case of Barcelona. *Journal of the Knowledge Economy, 4*(2), 135–148.
22. Marchesani, F., Masciarelli, F., & Quang, H. (2022). Innovation in cities a driving force for knowledge flows: Exploring the relationship between high-tech firms, student mobility, and the role of youth entrepreneurship. *Cities, 130, no. June*, 103852.
23. Lee, J., & Lee, H. (2014). Developing and validating a citizen-centric typology for smart city services. *Government Information Quarterly, 31*(Suppl. 1), S93–S105.
24. Pittaway, J. J., & Montazemi, A. R. (2020). Know-how to lead digital transformation: The case of local governments. *Government Information Quarterly, 37*, 101474.
25. Benevolo, C., Dameri, R. P., & Auria, B. D. (2016). *Empowering organizations: Enabling platforms and artefacts* (Vol. 11, p. 315).
26. Herrschel, T. (2013). Competitiveness AND sustainability: Can 'Smart City regionalism' square the circle? *Urban Studies, 50*(11), 2332–2348.
27. Trencher, G. (2019). Towards the smart city 2.0: Empirical evidence of using smartness as a tool for tackling social challenges. *Technological Forecasting and Social Change, 142*, 117–128.

28. Capdevila, I., & Zarlenga, M. I. (2015). Smart city or smart citizens? The Barcelona case. *Journal of Strategy and Management, 8*(3), 266–282.
29. Liu, C. Y. (2012). Intrametropolitan opportunity structure and the self-employment of Asian and Latino immigrants. *Economic Development Quarterly, 26*(2), 178–192.
30. Falco, E., Malavolta, I., Radzimski, A., Ruberto, S., Iovino, L., & Gallo, F. (2018). Smart City L'Aquila: An application of the 'Infostructure' approach to public urban mobility in a post-disaster context. *Journal of Urban Technology, 25*(1), 99–121.
31. Battarra, R., Gargiulo, C., Tremiterra, M. R., & Zucaro, F. (2018). Smart mobility in Italian metropolitan cities: A comparative analysis through indicators and actions. *Sustainable Cities and Society, 41*, 556–567.
32. Lee, J. H., Phaal, R., & Lee, S. H. (2013). An integrated service-device-technology roadmap for smart city development. *Technological Forecasting and Social Change, 80*, 286–306.
33. Barletta, V. S., Caivano, D., Dimauro, G., Nannavecchia, A., & Scalera, M. (2020). Managing a smart city integrated model through smart program management. *Applied Sciences, 10*(2), 1–23.
34. de Falco, S., Angelidou, M., & Addie, J. P. D. (2019). From the 'smart city' to the 'smart metropolis'? Building resilience in the urban periphery. *European Urban and Regional Studies, 26*(2), 205–223.
35. Garzoni, A., De Turi, I., Secundo, G., & Del Vecchio, P. (2020). Fostering digital transformation of SMEs: A four levels approach. *Management Decision, 58*(8), 1543–1562.
36. Contreras, G., & Platania, F. (2019). Economic and policy uncertainty in climate change mitigation: The London Smart City case scenario. *Technological Forecasting and Social Change, 142*, 384–393.
37. Hollands, R. G. (2020). Will the real smart city please stand up? In *The Routledge companion to smart cities*.
38. Almirall, E., et al. (2016). Smart cities at the crossroads: New tensions in city transformation. *California Management Review, 59*(1), 141–152.
39. Zheng, S., & Du, R. (2020). How does urban agglomeration integration promote entrepreneurship in China? Evidence from regional human capital spillovers and market integration. *Cities, 97*, 102529.
40. Camboim, G. F., Zawislak, P. A., & Pufal, N. A. (2019). Driving elements to make cities smarter: Evidences from European projects. *Technological Forecasting and Social Change, 142*, 154–167.
41. Florida, R., Adler, P., & Mellander, C. (2017). The city as innovation machine. *Regional Studies, 51*(1), 86–96.
42. Spicer, Z., Goodman, N., & Olmstead, N. (2021). The frontier of digital opportunity: Smart city implementation in small, rural and remote communities in Canada. *Urban Studies, 58*(3), 535–558.
43. Adler, P., Florida, R., King, K., & Mellander, C. (2019). The city and high-tech startups: The spatial organization of Schumpeterian entrepreneurship. *Cities, 87*, 121–130.
44. Cledou, G., Estevez, E., & Soares Barbosa, L. (2018). A taxonomy for planning and designing smart mobility services. *Government Information Quarterly, 35*, 61–76.
45. Leitheiser, S., & Follmann, A. (2020). The social innovation–(re) politicization nexus: Unlocking the political in actually existing smart city campaigns? The case of SmartCity Cologne, Germany. *Urban Studies, 57*(4), 894–915.
46. Caragliu, A., & Del Bo, C. F. (2019). Smart innovative cities: The impact of Smart City policies on urban innovation. *Technological Forecasting and Social Change, 142*, 373–383.
47. Cohen, B., Almirall, E., & Chesbrough, H. (2016). The city as a lab: Open innovation meets the collaborative economy. *California Management Review, 59*(1), 5–13.
48. Abid, N., Marchesani, F., Ceci, F., & Masciarelli, F. *Assessing capabilities to embrace digital transformation: The case of southern Italy*.
49. Levy, P. S., & Lemeshow, S. (2011). *Sampling of populations: Methods and applications* (4th ed.).

50. Berrone, P., Ricart, J. E., & Carrasco, C. (2016). The open kimono: Toward a general framework for open data initiatives in cities. *California Management Review, 59*(1), 39–70.
51. Betz, M. R., Partridge, M. D., & Fallah, B. (2016). Smart cities and attracting knowledge workers: Which cities attract highly-educated workers in the 21st century? *Papers in Regional Science, 95*(4), 819–841.
52. Oztemel, E., & Gursev, S. (2020). Literature review of Industry 4.0 and related technologies. *Journal of Intelligent Manufacturing, 31*(1), 127–182.

Exploring the Evolution of Digital Transformation Research in Non-profit Organisations: A Bibliometric Analysis

Michele Cipriano and Stefano Za

Abstract In recent years, research on Digital Transformation (DT) has increased significantly in relation to the need to manage uncertainty and unexpected events, such as the COVID-19 pandemic. In particular, among the studies examining economic, societal, and industry-related implications, DT initiatives emerge as a global priority in the "new normal" toward resilience, well-being, and Sustainable Development Goals (SDGs). Accordingly, although a significant number of reviews summarising the DT debate populating the literature, the IS community clamour for deepening the current knowledge of the DT process by advancing theoretical diversity. Among other, DT initiatives in non-profit organisations (NPOs) seems to be only partially explored. For this reason, our aim is to advance the comprehension of the DT process in NPOs by performing a bibliometric analysis of the literature debating this specific phenomenon. To this end, we extracted 586 contributions published from 1983 to 2022 using the Scopus database. Then, we investigate the conceptual structure of the DT discourse concerning NPOs. The outcome of this paper is twofold: (1) to quantitatively describe the existing research and its evolution by considering different sources; (2) to recognise the main topics characterising the DT discourse in NPOs by performing a co-word analysis. This preliminary study draws a more comprehensive overview of the debate compared to previous qualitative research, exploring some novel discussions that could not be still addressed in journal articles.

Keywords Digital transformation · Non-profit organisations · Bibliometric analysis · Co-words analysis · Social network analysis

---

M. Cipriano (✉) · S. Za
University "G. D'Annunzio" of Chieti-Pescara, Pescara, Italy
e-mail: michele.cipriano@unich.it; stefano.za@unich.it

A. M. Braccini et al. (eds.), *Technologies for Digital Transformation*, Lecture Notes in Information Systems and Organisation 64,
https://doi.org/10.1007/978-3-031-52120-1_13

1 Introduction

Over the last few years, the challenges triggered by uncertainty and unexpected events [1, 2], such as the covid-19 pandemic [3, 4], significantly affected the production of scientific-related research [5]. Among other aspects, in literature, several scholars focus on the need to understand [6], conceptualise [7], and manage [8] the changes affecting the organisational ecosystems [9]. In particular, although the Digital Transformation (DT) debate is a recurring topic among different fields of study, by exploring organisational antifragility [10, 11] and envisioning "a new normal" toward resilience, well-being, and Sustainable Development Goals (SDGs) [12–15], DT initiatives appear to be a global priority nowadays [16, 17]. The significance of DT initiatives could be seen in facilitating innovation, providing organisational flexibility [18], and their potential to generate social and economic value [19, 20]. For example, some organisations develop DT initiatives to enable organisational changes [21, 22], while others seek to improve their business opportunities [23, 24].

However, some scholars claim there are difficulties in conceptualising DT-enabled change management and change implementation [21, 22]. Specifically, a difficulty is that the DT phenomenon seems not yet well theorised [25]. Moreover, some information system (IS) context might not be well understood [17, 26], perhaps, due to not well-defined industry ecosystem [17, 27, 28]. Also, some top journal editorials [25], special issues [18, 29] and calls for paper,[1] especially from the IS community, invite researchers to deepen comprehension of the DT process. Then, it might be helpful to further analyse how to manage and sustain DT initiatives, focusing on how to implement, embed, integrate, and evaluate the resulting changes.

In addition, the literature also reveals that non-profit organisations (NPOs) deserve further investigations concerning the DT discourse [27, 28, 30] since a limited number of studies represent a poor examination of this organisational form. Still, several reasons could pave the attention for investigating DT in NPOs. First, NPOs play a significant role in building civil society, strengthening common well-being, social capital, and economic development [31]. For example, NPOs have undergone many challenges regarding work overload from increased societal demand because of the new challenges triggered by the COVID-19 pandemic [32–34]. Hence, as the DT phenomena also trigger broad-scale changes at the societal level [35], it might be significant to explore the implications of a digitalised society on the NPOs' work. Moreover, although NPOs could operate like any other industry [36], they differ in their unique nature [37, 38] based on the primacy of nonfinancial outcomes [39] and the absence of incentives to increase productivity [40]. Accordingly, NPOs might have unique objectives, organisational features, and operability assets [28, 31]. For all these reasons, we believe that NPOs might represent an IS context that is still poorly understood and an opportunity to enrich and improve further conceptualisation of DT.

[1] https://www.callforpapers.co.uk/managing-sustaining-digital-transformations

Thus, we propose a literature review based on bibliometric data analysis to advance an understanding of the themes concerning the evolution of research on DT in NPOs. Specifically, this study seeks to answer the following research question: What is the trend, and what are the main themes characterising the DT debate concerning NPOs?

For this aim, we first develop a descriptive analysis to investigate the scientific contributions discussing DT in NPOs, considering different sources and quality of publications, especially focusing on the IS field. We use the "bibliometrix" R package [41] in the R environment to perform the analysis, and the software "WOS viewer" [42] and "Ghepi" [43] for investigating the evolution of the topics over the years (conceptual analysis). The paper unfolds as follows. The next section summarises the theoretical underpinnings, followed by the methodology section and the literature search protocol. Next, descriptive and conceptual analyses are provided in the result section. Discussions and conclusions close the paper.

2 Theoretical Background

By exploring the literature, it appears that several scholars adopt a bibliometric approach to systematically study scientific publications in relation to a given domain [44–48]. Among other statistical techniques, this approach seems to be purposely valuable for exploring the history, development, and general state of the art of a specific research field, as well as the longitudinal evolution of terminology (or topics) [49–51]. In general, this technique is based on the analysis of bibliographic material, which is usually collected from online databases [50, 52]. It consists of different examinations that rely on more basic descriptive analysis of bibliometric data (performance analysis) [49, 53], and more accurate ones for investigating a scientific field and examining an area in relation to its knowledge structure and evolution (science mapping) [54, 55].

In particular, focusing on the DT literature, it appears that the proliferation of bibliometric studies has increased significantly in recent years with regard to multidisciplinary topics [56]. For example, Chawla and Goyal [57] analyse 234 journal articles published in the previous twenty years. Their research outlines the emerging trends in DT by investigating the citation, co-citation and keyword analysis [57]. De Bem Machado et al. [58] provide a structured literature review of 761 articles discussing knowledge management, DT, and Industry 4.0 (I4.0) to recognise the interactions and interdependencies of such research streams. These authors adopt a hybrid methodology using the "bibliometrix" R package to increase the study's rigour and decrease its bias [58]. In comparison, to develop a systematic literature review, Kraus et al. [59] adopt the VOS viewer software to analyse the author's keywords co-occurrences. Specifically, they present a qualitative classification of the DT discussion by recognising three clusters representing technological, business, and societal impacts [59]. Their research then provides helpful insights to government and private sectors in guiding the management of disruptive changes

[59]. Adekunle et al. [60] focus instead on the DT discussion concerning the construction industry. By classifying the discourse based on the co-occurrence of keywords (authors and journal indexed), their analysis shows an increasing interest in DT initiatives in such industry over the last ten years [60]. It also appears that some existing barriers limit the discussion in some countries. Then, the authors develop a supporting model and define some areas that require further research [60].

Furthermore, Pizzi et al. [61] performed a bibliometric analysis to investigate the impacts caused by DT on managerial auditing. These authors adopt a mixed approach based on bibliometric analysis and literature review to develop more focused research [61]. In particular, they perform a citation, keywords, and density analysis [61]. Their study proposes a research agenda in addition to outlining four independent research areas of interest: (1) continuous auditing, (2) fraud detection, (3) data analytics, and (4) technological innovation [61]. In comparison, Chinotaikul and Vinayavekhin [56] explore DT as a business and management research field. They focused mainly on the co-word network analyses for identifying the influential articles and the intellectual structure of the debate [56]. Chinotaikul and Vinayavekhin [56] claim that such a research field is an emerging field whose growing proliferation interested the last three to four years. Notably, they notice significant attention to the Internet of Things (IoT) and digital twin themes [56].

Then, the main purpose of this paper is to objectively explore the DT debate strictly focusing on NPOs. In this research, we consider the DT phenomena, as described by Vial [62], as a process that aims at improving an entity, focusing on its potential implications on the organisational change [62]. In particular, Wessel et al. [22] remark that the DT phenomenon differs from past IT-related organisational change [22] and Hanelth et al. [21] argue that it is challenging to analyse DT-enabled change management and change implementation since DT is triggered and shaped by the wide-spread diffusion of digital technologies [21]. Regarding the identification of the organisational context characterising the NPOs, this research adopts Salamon and Sokolowski's [63] conceptualisation. Specifically, one could identify an NPO when the following five characteristics are simultaneously verified: (1) *Institution* (or organisations that could be either formally or legally formed or not), (2) *Private* (institutionally separated and not controlled by the government), (3) *Self-governing* (able to control its activities without the operational control by any other entity, private, or governmental), (4) *Non-profit-distributing* (a legal prohibition is placed on any organisation's constituents or other stakeholders from receiving any quota of the surplus generated by the organisation's activities), and (5) *Without compulsion* (any participation with the organisation has to be voluntary as a matter of free choice). Following, the research method is presented.

3 Research Method

This study adopts a bibliometric approach to explore the most active research area and the foundations of the DT discourse in NPOs [64]. In examining the structure and characteristics of topics through the study of scientific publications [65, 66], we apply the bibliometric methods in two main usages, performance analysis and science mapping [50]. Our aim is to explore the conceptual evolution of DT in NPOs and uncover links between concepts through term co-occurrences. For this purpose, we first analyse and describe the publications distribution among journals, book chapters and conference proceedings. Specifically, we outline the extent of research proliferation in the major IS sources. Afterwards, we explore the longitudinal evolution of the terminology used by scholars [67, 68] and perform a co-word network analysis of the author's keywords [69–71]. We locate keyword networks strongly linked to each other [72], presenting the resulting diagram and distributing the keywords across the years. The research protocol we adopted for this study is based on the framework suggested by Za and Braccini [73], performing the following main steps:

1. Data setting
2. Dataset refining
3. Descriptive and conceptual analysis

The first step consists of the data collection. We developed a congruous source for the literature search, a comprehensive research query, and some manual refinement of the keywords of the query search. We used the Scopus database in collecting the corpus since it is an indexing platform highly deployed by academics and practitioners of social studies [74]. In particular, we iterated the research query several times, using different keywords, to include all the publications that do not focus on DT in any sector but are strongly related to NPOs. We did not include keywords such as "ICT" or "IT" as this research considers DT an exclusive phenomenon [21, 22]. Notably, this choice did not affect the dataset, as it includes contributions also focusing on those keywords (see Table A at the link https://bit.ly/Tables_DTNPOs). We searched for the terms *digitalisation* and *non-profit organisation* in the authors' keywords, title and abstract papers fields, using wildcards to include plurals and grammatical and spelling variations. A limitation was set on the language for retrieving papers written only in English. By running the query, we collected an initial dataset of 698 contributions concerning a period automatically established from the search (last updated on 30th May 2022).

Afterwards, we performed two main refinements of the dataset in the second step. We first defined the criteria for including or not a contribution. For example, we included journal articles, conference papers, books, book chapters, editorials and reviews. In contrast, we excluded conference reviews, notes, short surveys, data papers, erratum, and undefined (after analysing these contributions). Moreover, we excluded the contributions missing the authors' names after a manual check on the source page of the publications. As a result, we obtained a refined corpus of 633 papers. In the second round of refinement, we updated the number of citations for each document and homogenised some cited sources (e.g. VOLUNTAS—Voluntas—voluntas). We excluded some false positives (e.g. papers including the two keywords but not jointly discussing the two topics). In addition, we cleaned and updated some authors' keywords since we noticed that different keywords representing the same topic overlapped among the papers. In doing so, we refined an initial set of 1882 author's keywords (different occurrences) to a homogenised one

Table 1 Sample of the refined set of the most occurrence keywords (their number in brackets)

Original author's keywords	The adopted keywords
Non-profit (6)	Nonprofit (30)
Non-profits (2)	
Nonprofit (16)	
Nonprofits (5)	
Not-for-profit (1)	

composed of 1808. Moreover, since we noted that 170 contributions were missing the author's keywords but were apt for the analysis, we selected and added a set of representative keywords for each contribution. In other words, we added only homogenised keywords after reading the papers. Accordingly, the final dataset for the following step consisted of 586 papers. Table 1 shows a sample of the homogenised recurring keywords (see all keywords in Table A at the link https://bit.ly/Tables_DTNPOs).

Finally, in the third step, we employed the software VOS viewer [75, 76] and Ghepi [43, 77] in addition to R-studio with Bibliometrix package [41, 78] to perform the bibliometric analysis. We investigated the publications and citations [73, 79], stressing the analysis of the sources belonging to the IS field of study and the most locally cited publications [68]. Then, we developed a co-word analysis focusing on the most used author's keywords, their co-occurrences, and their distribution across the years [67].

4 Results

This section consists of two parts encompassing the two objectives of the study. The first provides the performance analysis, describing the trend of publications and citations by focusing on the most relevant sources, countries, authors, and local cited papers. The second carries on the science mapping analysis, investigating the most influential topics in our dataset based on the most recurring keywords used by authors. Specifically, it focuses on the trend of the most 41 used keywords and their co-occurrences.

4.1 Descriptive Analysis

We performed this analysis at the beginning of June 2022, focusing on the revised dataset of 586 papers distributed over 462 sources. Figure 1 depicts the annual scientific publication trend since 1983.

The diagram shows a growing interest in the DT discussion focused on NPOs over the last two decades, with a slight decrease in 2015 and 2019 (with respect to

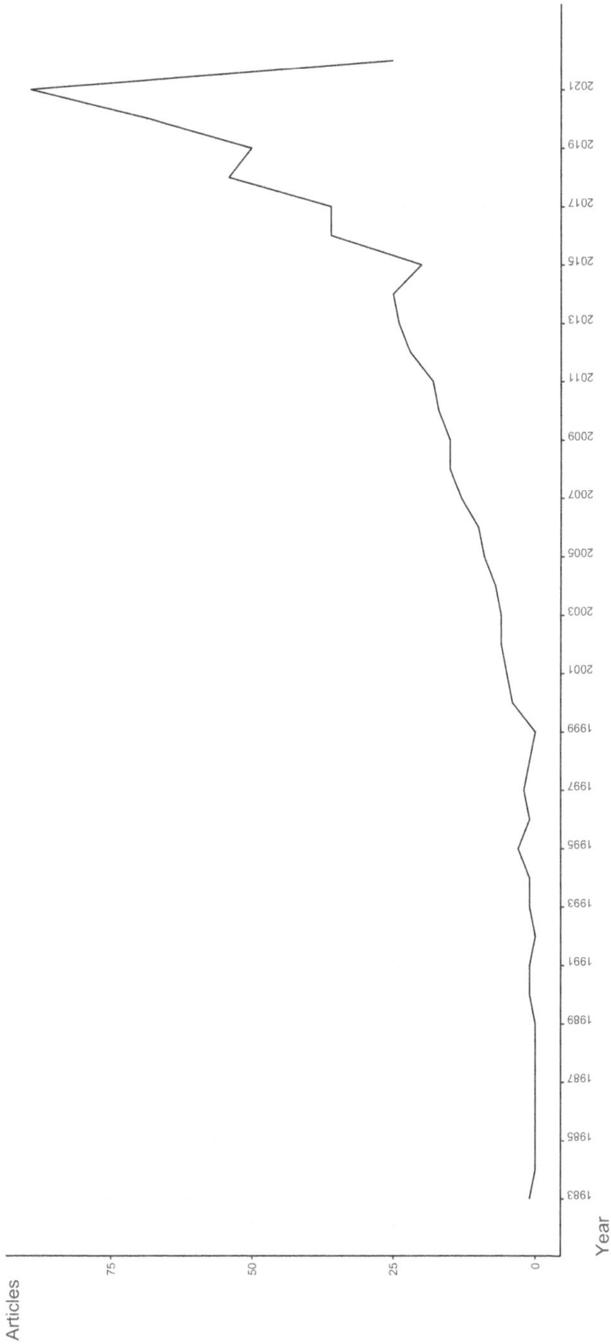

Fig. 1 Annual scientific production of the DT debate in NPOs from 1983

Table 2 Top 9 most relevant sources

Source	Articles
Acm International Conference Proceeding Series	8
Voluntas: International Journal of Voluntary and Nonprofit Organizations	7
Digital Journalism	6
Journalism	6
Proceedings of the Annual Hawaii International Conference on System Sciences (HICSS)	6
Telematics and Informatics	6
Ceur Workshop Proceedings	5
Journalism Practice	5
Nonprofit and Voluntary Sector Quarterly	5

the general trend). Regarding NPOs compared to the studies reported in the theoretical framework [56, 57], the DT debate shows an exponential increase (over the timespan) and a growing proliferation of the number of publications (in recent years). Almost 50% of the papers have been published in the last four years (2018–2021). Also, although 2022 is assigned 25 publications in late May, the number of contributions for this year may likely grow considering this trend. Moreover, considering the source of publications, the dataset is composed of 347 articles, 55 book chapters, 154 conference proceedings and 30 other sources.

Afterwards, by analysing the most relevant source, it appears that the corpus is distributed over various specialisations, developing a multidisciplinary discussion. We noticed that among 462 different sources, only 67 published more than one paper. Specifically, 41 out of 67 sources published two papers, 12 published three, and 5 published four. Table 2 shows the remaining top 9 sources publishing at least five papers each. Notably, the annual Hawaii international conference on system sciences (HIICSS) is one of the most prolific conference proceedings affiliated with the IS field.

Then, we further investigated the sources belonging to the IS field of study using the AIS eLibrary (the central repository for research papers and journal articles from the association of the IS academic community—AIS).[2] We considered the "list of premier journals" as the top journals in the IS field. This list was adopted by the College of Senior Scholars of the IS community to provide more consistency and meaningfulness to tenure and promotion cases.[3] Moreover, we used the Academic Journal Guide (AJG2021) released by the Chartered Association of Business Schools (CABS), which assesses the quality of journals, determines the excellence of business research, and the relative status of different business specialisations [80]. Among a set of 22 different fields of study, this guide ranks journals into five categories (i.e. 4*, 4, 3, 2, 1), where 4* is the top-level [74]. So, we examined the journal sources in the corpus to identify those belonging to the *Information*

[2] https://aisel.aisnet.org/?AISeLibrary

[3] https://aisnet.org/page/SeniorScholarListofPremierJournals

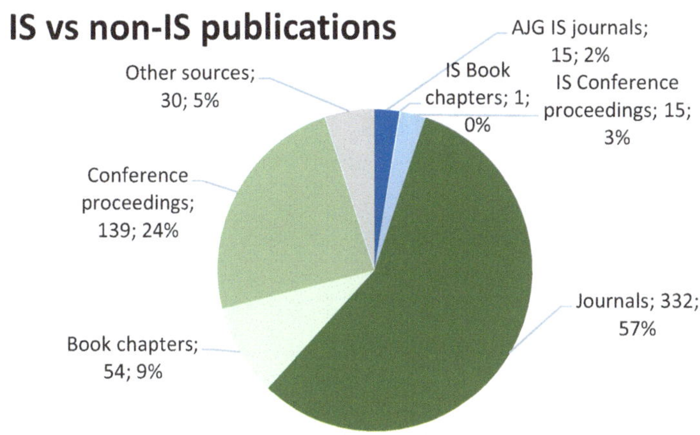

Fig. 2 Number of sources strictly related to the information systems academic community (AIS) and the Information Management field of study

Management field and assess their quality. Focusing on the primary three sources mentioned previously, Fig. 2 displays the publications' percentage of the sources relevant to the AIS community (in blue) and the others (not relevant, in green) composing the local dataset (of 586 papers). Then, 15 papers represent a conference proceedings publication, and one paper is a book chapter connected to the Italian Chapter of AIS. Afterwards, considering the journal articles, 15 publications are distributed in 9 different ranked journals (recognised as relevant by the AIS). Among the latter, the most prolific are *Government Information Quarterly* and *Computer in Human Behaviour*, with three publications each, classified as 3 and 2 in the AJG2021. In addition, the *Information Systems Research* journal, the only one belonging to the "list of premier journals" in IS, is assigned one publication and is classified as a 4* journal in the AJG2021.

Next, we examined the most productive countries in relation to the authors' affiliation (of the papers) included in the dataset. The graph in Fig. 3 distinguishes the publications whose authors belong to a single country (SCP) or multiple countries (MCP).

The MCP metric represents the publications in which at least one author is affiliated with a different country than the corresponding one, showing the intensity of international collaboration for each country. Interestingly, the DT debate in NPOs has been significantly developed in the USA with 157 contributions, followed by the UK and Germany with significantly fewer publications (approximately the 10% of the first country). However, considering the SCP, Spain is the second most productive country, with 13 articles overall. Among the other countries, Hong Kong, Hungary, and Switzerland are assigned one single and one multiple country publication. In comparison, Finland and South Africa are given one single and two multiple country publications.

Fig. 3 Most productive countries (with at least two publications)

Afterwards, we focused on the most productive authors. Figure 4 shows the 15 most productive authors with at least three publications in the local dataset. In particular, the dot size and the colour intensity are proportional to the number of papers published by an author. Considering the number of papers contributed, Patrick R. Ferrucci is the most productive author, with 7 articles published in different journals. Colby Mariva Riggs, John A. Campbell, and Marta Rey-Garcia follow with four publications. The remaining authors contributed instead with three publications.

Then, we provide a preliminary citation analysis to further explore the contributions that received more attention among scholars, [73, 79, 81, 82]. In this study, we decided to focus on the local citation (LC) metric [78], summarising the result of this analysis in Table 3. Specifically, we identified the 12 most locally cited papers receiving at least two local citations. In addition, for each paper, we report the year of publication, the number of global citations (GC), the ratio between local and global citations LCR (LC/GC), and the normalised number of local (Norm. LC) and global citations (Norm. GC). The local citation (LC) metric provides an understanding of how much a paper is significant (impact) within the specific dataset [78]. In other words, based on the whole references set in our local dataset (586 papers), we can identify the number of citations that the papers received from the others included in the same dataset (recognising their relevance for the selected literature sample). In comparison, the global citations (GC) metric (a cumulative one) measures the impact of a paper considering the whole bibliographic database (in this study, Scopus) [78]. Furthermore, the normalised metric (functioning the same for local and global citations) offers an unbiased comparison between papers published in different years [78]. That is, it compares the number of citations of an article (either LC or GC) to the global average of papers (either LC or GC) published in the same years. Finally, the Local Citation Rate (LCR), as the ratio (%) between LC over GC, represent the contribution of every paper to the research topic (DT in NPOs) according to its real relevance in this research area [83]. Therefore, Table 3 shows how a paper contributes to this highly selected sample of the literature, but also its contribution to other connected fields of research (with regard to all the papers indexed on Scopus) [83].

Interestingly, Nee R.C [84] is the author receiving the most significant number of local citations (nine). Still, Nee R.C. appears again as the most locally cited author for her publication in Journalism [85], with two citations. Then, Ferrucci P.R [86] followed with six local citations, while Konieczna M [87] received five. Interestingly, Ferrucci P.R. also appears as the most locally cited author for other three publications, receiving four citations for his publication in Journalism & Mass Communication Quarterly [88] and Electronic News [89] and additional two citations for his publication in Journalism Studies [90], respectively. Moreover, Yoo S-C [91] received four local citations, followed by Smith J.N [92] and Burger T [93] with three citations, respectively. Raman A [94] received two local citations as Voida A [95], which is also the author collecting the highest number of general citations among the 12 authors (in Table 3). As a way of exemplification, the most cited paper in our dataset is Bakir V [96], with 272 total citations overall in 2018 for his

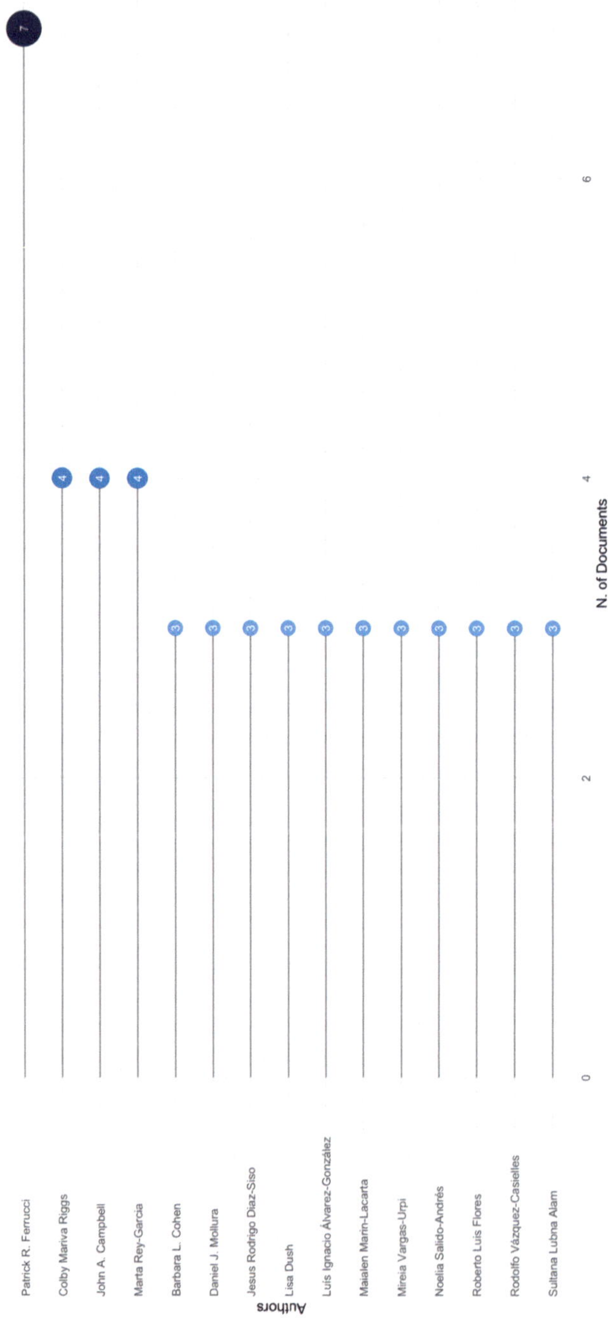

Fig. 4 The 15 most productive authors

Table 3 Top 12 most local cited papers with at least two local citations

Paper	Year	LC	GC	LCR (LC/GC)	Norm. LC	Norm. GC
Nee R.C. 2013, Jmm Int J Media Manage	2013	9	63	14.29	21.60	5.09
Ferrucci P.R. 2015, Journalism	2015	6	32	18.75	9.23	4.60
Konieczna M. 2014, Journalism	2014	5	32	15.63	15.63	4.23
Yoo S-C. 2018, Nonprofit Manage Leadersh	2018	4	21	19.05	18.00	1.35
Ferrucci P.R. 2017, Journal Mass Commun Q	2017	4	26	15.38	20.57	2.76
Ferrucci P.R. 2015, Electron News	2015	4	16	25.00	6.15	2.30
Smith J.N. 2018, J Nonprofit Public Sect Mark	2018	3	20	15.00	13.50	1.28
Bürger T. 2015, Public Relat Rev	2015	3	13	23.08	4.62	1.87
Ferrucci P.R. 2017, Journal Stud	2017	2	15	13.33	10.29	1.59
Raman A. 2016, Inf Technol Dev	2016	2	14	14.29	18.00	1.36
Nee R.C. 2014, Journalism	2014	2	26	7.69	6.25	3.44
Voida A. 2011, Conf Hum Fact Comput Syst Proc	2011	2	65	3.08	12.00	4.61

publication in *Digital Journalism*. Hence, these 12 authors received the highest number of local citations, representing the ones that have been mostly cited in this selected sample of the literature. However, since Ferrucci P.R. and Nee R.C. appear in 6 cases over 12, this could mean these authors have cited their own works several times, leaving room for further investigation on these aspects.

4.2 Conceptual Analysis

To investigate the most important topic concerning the discussion on DT in NPOs, we analysed the most recurring keyword used by the authors. By developing this analysis, we can recognise insights regarding the content and the relations between the topics discussed in our dataset. Specifically, we first analyse the trend topic (where each author's keyword represents a topic). For this analysis, we considered the top 41 most used author's keywords with at least eight occurrences (meaning an author's keyword is included at least in eight papers) (Fig. 5). Then, we explore the network of these author's keywords co-occurrences over the years (Fig. 6).

The scatter diagram in Fig. 5 displays the trend topic graph based on time (the years are on the x-axis) and term (the authors' keywords are on the y-axis). In particular, the reference year for each term is identified using the median of the distribution of occurrences over the period from 1994 to 2021 (automatically established given the threshold set on eight occurrences minimum for an author's keyword) [78]. Accordingly, for each year, it is possible to recognise the terms in decreasing order of frequency [78]. Moreover, for each author's keyword, the dot size is

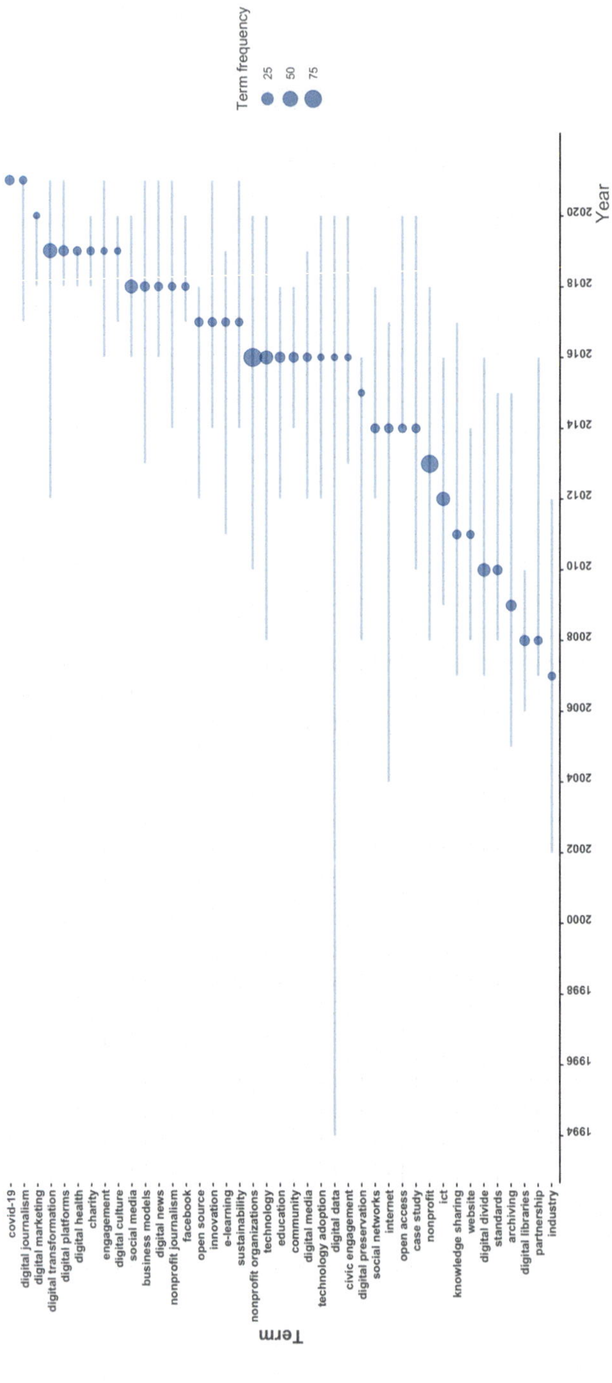

Fig. 5 Top 41 used keywords

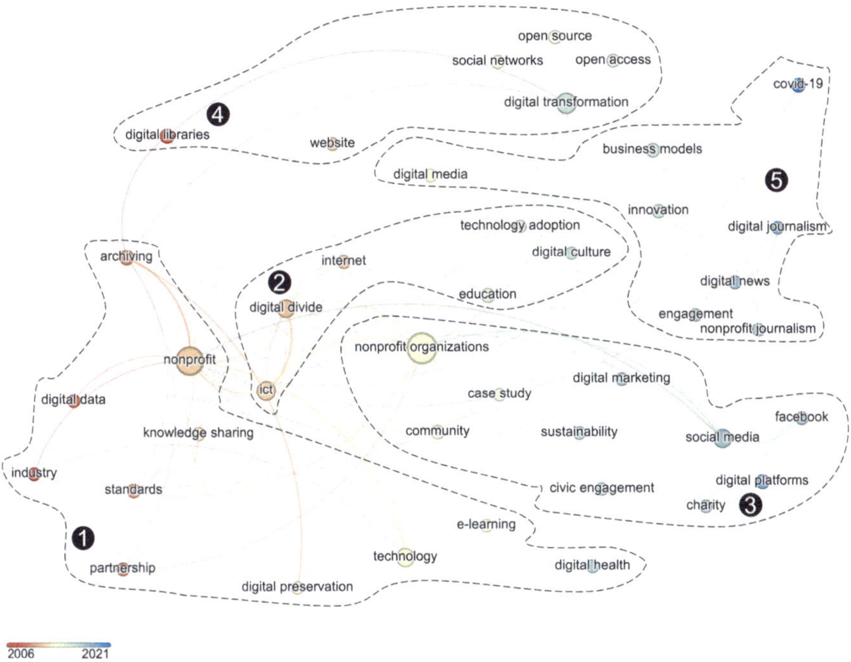

Fig. 6 Author's keywords co-occurrences network through a longitudinal lens

proportional to the total number of its occurrences. At the same time, the line represents the specific period in which the authors used such a keyword.

Observing the 41 most used keywords by authors over the years, *nonprofit organizations* is the most frequent keyword, with 91 occurrences. *Nonprofit* and *digital transformation* follow with 77 and 42, respectively (this is not surprising since these are the primary keywords used for the search). Moreover, with less frequency, *ict*, *technology*, *social media*, and *digital divide* are the other keywords with at least 30 occurrences (36, 34, 33, and 30, respectively). Regarding the frequency of the 41 keywords, it appears that it significantly intensified between 2016 and 2021, with a lower extant in 2014. In particular, this period shows a higher concentrated level of occurrences concerning multidisciplinary topics related to DT and NPOs. For example, some frequent keywords are *digital platform*, *digital health*, *nonprofit journalism*, *charity*, *education* and *community*. Besides, *digital data* is the authors' keyword covering the most extended period (from 1994 to 2020), with the median of its distribution in 2016.

Furthermore, considering the median of distributions of the whole set of authors' keywords, it is possible to recognise three main periods over the debate on DT in NPOs and the terms that characterised its evolution. Focusing on the three most frequent keywords, we can see that *nonprofit* and the descending other keywords such as *knowledge sharing*, *website*, *archiving*, and *digital libraries* represent the period in which researchers started to increasingly investigate the impact of technology on NPOs [35, 97]. Considering *nonprofit organizations*, a second period refers to the studies exploring the development and adoption of digitalised channels in NPOs where typical authors' keywords are *community, digital media, social networks, technology adoption* and *internet* [35, 98]. In comparison, *digital transformation*, the third most frequent authors' keyword, has been used significantly from 2018 to 2021. Accordingly, we can notice the related topics by considering authors' keywords such as *digital platform, engagement, nonprofit journalism, business model, innovation* and *covid-19*. Unsurprisingly, the authors used those keywords, considering the many challenges triggered by the pandemic. These results highlight the terms that have been discussed over time, and the ones in addition to the keyword *covid-19*, also recognising the impact of disruption and unexpected events on the DT debate concerning NPOs.

The next step consists of the keywords co-occurrence analysis [65, 81]. The latter aims to investigate the connections among the main topics discussed in the dataset. We created the co-occurrence network (Fig. 6) based on the 41 most recurring keywords (see Fig. 5). For this purpose, we employed VOS viewer [75, 76] and Gephi [43, 77] to create a graph which displays the resulting network. Specifically, the network is a graphical representation of how each keyword has been mentioned together with another one [78]. Then, the keywords are the node (where the size represents the median of citations for each keyword) [67]. Then, if two keywords have been mentioned together in a publication, there is a tie between them (co-occurrence) [78]. The more the thickness of a tie, the more the number of connections between the pair of keywords (based on the number of papers including the pair of keywords). Moreover, the colour represents the temporal indications of the most occurrences (red if the median of total mentions ran toward 2006 and blue if it ran toward 2021) [67]. Overall, observing the connections among the keywords in Fig. 6, it is possible to recognise the temporal evolution of the terminology used in the debate on DT in NPOs. At the same time, we also recognise five clusters of authors' keywords co-occurrences (automatically generated by the software) that provide instead the statical picture of the co-occurrences network. In other words, Fig. 6 shows the temporal evolution of the terms concerning the DT discussion in NPOs, and the terms that have been discussed together with high frequency in the local dataset (which represent significant sub-debates).

Regarding the temporal evolution of the terms, Fig. 6 outlines the more recent use of *digital transformation* and the keywords like *non-profit organisations, covid-19, Open Access* , *business models, digital platforms*, and *social media*. Similarly, *non-profit organisations* appear from 2010 to date alongside keywords such as *ict, technology, internet, website, digital media, digital platform*, and *social media*. In addition, it is also possible to identify some older terms that are used together with newer ones. For example, terms like *archiving* or *digital libraries* show a connection with *digital transformation*, while *digital journalism* is connected with *e-learning* and *ict*. In other words, Fig. 6 paves the groundwork for future research avenues by showing the many connections that occurred among the keywords (different terminology) over the years, outlining also those appearing together in the same period.

Besides, considering the five clusters grouping the pair of keywords mostly used by authors, we provide a brief description of each cluster hereafter:

1. This cluster is related to the nonprofit topic to a more general extent concerning the digitalisation of activities for social purposes, common utility, and well-being. This cluster includes keywords such as *partnership*, *knowledge sharing*, *e-learning*, and *digital health*. The most occurred keywords are *nonprofit*, *technology*, and *archiving*, with 77, 34, and 17 occurrences, respectively.
2. This cluster is focused on digital technologies adoption considering the commitment of NPOs to limiting issues related to the digital divide. The most occurred keywords in this cluster are *ict* and *digital divide*, with 36 and 30 occurrences, respectively.
3. This cluster refers to more specific digital transformation initiatives concerning NPOs, including aspects strictly related to the public benefit and the use of digitalised channels and social media. Some keywords included, in addition to the most occurred, *non-profit organisation* and *social media*, are *digital platforms, and community,* with 99, 33, 15, and 14, respectively.
4. This cluster recognises some DT initiatives discussed mainly concerning NPOs, considering the computed number of co-occurrences between the keywords in such a cluster. These discussions focus on the involvement of NPOs in the digitalisation of public knowledge and related issues such as sources or asses. For this cluster, the most occurred keywords are *digital transformation*, *digital libraries*, *social networks*, and *open sources*, with 42, 16, 11, and 11 occurrences, respectively.
5. This cluster refers to the most recent debate concerning the DT in NPOs, especially considering the keyword *covid-19*. In particular, it explores the digital impact affecting the news business and journalism practices and changes affecting the NPOs ecosystem. Then, the most occurred keywords are *covid-19*, *business models*, and *innovation,* with 13, 13, and 11 occurrences, respectively.

5 Discussion and Conclusions

In this study, we performed a bibliometric analysis to examine the evolution of the digital transformation debate in non-profit organisations. Based on 586 contributions, we first developed a descriptive analysis and a conceptual analysis afterwards. The findings of the descriptive analysis depict the growing interest in this stream of research, with approximately 50% of the overall contributions published in the last four years. Moreover, the different analyses show that concerning NPOs, the DT debate has been affected significantly in relation to the need to manage uncertainty and unexpected events triggered by the Covid-19 pandemic [3, 4].

To better understand the DT debate in NPOs, we analysed the most used authors' keywords in the local dataset. By focusing on the 41 most occurred keywords over time, we discussed their different frequency. Then, we developed the keywords co-occurrence analysis [65, 81] to explore the connections among the main terms discussed in the dataset. The findings show terms used several years ago, such as *industry* or *archiving*, and others used mainly in recent years, such as *covid-19* and *nonprofit journalism*. At the same time, other insights are related to terms being popular some time ago, showing a connection with current terminology. For example, *archiving* or *digital libraries* are linked with *digital transformation*, or *digital journalism* is connected with the terms *e-learning* and *ict*. Hence, this study aims to support current researchers examining the DT in NPOs to acknowledge all the relevant contributions (from previous studies), also considering the ones published under other terms.

This study contributes to the research field of DT strictly focused on the literature on NPOs by providing insight into the relationships of different terms used over time (how they are connected). In particular, the local citation analysis could represent a starting point for further researchers in addition to the time course of authors' keywords and related associations (beneficial to select the keywords for additional research).

As a contribution, this research investigated the scientific production related to the main sources of the IS community. As a result, we claim that the IS community seems to pay limited attention to the DT debate in NPOs due to the limited number of studies published in sources belonging to such a domain.

Moreover, this review could support NPOs' managers, policymakers or governmental institutions to better explore the most important publications, cited authors, and terminology related to the DT in NPOs through a longitudinal lens.

Finally, this paper has some limitations. First, this research is based only on Scopus and does not use other databases to integrate the corpus. Second, we focused on the co-word analysis, providing a preliminary citation analysis. So, in a future step, we could perform a complete citation and co-citation analysis to better describe the evolution of topics about citation patterns and recognise co-citation networks and different communities. Moreover, as a further step, we could also develop a thematic map to deeply investigate the conceptual structure, evolution, and relations between themes, further recognising a topic's relevance and novelty.

References

1. Weick, K. E., & Sutcliffe, K. M. (2015). *Managing the unexpected: Sustained performance in a complex world*. Wiley.
2. Aria, M., Cuccurullo, C., D'Aniello, L., Misuraca, M., & Spano, M. (2022). Thematic analysis as a new Culturomic tool: The social media coverage on COVID-19 pandemic in Italy. *Sustainability., 14*, 3643. https://doi.org/10.3390/su14063643
3. Hai, T. N., Van, Q. N., & Thi Tuyet, M. N. (2021). Digital transformation: Opportunities and challenges for leaders in the emerging countries in response to Covid-19 pandemic. *Emerging Science Journal, 5*, 21–36. https://doi.org/10.28991/esj-2021-SPER-03

4. Nagel, L. (2020). The influence of the COVID-19 pandemic on the digital transformation of work. *International Journal of Sociology and Social Policy, 40*, 861–875. https://doi.org/10.1108/IJSSP-07-2020-0323
5. Ali, M. F. (2022). Between panic and motivation: Did the first wave of COVID-19 affect scientific publishing in Mediterranean countries? *Scientometrics, 127*, 3083–3115. https://doi.org/10.1007/s11192-022-04391-w
6. Hausberg, J. P., Liere-Netheler, K., Packmohr, S., Pakura, S., & Vogelsang, K. (2019). Research streams on digital transformation from a holistic business perspective: A systematic literature review and citation network analysis. *Journal of Business Economics, 89*, 931–963. https://doi.org/10.1007/s11573-019-00956-z
7. Jöhnk, J., Oesterle, S., Ollig, P., & Riedel, L. (2020). The complexity of digital transformation: Conceptualizing multiple concurrent initiatives. In Finance & Information Management (Ed.), *15th International Conference on Wirtschaftsinformatik*. https://doi.org/10.30844/wi_2020_j8-joehnk
8. Benbunan-Fich, R., Desouza, K. C., & Andersen, K. N. (2020). IT-enabled innovation in the public sector: Introduction to the special issue. *European Journal of Information Systems, 29*, 323–328. https://doi.org/10.1080/0960085X.2020.1814989
9. vom Brocke, J., Jans, M., Mendling, J., & Reijers, H. A. (2021). A five-level framework for research on process mining. *Business and Information Systems Engineering, 63*, 483–490. https://doi.org/10.1007/s12599-021-00718-8
10. Munoz, A., Todres, M., & Rook, L. (2021). Empowering organisations to gain from uncertainty: A conceptualisation of antifragility through leveraging organisational routines in uncertain environments. *Australasian Accounting, Business and Finance Journal, 15*, 23–42. https://doi.org/10.14453/aabfj.v15i3.3
11. Munoz, A., Billsberry, J., & Ambrosini, V. (2022). Resilience, robustness, and antifragility: Towards an appreciation of distinct organizational responses to adversity. *International Journal of Management Reviews, 24*, 181–187. https://doi.org/10.1111/ijmr.12289
12. Obradović, T., Vlačić, B., & Dabić, M. (2021). Open innovation in the manufacturing industry: A review and research agenda. *Technovation, 102*, 102221. https://doi.org/10.1016/j.technovation.2021.102221
13. d'Orville, H. (2020). COVID-19 causes unprecedented educational disruption: Is there a road towards a new normal? *Prospects, 49*, 11–15. https://doi.org/10.1007/s11125-020-09475-0
14. Rapanta, C., Botturi, L., Goodyear, P., Guàrdia, L., & Koole, M. (2021). Balancing technology, pedagogy and the new normal: Post-pandemic challenges for higher education. *Postdigital Science and Education, 3*, 715–742. https://doi.org/10.1007/s42438-021-00249-1
15. Ameli, M., Shams Esfandabadi, Z., Sadeghi, S., Ranjbari, M., & Zanetti, M. C. (2022). COVID-19 and sustainable development goals (SDGs): Scenario analysis through fuzzy cognitive map modeling. *Gondwana Research, 114*, 138–155. https://doi.org/10.1016/j.gr.2021.12.014
16. Pee, L. G., Pan, S. L., Wang, J., & Wu, J. (2021). Designing for the future in the age of pandemics: A future-ready design research (FRDR) process. *European Journal of Information Systems, 30*, 157–175. https://doi.org/10.1080/0960085X.2020.1863751
17. Carroll, N. (2020). Theorizing on the normalization of digital transformations. In *Twenty-Eighth European Conference on Information Systems (ECIS) - A Virtual AIS Conference*.
18. Nicholson, B., Nielsen, P., & Saebo, J. (2021). Special issue: Digital platforms for development. *Information Systems Journal, 31*, 863–868. https://doi.org/10.1111/isj.12364
19. Madon, S., & Schoemaker, E. (2021). Digital identity as a platform for improving refugee management. *Information Systems Journal, 31*, 929–953. https://doi.org/10.1111/isj.12353
20. Uzcanga, C., & Oiarzabal, P. J. (2019). Associations of migrants in Spain: An enquiry into their digital inclusion in the "network society" in the 2010s. *Voluntas: International Journal of Voluntary and Nonprofit Organisation, 30*, 947–961. https://doi.org/10.1007/s11266-019-00162-z

21. Hanelt, A., Bohnsack, R., Marz, D., & Antunes Marante, C. (2021). A systematic review of the literature on digital transformation: Insights and implications for strategy and organizational change. *Journal of Management Studies, 58*, 1159–1197. https://doi.org/10.1111/joms.12639
22. Wessel, L., Baiyere, A., Ologeanu-Taddei, R., Cha, J., & Blegind Jensen, T. (2021). Unpacking the difference between digital transformation and IT-enabled organizational transformation. *Journal of the Association for Information Systems, 22*, 102–129. https://doi.org/10.17705/1jais.00655
23. Nwankpa, J. K., & Roumani, Y. (2016). IT capability and digital transformation: A firm performance perspective. In *37th International Conference on Information Systems* (pp. 1–16).
24. Schallmo, D., Williams, C. A., & Boardman, L. (2017). Digital transformation of business models - best practice, enablers, and roadmap. *International Journal of Innovation Management, 21*, 1740014. https://doi.org/10.1142/S136391961740014X
25. Markus, M. L., & Rowe, F. (2021). Guest editorial: Theories of digital transformation: A progress report. *Journal of the Association for Information Systems, 22*, 273–280. https://doi.org/10.17705/1jais.00661
26. Rowe, F. (2018). Being critical is good, but better with philosophy! From digital transformation and values to the future of IS research. *European Journal of Information Systems, 27*, 380–393. https://doi.org/10.1080/0960085X.2018.1471789
27. Cipriano, M., & Za, S. (2022). A cluster analysis for research on digital transformation in non-profit organisations. Proceedings of the *Thirtieth European conference on information systems (ECIS 2022)*, Timisoara, Romania. https://doi.org/https://aisel.aisnet.org/ecis2022_rip/54
28. Cipriano, M., & Za, S. (2022). Which digital transformation strategy for non-profit organisations non-profit organisations? Proceedings of the *Thirtieth European Conference on Information Systems (ECIS 2022)*, Timisoara, Romania. https://doi.org/https://aisel.aisnet.org/ecis2022_rp/153
29. vom Brocke, J., Winter, R., Hevner, A., & Maedche, A. (2020). Special issue editorial – Accumulation and evolution of design knowledge in design science research: A journey through time and space. *Journal of the Association for Information Systems, 21*, 520–544. https://doi.org/10.17705/1jais.00611
30. Cipriano, M., & Za, S. (2021). Exploring the discourse on digital transformation in the domain of non-profit organisations. In F. Ceci, A. Prencipe, & P. Spagnoletti (Eds.), *Exploring innovation in a digital world. Lecture notes in information systems and organisation* (Vol. 51, pp. 198–231). Springer. https://doi.org/10.1007/978-3-030-87842-9_15
31. Nahrkhalaji, S. S., Shafiee, S., Shafiee, M., & Hvam, L. (2019). Challenges of digital transformation: The case of the non-profit sector. In *Proceedings of 2018 IEEE International Conference on Industrial Engineering and Engineering Management (IEEM)*. https://doi.org/10.1109/IEEM.2018.8607762
32. Hu, Q., Zhang, H., Kapucu, N., & Chen, W. (2020). Hybrid coordination for coping with the medical surge from the COVID-19 pandemic: Paired-assistance programs in China. *Public Administration Review, 1–7*, 895–901. https://doi.org/10.1111/puar.13253
33. Deitrick, L., Tinkler, T., & Young, E. (2020). *Unprecedented disruption: COVID-19 impact on San Diego nonprofits*.
34. Barhate, B., Hirudayaraj, M., Gunasekara, N., Ibrahim, G., Alizadeh, A., & Abadi, M. (2021). Crisis within a crisis: Migrant workers' predicament during COVID-19 lockdown and the role of non-profit organizations in India. *Indian Journal of Human Development, 15*, 151–164. https://doi.org/10.1177/0973703021997624
35. McNutt, J., Guo, C., Goldkind, L., & An, S. (2018). Technology in nonprofit organizations and voluntary action. *Voluntaristics Review, 3*, 1–63. https://doi.org/10.1163/24054933-12340020
36. Vogelsang, K., Packmohr, S., & Brink, H. (2021). Challenges of the digital transformation – Comparing nonprofit and industry organizations. In *Lecture Notes in Information Systems and Organisation* (pp. 297–312). https://doi.org/10.1007/978-3-030-86790-4_21

37. Bekkers, R., & Wiepking, P. (2011). A literature review of empirical studies of philanthropy: Eight mechanisms that drive charitable giving. *Nonprofit and Voluntary Sector Quarterly, 40*, 924–973. https://doi.org/10.1177/0899764010380927
38. Hansmann, H. B. (1981). *Reforming nonprofit corporation law* (Vol. 129, p. 497). HeinOnline.
39. Taylor, R. (2010). Moving beyond empirical theory. In *Third sector research* (pp. 1–9). Springer. https://doi.org/10.1007/978-1-4419-5707-8_1
40. Bartosova, V., & Podhorska, I. (2021). The importance of non-profit organization in Globalized World: International comparison of American and European continent. *SHS Web Conf. 92*, 07008. https://doi.org/10.1051/shsconf/20219207008
41. Aria, M., & Cuccurullo, C. (2022). *Comprehensive science mapping analysis.*
42. van Eck, N. J., & Waltman, L. (2010). Software survey: VOSviewer, a computer program for bibliometric mapping. *Scientometrics, 84*, 523–538. https://doi.org/10.1007/s11192-009-0146-3
43. Bastian, M., Heymann, S., & Jacomy, M. (2009). Gephi: An open source software for exploring and manipulating networks. BT - International AAAI Conference on Weblogs and Social. In *International AAAI Conference on Weblogs and Social Media* (pp. 361–362).
44. Scornavacca, E., Paolone, F., Za, S., & Martiniello, L. (2020). Investigating the entrepreneurial perspective in smart city studies. *International Entrepreneurship and Management Journal, 16*, 1197–1223. https://doi.org/10.1007/s11365-019-00630-4
45. Lamboglia, R., Lavorato, D., Scornavacca, E., & Za, S. (2021). Exploring the relationship between audit and technology. A bibliometric analysis. *Meditari Accountancy Research, 29*, 1233–1260. https://doi.org/10.1108/MEDAR-03-2020-0836
46. Cobo, M. J., Jürgens, B., Herrero-Solana, V., Martínez, M. A., & Herrera-Viedma, E. (2018). Industry 4.0: A perspective based on bibliometric analysis. *Procedia Computer Science, 139*, 364–371. https://doi.org/10.1016/j.procs.2018.10.278
47. Bracarense, N., Bawack, R., Wamba, S. F., & Carillo, K. D. A. (2022). Artificial intelligence and sustainability: A bibliometric analysis and future research directions. *Pacific Asia Journal of the Association for Information Systems, 14*, 136–159. https://doi.org/10.17705/1pais.14209
48. Za, S., & Spagnoletti, P. (2013). Knowledge creation processes in information systems and management: Lessons from simulation studies. In *Lecture Notes in Information Systems and Organisation* (pp. 191–204). https://doi.org/10.1007/978-3-642-37228-5_19
49. Aria, M., Misuraca, M., & Spano, M. (2020). Mapping the evolution of social research and data science on 30 years of social indicators research. *Social Indicators Research, 149*, 803–831. https://doi.org/10.1007/s11205-020-02281-3
50. Cobo, M. J., López-Herrera, A. G., Herrera-Viedma, E., & Herrera, F. (2011). An approach for detecting, quantifying, and visualizing the evolution of a research field: A practical application to the fuzzy sets theory field. *Journal of Informetrics, 5*, 146–166. https://doi.org/10.1016/j.joi.2010.10.002
51. Za, S., Ghiringhelli, C., & Virili, F. (2020). Organizational change and learning: An explorative bibliometric-based literature analysis. In *Lecture Notes in Information Systems and Organisation* (pp. 429–442). https://doi.org/10.1007/978-3-030-23665-6_31
52. Donthu, N., Kumar, S., & Pattnaik, D. (2020). Forty-five years of journal of business research: A bibliometric analysis. *Journal of Business Research, 109*, 1–14. https://doi.org/10.1016/j.jbusres.2019.10.039
53. White, H. D., & McCain, K. W. (1998). Visualizing a discipline: An author co-citation analysis of information science, 1972–1995. *Journal of the American Society for Information Science, 49*, 327–355. https://doi.org/10.1002/(SICI)1097-4571(19980401)49:4<327::AID-ASI4>3.0.CO;2-W
54. Small, H. (1999). Visualizing science by citation mapping. *Journal of the American Society for Information Science, 50*, 799–813. https://doi.org/10.1002/(SICI)1097-4571(1999)50:9<799::AID-ASI9>3.0.CO;2-G
55. Börner, K., Chen, C., & Boyack, K. W. (2005). Visualizing knowledge domains. *Annual Review of Information Science and Technology, 37*, 179–255. https://doi.org/10.1002/aris.1440370106

56. Chinotaikul, P., & Vinayavekhin, S. (2020). Digital transformation in business and management research: Bibliometric and co-word network analysis. In *2020 1st International Conference on Big Data Analytics and Practices (IBDAP)* (pp. 1–5). IEEE. https://doi.org/10.1109/IBDAP50342.2020.9245456
57. Chawla, R. N., & Goyal, P. (2022). Emerging trends in digital transformation: A bibliometric analysis. *Benchmarking: An International Journal, 29*, 1069–1112. https://doi.org/10.1108/BIJ-01-2021-0009
58. de Bem Machado, A., Secinaro, S., Calandra, D., & Lanzalonga, F. (2022). Knowledge management and digital transformation for Industry 4.0: A structured literature review. *Knowledge Management Research and Practice, 20*, 320–338. https://doi.org/10.1080/14778238.2021.2015261
59. Kraus, S., Jones, P., Kailer, N., Weinmann, A., Chaparro-Banegas, N., & Roig-Tierno, N. (2021). Digital transformation: An overview of the current state of the art of research. *SAGE Open, 11*, 215824402110475. https://doi.org/10.1177/21582440211047576
60. Adekunle, S. A., Aigbavboa, C. O., Ejohwomu, O., Adekunle, E. A., & Thwala, W. D. (2021). Digital transformation in the construction industry: A bibliometric review. *Journal of Engineering, Design and Technology*. https://doi.org/10.1108/JEDT-08-2021-0442
61. Pizzi, S., Venturelli, A., Variale, M., & Macario, G. P. (2021). Assessing the impacts of digital transformation on internal auditing: A bibliometric analysis. *Technology in Society, 67*, 101738. https://doi.org/10.1016/j.techsoc.2021.101738
62. Vial, G. (2019). Understanding digital transformation: A review and a research agenda. *The Journal of Strategic Information Systems, 28*, 118–144. https://doi.org/10.1016/j.jsis.2019.01.003
63. Salamon, L. M., & Sokolowski, S. W. (2016). Beyond nonprofits: Re-conceptualizing the third sector. *Voluntas: International Journal of Voluntary and Nonprofit Organizations, 27*, 1515–1545. https://doi.org/10.1007/s11266-016-9726-z
64. Castriotta, M., Loi, M., Marku, E., & Naitana, L. (2019). What's in a name? Exploring the conceptual structure of emerging organizations. *Scientometrics, 118*, 407–437. https://doi.org/10.1007/s11192-018-2977-2
65. Zupic, I., & Čater, T. (2015). Bibliometric methods in management and organization. *Organizational Research Methods, 18*, 429–472. https://doi.org/10.1177/1094428114562629
66. Ferreira, M. P., Santos, J. C., de Almeida, M. I. R., & Reis, N. R. (2014). Mergers & acquisitions research: A bibliometric study of top strategy and international business journals, 1980–2010. *Journal of Business Research, 67*, 2550–2558. https://doi.org/10.1016/j.jbusres.2014.03.015
67. Scornavacca, E., Kollmann, T., Za, S., Kleine-Stegemann, L., & Strauss, C. (2022). Exploring the field of digital entrepreneurship: A bibliometric analysis. In M. Keyhani, T. Kollmann, A. Ashjari, A. Sorgner, & C. E. Hull (Eds.), *Handbook of digital entrepreneurship* (pp. 74–90). Edward Elgar Publishing.
68. Campra, M., Riva, P., Oricchio, G., & Brescia, V. (2022). Bibliometrix analysis of medical tourism. *Health Services Management Research, 35*, 172–188. https://doi.org/10.1177/09514848211011738
69. Caputo, A., Marzi, G., Maley, J., & Silic, M. (2019). Ten years of conflict management research 2007-2017. *International Journal of Conflict Management, 30*, 87–110. https://doi.org/10.1108/IJCMA-06-2018-0078
70. Marzi, G., Caputo, A., Garces, E., & Dabic, M. (2020). A three decade mixed-method bibliometric investigation of the IEEE transactions on engineering management. *IEEE Transactions on Engineering Management, 67*, 4–17. https://doi.org/10.1109/TEM.2018.2870648
71. Huang, J.-H., Duan, X.-Y., He, F.-F., Wang, G.-J., Hu, X.-Y. (2021). A historical review and bibliometric analysis of research on weak measurement research over the past decades based on Biblioshiny, 1–19.
72. Callon, M., Courtial, J. P., & Laville, F. (1991). Co-word analysis as a tool for describing the network of interactions between basic and technological research: The case of polymer chemistry. *Scientometrics, 22*, 155–205. https://doi.org/10.1007/BF02019280

73. Za, S., & Braccini, A. M. (2017). Tracing the roots of the organizational benefits of IT services. In *Exploring Services Science* (pp. 3–11). https://doi.org/10.1007/978-3-319-56925-3_1
74. Rahal, A., & Zainuba, M. (2019). The rating dilemma of academic management journals: Attuning the perceptions of peer rating. *Advances in Business Research, 9*, 26–45.
75. Perianes-Rodriguez, A., Waltman, L., & van Eck, N. J. (2016). Constructing bibliometric networks: A comparison between full and fractional counting. *Journal of Informetrics, 10*, 1178–1195. https://doi.org/10.1016/j.joi.2016.10.006
76. van Eck, N. J., & Waltman, L. (2014). Visualizing bibliometric networks. In *Measuring scholarly impact* (pp. 285–320). Springer International Publishing, Champions. https://doi.org/10.1007/978-3-319-10377-8_13
77. Bastian, M., & Heymann, S. (2014). *Gephi: An Open Source Software for Exploring and Manipulating Networks* (pp. 4–6). https://doi.org/10.13140/2.1.1341.1520
78. Aria, M., & Cuccurullo, C. (2017). Bibliometrix: An R-tool for comprehensive science mapping analysis. *Journal of Informetrics, 11*, 959–975. https://doi.org/10.1016/j.joi.2017.08.007
79. Baier-Fuentes, H., Merigó, J. M., Amorós, J. E., & Gaviria-Marín, M. (2019). International entrepreneurship: A bibliometric overview. *The International Entrepreneurship and Management Journal, 15*, 385–429. https://doi.org/10.1007/s11365-017-0487-y
80. Walker, J., & Wood, G. (2021). Methodology. *Academic Journal Guide*. https://charteredabs.org/wp-content/uploads/2021/06/Academic_Journal_Guide_2021-Methodology.pdf. https://doi.org/10.36548/jitdw.2021.2
81. Za, S., Pallud, J., Agrifoglio, R., & Metallo, C. (2020). Value co-creation in online communities: A preliminary literature analysis. In *Lecture Notes in Information Systems and Organisation* (pp. 33–46). https://doi.org/10.1007/978-3-030-23665-6_4.
82. Merigó, J. M., Mas-Tur, A., Roig-Tierno, N., & Ribeiro-Soriano, D. (2015). A bibliometric overview of the Journal of Business Research between 1973 and 2014. *Journal of Business Research, 68*, 2645–2653. https://doi.org/10.1016/j.jbusres.2015.04.006
83. Batista-Canino, R. M., Santana-Hernández, L., & Medina-Brito, P. (2023). A scientometric analysis on entrepreneurial intention literature: Delving deeper into local citation. *Heliyon., 9*, e13046. https://doi.org/10.1016/j.heliyon.2023.e13046
84. Nee, R. C. (2013). Creative destruction: An exploratory study of how digitally native news nonprofits are innovating online journalism practices. *International Journal on Media Management, 15*, 3–22. https://doi.org/10.1080/14241277.2012.732153
85. Coates Nee, R. (2014). Social responsibility theory and the digital nonprofits: Should the government aid online news startups? *Journalism, 15*, 326–343. https://doi.org/10.1177/1464884913482553
86. Ferrucci, P. (2015). Public journalism no more: The digitally native news nonprofit and public service journalism. *Journalism, 16*, 904–919. https://doi.org/10.1177/1464884914549123
87. Konieczna, M., & Robinson, S. (2014). Emerging news non-profits: A case study for rebuilding community trust? *Journalism, 15*, 968–986. https://doi.org/10.1177/1464884913505997
88. Ferrucci, P. (2017). Exploring public service journalism. *Journalism & Mass Communication Quarterly, 94*, 355–370. https://doi.org/10.1177/1077699016681968
89. Ferrucci, P. (2015). Murder Incorporated. *Electronic News, 9*, 108–121. https://doi.org/10.1177/1931243115581414
90. Ferrucci, P., Russell, F. M., Choi, H., Duffy, M., & Thorson, E. (2017). Times are a Changin. *Journalism Studies, 18*, 247–264. https://doi.org/10.1080/1461670X.2015.1065197
91. Yoo, S.-C., & Drumwright, M. (2018). Nonprofit fundraising with virtual reality. *Nonprofit Management & Leadership, 29*, 11–27. https://doi.org/10.1002/nml.21315
92. Smith, J. N. (2018). The social network?: Nonprofit constituent engagement through social media. *Journal of Nonprofit & Public Sector Marketing, 30*, 294–316. https://doi.org/10.1080/10495142.2018.1452821
93. Bürger, T. (2015). Use of digital advocacy by German nonprofit foundations on Facebook. *Public Relations Review, 41*, 523–525. https://doi.org/10.1016/j.pubrev.2015.07.007

94. Raman, A. (2016). How do social media, mobility, analytics and cloud computing impact nonprofit organizations? A pluralistic study of information and communication technologies in Indian context. *Information Technology for Development, 22*, 400–421. https://doi.org/10.1080/02681102.2014.992002
95. Voida, A., Harmon, E., & Al-Ani, B. (2011). Homebrew databases. In *Proceedings of the SIGCHI Conference on Human Factors in Computing Systems* (pp. 915–924). ACM. https://doi.org/10.1145/1978942.1979078
96. Bakir, V., & McStay, A. (2018). Fake news and the economy of emotions. *Digital Journalism, 6*, 154–175. https://doi.org/10.1080/21670811.2017.1345645
97. Te'eni, D., & Young, D. R. (2003). The changing role of nonprofits in the network economy. *Nonprofit and Voluntary Sector Quarterly, 32*, 397–414. https://doi.org/10.1177/0899764003254900
98. Guo, C., & Saxton, G. D. (2014). Tweeting social change. *Nonprofit and Voluntary Sector Quarterly, 43*, 57–79. https://doi.org/10.1177/0899764012471585

How to Unlock the Value of Your Data: Six Design Guidelines for Implementing Data Strategies

Jörg H. Mayer, Marc Lanzerath, Juliane Wutzler, Reiner Quick, and Marcus Peruscha

Abstract Companies struggle to exploit the value of their data. Data strategies define the scope and provide a roadmap for a company's data management. However, most companies remain behind the curve. Based on structured expert interviews, we provide six design guidelines for implementing data strategies. They are applicable across industries and at all levels of a company's data management: (1) Define effectiveness as the overarching project goal. In doing so, focus on better insights by leveraging advanced analytics for big data. (2) Implement data strategies across the company, ideally with a board member's commitment. (3) Create diverse project teams. IT should not be the sole project leader. (4) Follow a top-down project approach, supplemented by quick wins covering a company's current pain points. (5) Ensure data quality, integrate your data then, and assign roles and responsibilities. (6) There is no one size fits all. Accordingly, consider digital technologies and align them with your information system backbone.

Keywords Data strategy · Digital technologies · Design guidelines · Structured expert interviews · Design science research in information systems

1 Introduction

Across all industries, less than two-thirds of companies' structured data is actively analyzed and less than 18% of its unstructured data is used at all [1]. 85% of all stored data is unidentified [2]. Accordingly, data analysts spend 80% of their time

J. H. Mayer (✉) · M. Lanzerath · R. Quick
Darmstadt University of Technology, Darmstadt, Germany

J. Wutzler
Worms University of Applied Sciences, Worms, Germany

M. Peruscha
Döhler SE, Darmstadt, Germany

A. M. Braccini et al. (eds.), *Technologies for Digital Transformation*, Lecture Notes in Information Systems and Organisation 64,
https://doi.org/10.1007/978-3-031-52120-1_14

discovering and preparing data—not the analysis itself [3]. In other words, when it comes to *managing data effectively*, most companies remain behind the curve. Data breaches are common, rogue data sets are propagated in silos, and information systems (IS) fail to meet the requirements.

In order to unlock its value, *data has to be managed as an asset* [4]. For example, manufacturing companies significantly increase their productivity when they are able to rely on data-driven decision making [5, 6]. Another example is the COVID-19 vaccine development within months. The adaptation to the Omicron variant would not have been possible without sound *data management.* It covers the effective use of data within an organization [4], in particular, it enables advanced analytics for big data [7].

As the annually generated data volume is expected to reach 175 zettabytes by 2025, companies will need to consider how to leverage digital technologies [8]. In doing so, *data strategies* are a prerequisite. They not only define the scope and provide a roadmap for a company's data management, but even deal with alternatives, ultimately ensuring relevant data management capabilities [9, 10].

Although companies acknowledge the need for a data strategy [11], the majority has neither developed nor implemented one [12]. We examined models such as the Data Excellence Model (DXM) or the Corporate Data Quality Management (CDQM) reference model. However, they do not provide design guidelines (DGs) for implementing data strategies nor incorporate associated instantiations [10]. This is even true for data management frameworks such as the Data Management Body of Knowledge (DMBOK) guide [13] or the Data Management Model of the Capability Maturity Model Institute (CMMI-DMM) [14]. Furthermore, these models lack an up-to-date approach for leveraging digital technologies, i.e., applying advanced analytics to big data [15, 16].

Accordingly, the objective of this article is to present *design guidelines for implementing data strategies*. They should be applicable across industries and at all levels of a company's data management. In doing so, we conduct structured expert interviews and use a food and beverage company as our reference for evaluation. We pose two research questions (RQ):

- What constitutes *design guidelines* for data strategy implementation?
- Do the proposed design guidelines actually do what is intended (*validity*) and are they useful beyond the environment in which they were initially developed (*utility*)?

To create things that serve human purposes [17], ultimately to build a better world [18], we follow Design Science Research (DSR) in IS [19, 20], for which the publication scheme from Gregor and Hevner [21] gave us direction. We motivate this article with companies' revealed need to better implement data strategies (*introduction*). Highlighting research gaps, we contextualize our research questions (*literature review*). Addressing these gaps, we conduct structured expert interviews (*method*). Emphasizing a staged research process with iterative "build" and "evaluate" research activities [22], we come up with the proposed design guidelines (*artifact description*, related to RQ 1). We then conduct a case study as our reference for *evaluation* (related to RQ 2). Comparing our results with prior work and examining how they relate back to the article's objective and research questions, we close with a summary, limitations of our work, and avenues for future research (*discussion and conclusion*) [23].

2 Literature Review

Following Webster and Watson [24] as well as vom Brocke [25, 26], we identified relevant articles in a four-stage process. (1) We focused on leading IS journals as well as selected business, management, and accounting journals, complemented by proceedings from major IS conferences (*outlet search*). For a practitioners' perspective, we considered journals such as MIS Quarterly Executive and Harvard Business Review. (2) Accessing the identified outlets, we used ScienceDirect, EBSCOhost, Springer Link, AIS eLibrary, and ACM Library (*database search*). (3) Then, we searched for articles through their titles, abstracts, and keywords (*keyword search*)—limiting the results to the last ten years.

Integrating this strategy for our research, we combined the keywords "data" and "strategy," which yielded about 800 hits. We then combined data with either "management," "governance," "better insights," "decision making," "integration," or "architecture" as well as "strategy" with "digital," "information," or "technology" (Fig. 1). This led to 27 relevant hits.

Finally, we conducted a (4) *backward and forward search*. With references from all relevant publications, we identified another 11 publications such as Pentek et al. [10] and Gür et al. [15] ending up with *38 publications* in total. Figure 1 depicts our search string with the number of relevant publications.

For our gap analysis, we structured relevant publications into three clusters:

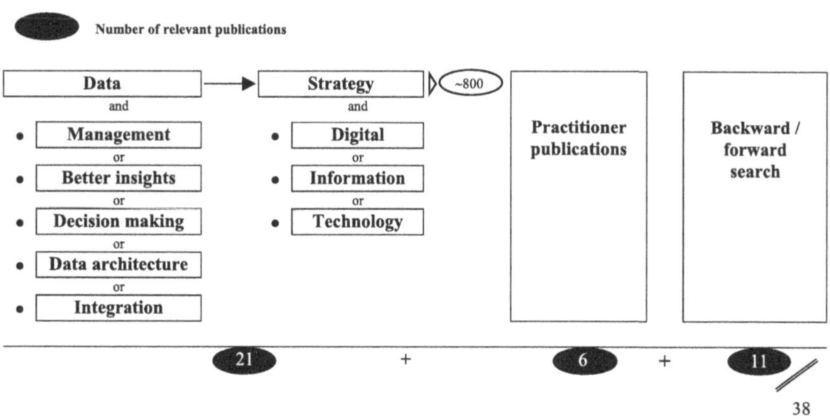

Fig. 1 Search strategy

1. **Reference Models**: In order to build data management capabilities, 11 conceptual frameworks have been established to provide "descriptions of an application domain" [15, 27]. However, only the DXM provides a systematic scientific framework. It is based on the Hüner et al. [28] CDQM model and has recently been adapted to consider the impact of big data and artificial intelligence (AI) [10, 27]. It covers 11 design areas that are clustered into goals, results, and enablers [10]. Enablers include performance management, organization, processes and methods, data architecture, data management applications, data lifecycle, as well as *data strategy*. The latter is crucial for the model. Within these design areas, companies strive for data and business capabilities (*goals*) ultimately leading to data excellence and business value (*results*) [10].

   While the DXM structures design areas of data management, it does not detail scope and deliverables for each design area nor patterns of action [29]. We address a first research gap by developing *design guidelines* when applying proven concepts for data management. In contrast to design principles which are "statements that prescribe what and how to build an artifact in order to achieve a preferred design goal" [30, 31], design guidelines have a more recommendatory and adaptive character [19]. For research purposes, design guidelines contribute to theories that specify how artifacts should be designed on the basis of kernel theories [32].
2. **Data Strategy Implementation**: We identified three focus areas that are key for implementing data strategies. Thus, we apply this structure in our interview guide as follows (Sect. 3): We begin with *reasons for action.* Companies often pay little attention to the use of data, which results in data breaches, silos [33–35], or strategic risks [36–38]. However, not all companies successfully implement data strategies [35]. By examining our interviewees' *motivations*, we aim to identify what drives companies to finally take action to implement data strategy projects *now.*

   After starting data strategy implementations, companies need to ensure *alignment with other strategy aspects*. As digital technologies are currently reshaping corporate strategies, business models, and processes, aligning business and IT strategy effectively is important [39, 40]. Data strategy needs to be a substantial part of such alignment [41, 42]. A cross-functional alignment process is therefore key, focusing on processes across different business units or product lines [43, 44]. Hence, we question which functions and departments need to be involved when implementing data strategies.

   Finally, the overarching goal of a data strategy is to *build data capabilities* such as data processing or modelling [10]. Simultaneously, the maturity-level of a company's data capabilities determines the orientation of its data strategy in the design phase [45]. Thus, there is an interdependence between data strategy and capabilities. Focusing on such implications, Halaweh and El Massry [41] developed a model describing eight success factors grouped into four main dimensions. The first dimension contains success factors such as top management support, organizational change, and the need for skilled professionals [41]. Other authors have agreed on the lack of a data-driven culture [33, 46] or human talent [40] as barriers to building data capabilities.

The second dimension covers the required IS *infrastructure* and *data analytics* necessary to extract value from data within a company [41, 47]. The third dimension deals with the *data content* itself, considering data quality and data veracity [41]. Other authors add data integration [40] and data accessibility [48]. This results in requirements for the governance of roles and responsibilities, given that expanding data accessibility requires a detailed data ownership concept [49, 50]. Accordingly, the fourth dimension of Halaweh and El Massry [41] is data-related processes, procedures, and policies and focuses on data security, data privacy, and data strategy.

However, the relations between different data capabilities and their success factors remain unclear [51]. Addressing this topic, we provide a *systematic approach for implementing data strategies* by identifying and prioritizing design guidelines that can help companies ask the right questions at the right time [16, 52]. We address our second research gap, which is the lack of instructions for implementing data strategies, by proposing design guidelines to apply proven concepts.

3. **Research Method**: Prior research applies a broad mix of research methods in the context of data strategies. While a minority of publications such as Tallon [43] used quantitative methods or event studies like Gwebu et al. [38], other publications applied qualitative methods. Ross et al. [44] conducted interviews with senior executives from 27 companies. Other authors used focus group observations of IT and data experts [28], a (multi-)*case study* from different industries [49], secondary data analysis [12], or researcher's opinion [3]. Additionally, we assessed six literature reviews such as Legner et al. [27] or Mazzei and Noble [53].

Pentek et al. [10] applied a consortium research approach to develop the DXM. DalleMule and Davenport [3] introduced a framework that distinguishes between defensive and offensive approaches. Much of the examined literature provided a series of insights into data strategies. Lefebvre et al. [48] focused on data democratization, Lakoju and Serrano [42] examined big data. Other studies including Wilberg et al. [16] or Himmi et al. [45] focused solely on data strategy and only provide granular findings.

Mitigating the third and final research gap (RQ 1, Sect. 4), we opted for a *method mix* [54] combining structured expert interviews across industries with an in-depth case analysis of our reference company to arrive at design guidelines. We use a food and beverage company, which is currently setting up a data strategy, as our reference, followed by a second round of expert interviews to corroborate our results and ensure their external validity (RQ 2, Sect. 5).

3 Method

Following the three themes identified in the literature review (Sect. 2), we prepared a *series of 16 questions* which took about 45 min to answer. Some questions provided a selection of pre-determined answers, whereas others left room for individual explanations (i.e., open questions). Following Fontana and Frey [55], the interviewers never deviated from this predetermined sequence of questions as follows: The interviewers started asking if the interviewees were currently implementing a data strategy project or planning to do so. To verify motivations for implementing data strategies, the first cluster of questions focused on "*why the need for a data strategy now*", what the perceived benefits are, and how its success should be measured (six questions).

The second cluster focused on establishing the link between data strategies and other strategy components. It was about "*who does it affect*", covering questions about the project scope, project leader(s), and about project team members (five questions). The third and final cluster focused on *how to start data strategy* projects at the beginning and applying useful IT architectures (four questions).

We started our method mix by interviewing *21 management accounting and data experts* from different companies (Table 1) who belong to the Schmalenbach working group "Digital Finance" [56], which comprises medium to large organizations across all industries in Germany. Selecting a broad range of companies from different industries for the interviews that build the foundation for our design guidelines ensures generalizability of the research result.

Following Mayring [57], a *coding scheme* was developed in order to capture the answers from the qualitative questions. Interviews were conducted by two members of the research team (authors of the article). We thereby aimed to ensure the accuracy and completeness of the interview protocols. Based on the answers, we laid out six design guidelines for implementing a data strategy (Sect. 4).

Evaluating artifacts is a major activity in DSR in IS [58]. In doing so, we evaluate and adjust these design guidelines through an interview-based *single case study* with a global food and beverage company (sales: 2.2 billion euros; 8500 employees). The company represents an ideal subject for research as it has already laid the foundations through a single ERP system and is moving from the design to the

Table 1 Overview of interviewees (participating companies)

n = 21	Mean	Median	Min	Max
Sales in €	39 billion	10 billion	0.9 billion	250 billion
Employees	93,000	30,000	3,500	670,000
Industries	• Machinery (20%)	• Chemicals (16%)		
	• Infrastructure (12%)	• Electrical equipment (8%)		
	• Automotive (8%)	• Consumer goods (8%)		
	• ICT service activities (4%)	• Food and beverages (4%)		
	• Retail trade (4%)	• Real estate (4%)		
	• Others (12%)			

implementation phase of their data strategy. As a global supplier of natural ingredients and nutrition solutions, the company has identified large sales potential among existing customers currently sourcing some components from competitors. Overall, our reference company strives to become a *digital leader in the industry,* causing them to aim for a holistic data strategy that allows exploiting data as a strategic resource.

Case studies are "examinations of a contemporary phenomenon within its real-life context" [59]. They play an important role in bridging the gap between theory and practice [60]. Compared to surveys, they provide substantial in-depth information and enable researchers to study their artifacts in a natural setting [61].

Using *structured expert interviews,* we evaluate our research results through an in-depth analysis of the design guidelines in the context of our reference company. During these interviews, we gathered feedback about the design guidelines' utility and validity. We considered *interviews,* as their purpose is to draw on the interviewee's knowledge as comprehensively as possible [62]. In comparison to surveys, they enable us to delve deeper into a given subject matter. We applied *semi-structured expert interviews,* because they combine a comparable structure within a series of interviews, whilst being flexible when interviewees wish to share their way of thinking and any hidden facets, they are aware of [63].

To ensure that the design guidelines are not specific to the needs of our reference company only, we corroborate our results by conducting interviews with data management experts beyond the reference company [64]. Using semi-structured expert interviews for the reasons outlined above, we again gathered feedback about the design guidelines' utility and validity.

4 Artifact Description

We follow the threefold structure of our expert interviews (Sect. 3) throughout the qualitative content analysis and define design guidelines as follows: (1) Why are companies implementing a data strategy now; (2) Which functions and departments need to be involved; (3) How to translate data strategies into action?

4.1 Why Are Companies Implementing a Data Strategy Now

Regarding the **motivation** for implementing a data strategy, we revealed three key reasons: (1) Companies expected data analytics to cope with big data fostering better decision-making. Accordingly, *enabling advanced analytics and other digital technologies* was key (86%). (2) *Data accessibility and quality* were mentioned by 43% of respondents. This includes treating not only data as an asset but democratizing it to make it widely accessible. In addition, respondents strived for data accuracy, consistency, completeness, and timeliness as a result of an appropriate data

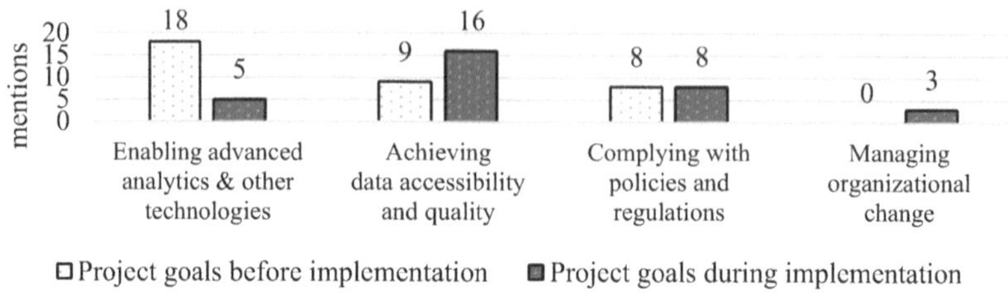

Fig. 2 Project goals before and during data strategy implementation

strategy. (3) Finally, missing data governance leads to an absence of responsibilities and increases the likelihood of data breaches. Thus, *data compliance* was mentioned by 38% of the respondents as another goal for successfully implementing data strategies. Figure 2 presents the goals considered before starting a data strategy project.

We then asked respondents how to measure a **project's success**, which covers *efficiency, effectiveness, experience* [65], as well as *compliance* as an alternative goal. Our results showed that *effectiveness* through better insights was perceived to be the most relevant (67%). The second important success measurement was *experience* (19%) to enable future economies of scale in digital technologies and data usage. *Efficiency*—was in third place. Only 5% considered efficiency to be most useful for measuring the success of a data strategy project. Accordingly, reducing full-time equivalents with a data strategy project was not in focus at all. Instead, business process acceleration (86% of respondents) mattered. We observed that companies implementing data strategies are driven by *better insights leveraging advanced analytics for big data*. We derive a first design guideline:

Design guideline #1: Define effectiveness as the overarching project goal. In doing so, focus on better insights by leveraging advanced analytics for big data.

4.2 Which Functions and Departments Need to Be Involved

Examining the appropriate **depth** of a data strategy project, the respondents agreed that a data strategy must be implemented at *all company levels* from the beginning of the project (86%). Regarding the project's **breadth**, the interviewees answered heterogeneously. *Finance* (86%) and *IT* (81%) are crucial domains that should be covered within the project. They were supplemented by functional areas such as production/operations (57%), marketing and sales (48%), procurement (43%), and supply-chain-management (38%). 24% of interviewees argued for a more comprehensive approach including all company departments right from the beginning of the project.

In line with the importance of a company-wide project scope, 67% of our sample companies had a board member as **project sponsor**. The sponsor typically belonged to the Finance (81%) or IT (43%) domain. In order to ensure a comprehensive approach and reap all potential benefits of a data strategy, data strategy projects need a strong sponsor. He/she should be able to define binding standards for the entire company. Analyzing the answers, we strongly recommend the CFO, as he/she is not only responsible for the Finance department, but usually controls even the IT budget. We derive a second design guideline:

Design guideline #2: Implement data strategies across the company, ideally with a board member's commitment.

Composing the **project team**, IT was involved in 95% of cases, followed by Finance (90%) and supplemented with expertise from other departments, i.e., production/operations (33%), marketing/sales (33%), supply chain management (24%), or procurement (19%). Hence, mixed teams should be central to project implementation.

Project heads from either Finance (57%) or IT (43%) were shown to take the **lead**. Since value creation from data strategy implementation takes place within the business processes itself, neither the project sponsor (#9) nor the project lead (#12) should be from the IT department. This leads us to a third design guideline:

Design guideline #3: Create diverse project teams. IT should not be the sole project leader.

4.3 How to Translate Data Strategies into Action

We then asked for *focus topics* that arise during the project. In particular, we analyzed how the focus has shifted from the initial motivations over time (Sect. 4.1, Fig. 2). While enabling data analytics was most common for starting a data strategy project, in turn, when it comes to implementation, companies recognized the need for *better data quality and accessibility*. 76% of the interviewees stated that the project had revealed low data quality, e.g., data inconsistency and intransparency. Accordingly, only 24% maintained data analytics as the most common project goal, *compliance with policies and regulations* remained relevant (in line with the initial motivation, 38% of respondents).

As data are gathered in different departments, we questioned whether a top-down approach is appropriate. Hence, we asked participants *how they initiated a data strategy project* (#11). The majority of interviewees implemented data strategies top-down (43%) or as a combination of top-down and bottom-up approaches (43%). In contrast, a minority approached data strategy implementation bottom-up solely focusing on individual use cases (14%). Considering these findings, we recommended a top-down approach for the implementation phase, which enables achieving the goal of *data accessibility and quality*. We conclude a fourth design guideline:

Design guideline #4: Follow a top-down project approach.

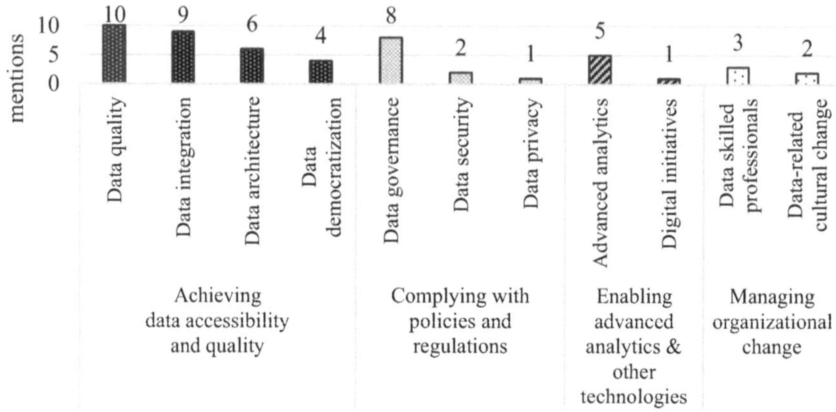

Fig. 3 Success factors for data capability building

We then asked for a prioritization of relevant **success factors** for data strategy implementation (Fig. 3). To translate a top-down approach (DG#4) into action, a clear target picture of the data architecture (29%) and breakdown of silos through data integration (43%) was key. This included *scouting and evaluating (digital) focus technologies*. Thus, in the beginning of data strategy projects, companies needed to focus on the basics, aiming to achieve high data quality (48%) for advanced topics such as AI projects.

Promising success factors are as follows: Establish centralized *data governance* first, ensuring *data quality* and clarifying roles and responsibilities. *Data integration* initiatives then break down data silos to make the data accessible and democratize knowledge locked in the data systems. We derive a fifth design guideline:

Design guideline #5: Ensure data quality, integrate your data then, and assign roles and responsibilities.

To determine appropriate underlying IT architectures, our penultimate question dealt with **IT concepts**. Data lakes (86%) and data warehouses (81%) were considered to be relevant for data strategy implementation. A frequently cited reason for data lakes was the associated ability to integrate multiple data sources such as structured and unstructured data into a single source of truth. Nevertheless, companies do not see a data lake as a standalone approach, as data scientists are needed to handle the high volume of structured and unstructured data.

Data warehouses, on the other hand, were rated as well known and widely used. Newer concepts like a data mesh (29%) or data fabric (19%) were considered less frequently. Their future role remained unclear. Enterprise knowledge graphs (19%) represent a more sophisticated but early-stage concept. Depending on a company's needs and current IT landscape, the benefits of these technologies are weighed differently. Therefore, the sixth design guideline states:

Design guideline #6: There is no one size fits all. Accordingly, consider digital technologies.

5 Evaluation

Evaluating our design guidelines, we gathered feedback by conducting four semi-structured in-depth expert interviews of about 45 min with the IT Team Leader BI Data Engineering and the Head of Data Governance and Data Quality of the reference company. To avoid bias, the interviewees were not part of the interviews for the design guidelines (Sect. 4). We included an external perspective in the evaluation phase by conducting interviews with a Senior Data Excellence Specialist from a chemicals company and a Data Management Principal from an information and communications technology company. The latter interviews helped us to avoid an undue emphasis on the reference company's industry- and company-specific focus areas. Cross-checking the experts' answers with our findings (Sect. 4), we reworked three design guidelines.

We began the expert interviews with questions about the design guidelines' *understandability and completeness*, followed by their *potential for implementation*. All agreed that the design guidelines were easy to understand. However, the Data Excellence Specialist would prefer additional clarification on design guideline #5 (i.e., a clearer link between data integration and data architecture). Three participants mentioned additional topics such as task and behavioral capabilities of the project leader and data criticality which describes how vital data is to the companies' processes. According to the Data Excellence Specialist, the design guidelines can lead the way, but "[...] the implementation might not necessarily be easy." He elaborated that a lack of top management support makes it difficult to implement a top-down approach to long-term data strategy, as management's focus changes over time.

We then gathered feedback about the **validity** of the design guidelines (RQ 2). We structured our evaluation using a presentation of each design guideline followed by the assessment of three statements to which the interviewees indicated their agreement. The level of agreement was high, with an average of at least 4.25 out of five (Table 2).

Referring to design guideline #1, three participants strongly agreed that *effectiveness* is the overarching goal for data strategy projects. The Team Leader IT Data Engineering stated that "[...] better insights provide the basis for deriving actions based on data." Both external data management experts added that "[...] data is not an end in itself," so while looking for better insights, the data strategy must be aligned with business strategy in order to achieve goal-oriented resource allocation. The Head of Data Governance confirmed that effectiveness is part of the project goal but added that a data strategy should not ignore the cost factor. Accordingly, we validate design guideline #1.

Regarding design guideline #2, all participants strongly agreed that a data strategy must include the *entire company*. The support of a board member is required. The Head of Data Governance and the Data Management Principal confirmed that management support is mandatory, as it ensures that there is continued momentum in implementation.

Table 2 Agreement of the interviewees

	Validity						Utility		
n = 4	DG1	DG2	DG3	DG4	DG5	DG6	S1	S2	S3
Interviewee #1	5	5	5	5	5	5	4	4	4
Interviewee #2	3	5	5	3	5	5	5	4	2
Interviewee #3	5	5	5	4	4	5	5	4	2
Interviewee #4	5	5	5	5	5	5	4	4	2
Median	5	5	5	4	5	5	4	4	2
Mean	4,5	5	5	4.25	4.75	5	4.5	4	2.5

Strongly Agree—5; Agree—4; Neutral—3; Disagree—2; Strongly Disagree—1

The Digital Excellence Specialist noted that it is beneficial to maintain an overall sense of urgency, e.g., by linking data strategy with topics such as compliance or sustainability. Especially the COVID-19 pandemic has increased the importance of digitalization regarding data strategy projects. This feedback validates design guideline #2.

Concerning leadership and the project team composition (design guideline #3), the Head of Data Governance and the Data Excellence Specialist explained that business and IT must work together and share the project lead, where one must ensure alignment with the overall business strategy. The Data Management Principal is in favor of project team members coming from the business. Accordingly, we validate design guideline #3.

Our fourth design guideline proposed a top-down project approach. All interviewees agreed with this statement. Nevertheless, they pointed out that enhancing the top-down approach with companies' *individual use cases* and fostering a combined approach, is likely to improve effectiveness—as a data strategy project typically takes 2 to 3 years. Consequently, it is important to show project results early on, meaning quick-wins to secure continued sponsorship from the organization. Their focus should be on the identification of common pain points. We adjust our design guideline #4 as follows.

Adjusted design guideline #4: Follow a top-down project approach, supplemented by quick wins covering a company's current pain points.

Introducing relevant success factors, we leave design guideline #5 as it is. All participants agreed that data quality, data integration, and data governance are key, so that the data strategy must provide concepts and methods. The Data Management Principal placed special emphasis on data governance. When implementing data governance structures, three interviewees recommended focusing on an *end-to-end process design*. The Head of Data Governance and the Data Excellence Specialist explained that the correct design of processes heavily influences the resulting flow of data. Accordingly, responsibilities are automatically assigned to appropriate roles. He further elaborated that efficient data delivery channels between data consumer and supplier are at the center of their data strategy. This results in challenges regarding integrating different data sources and the structure of a data architecture, said the Data Excellence Specialist. When it comes to *data quality*, the Data Management Principal noted that key performance indicators must be in place.

To support data strategies, *digital technologies* are important (Sect. 1). All interviewees agreed with design guideline #6 that there is no "must have" technology. Instead, every company has to consider it individually. The Data Management Principal argued that there are several factors influencing the choice, namely budget, company size, data volume, and preferences for or against cloud technologies.

Additionally, an important factor is the existing IS backbone (Data Excellence Specialist; Data Management Principal). While the business should determine functional requirements, IT should be responsible for the IS backbone. The Head of Data Governance highlighted *data granularity* as an important technical requirement. Enterprise Knowledge Graphs are currently in the proof-of-concept phase and therefore do not yet play a major role, according to the BI Team Leader Data Engineering. Summarizing this feedback, we enrich design guideline #6 as follows:

Adjusted design guideline #6: There is no one size fits all. Accordingly, consider digital technologies and align them with your information system backbone.

Regarding the **utility** of the design guidelines, we asked the interviewees if they were suitable beyond their intended purpose. The Head of Governance and the Data Excellence Specialist agreed that the design guidelines were helpful in developing patterns of action, thus increasing the transparency of implementation. The BI Team Leader Data Engineering agreed on their helpfulness as he described the design guidelines as "concise and accurate." Furthermore, they support the data strategy implementation by addressing the corresponding necessary process steps.

In addition, all interviewees agreed that they are evaluating the design guidelines as a basis for other IS projects such as Environmental, Social, and Governance reporting and would apply them in similar ways. However, when applying the design guidelines to other use cases, despite remaining a good starting point, they must be modified. Accordingly, the utility of the design guidelines was assessed as good, especially when patterns of actions must be defined and implemented.

6 Discussion and Conclusion

The objective of this paper was to present design guidelines on how to implement data strategies. Covering the three major topics of project management, that is why companies are implementing a data strategy (Sect. 4.1), which functions and departments need to be involved (Sect. 4.2), and how to translate data strategies into action (Sect. 4.3), we derived our findings based on structured expert interviews across companies from different industries.

For practice, the design guidelines should help on implementing data strategies. By incorporating contributions from multiple companies at different stages of implementation and various focus areas of action, the design guidelines should foster the dissemination of data strategies across industries and at all levels of a company's data management activities. They provide a good foundation, furthermore they are scalable and can, thus, be applied to other IS projects with the necessary modifications.

For research purposes, our work takes a step towards aligning academic knowledge on data management reference models and lessons learned from practice [27]. We thereby complement existing reference models such as the DXM [10] with prescriptive knowledge by providing principles and methods describing *how to do* something [66]. Hence, our design guidelines support the transformation of conceptual models, which most often describe the "what to do" [29]. Compared to the DAMA-DMBOK [13], our design guidelines are based on a quantitative and qualitative content analysis.

Unlike specific guidance on strategy design, our design guidelines provide instructions for implementing data strategy projects threefold in terms of project approach, team composition, and project lead (Sect. 4). In doing so, the design guidelines can be applied regardless of a company's data management maturity—from "digital beginners" to "digital masters" [67]. They even support a specialization of the CMMI-DMM framework [8] as they provide insights into the IS architecture used and help to enrich the technological change by a new scientific field of data strategy [15].

However, our research inevitably reveals certain *limitations* which open up avenues for future research. Data strategies leveraging digital technologies are a new phenomenon that companies have to manage. With regards to the selected IS architectures, we were unable to derive meaningful reasons as to why a certain IS is considered. We, thus, recommend monitoring developments of emerging IS architectures such as knowledge graphs. The latter could represent a promising database solution. Due to the early stage of data strategy implementation in the examined companies, we were unable to draw conclusions which subprojects are performing well and why. As these projects progress, it will become possible to gain deeper insights into their implementation. Finally, in terms of the method applied (Sect. 3), there are limitations to structured interviews as they neglect deeper social interactions and emotional dimensions [55].

References

1. Smith, T., Stiller, B., Guszcza, J., & Davenport, T. (2019). *Analytics and AI-driven enterprises thrive in the age of with*. Accessed 2021/12/21, from https://www2.deloitte.com/us/en/insights/topics/analytics/insight-driven-organization.html
2. Sangani, P. (2016). *85% stored data is dark or redundant*. Accessed 2022/05/05, from https://economictimes.indiatimes.com/technology/data-overload-could-cost-cos-up-to-3-3-trillion-by-2020/articleshow/51406951.cms
3. DalleMule, L., & Davenport, T. H. (2017). What's your data strategy? *Harvard Business Review, 95*(3), 112–121.

4. Wang, R. Y. (1998). A product perspective on total data quality management. *Communications of the ACM, 41*(2), 58–65.
5. Brynjolfsson, E., & McElheran, K. (2019). *Data in action: Data-driven decision making and predictive analytics in U.S. manufacturing*. Accessed 2021/12/15, from https://papers.ssrn.com/sol3/papers.cfm?abstract_id=3422397
6. Brynjolfsson, E., & McElheran, K. (2016). The rapid adoption of data-driven decision-making. *The American Economic Review, 106*(5), 133–139.
7. HBR Analytic Services. (2021). *The Data Dividend: Unlocking Performance Intelligence with Data-DrivenIndustrialSoftware*.Accessed2021/12/19,fromhttps://hbr.org/sponsored/2021/12/the-data-dividend-unlocking-performance-intelligence-with-data-driven-industrial-software
8. Fleckenstein, M., & Fellows, L. (2018). *Modern data strategy* (1st ed.). Springer Nature.
9. Falge, C., Otto, B., & Österle, H. (2013). Towards a strategy design method for corporate data quality management. In *11th conference on Wirtschaftsinformatik* (Vol. 51, pp. 801–815).
10. Pentek, T., Legner, C., & Otto, B. (2017). Towards a reference model for data management in the digital economy. In A. Maedche, J. vom Brocke, & A. R. Hevner (Eds.), *Designing the Digital Transformation: DESRIST 2017 Research in Progress Proceedings of the 12th International Conference on Design Science Research in Information Systems* (pp. 73–82).
11. HBR Analytic Services. (2019). *Critical success factors to achieve a better enterprise data strategy in a multi-cloud environment*. Accessed 2022/01/30, from https://hbr.org/sponsored/2019/09/critical-success-factors-to-achieve-a-better-enterprise-data-strategy-in-a-multi-cloud-environment
12. Davenport, T. H., & Bean, R. (2018). *Big companies are embracing analytics, but most still don't have a data-driven culture*. Accessed 2022/02/08, from https://hbr.org/2018/02/big-companies-are-embracing-analytics-but-most-still-dont-have-a-data-driven-culture
13. DAMA. (2017). *DAMA-DMBOK. Data management body of knowledge* (2nd ed.). Technics Publications.
14. CMMI. (2006). *CMMI for Development*. Accessed 08.05.2022, from https://resources.sei.cmu.edu/library/asset-view.cfm?assetid=8091
15. Gür, I., Spiekermann, M., Arbter, M., & Otto, B. (2021). Data strategy development: A taxonomy for data strategy tools and methodologies in the economy. In *Wirtschaftsinformatik Proceedings* (pp. 1–16).
16. Wilberg, J., Triep, I., Hollauer, C., & Omer, M. (2017). Big data in product development: Need for a data strategy. In *Proceedings of PICMET '17: Technology Management for Interconnected World* (pp. 1–10).
17. Simon, H. A. (1996). *The science of the artificial* (3rd ed.). MIT Press.
18. Walls, J. G., Widmeyer, G. R., & El Sawy, O. A. (1992). Building an information system design theory for vigilant EIS. *Information Systems Research, 3*(1), 36–59.
19. Hevner, A. R., March, S. T., Park, J., & Ram, S. (2004). Design science in information systems research. *MIS Quarterly, 28*(1), 75–105.
20. vom Brocke, J., Winter, R., Hevner, A., & Maedche, A. (2020). Accumulation and evolution of design knowledge in design science research - A journey through time and space. *Journal of the Association for Information Systems 21*(3), 520–544.
21. Gregor, S., & Hevner, A. R. (2013). Positioning and presenting design science research for maximum impact. *MIS Quarterly, 37*(2), 337–355.
22. Peffers, K., Tuunanen, T., Rothenberger, M. A., & Chatterjee, S. (2007). A design science research methodology for information systems research. *Journal of Management Information Systems, 24*(3), 45–77.
23. Mayer, J. H., Quick, R., Sayar, S., & Siebert, J. (2022). Switching to flipped classrooms – One and the same training challenged by practitioners and students. *Accounting Education, 31*(1), 1–23.
24. Webster, J., & Watson, R. T. (2002). Analyzing the past to prepare for the future: Writing a literature review. *MIS Quarterly, 26*(2), 13–23.

25. vom Brocke, J., Simons, A., Niehaves, B., Riemer, K., Plattfaut, R., & Cleven, A. (2009). Reconstructing the giant: On the importance of rigour in documenting the literature search process. In S. Newell, E. A. Whitley, N. Pouloudi, J. Wareham, & L. Mathiassen (Eds.), *Proceedings of the 17th European Conference on Information Systems (ECIS 2009).*
26. vom Brocke, J., Simons, A., Riemer, K., Niehaves, B., Plattfaut, R., & Cleven, A. (2015). Standing on the shoulders of giants: Challenges and recommendations of literature search in information systems research. *Communications of the Association for Information Systems 37*(1), 205–224.
27. Legner, C., Pentek, T., & Otto, B. (2020). Accumulating design knowledge with reference models: Insights from 12 years' research into data management. *Journal of the Association for Information Systems, 21*(3), 735–770.
28. Hüner, K.M., Ofner, M., & Otto, B. (2009). Towards a maturity model for corporate data quality management. In *SAC '09: Proceedings of the 2009 ACM symposium on Applied Computing* (pp. 231–238).
29. Frank, U. (2007). Evaluation of reference models. In P. Fettke & P. Loos (Eds.), *Reference modeling for business systems analysis* (pp. 118–140). IGI Global.
30. Chandra, L., Seidel, S., & Gregor, S. (2015). Prescriptive knowledge in IS research: Conceptualizing design principles in terms of materiality, action, and boundary conditions. In T. X. Bui & R. H. Sprague (Eds.), *2015 48th Hawaii International Conference on System Sciences (HICSS 2015).* Kauai, Hawaii, USA, 5–8 January 2015 (pp. 4039–4048). IEEE.
31. Seidel, S., Chandra Kruse, L., Székely, N., Gau, M., & Stieger, D. (2018). Design principles for sensemaking support systems in environmental sustainability transformations. *European Journal of Information Systems, 27*(2), 221–247.
32. Vaishnavi, V. K., & Kuechler, W. (2015). *Design science research methods and patterns. Innovating information and communication technology* (2nd ed.). CRC Press.
33. Redman, T. C. (2018). *5 ways your data strategy can fail.* Accessed 2022/02/22, from https://hbr.org/2018/10/5-ways-your-data-strategy-can-fail
34. Tanriverdi, H., Roumani, Y., & Nwankpa, J. (2019). Structural complexity and data breach risk. In *40th International Conference on Information Systems 2019.*
35. Hurley, J. (2018). *Why your data strategy is your B2B growth strategy.* Accessed 2022/02/22, from https://hbr.org/sponsored/2018/02/why-your-data-strategy-is-your-b2b-growth-strategy
36. Clarke, R. (2016). Big data, big risks. *Information Systems Journal, 26*(1), 77–90.
37. Wrona, T., & Reinecke, P. (2019). The "dark side" of big data analytics - Uncovering path dependency risks of BDA-investments. In *27th European conference on Information Systems* (pp. 1–10).
38. Gwebu, K. L., Wang, J., & Wang, L. (2018). The role of corporate reputation and crisis response strategies in data breach management. *Journal of Management Information Systems, 35*(2), 683–714.
39. Bharadwaj, A., El Sawy, O. A., Pavlou, P. A., & Venkatraman, N. (2013). Digital business strategy: Towards a next generation of insights. *MIS Quarterly, 37*(2), 471–482.
40. Grover, V., Chiang, R. H., Liang, T.-P., & Zhang, D. (2018). Creating strategic business value from big data analytics: A research framework. *Journal of Management Information Systems, 35*(2), 388–423.
41. Halaweh, M., & El Massry, A. (2017). A synergetic model for implementing big data in organizations: An empirical study. *Information Resources Management Journal, 30*(1), 48–64.
42. Lakoju, M., & Serrano, A. (2016). A strategic approach for visualizing the value of big data (SAVV-BIGD) framework. In *IEEE International Conference on Big Data* (pp. 1334–1339).
43. Tallon, P. P. (2008). A process-oriented perspective on the alignment of information technology and business strategy. *Journal of Management Information Systems, 24*(3), 227–268.
44. Ross, J. W., Sebastian, I. M., Beath, C., Mocker, M., Moloney, K., & Fonstad, N. (2016). Designing and executing digital strategies. In *37th International Conference on Information Systems* (pp. 1–17).

45. Himmi, K., Arcondara, J., Guan, P., & Zhou, W. (2017). Value oriented big data strategy: Analysis & case study. In *Proceedings of the 50th Hawaii International Conference on Information Systems* (pp. 1053–1062).
46. Davenport, T. H., & Mittal, N. (2020). *How CEOs can lead a data-driven culture*. Accessed 2022/01/28, from https://hbr.org/2020/03/how-ceos-can-lead-a-data-driven-culture
47. LaValle, S., Lesser, E., Shockley, R., Hopkins, M. S., & Kruschwitz, N. (2011). Big data, analytics and the path from insights to value. *MIT Sloan Management Review, 52*(2), 21–32.
48. Lefebvre, H., Legner, C., & Fadler, M. (2021). Data democratization: Toward a deeper understanding. In *42nd international conference on information systems* (pp. 1–17).
49. Fadler, M., & Legner, C. (2020). Who owns data in the enterprise? Rethinking data ownership in times of big data and analytics. In *28th European conference on information systems* (pp. 1–16).
50. Labadie, C., Legner, C., Eurich, M., & Fadler, M. (2020). FAIR enough? Enhancing the usage of enterprise data with data catalogs. In *IEEE 22nd Conference on Business Informatics* (pp. 201–210).
51. Gür, I., Guggenberger, T., & Altendeitering, M. (2021). Towards a data management capability model. In *27th Americas Conference in Information Systems* (pp. 1–5).
52. Lakoju, M., & Serrano, A. (2017). A framework for aligning big-data projects with organizational strategy. In *AMCIS 2017 Proceedings* (pp. 1–10).
53. Mazzei, M. J., & Noble, D. (2017). Big data dreams: A framework for corporate strategy. *Business Horizons, 60*(3), 405–414.
54. Teddlie, C., & Tashakkori, A. (2009). *Foundations of mixed methods research. Integrating quantitative and qualitative approaches in the social and behavioral sciences*. Sage.
55. Fontana, A., & Frey, J. (1994). Interviewing - The art of science Denzin. In N. K. (Ed.), *The handbook of qualitative research* (pp. 361–376).
56. Schmalenbach Arbeitskreis Digital Finance: Digital Finance. (2022). Accessed 03.02.2022, from https://www.schmalenbach.org/index.php/arbeitskreise/finanz-und-rechnungswesen-steuern/digital-finance
57. Mayring, P. (2015). Qualitative Inhaltsanalyse. In U. Flick, E. von Kardoff, H. Keupp, L. von Rosenstiel, & S. Wolff (Eds.), *Handbuch qualitative Forschung: Grundlagen, Konzepte, Methoden und Anwendungen* (pp. 209–213).
58. Venable, J., Pries-Heje, J., & Baskerville, R. (2016). FEDS: A framework for evaluation in design science research. *European Journal of Information Systems, 25*(1), 77–89.
59. Myers, M. D. (1997). Qualitative research in information systems. *MIS Quarterly, 21*(2), 241–242.
60. Flyvbjerg, B. (2018). Case study. In N. K. Denzin & Y. S. Lincoln (Eds.), *The SAGE handbook of qualitative research* (pp. 301–316). Sage.
61. Dul, J., & Hak, T. (2007). *Case study methodology in business research*. Routledge.
62. Kvale, S. (1996). *Interviews. An introduction to qualitative research interviewing*. Sage.
63. Qu, S. Q., & Dumay, J. (2011). The qualitative research interview. *Qualitative Research in Accounting & Management, 8*(3), 238–264.
64. Prat, N., Comyn-Wattiau, I., Akoka, J. (2014). Artifact evaluation in information systems design-science research - A holistic view. In *PACIS 2014 Proceedings* (23), 1–16.
65. Mayer, J. H., Ulusoy, B., Esswein, M., & Quick, R. (2021). Receiving a triple "E" rating – Measuring IS success by balancing efficiency, effectiveness, and experience criteria. In J. Valacich, A. Baraua, & R. Wright (Eds.), *Building Sustainability and Resilience with IS: A Call for Action. Proceedings of the 42nd International Conference On Information Systems (ICIS)* (pp. 1–16). Austin, Texas.
66. Gregor, S. (2006). The nature of theory in information systems. *MIS Quarterly, 30*(3), 611–642.
67. Mayer, J. H., Göbel, M., Esswein, M., & Quick, R. (2021). Getting digital technologies right – A forward-looking maturity model for enterprise performance management. In R. Cuel & R. Winter (Eds.), *Digital resilience and sustainability: People, organizations, and society. Proceedings of the Eighteenth Conference of the Italian chapter of (ItAIS)* (pp. 1–14). Trento.

Data-Driven Failure Management: An Ontology-Based Speech Recognition App for Failure Capturing in Manufacturing Processes

Philipp Scharfe, Heiner Ludwig, Katja Bley, Martin Wiener, and Thorsten Schmidt

Abstract Manufacturing processes are characterized by an increasing complexity, making them susceptible to failures. An effective strategy to avoid such failures, or at least to minimize their impact, is data-driven failure management. However, for many small and medium sized manufacturers, this strategy is not feasible due to a paucity of relevant failure data, which can be explained by the severe limitations and shortcomings of available solutions: ranging from the error proneness and high efforts of manual solutions to the high costs and implementation efforts of automated solutions. Against this backdrop, our study follows a design science research approach to design, develop, and evaluate a novel ontology-based speech recognition app that addresses key shortcomings of currently available solutions. Main contributions of our study are the development of design requirements and principles, as well as their instantiation in an app prototype for collecting failure data in the context of manufacturing processes.

Keywords Data-driven failure management · Manufacturing-failure capturing · Speech recognition app · Ontology · Design science

P. Scharfe (✉) · M. Wiener
Business Information Systems, esp. Business Engineering, TU Dresden, Dresden, Germany
e-mail: philipp.scharfe@tu-dresden.de; martin.wiener@tu-dresden.de

H. Ludwig · T. Schmidt
Institute of Material Handling and Industrial Engineering, TU Dresden, Dresden, Germany
e-mail: heiner.ludwig@tu-dresden.de; technische.logistik@tu-dresden.de

K. Bley
Business Information Systems, esp. IS in Trade and Industry, TU Dresden, Dresden, Germany

Department of Computer Science, Norwegian University of Science and Technology, Trondheim, Norway
e-mail: katja.bley@ntnu.no

A. M. Braccini et al. (eds.), *Technologies for Digital Transformation*, Lecture Notes in Information Systems and Organisation 64,
https://doi.org/10.1007/978-3-031-52120-1_15

1 Introduction

Nowadays, manufacturing processes are characterized by a high complexity since they need to meet rising demands in terms of productivity, quality, and flexibility [1, 2]. As a result of this complexity, manufacturing processes are becoming increasingly prone to failures [1, 2]. In a manufacturing context, a failure can be broadly defined "as an unforeseen deviation from the planned manufacturing process" [2, p. 92]. Such failures (e.g., a machine breakdown) can lead to serious consequences, such as missed delivery dates, lost business, or significant expenditures for failure fixing [3]. To minimize the negative consequences of manufacturing process failures, an effective data-driven failure management is necessary [4]. A critical requirement for, and first step toward, a data-driven failure management pertains to the collection of accurate failure data, including failure type, object, etc. In the short term, such collected failure data can help workers to resolve failures faster (e.g., by using failure data to decide on the 'right' countermeasures). Further, in the mid to long term, manufacturing managers can use collected failure data to develop models to predict future failures, as well as, to identify and eliminate failure root causes [4]. However, even the first step (i.e., collection of failure data) is already challenging for many manufacturing firms, given the partly severe limitations of the solutions currently available.

Based on their automation level, existing data-collection solutions can be classified into manual, semi-automated, and automated solutions. Generally, manual solutions lead to high efforts, delays, and are error-prone [5]. In contrast, automated solutions avoid key shortcomings of manual solutions, but tend to be very complex and expensive, limiting the use of such solutions in the manufacturing industry, which is still dominated by small and medium-sized enterprises (SMEs) [6]. In this regard, semi-automated solutions represent a compromise between manual and automated solutions [5]. Existing semi-automated solutions can be further classified into typing-based and speech recognition-based solutions. Since the latter minimizes key shortcomings of the former (e.g., worker distraction) [5, 7], speech recognition-based systems represent a promising approach for the collection of failure data in the manufacturing industry. Despite this potential, speech recognition-based data collection systems are not widely used in the manufacturing domain yet [8]. Only a few studies propose the design of speech recognition-based systems for the collection of failure data in this domain [7, 9]. However, these systems collect data along a fixed set of a few general failure attributes, which is problematic since relevant attributes can vary significantly across failure types [4, 10]. To overcome this shortcoming and collect for each failure type specific attributes a more complex underlying failure data structure is necessary, which is difficult to implement with the typically relational-based data structures used in existing solutions. In this regard, an ontology-based data structure represents a well-suited alternative to handle the complexity of manufacturing failure data [11].

Against this backdrop, the objective of this study is to design, instantiate, and evaluate an ontology-based speech recognition app as an assistance system for collecting failure data in manufacturing processes. To do so, we follow the design science research (DSR) cycle proposed by Sonnenberg and vom Brocke [12] and describe the respective design and evaluation steps for the development of our solution artifact. In this context, our study contributes design requirements and design principles for the instantiation of such artifacts [13] and furthermore provides contributions to the body of knowledge in IS. In this paper, we first outline the study foundations (Sect. 2), followed by a presentation of our DSR approach (Sect. 3), the derived design requirements and principles (Sect. 4), the design of the main app artifact (Sect. 5), the app artifact evaluation (Sect. 6), and discussion (Sect. 7).

2 Foundations and Related Work

2.1 Manufacturing Processes and Existing Solutions for Failure Data Collection

Generally, manufacturing refers to processes that convert "raw materials into useful products" [14, p. 69] by carrying out a set of activities. As already mentioned, manufacturing processes (e.g., casting or drilling) are becoming increasingly prone to failures (i.e., deviations from the optimal manufacturing process and its results [2]). In this context, data-driven failure management is considered an effective strategy to avoid such failures, or at least to minimize their negative impacts. As indicated above, existing solutions for the collection of manufacturing process (failure) data can be classified into three main groups based on their level of automation [5].

Manual solutions rely on text- or spreadsheet-based forms and reports, or basic data-entry terminals, and continue to be widely used for the collection of failure data, especially in the SME-dominated manufacturing industry. However, the high human dependency of manual data collection procedures leads to high efforts and delays (e.g., if the data has to be reentered into a software system later on), as well as to errors (resulting from subjectivity, negligence, or malice) [5]. In contrast to manual solutions, automated solutions (e.g., advanced sensor systems, camera-based vision systems) do not rely on human-based data collection, thereby avoiding a key source of (future) data problems. However, since automated solutions are often complex and difficult to setup and maintain, manufacturing SMEs tend to lack the financial resources and internal capabilities required to acquire and implement these solutions [5, 6]. Semi-automated solutions still rely on manual data collection but use information technology to reduce manual efforts by partly automating the data collection process (e.g., by offering menu-based data entry) [5]. Since semi-automated solutions are not as difficult to implement and maintain as automated ones (in terms of required capabilities and resources), they tend to be well-suited for

SMEs. Semi-automated solutions can be further divided into typing-based and speech recognition-based solutions [5–7].

2.2 Typing-Based Vs. Speech Recognition-Based Solutions

Generally, speech-recognition based solutions recognize spoken words, translate them into character strings, and make these strings available for further data processing, thereby avoiding several shortcomings of typing-based solutions. In particular, since people talk faster than they type, speech recognition has a higher data collection speed. Moreover, speech recognition avoids navigation through complex graphical menus and instead provide the necessary information and parameters in just a few sentences [15]. Speech recognition is also more convenient, since keyboards for typing are often small (e.g., on a smartphone screen). Keyboards also require visual attention and the use of hands, leading to work interruptions and distractions. In addition, workers often wear gloves, which makes typing difficult. Speech recognition avoids these shortcomings [7, 16]. As well, given their inherent flexibility, speech recognition systems are able to collect very heterogeneous data (e.g., as opposed to sensors that can only measure predefined values).

Given the above, earlier studies point to the use of speech recognition as a promising solution approach for the effective and efficient collection of failure data in the context of manufacturing processes. For example, Camba et al. [17] present a system that can record manufacturing product failure descriptions by speech and link them as annotations to the relevant elements in computer-aided design (CAD) drawings. Their system, however, just transforms the recorded failure descriptions into simple text strings. To extract relevant data from the text strings, elaborated methods (e.g., text mining) are necessary [18]. Also, the system does not verify that all relevant data for the failure description is included in the annotation. Another example is Fischer et al. [7] who propose a system where workers can record the location, cause, and handling of each failure in a production line via speech recognition. Similarly, Sim et al. [9] describe a system where workers can use speech recognition to collect data about machine failures (e.g., breakdown time, failure reason, etc.). In both systems [7, 9], only a few, and always the same, attributes are captured for any failure (e.g., location, breakdown time, etc.). However, for an effective data-driven failure management, the manufacturing process failure data collection should be tailored to the specific characteristics of a given failure (i.e., for each failure, data about the failure type-specific attributes should be collected) [4, 10]. For example, to describe a machine pump overheating, other attributes will be relevant than for describing a "missing information" failure in an assembly instruction. On this basis, we argue that speech recognition-based solutions proposed in earlier studies fail to meet a key requirement of effective data-driven failure management, as they lack the ability to collect failure type-specific data (and thus treat any failure the same).

2.3 *Ontologies as Data Model*

For mapping data, a distinction can be made between relational and non-relational data structures. Among the latter exist graph-based data structures that are well suited for mapping complex data with many connections. Knowledge graphs that form the basis of graph-based data structures consist of two nodes connected by a named edge (e.g., the named edge 'is at' connects the nodes 'sawing machine 1' and 'workplace 1'). Simplified, an ontology consists of multiple knowledge graphs [11, 19]. For ontology description, the Web Ontology Language (OWL) is widely used. OWL organizes data in classes, individuals, and properties [11]. A class (e.g., 'machine') can have subclasses (e.g., 'sawing machine') to which individuals (e.g., 'sawing machine 1') belong [19]. In terms of properties, a distinction can be made between object properties and data properties. Object properties predefine how classes relate to each other (e.g., 'worker' work(s) on 'machine' and 'machine' is at 'workplace'). Object property assertions then connect the corresponding individuals within the classes to each other (e.g., 'worker 1' work(s) on 'sawing machine 1' and 'sawing machine 1' is at 'workplace 1'). Data properties define the attributes that the individuals of a class can have, as well as, the attributes data type. Data property assertions then link the individuals and corresponding attributes with their values [11, 19].

The mentioned named edges are useful for targeted querying, since nodes can have multiple edges with different names. This enables inferring by querying along multiple edges (e.g., worker 1 is at workplace 1). Moreover, ontologies enable reasoning, which means initial rules for modelling the ontology can be defined and their compliance can be checked (e.g. that certain classes must be connected by an object property). For ontologies exist the free modeling tool Protégé, which we used in this project and considered to be well usable also for novice users, since it allows graphical modelling (i.e., without coding) [11]. Moreover, from our experience, the SPARQL language, that we used to query ontology data stored in Resource Description Framework (RDF) graph databases, is well readable because the queries are based on the simple structure of knowledge-graphs. Because of the described advantages, we decided to use ontologies to model, store, and query the complex and highly networked manufacturing process failure data structure within our system. Other researchers have also used ontologies as data structure for their failure data collection tools for the same reasons (e.g., [20, 21]).

3 Research Approach

The overall objective of our study is to propose a new IT artifact for the collection of process failure data, with a particular focus on the specific context of the SME-dominated manufacturing industry. To do so, we follow a DSR approach, which is a fundamental paradigm in IS research that concerns the construction of IT artifacts in order to address organizational problems and deduce prescriptive design knowledge [12, 13]. Specifically, our study follows the cyclic DSR process proposed by Sonnenberg and vom Brocke, which includes the activities problem identification, design, construction, and use. Each activity is followed by an evaluation (see Fig. 1). Ex ante/ex post evaluations are conducted before/after any artifact construction [12]. We choose this DSR process since it provides an individual evaluation cycle after each design activity. We consider these evaluation cycles of essential importance when developing a design science artifact, since the artifact design is justified and validated even before it is put into use. This ensures that the developed artifact continuously meets the user needs and thereby provides solution for the problem class. Further, we followed a human risk and effectiveness evaluation strategy since the main design risk stems from the perception of the artifact user [22]. We implemented this strategy with multiple formative evaluation cycles at the beginning and one summative evaluation workshop at the end of our research project.

For this project, we collaborated closely with three SME manufacturers (SURF, SHELF, and PROT) as part of a 2-year, publicly-funded research project. The three participating companies manufacture different products (SURF: surface coating machines; SHELF: store shelves; PROT: wood prototypes) and have a large number of different failure types. Since these companies lack appropriate solutions to collect failure data, they were well suited for participating in our research project. In each company, there were two main project liaisons: the Heads of Production and Industry 4.0 at SHELF (referred to as SHELF1 and SHELF2); the Heads of Production and Assembly at SURF; as well as the CEO and the CTO at PROT.

According to the design-evaluation cycle by Sonnenberg and vom Brocke [12] in the first activity and prior to the artifact development itself, we identified problems of existing solutions for manufacturing process failure data collection. This step is crucial to be able to develop an artifact, which provides an improvement to existing approaches. Based on our identified shortcomings we were afterwards able to formulate design requirements (DRs). To do so, we iteratively reviewed relevant literature (see Sect. 2), conducted a group workshop with all company representatives,

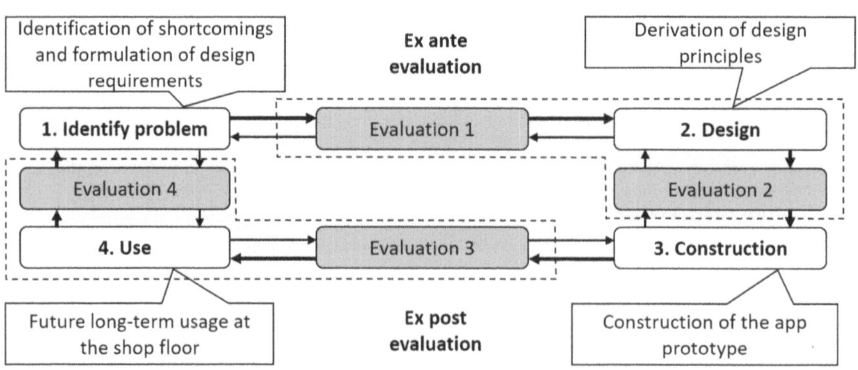

Fig. 1 Research process based on Sonnenberg and vom Brocke [12]

and three dedicated interviews with the liaisons of the three SME partner companies. This step is considered as first evaluation (Eval. 1) and investigates whether the identified problems are relevant and result from inabilities of existing solutions [12].

In the second design activity, we translated the identified and evaluated DRs into design principles (DPs) for the IT artifact to be developed. For the DP formulation, we reviewed relevant literature (e.g., [7, 15, 20]), conducted one interview per company, as well as one group meeting with all company representatives. The formulation of DPs was finalized when all company liaisons were satisfied. With this iterative procedure we examined (Eval. 2) the clarity, feasibility, applicability, and internal consistency of our DPs [12].

In the third activity, we constructed our app prototype based on the DPs. After this construction process we initiated the ex post evaluation of our artifact (Eval. 3). Thus, we conducted three interviews with the liaisons of each partner company to evaluate the feasibility and suitability of specific app components and functions (e.g., of the final ontology structure). Further, we conducted a workshop to investigate the practical applicability of our app prototype (see Sect. 6).

The fourth activity—use—is not part of this research approach and will be conducted in the future when one of the participating companies implement our app and provides us with the respective results (Eval. 4). This will give us the opportunity for a long-term evaluation of our app artifact in a naturalistic setting.

4 Design Requirements and Principles

In the first activity of our research process, we derived seven key DRs for our artifact, based on the shortcomings of existing solutions.

DR 1: *Minimize work interruptions for data collection.* Our project liaisons demanded the to-be-developed solution should minimize work interruptions of existing (in particular manual) solutions. To reach this, the time for the data collection on the system itself should be minimized and it should be avoided that workers have to go to a fixed terminal that is often not close to their actual work place [5].

DR 2: *Increase correctness of collected data.* Our project liaisons also explained that due to high efforts for failure data collection, as well as, missing structures how failures should be described in existing solutions, collected failure data is often not correct, too superficial, or the failures are not even recorded at all [5].

DR 3: *Limit implementation/set-up costs and efforts.* Automated solutions for collecting manufacturing process failure data tend to be too expensive and require too high implementation efforts for SME manufacturers [6] (e.g., SHELF was offered a software solution that automatically collects machine failure data. However, this software is too expensive).

DR 4: *Enable capturing of failure type individual attributes.* Existing solutions for manufacturing process failure data collection (i.e., the speech recognition-based systems mentioned in Sect. 2 and widely used standard enterprise resource planning (ERP) systems [cf. 10]) usually lack the ability to capture failure type individual attributes (i.e., they collect for all failures the same few attributes).

DR 5: *Minimize manual efforts for data retrieval.* In existing solutions failure data is often retrieved manually, leading to high efforts, delays, and errors. For example, at PROT failures are noted in spreadsheets, from which information is manually retrieved.

DR 6: *Operate in loud environment.* Since we planned to use speech recognition in manufacturing, the practitioners demanded that the to-be-developed artifact should have a high accuracy also in noisy environments.

DR 7: *Ensure a high data security and privacy level.* A high data security and privacy level is crucial for manufacturing firms (e.g., to avoid industrial espionage) [23] and should therefore be considered in the artifact design.

Based on the results of our first evaluation cycle, we were able to use the seven identified DRs to derive six DPs, which meet the formulated DRs in the second activity of our research process. For the DP formulation, we followed the recommendations of Chandra et al. [24] and derived action and materiality oriented DPs that are both precise and clear.

DP 1: *Provide the artifact with a mobile device app to enable workplace-independent data collection and effortless, cost-effective setup.* To reduce work interruptions (DR 1), an app installed on mobile devices (e.g., smartphone or tablet) seems suitable, since it avoids workers going to a fixed station. Further, mobile device apps limit set-up efforts and costs (DR 3) since they can easily be installed, their handling is well known from everyday life, and the required devices are financially affordable for SMEs.

DP 2: *Provide the artifact with an ontology-based data structure to map, model, and query the complexity of manufacturing process failure data.* To capture manufacturing process failure data with their multiple failure (type individual) attributes (DR 4) a complex data structure is necessary, which can be mapped by ontologies [cf. 20, 21]. Further, ontology-based data structures can be modelled and queried with limited manual efforts (see Sect. 2; DR 3 + 5). Ontologies also enable inferring. For example, if the failure location is captured, failure objects that are only possible for this location can be inferred and presented to the user. Choosing only from such a limited number reduces work interruption and increases correctness (DR 1 + 2).

DP 3: *Provide the artifact with a guided question-answer conversation flow to capture all failure type relevant attributes in a short time.* A guided question-answer flow enables the artifact to ask for the relevant attributes of the occurred failure type (DR 4). Since no relevant attribute is missed out and the artifact only asks for relevant attributes, correctness is increased while at the same time work interruption is minimized (DR 1 + 2).

DP 4: *Provide the artifact with well selected components to ensure a high data security and privacy level.* The artifact software and hardware components should be well selected, to meet the high data security and privacy demands of manufacturing firms (DR 7) [23].

DP 5: *Provide the artifact with speech recognition backed by a Graphical User Interface (GUI) for data collection to reduce work interruptions but also enable data collection in loud environments.* To reduce work interruptions speech recognition seems a suitable solution, given no/little visual attention is needed and the workers have their hands free for their manual task (DR 1) [7, 15]. However, to account for risks of speech recognition (e.g., reduced correctness in very loud environments), a GUI as backup should be used (DR 6).

DP 6: *Provide the artifact with report and query functions to minimize data retrieval efforts.* To do so (DR 5), query and report functions should automatically search for relevant data and present large amounts of information in a standard format (e.g., in a dashboard). These retrieval functions can be part of the app itself and/or on another device (e.g., a computer with a larger screen in a less noisy office off the shop floor).

5 Artifact Instantiation

Our design artifact is a blueprint for the instantiation of an ontology-based speech recognition app prototype, whose key functions are the collection and storage of manufacturing process failure data. In the following, we describe the instantiated artifact, which is based on the derived DRs and DPs, with a particular focus on its two main components, namely: the ontology-based data structure (data storage) and the speech recognition-based user interface (data collection). In addition, we describe three tools for data retrieval/analysis, which are embedded in our artifact. The developed app prototype is Android-based, so it can be installed on different kinds of smartphones/tablets. For the actual transformation of spoken words into machine-readable text, we decided to use the Google speech-to-text API, since this API is free, has a high accuracy—also in noisy environments (as indicated in relevant discussion forums), and used to be "offline-capable" (mitigating data security and privacy concerns). Besides the speech interface, the app has a GUI.

5.1 Data Storage: Ontology-Based Data Structure

The ontology underlying our speech recognition app is used to structure relevant failure data/information. Our system contains an 'initial' ontology including four classes (failure location, object, type, and collecting employee; see Fig. 2) and their connecting object properties [20, 25]. This 'initial' ontology can be adapted to the particularities of the using firm in the following ways. The four top classes of the initial ontology cannot be changed. To the classes failure location and failure object can additional subclasses and individuals be added in a hierarchical manner (e.g.,

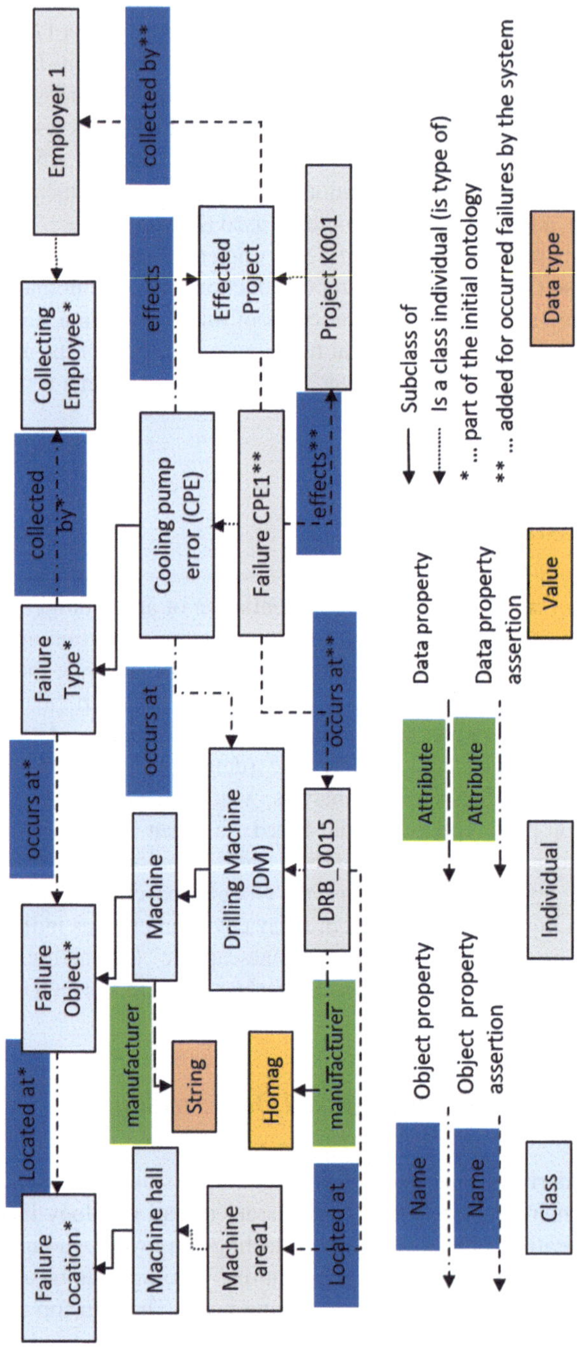

Fig. 2 Ontology-based data structure

the subclass drilling machine (DM) with the individual DM DRB_0015). To the class failure type can only subclasses (e.g., cooling pump error; CPE) be added. To the class collecting employee can only individuals be added, which each represent one employee. Moreover, classes that represent attributes to describe specific failure types in a more detailed manner can also be created (e.g., for CPE it is important to describe which project this failure type effects). In addition, object properties (assertions) connect the created (sub)classes and individuals. Initially each failure type has to be connected to a failure object (e.g., a CPE can occur at a DM), each failure object has to be connected to a failure location (e.g., DRB_0015 is at machine area 1), and failure type subclasses are connected to their individual attribute subclasses (e.g., a CPE effects a project). We implemented the described ontology structure requirements in reasoning rules. This ensures that the ontologies modeled by the firms meet the requirements and that the app thus works.

If occurred failures are collected, this initial ontology is extended in the following ways: For the failure type a new individual is created. Each individual represents one occurred failure of the corresponding class/failure type (e.g., Failure CPE1 is an occurred CPE). The created failure type individual is connected to its failure object (for Failure CPE1 this is DRB_0015); to its collecting employee (Failure CPE 1 was collected by employer 1) and to its attribute that describes the corresponding failure type in a more detailed manner (e.g., Failure CPE1 effects Project K001).

5.2 *Speech Recognition-Based User Interface*

Since the main task of the speech recognition-based user interface is the data collection, we describe this component along the individual steps of the data-collection process. Before the app can collect failures, the user has to choose his name and location. Then the app is ready for the three-step data collection process. To start this process, the user need to press a button on its headset. Then the app asks within the first step "What is the failure object?". The user's response is processed by the speech-to-failure-object algorithm, which compares the response with the failure objects that are theoretically possible for the user's location (i.e., objects whose individual names, class names, or data property values are part of the preprocessed input words). Since objects in manufacturing often have abstract (technical) names, there exist data property values for additional attributes. Therefore, our speech-to-failure-object algorithm searches not only by individual or class names, but also by data property values (e.g., Homag as manufacturer). Ideally, the speech-to-failure-object algorithm will identify only (one)single failure object; otherwise the speech-to-failure-object algorithm will generate a candidate list with all failure objects matching the provided information. The user can select the appropriate failure object from that candidate list (by speech for a maximum of three failure objects; otherwise using the GUI). If no failure object is identified, the user is asked to use other words to describe the failure object. In the second step, the app asks the user "What was the failure type?" and compares the user response with the failure types possible for the failure object. If the app can identify the failure type, it will continue with the next step; otherwise, the user has to select the failure type via speech or GUI (for more than three possible failure types). In the third and last step, the app asks for individual attributes of the occurred failure type. In case of CPE1, the app would ask the user which project was affected, and the user can then select 'Project K001'.

5.3 Data Retrieval Tools

The collected data must be transmitted to a computer for retrieval. A company internal Wi-Fi should be used to ensure data transmission in a fast, reliable, and secure way. On the computer the data can be analyzed on a Power Bi dashboard or queried in an RDF graph database using the SPARQL language. For short-term evaluation, the Power Bi dashboard contains a list of all failures recorded on the current working day. For long-term evaluation exist on the dashboard multiple diagrams (e.g., showing failure frequency per failure object, location, type etc.). The querying enables a targeted data retrieval. For example, by inferring along the data property assertions it is possible to query which failures on which machine areas effect a project or to query along class hierarchies (e.g., all failures on individuals that belong to the class machine; Fig. 2). Moreover, with the question "What happened?" the app enumerates to the user all failures recorded on the current day.

6 Artifact Evaluation

According to the build-evaluate cycle following Sonnenberg and vom Brocke [12] in Fig. 1, we already evaluated the DRs (Evaluation 1) and the corresponding DPs (Evaluation 2) as ex ante evaluations based on previous findings, which were derived from a systematic literature review and expert interviews. Based on these results, the current research approach now focuses on the instantiation of the app prototype artifact, and we further describe the ex post evaluation of the artifact against the DRs (Evaluation 3). To do so, we conducted a workshop with one of our company partners (SHELF). The objective of this workshop was to evaluate the practical applicability of our app prototype in a real-world setting [22]. Before the workshop, we developed a company-specific ontology together with our main liaisons at SHELF. Three SHELF employees participated in the workshop (hereafter referred to as SHELF 1–3), including one shop-floor worker (SHELF 3), which is important, given that shopfloor workers are the designated app users. The workshop consisted of three parts: First, after explaining the app's technical components and their installation, we showed the workshop participants how to use the Protégé tool for building a company-specific ontology, as well as how to collect failure data with the app (see three-step process outlined in Sect. 5.2). Furthermore, we showed them the dashboard and how to query data using the SPARQL language. In the second part, we asked each participant to use the app and to capture multiple failures. As the participants got increasingly familiar with the app, the data collection process (again, see Sect. 5.2) worked fast and almost flawlessly. In the third part, we visited SHELF's shop floor to assess whether the app can understand speech input even in the presence of loud background noise. Throughout the workshop, we kept asking the participants questions in relation to the different DRs and took detailed notes of their answers/feedback (as well as of their app usage behaviors).

Within the workshop, the company participants confirmed that our app would enable them to minimize work interruptions (DR 1). Here, they emphasized two aspects. First, the app installed on a smartphone allows data collection directly at every workplace. Therefore, workers no longer have to go to the fixed terminal in the production hall. Second, SHELF 3 emphasized, that the developed app enables him almost hands-free data collection. Therefore, he is able to continue tasks (e.g., load machine with material) and collect failure data in parallel. The participants further highlighted the ability to increase correctness and avoid incompleteness of collected data (DR 2), since instead of writing in 'free-text-fields' only predefined attributes can be selected. Furthermore, the participants confirmed that the implementation costs for our artifact are low since they already have all required devices on-site (headsets) or they are affordable for them (tablets/smartphones). Therefore, SHELF is planning to use our app for machine failure tracking after the workshop since the "price of the [corresponding machine manufacturer] software alone is a criterion that leads to failure". They also found that the described set-up steps are doable with their IT expertise. The participants also confirmed the Protégé tool as useful for the modelling of ontologies since no coding is required (DR 3). Further, the company participants highlighted that our app would enable them to capture failure type-specific data/information (DR 4), which represents a significant improvement over their existing systems. For example, they can use our app to specify the cause for the failure type "vacuum is not applied", which could be "diaphragm defective, valve open, or vacuum pump defective" (SHELF 1). Further, the participants confirmed that our artifact minimizes manual efforts and time delays to retrieve and analyze collected data (DR 5). In the short run, SHELF 1 wants to monitor actual occurred failures on the dashboard to assign workers to troubleshoot these failures. For long run evaluations, SHELF wants to query the collected failure data and combine it with the tracked machine running times to "evaluate which failures typically cause machine work interruptions" (SHELF 2). Moreover, we concluded that the speech recognition of our app works well within noisy environments (DR 6) since the app collected at the shopfloor volume test (fourth workshop step) 28 of 30 failures correctly (at 2 failures we spoke unclearly). For this test, we wore a noise cancellation headset of the company BOSE and we measured a background noise level of 75 dB. This type of headset is typically worn by the shop floor workers of SHELF. SHELF 2 also confirmed that since no internet connectivity is required and therefore no external access to the data is possible our artifact ensures data security and privacy (DR 7). Based on this feedback, we conclude that the instantiated app fulfills the seven DRs. Thereby we were able to confirm these DRs for the intended artifact. Thereby, we furthermore indirectly evaluated the six derived DPs since the instantiation, thus the development of the app prototype, is based on them. Consequently, we concluded that if the DRs are met in the instantiated artifact, the method of development, which relied on the DPs, can be considered as being effective.

7 Discussion and Outlook

In this study, we followed a DSR approach [12] to present the design, development, and evaluation of an SME tailored ontology-based speech recognition app as an assistance system for the collection of failure data in manufacturing processes. Our study contributes to the body of knowledge in IS in several ways. First, we contribute an improved and relevant solution that solves shortcomings of existing solutions for manufacturing process failure data collection (e.g., high efforts for failure data collection and data retrieval) [13, 26]. In particular, we investigated the problem domain, formulated seven DRs, derived six DPs and instantiated them in a software artifact. The derived DRs and DPs can be transferred to other domains with a high proportion of manual work and many different failure types (e.g., construction industry), that face the same problem class of failure data collection. Second, since we instantiated the practical-oriented artifact build-evaluation design cycle [26] proposed by Sonnenberg and vom Brocke [12] and furthermore followed the evaluation strategy presented by Venable et al. [22], as enhancements of traditional DSR approaches, we met a research gap and the demand for "evidence-based design knowledge rooted in the design, implementation, and evaluation of real-world service systems" [27, p. 74]. Third, we contribute an ontology-structure that can be used by other researchers for the development of their own failure ontology, in particular since our structure is able to map failure type specific attributes. Overall, our study adds knowledge to the knowledge base with different levels of inquiry: nomothetic design knowledge (the general design requirements and principles), idiographic design knowledge (our individual artifact with all its components), and nomothetic scientific knowledge (the general failure ontology structure with the formalized relationships of failure characteristics) [28].

As with any research, our study has several limitations. First, the app evaluation is limited to a set of rather generic criteria. Thus, further evaluations are needed, including a more detailed comparison with existing (manual) solutions for the collection of manufacturing process failure data (e.g., in terms of total collection efforts). Also, since the evaluation only involved one workshop, our study would benefit large-scale evaluations on the shop floor. As mentioned, SHELF is planning to introduce our app, which would give us the opportunity for such an evaluation. We could get feedback from multiple workers, who would use our artifact. For such evaluation could serve the Technology Acceptance Model as theoretical foundation [29]. Second, the evaluation scope in our study is on technical and functional aspects. Further evaluations should also focus on organizational aspects (e.g., app acceptance). In this context, we would like to encourage future studies on the topic of speech recognition in manufacturing in general. For example, a longitudinal study might help clarify the specific characteristics of speech recognition that influence its acceptance, continuous use, and efficiency.

Furthermore, all three case firms saw a high relevance in an additional function where in particular new workers with little experience can access troubleshooting instructions via the app and follow them while solving the failure. Further, such a function is relatively easy to realize based on the ontology-based data structure, since the instructions can be assigned to the respective failure types in the ontology.

In conclusion, we hope that our results can serve as a reference point for future research on the design and use of ontology-based speech recognition apps for manufacturing process failure data collection.

References

1. Bokrantz, J., Skoogh, A., Ylipää, T., & Stahre, J. (2016). Handling of production disturbances in the manufacturing industry. *Journal of Manufacturing Technology Management, 27*(8), 1054–1075.
2. Bergers, T., Stauder, L., Grünbaum, T., & Barth, S. (2021). Adaptive design of manufacturing process sequences in case of short-term disruptions in the production process. *Manufacturing Letters, 27*, 92–95.
3. Servicemax. Accessed 2020/07/05, from https://www.servicemax.com/de/unplanned-downtime
4. Stich, V., Jordan, F., Birkmeier, M., Oflazgil, K., Reschken, J., & Diews, A. (2015). Big data technology for resilient failure management in production systems. In S. Umeda, M. Nakano, H. Mizuyama, N. Hibino, D. Kiritsis, & G. von Cieminski (Eds.), *Advances in production management systems: Innovative production management towards sustainable growth. APMS 2015. IFIP advances in information and communication technology* (Vol. 459, pp. 447–454). Springer.
5. Cwikla, C. (2014). Methods of manufacturing data acquisition for production management – A review. *Advanced Materials Research, 837*, 618–623.
6. Ghmire, S., Melo, R., Ferreira, J., Agostinho, C., & Goncalves, R. (2015). Continuous data collection framework for manufacturing industries. In I. Ciuci, H. Panetto, C. Debruye, A. Aubry, et al. (Eds.), *On the move to meaningful internet systems: OTM 2015 workshops, LNCS* (Vol. 9416, pp. 29–40). Springer.
7. Fischer, J., Pantförder, D., & Vogel-Heuser, B. (2017). Improvement of maintenance through speech interaction in cyber-physical production systems. In *IEEE 15th International Conference on Industrial Informatics (INDIN)* (pp. 290–295). IEEE, Emden.
8. Cloudflight. Accessed 2020/07/05, from https://de.cloudflight.io/presse/hallo-iot-warum-scheitert-die-konversation-mit-dingen-der-industrie-35368/
9. Sim, E.-S., Lee, H.-G., Lee, J.-C., & Park, J.-W. (2006). Efficient work measurement system of manufacturing cells using speech recognition and digital image processing technology. *The International Journal of Advanced Manufacturing Technology, 29*(7), 772–785.
10. Westkämper, E., & Löffler, C. (2016). *Strategien der Produktion. Technologien, Konzepte und Wege in die Praxis*. Springer.
11. Stuckenschmidt, H. (2009). *Ontologien*. Springer.
12. Sonnenberg, C., & vom Brocke, J. (2012). Evaluations in the science of the artificial – Reconsidering the build-evaluate pattern in design science research. In K. Peffers, M. Rothenberger, & B. Kuechler (Eds.), *DESRIST 2012* (Vol. 7286, pp. 381–397). Springer.

13. Gregor, S., & Hevner, A. R. (2013). Positioning and presenting design science research for maximum impact. *MIS Quarterly: Management Information Systems, 37*, 337–355.
14. Dahotre, N. B., & Harimkar, S. P. (2008). Manufacturing processes. In *Laser fabrication and machining of materials* (pp. 69–96). Springer.
15. Kasper, G. M., & Morris, A. H. (1988). The effect of presentation media on recipient performance in text-based information systems. *Journal of Management Information Systems, 4*(4), 25–43.
16. Udoka, S. J. (1991). Automated data capture techniques: A prerequisite for effective integrated manufacturing systems. *Computers & Industrial Engineering, 21*, 217–221.
17. Camba, J., Naya, F., Perez-Lopez, D., & Contero, M. (2020). From voice to knowledge: A proposal for a voice annotation system to support collaborative engineering design processes. In *Proceedings of the 53th HICSS* (pp. 385–394). IEEE, Maui, Hawaii.
18. Allahyari, M., Pouriyeh, S.A., Assefi, M., Safaei, S., Trippe, E.D., Guttierez, J., & Kochut, K. (2017). A brief survey of text mining: Classification, clustering and extraction techniques. In *Proceedings of KDD bidgas*. Association for Computing Machinery.
19. W3C. Accessed 2021/04/10, from https://www.w3.org/TR/owl-ref/#Individual
20. Ali, N., & Hong, J.-E. (2018). Failure detection and prevention for cyber-physical systems using ontology-based knowledge base. *Computers, 7*(4), 1–16.
21. Park, C.-S., Lee, D.-Y., Kwon, O.-H., & Wang, X. (2018). A framework for proactive construction defect management using BIM, augmented reality and ontology-based data collection template. *Automation in Construction, 33*, 61–67.
22. Venable, J., Pries-Heje, J., & Baskerville, R. (2016). FEDS: A framework for evaluation in design science research. *European Journal of Information Systems, 25*(1), 77–89.
23. Deloitte. Accessed 2020/12/06. https://www2.deloitte.com/content/dam/Deloitte/us/Documents/manufacturing/us-manu-cyber-risk-in-advanced-manufacturing.pdf
24. Chandra, L., Seidel, S., & Gregor, S. (2015). Prescriptive knowledge in IS research: conceptualizing design principles in terms of materiality, action, and boundary conditions. In *Proceedings of the 48th HICSS* (pp. 4039–4048). IEEE, Kauai, Hawaii.
25. Meyer, G., Knüppel, K., Busch, J., Jakob, M., & Nyhuis, P. (2014). Störgrößenmanagement-Systematik. *Zeitschrift für wirtschaftlichen Fabrikbetrieb, 109*(10), 704–707.
26. Hevner, A. (2007). A three cycle view of design science research. *Scandinavian Journal of Information Systems, 19*(2), 87–92.
27. Böhmann, T., Leimeister, J. M., & Möslein, K. (2014). Service systems engineering. *Business & Information Systems Engineering, 6*(2), 73–79.
28. Baskerville, R., Kaul, M., & Storey, V. (2015). Genres of inquiry in design-science research: Justification and evaluation of knowledge production. *MIS Quarterly: Management Information Systems, 39*(3), 541–564.
29. Davis, F. D. (1989). Perceived usefulness, perceived ease of use, and user acceptance of information technology. *MIS Quarterly: Management Information Systems, 13*(3), 319–340.

Evaluation of Innovativeness as the Success Factor of Innovative Start-Ups: Evidence from Literature

Francesco Bellini, Fabrizio D'Ascenzo, Irina Gorelova, Adriano Fabbri, and Giuseppe Ventrice

Abstract Innovation has become a driving force for all spheres of contemporary society, including entrepreneurial activities in start-ups. Evidence from the scientific literature shows how innovative start-ups play an important role in economic, technological and social development. Innovation is the ability of start-ups to face challenges by creating new solutions. Despite the fact that the evaluation model is in all respects necessary to measure the innovativeness of start-ups, no comprehensive attempts have been found in the literature to conduct this type of research. This paper represents a preliminary study that aims to develop an evaluation model of the innovativeness of innovative start-ups; it is an attempt to construct a framework of variables that could be useful for assessing innovativeness capability of start-ups. The results of this research must be evaluated in the future by conducting round tables and interviews with economic operators who will provide the academic community with sufficient evidence on the method of evaluating innovativeness from the practical side.

Keywords Innovativeness · Innovative start-ups · Success factors · Indicatoring innovativeness

F. Bellini · F. D'Ascenzo · I. Gorelova (✉) · A. Fabbri
Department of Management, Sapienza University of Rome, Rome, Italy
e-mail: francesco.bellini@uniroma1.it; fabrizio.dascenzo@uniroma1.it; irina.gorelova@uniroma1.it; adriano.fabbri@uniroma1.it

G. Ventrice
Department of Business and Economic Studies, Parthenope University of Naples, Naples, Italy
e-mail: giuseppe.ventrice001@studenti.uniparthenope.it

A. M. Braccini et al. (eds.), *Technologies for Digital Transformation*, Lecture Notes in Information Systems and Organisation 64,
https://doi.org/10.1007/978-3-031-52120-1_16

1 Introduction

Innovation has become a driving force for all areas of contemporary society nowadays. The modern world cannot be imagined without future innovations. The scientific community agrees that innovation has become the main driving force of economic development. Innovation processes have brought the world community to a new, higher level of development. Innovations are applied in almost all fields, being a topic of discussion at both a scientific and managerial level, including governments and international organizations. United Nations Sustainable Development Goal (UN SDG) number 9 is dedicated to industry, innovation and infrastructure. Objective 9.5 of SDG 11 is focused on improving scientific research, updating the technological capabilities of industrial sectors and encouraging innovation; Objective 9.b supports domestic technological development, research and innovation in developing countries, while ensuring a policy environment conducive to industrial diversification and adding value to goods [1]. The United Nations Department of Economic and Social Affairs (UN DESA) contributes to the promotion of innovation by promoting cooperation in the science-policy-society interface and in multi-stakeholder engagement on science, technology and innovation for the SDGs, areas of work established through the Rio+20 Conference and the 2030 Agenda for Sustainable Development. The European Union (EU) sees innovation as one of the pillars of its industrial development. According to the European Commission (EC), the adoption of product and service innovations, the use of innovative production technologies and the introduction of new business models are necessary to promote the modernization of the EU industry. The EC develops policies that help accelerate the broad commercialization of innovation and engages in many activities in support of innovation in the EU. EC directions and actions to accelerate innovation include social innovation, workplace innovation, the Business Innovation Observatory, the European Innovation Scoreboard and the European Innovation Scoreboard of regional innovation.[1]

Innovation has a significant impact on entrepreneurship across a wide range of applications. Along with delivering high quality products and services to the market, innovation also brings profit to businesses by increasing competitiveness and helping to explore or create new markets [2]. Innovators engage in the process of generating and executing new, contextually beneficial ideas [3–5]. There is a close link between innovation and start-ups revealed in the literature [6–8]. At the same time, the evidence gleaned from the literature shows that only a small number of start-ups are innovative, but they nevertheless play an important role in economic, technological and social development [9–11]. Innovative start-ups are new companies that produce, develop and market innovative goods or services with a high technological value [12]. The Ministry of Economic Development in its report "The Italian legislation in support of innovative startups, executive summary" defines innovative start-ups as new innovative companies with high technological value

[1]European Commission. Internal Market, Industry, Entrepreneurship and SMEs. https://single-market-economy.ec.europa.eu/industry/strategy/innovation_en

[13]. Innovative start-ups can be seen both as a distinct form of entrepreneurship and as a distinct mechanism for developing innovations [9]. Innovation is the ability of a company to implement "creative and innovative solutions to the challenges the company faces" [14]. Another group of researchers [15] argues that it is important to develop "a comprehensive composite index of innovativeness" based on readily available and reliable indicators.

Despite the fact that innovation and innovativeness of start-ups occupy a significant place in the literature, to the knowledge of the authors there have been no full-fledged attempts to evaluate the innovativeness of innovative start-ups. This study is a first step in building such a complete system. To achieve this the authors asked the following research questions:

RQ1: what are the innovativeness variables presented in the literature?
RQ2: what is the state of the art of the literature on the evaluation of variables?
RQ3: what are the possible evaluations of the innovativeness variables?

The paper is organized as follows: Sect. 2 provides the methodology applied for this research; the results and discussion are represented in Sect. 3; Sect. 4 outlines the conclusions and future research paths.

2 Research Methodology

The nature of the study is exploratory and it aims to obtain the first raw evidence on possible ways to evaluate the innovativeness of start-ups pursuing the further aim of developing a complete index of innovativeness. This research was inspired by the paper of Bellini et al. (2022) [6] which provides the broadest currently available taxonomy of the success factors of innovative start-ups. We categorise the success factors following the approach used in Bellini et al. (2022) [6] for the two main reasons: on the one hand, this research is one of the most recent and up-to-date works on the innovative start-ups' success factors; on the other hand, this study represents a systematic literature review in order to define a taxonomy of success factors (that taxonomy has represented our starting point to classify the factors because). The authors of the paper divided the success factors of innovative start-ups into three macro-areas—(1) Propensity for innovation; (2) Open Innovation and (3) Sustainability. As reported in Bellini et al. (2022) [6], the three identified sub-factors of innovativeness are well documented; hence, there is solid evidence in the current literature for those factors. Regarding the process we have followed, we defined by ourselves the possible variables to use: we have read the articles focused on the innovativeness from Bellini et al. (2022) [6] and we have extracted variables from there. The first step of our research was to extract the innovation variables corresponding to each macro-area from the scientific literature. To this end, the articles previously mentioned in the research by Bellini et al. (2022) [6] were used since this research group has already conducted a complete review of the literature on the subject; the evidence found in this literature has been corroborated by some additional studies (you can see them in Table 1 in the "Result and discussion" section).

Table 1 Variables and related measures

Variable	Measure	Variable references
Propensity for innovation		
Innovation—Imitation	Discrete variable: 1—if the entrepreneurial activity is innovative or 0—if it is imitative	[16, 60]
Organizational willingness to change	Likert: 1—The members of the organization do not want to implement change, 6—The members of the organization are strongly oriented towards change	[17, 19, 20]
Awareness of the resources used	Likert: 1—Low level of awareness of the resources used, 6—High level of awareness of the resources used	[22]
Entrepreneurial motivation for innovation	Likert: 1—The entrepreneur/s is not so innovation-oriented, 6—The entrepreneur/s is strongly innovation-oriented	[23]
Progressive thinking	Likert: 1—There is no flexible and open culture on the part of company members, 6—Members have a maximally flexible and open organizational culture	[23]
Self-development	Discrete variable: 1—There is at least one active learning program for members, 0—There are no active learning programs	[23]
Commercialization of ideas	Numeric variable: Number of ideas placed on the market	[23]
Market-oriented change of opportunity	Discrete variable: 1—A flexible business model is used, 0—In all other cases	[23]
Innovation development stage	Innovation development phase: 1—Under development, 2—Developed but not exploited, 3—Under exploitation	[24]
Learning model for trials and errors	The start-up adopts a learning model for trials and errors, 0—The start-up adopts another model	[25]
Open innovation		
Knowledge absorption capacity	Likert: 1—Low level of knowledge absorption capacity, 6—High level of knowledge absorption capacity	[7, 27]
Start-ups' Network	Numeric variable: Network size—the number of partners in the network	[28]
Search breadth	Range: 0 to 5	[29]
Search depth	Range: 0 to 5	[29]
Number of activities for the transfer of project results	Numeric variable: Number of activities focused on the transfer of project results	[30]
Scientists founders	Discrete variable: 1—if at least two scientists have founded the innovative start-up, 0—if one (or none) scientist has founded the innovative start-up	[30]
Competitions/Prize competitions	Dummy: 1—At least one program related to innovative challenges is available; 0—There is no program linked to innovative challenges	[26, 31]
Crowdsourcing and community use	Discrete variable: 1—There is at least one outsourced task 0—No task is outsourced	[26, 31]

Table 1 (continued)

Variable	Measure	Variable references
Dyadic co-creation/ co-development in the upstream-downstream network	Discrete variable: 1—There is at least one supplier-customer-user-lead user involved in an innovative process 0—No external actor is involved in the innovative process	[29, 31–35]
Informal external networking	Likert: 1—No activities are carried out to acquire and maintain links with external sources of knowledge, 6—There is a large number of activities to acquire and maintain links with external sources of knowledge	[29, 31, 34]
Collaboration on R&D and technology alliances/ consortia	Discrete variable: 1—There is at least one R&D cooperation project (without shareholding) between non-competitors, 0—Otherwise	[29, 31, 33, 36]
Information networking	Discrete variable: 1—There is at least one person responsible for researching new trends or technologies on the Internet, magazines and other organizations, 0—In all other cases	[29, 32]
Technology brokering	Discrete variable: 1—There is at least one person responsible for technological intermediation, 0—In all other cases	[29, 37]
Ability to seize and use market opportunities	Likert: 1—inability to seize and use market opportunities, 6—high ability to seize and use market opportunities	[23]
Team Openness	Likert: 1—The team does not leverage external sources of knowledge and innovation, 6—The team heavily leverages external sources of knowledge and innovation	[38–41]
Research and communication channels for openness	Discrete variable for each element used: IP in—licensing (1—Yes, 0—No), Scientific knowledge sourcing (1—Yes, 0—No), R&D alliances (1—Yes, 0—No), Cooperation agreements (1—Yes, 0—No), Technology selling (1—Yes, 0—No), IP out—licensing (1—Yes, 0—No), Market knowledge sourcing (1—Yes, 0—No), Strategic partnerships (1—Yes, 0—No)	[38]
Dimension of the Open innovation process	Likert: 1—The start-up explores and acquires external knowledge for internal use only but does not exploit internal knowledge for external use; 6—The start-up exploits internal knowledge for external use only but does not explore and acquire external knowledge for internal use	[43]
Exploration	Likert: 1—The start-up has a low level of exploration, 6—The start-up has a high level of exploration	[38, 44, 45]
Exploitation	Likert: 1—The start-up has a low level of exploitation, 6—The start-up has a high level of exploitation	[38, 44, 45]

(continued)

Table 1 (continued)

Variable	Measure	Variable references
Number of people to be dedicated to the enhancement and transfer of innovation	Numeric variable: People to be dedicated to the enhancement and transfer of innovation	[46]
Number of patents deriving from R&D collaborations	Numeric variable: Number of patents deriving from collaborative R&D activities/Total number of patents	[47, 61]
Number of external ideas—or technologies—flowing into an organization	Numeric variable: Number of external ideas—or technologies—that flow into an organization	[48]
Number of internal ideas—or technologies—that come out of an organization	Numeric variable: Number of internal ideas—or technologies—that come out of an organization	[48]
Number of new collaboration links established by the start-up with local actors in a specific context	Numerical variable: Number of new collaboration links established by the start-up with local actors in a specific context	[46]
Open partnership	Numeric variable: 0—if there were no Research and Development collaborations, 1—if the partnership involved only industrial partners, 2 if the partnership only involved scientific organizations, 3 if both types of partners are present	[47]
Self-assessment of the project on the quality of the new links	Likert: 1—Low quality level of the new collaboration links established by the start-up with local actors, 6—High level of new collaboration links established by the start-up with local actors	[46]
Sustainability		
Green Revenues %	(Total revenue from sustainable activities / Total revenue) × 100	[51]
Availability of scientific and technological knowledge	Likert: 1—Scarce availability of scientific and technological knowledge deriving from universities and external companies; 6—Abundant availability of scientific and technological knowledge deriving from universities and external companies	[52]
Technical universities	Discrete variable: 1—if there is at least one university in the province that produces high-quality research in the field of engineering and other technical sciences, 0—In all other cases	[52]
Environmental awareness	Likert: 1—There is no adequate sensitivity to environmental issues on the part of local administrations, businesses and residents in the area where the company is located; 6—There is a high sensitivity to environmental issues on the part of local administrations, businesses and residents in the area where the company is located	[52]

Table 1 (continued)

Variable	Measure	Variable references
Ecopreneurs	Likert: 1—The founder (or founders) of the start-up is not interested in the "green" aspect of his business; 6—The founder (or founders) of the start-up is totally focused on the "green" aspect of his business	[53]
The climatic performance	Likert: 1—Very low climatic performance, 6—Very high climatic performance	[52, 55–57]
Social impact of the product	Likert: 1—The start-up product has no social impact, 6—The start-up product has a high social impact	[58]
Consumption of non-renewable resources	Likert: 1—The start-up needs a wide use of non-renewable resources; 6—The start-up does not use non-renewable resources	[59]
Emissions	Likert: 1—The start-up has a high level of solid, liquid and gaseous emissions; 6—The start-up does not use non-renewable resources	[59]

After performing this step and extracting the variables along with their definitions and characteristics, the authors proceeded to search for the evaluation references of each variable. Since a direct evaluation of the variables has not been found in the literature, as a third step the authors proposed their own possible evaluation method using discrete variables, numerical variables and the Likert Scale as measures. The main difference of our study compared to that of Bellini et al. (2022) [6] relies on the fact that our study is based on the creation of variables to evaluate the innovative start-ups' success factors whereas the work of Bellini et al. (2022) [6] is focused just on the definition of a two-level taxonomy of those factors. We went deeper with the analysis by creating variables to evaluate the areas of the success factors identified. The variables we have identified represent a new step of the work in order to define possible success factors and they must be evaluated in future research with round tables and interviews with economic operators. The results of this study are presented below.

3 Results and Discussions

Our research focuses on the innovativeness success factors of innovative start-ups with a specific focus on three key aspects (macro-areas): "Propensity for innovation", "Open Innovation" and "Sustainability" [6]. For each of the macro-areas, we have studied the scientific literature with the aim to isolate possible variables in order to offer a methodology of innovativeness evaluation of innovative start-ups later on. In this paragraph, the variables and their relative measures will be discussed, ending with a summary table of what has been observed.

3.1 Propensity for Innovation

As regards the propensity for innovation, we have isolated the following 10 variables: *"Innovation—Imitation"*, *"Organizational willingness to change"*, *"Awareness of the resources used"*, *"Entrepreneurial motivation for innovation"*, *"Progressive thinking"*, *"Self -development"*, *"Commercialization of ideas"*, *"Market-oriented change of opportunity"*, *"Development phase of innovation"*, *"Learning model for trials and errors"*.

The "innovation-imitation" variable simply refers to the propensity of the start-up and is constructed as a discrete variable (1 if the start-up activity is innovative and 0 if it is imitative). This is a relevant point from which to start: innovative activity is much more risky, non-linear and complicated [16], and it is essential to know which path has been taken on a strategic level. The "organizational readiness to change" is closely linked to the innovative process, in fact the latter refers to a dynamic process [17] and strongly impact on the efficiency of a firm [18]; readiness for change could be observed at any level—office, department, business unit [19]—but in this specific case we refer to organizational readiness for change as a shared resolution by members of the organization to implement the change [20]. As reported in [21], the greater the organizational readiness for change, the greater the cooperation, effort and persistence of team members. Consistently with all of this, we have decided to use a Likert scale to measure organizational readiness for change. The "Awareness of the resources used" is one of the categories identified in [22] in their qualitative survey: we decided to include this variable as it can be a valid proxy for the company's propensity for innovation; also in this case we used a Likert scale to measure the level of awareness of the resources used and implemented by the entrepreneur (s). The "entrepreneurial motivation for innovation" [23] is an intuitive variable (which refers to the motivation of an entrepreneur regarding the innovation measured with a Likert scale), while " progressive thinking" is one of the key factors of a technology start-up, as reported by Kim et al. (2018) [23]: it concerns a flexible organization and open-mindedness of its members; a Likert scale was also used for these two variables. "Self-development" (measured as a discrete variable) refers to the learning and development of organization members [23] so that this can benefit the innovative start-up, while the "Commercialization of ideas" concerns the ideas actually marketed by the company [23] and it is considered as a numerical variable. The "Market-oriented change of opportunity" refers to the usage by the start-up of a highly flexible business model, which can dynamically respond to market needs [23]. While the "Innovation development phase" [24] directly concerns the innovative level in which the start-up is operating (we used a multiple numerical variable which indicates: 1—Innovation in development, 2—Developed but not commercially exploited, 3—Introduced in the market), the "Learning model for trials and errors" [25] concerns a flexible model through which it is possible to modify what has been established even in progress, and this is of considerable importance for a start-up that take the path of innovation.

3.2 Open Innovation

Theorized in [26], Open innovation concerns a new way of conceiving innovation, based on a company with porous borders (so the projects the company is engaged in could have both external and internal nature), on the exploitation of externality and on a highly collaborative approach. For this specific section, the following 26 variables have been isolated: *"Knowledge absorption capacity"*, *"Start-ups' Network"*, *"Search breadth"*, *"Search depth"*, *"Number of activities for the transfer of project results"*, *"Scientists founders"*, *"Competitions/awards"*, *"Crowdsourcing and community use"*, *"Dyadic co-creation/co-development in the upstream-downstream network"*, *"Informal external networking"*, *"Collaboration on R&D and technology alliances/consortia"*, *"Information networking"*, *"Technology brokering"*, *"Ability to seize and use market opportunities"*, *"Team Openness"*, *"Research and communication channels for Openness"*, *"Dimension of the open innovation"*, *"Exploration"*, *"Exploitation"*, *"Number of people to devote to the enhancement and transfer of innovation"*, *"Number of patents deriving from R&D collaborations"*, *"Number of external ideas—or technologies—that converge in an organization"*, *"Number of internal ideas—or technologies—coming out of an organization"*, *"Number of new collaboration links established by the start-up with local actors in a specific context"*, *"Open partnership"*, *"Project self-assessment on the quality of new bonds"*.

The "Knowledge absorption capacity" [7] is of fundamental importance for an innovative start-up that link the company's survival and growth to this variable [27]—and a Likert scale has also been adopted for it which can intercept how well the company is able to absorb this knowledge; the "Start-up network" variable [28] is more intuitive and is divided into two sub-variables: the number of partners in the network and the strength of the links with them. Two key concepts that emerged from the research concern "Search breadth" and "Search depth" [29]: the first refers to the "variety" of external sources used by a company for innovation purposes (measuring the number of external sources of knowledge that the company integrates within it for innovative activities) while the second to the "depth" or the number of different sources to which the start-up addresses through frequent and repeated interactions. Both of these variables were measured over a range of values from 0 to 5 as suggested by the authors themselves. The "Number of activities for the transfer of project results" [30] is an intuitive variable measured with a number in absolute value. As reported in [30], the presence of only one scientist among the founders shows no difference compared to the situation in which there is none; however, as the number of the same increases, the search breadth and search depth also increase, for this reason a discrete measure was used for the variable "Scientists Founders" where 1 corresponds to the situation in which there are at least two scientists among the founders and 0 where instead in case there is only one (or none). Several relevant aspects have been identified in [31] as regards Open Innovation: for the following seven variables we followed the approach of the authors mentioned. For these seven variables, Likert scales and discrete variables were used as measures alternatively. A first variable that emerged from this research concerns the "Competitions/prize competitions" that the start-up can run in order to collect ideas and innovations from the outside [26, 31]; the same authors have then identified in the activity of "Crowdsourcing and use of communities" an important lever for Open Innovation, being able to exploit the potential outside the company for problem solving. Another important aspect is that identified by numerous authors [26, 31–35] as "Dyadic co-creation/co-development in the upstream-downstream network": this variable essentially refers to the involvement and integration of other actors (suppliers, customers, users, lead users) who can support the innovative process. Then the two variables of "Informal external networking" emerged, i.e. the various activities to acquire and maintain links with external sources of knowledge [26, 31, 34], and "Collaboration in R&D and technological alliances/consortia", connected to collaboration and cooperation between companies for innovative purposes [26, 31, 33, 36]. Finally, the variables "Information networking"—concerning the investigation activity on the internet, magazines and other organizations in search of relevant trends and technologies [31, 32]—and "Technology brokering"—were used to analyze various sectors to see how existing technologies could be used in other markets for new solutions [31, 37]. The "Ability to seize and use market opportunities" [23] assumes considerable importance for a start-up that wants to be able to expand its business, as does the "Team Openness" which refers to the aptitude to use external sources of innovation [38] can be considered a very important element for a nascent company, as reported in numerous studies [39–41]; we used a Likert Scale for both these variables. "Research and communication channels for Openness" take on a concrete role for the "Team Openness"; following the approach of [38, 42] a discrete variable is used here to understand whether or not the start-up uses each of the following tools: IP in—licensing, Scientific knowledge sourcing, R&D alliances, Cooperation agreements, Technology selling; IP out—licensing, Market knowledge sourcing, Strategic partnerships. "The dimensions of Openness" [43] concern the two possible different modes of openness (towards internal or external environment) and depending on the value indicated on the measurement scale it will be possible for the start-up to understand whether it is more oriented towards acquisition and exploration of external resources or whether on the contrary it is more shifted towards external exploitation of its own resources. "Exploration" and "Exploitation" relate precisely to the innovative activity of the start-up, in fact, as found in [44, 45], a diversified access to distributed knowledge is fundamental for the performance of a company [38]. In addition, in this case a Likert scale was used to measure the degree of Exploration and Exploitation of the company. Numerical variables (in absolute value) were instead used as regards: "Number of people to be dedicated to exploitation and transfer of innovation" [46], "Number of patents deriving from R&D collaborations" [47], "Number of external ideas—or technologies—that flow into an organization" [48], "Number of internal ideas—or technologies—coming out of an organization" [48], "Number of new collaboration ties established by the start-up with local actors in a specific context" [46]. As regards the "Open Partnership" of the start-up, taking up the approach present in [47] this variable can have a fourfold value: 0—if there were no Research and Development collaborations, 1—if the partnership involved only industrial partners, 2—if the partnership only involved scientific organizations, 3—if both types of partners are present. Finally, "Project self-assessment on the quality of new ties" [46] concerns the collaborations established by the start-up with other actors in a specific context: the self-assessment will be possible through a Likert scale as specified in Table 1.

3.3 Sustainability

Start-ups are an important driver for sustainability and help to respond to environmental and social problems nowadays [49, 50]. The following variables have been identified in this sub-category: *"Green Revenues%", "Availability of scientific and technological knowledge", "Technical University", "Environmental awareness", "Ecopreneurs", "Sustainable start-ups", "Climate performance", "Social impact of the product", "Consumption of non-renewable resources" and "Emissions".*

The first variable on this list—"Green Revenues%"—was reworked from the metrics identified in the document "MSCI ESG and SFDR Index Metrics Calculation Methodology 2021" [51]; it measures the percentage of revenues deriving from the following activities: green building, sustainable agriculture, use of alternative energies, energy efficiency and pollution reduction activities. As reported in [52], the "Availability of scientific and technological knowledge" that spreads from universities or other companies has a positive impact on the creation of cleantech start-ups, as well as "Environmental awareness", understood as environmental awareness on the part of businesses, organizations, institutions and residents of a specific place. For both of these factors a Likert scale was used to measure the degree of knowledge availability and environmental awareness in the area in which the start-up operates. Also in [52] a statistically significant correlation was found between the presence of "Technical universities" and the creation of cleantech start-ups: a discrete variable was adopted for it where 1 corresponds to the presence of at least one polytechnic in the reference area and 0 in case there is none. The variable "Ecopreneurs", taken up in [53], refers to the entrepreneur who does not limit himself to supporting environmental issues, but creates "green-green companies in order to radically transform the economic sector in which he operates". For this variable, it is required to what extent the company's activity is actually set up for this purpose. A more attenuated variable than the previous one is "Climate performance" which contains several aspects: that the business model of the start-up has the potential to reduce greenhouse gas emissions [54], but also that this model is sustainable and scalable [55–57] in order to have a significant impact on society. Finally, we will evaluate the "Social impact of the product" [58] as well as the "Consumption of non-renewable resources" [59] and the "Emissions" [59] that characterize the activity of the start-up: in this way, we will also have a first reference on how the company is actually affecting on society and in its reference context. For the latter three variables, a Likert scale was adopted to give an initial indication of the level of the social impact of the start-up product, of the consumption of resources and of emissions.

Table 1 shows the list of the variables identified and the relative measures adopted. The first column lists all the variables extracted from the analyzed papers, while the second column shows the measures adopted (numerical variables, discrete variables and Likert scale). In the last column, the bibliographic references regarding the publications from which the variables were extracted are represented. The summary reported here must be considered as a first attempt to define an evaluation framework for innovative start-ups. This research is in fact preparatory to the next works that will be conducted, in which we will proceed to collect data from primary sources by conducting round tables and interviews with the stakeholders of the ecosystem in order to validate or modify these measures and redefine the framework according to what will be obtained.

The 45 variables identified here offer a first overview of the phenomenon under investigation and can provide a first indication of the innovativeness level of the innovative start-up.

4 Conclusions

The research conducted on the innovativeness evaluation of innovative start-ups covered three macro-areas: Propensity for innovation, Open Innovation and Sustainability. For each thematic area, we have studied various publications in order to identify possible variables with which to build measures and indicators. The survey revealed 45 variables described in the previous paragraph. Based on the evidence we obtained, we then proceeded to create measures that could provide a first evaluation of the phenomenon under investigation.

For the construction of the set of measures and indicators, numerical variables, discrete variables, Likert scales (with a value between 1 and 6 so as to be able to avoid average values) and percentage indicators were used. By means of the value assigned to each variable, the start-up will be able to have a first overview of its work in the innovative field. Since the innovative activity is risky and complex, management will thus be able to take advantage of concrete support for the decision-making process, arriving at more accurate and precise choices.

The main difficulty and hence the limitation we encountered while conducting the research concerned the scarcity of concrete indications, metrics and quantitative data with which to proceed with an assessment of the company regarding its innovative activity (instead, the measures regarding the sustainability subsection are more widespread); it was therefore necessary to provide for this lack by arbitrarily establishing a first nucleus of variables and measures from which to start. Precisely in this sense, a first research gap that we tried to fill was to provide a practically usable measure to begin to understand how start-ups are operating in the innovative field.

This research will serve as a support for the subsequent research on the subject, in which we will try to validate the measures arbitrarily constructed here. To do so, the future research will collect data and information from primary sources in order to understand whether these measures could be used for monitoring and evaluating an innovative start-up. For the evaluation, in-depth surveys and workshops with innovative start-ups will be conducted, in order to then proceed with their expansion and/or their eventual modification depending on what is detected. Once the evaluation framework of the start-ups' innovativeness is defined it could be used by the practitioners (entrepreneurs, investors, mentors) to verify the effectiveness of the start-ups in order to adjust the activities. The verified framework will also represent a floor for discussion for the academicians by providing the evidence on the interrelation and measurement of innovativeness variables and their application in the future studies.

References

1. Transforming our world: The 2030 Agenda for Sustainable Development. (2015). UN.
2. Brancati, E., Brancati, R., Guarascio, D., et al. (2022). Innovation drivers of external competitiveness in the great recession. *Small Business Economics, 58*, 1497–1516.
3. Selznick, B. S., Mayhew, M. J., Christa, W., & McChesney, E. (2022). Developing innovators: A longitudinal analysis over four college years. *Frontiers in Education, 7*(854436).
4. Selznick, B. S., & Mayhew, M. J. (2019). Developing first-year students' innovation capacities. *Review of Higher Education, 42*(4), 1607–1634.
5. Wagner, T. (2012). *Creating innovators: The making of young people who will change the world* (1st ed.). Simon&Schuster.
6. Bellini, F., Rudko, I., Bonab, B. A., Amendola, C., & Ventrice, G. (2022). Success factors of innovative start-ups: A systematic literature review. In *39th EBES Conference*.
7. Santisteban, J., Mauricio, D., & Cachay, O. (2021). Critical success factors for technology-based startups. *International Journal of Entrepreneurship and Small Business, 42*(4), 397–421.
8. Xu, B., Yang, J., & Dasí-Rodríguez, S. (2020). Determinants of credit availability for high-tech start-ups. *International Entrepreneurship and Management Journal, 16*(4), 1483–1501.
9. Audretsch, D., Colombelli, A., Grilli, L., Minola, T., & Rasmussen, E. (2020). Innovative start-ups and policy initiatives. *Research Policy, 49*(10), 104027.
10. Autio, E., Kenney, M., Mustar, P., Siegel, D., & Wright, M. (2014). Entrepreneurial innovation: The importance of context. *Research Policy, 43*(7), 1097–1108.
11. Baumol, W. J., & Strom, R. J. (2007). Entrepreneurship and economic growth. *Strategic Entrepreneurship, 1*(3–4), 233–237.
12. Del Bosco, B., Mazzucchelli, A., Chierici, R., et al. (2021). Innovative startup creation: The effect of local factors and demographic characteristics of entrepreneurs. *The International Entrepreneurship and Management Journal, 17*, 145–164.
13. Italian Ministry of economic development. The Italian legislation in support of innovative startups. Accessed 7 Jun 2020, from https://www.mise.gov.it/images/stories/documenti/Executive-Summary-of-Italy-s-Startup-Act-new-format-23_02_2017.pdf
14. Knight, G. A. (1997). Cross-cultural reliability and validity of a scale to measure firm entrepreneurial orientation. *Journal of Business Venturing, 12*(3), 213–225.
15. Nasierowski, W., & Arcelus, F. J. (2013). What is innovativeness: Literature review. *Foundations of Management, 4*(1), 63–74.
16. Hyytinen, A., Pajarinen, M., & Rouvinen, P. (2015). Does innovativeness reduce startup survival rates? *Journal of Business Venturing, 30*(4), 564–581.

17. Damanpour, F. (1991). Organizational innovation: A meta-analysis of effects of determinants and moderators. *The Academy of Management Journal, 34*(3), 555–590.
18. Cunha-Cruz, J., Huebner, E. C., Milgrom, P., & Scott, J. M. (2017). Care delivery and compensation system changes: A case study of organizational readiness within a large dental care practice organization in the United States. *BMC Oral Health, 17*(1), 157.
19. Alolabi, Y. A., Kartinah, A., & Muneer, A. D. (2021). Issues and implications of readiness to change. *Administrative Sciences, 11*(140).
20. Almaamari, Q., Kassim, R. M., Raju, V., & Al-Tahitah, A. N. (2018). Factors affecting individual readiness for change: A conceptual framework. *International Journal of Management and Human Science, 2*(1), 13–18.
21. Weiner, B. J., Mettert, K. D., Dorsey, C. N., Nolen, E. A., Stanick, C., Powell, B. J., & Lewis, C. C. (2020). Measuring readiness for implementation: A systematic review of measures' psychometric and pragmatic properties. *Implementation Research and Practice, 1*, 263348952093389.
22. Vnoučková, L. (2018). Criteria of innovativeness and creativity in start-ups and innovative entrepreneurship. *Quality Innovation Prosperity-Kvalita Inovacia Prosperita, 22*(1), 27–43.
23. Kim, B., Kim, H., & Jeon, Y. (2018). Critical success factors of a design startup business. *Sustainability, 10*(9), 2981.
24. Gupta, M. (2018). The innovation process from an idea to a final product: A review of the literature. *International Journal of Comparative Management, 1*(4), 400–421.
25. Sommer, S. C., & Loch, C. H. (2004). Selectionism and learning in projects with complexity and unforeseeable uncertainty. *Management Science, 50*(10), 1334–1347.
26. Chesbrough, H. W., & Brunswicker, S. (2014). A fad or a phenomenon?: The adoption of open innovation practices in large firms. *Research Technology Management, 57*(2).
27. Lasch, F., Le Roy, F., & Saïd Yami, F. (2007). Critical growth factors of ICT start-ups. *Management Decision, 45*(1), 62–75.
28. Spender, J. C., Corvello, V., Grimaldi, M., & Rippa, P. (2017). Startups and open innovation: A review of the literature. *European Journal of Innovation Management, 20*(1), 4–30.
29. Laursen, K., & Salter, A. (2005). Open for innovation: The role of openness in explaining innovation performance among U.K. manufacturing firms. *Strategic Management Journal, 27*(2), 131–150.
30. Hahn, D., Minola, T., & Eddleston, K. A. (2019). How do scientists contribute to the performance of innovative start-ups? An imprinting perspective on open innovation. *Journal of Management Studies, 56*(5), 895–928.
31. Battistella, C., De Toni, A. F., & Pessot, E. (2017). Open accelerators for start-ups success: A case study. *European Journal of Innovation Management, 20*(1), 80–111.
32. Burcharth, A., Knudsen, M. P., & Søndergaard, H. A. (2014). Neither invented nor shared here: The impact and management of attitudes for the adoption of open innovation practices. *Technovation, 34*(3), 149–161.
33. Gassmann, O., & Enke, E. (2004). Towards a theory of open innovation: Three Core process archetypes. In *R&D Management Conference (RADMA)*.
34. Van de Vrande, V., De Jong, P. J., Vanhaverbeke, W., & De Rochemont, M. (2009). Open innovation in SMEs: Trends, motives and management challenges. *Technovation, 29*(6–7), 423–437.
35. Brunswicker, S., & Vanhaverbeke, W. (2014). Open innovation in small and medium-sized enterprises (SMEs): External knowledge sourcing strategies and internal organizational facilitators. *Journal of Small Business Management, 53*(4).
36. West, J., & Bogers, M. (2013). Leveraging external sources of innovation: A review of research on open innovation. *Journal of Product Innovation Management, 31*(4), 814–831.
37. Hargadon, A. S., & Sutton, R. I. (1997). Technology brokering and innovation in a product development firm. *Administrative Science Quarterly, 42*(4), 716–749.

38. Marullo, C., Casprini, E., Minin, A. D., & Piccaluga, A. (2018). 'Ready for take-off': How open innovation influences startup success. *Creativity and Innovation Management, 27*(4), 476–488.
39. Heirman, A., & Clarysse, B. (2004). How and why do research-based start-ups differ at founding? A resource-based configurational perspective. *The Journal of Technology Transfer, 29*(3–4), 247–268.
40. Ketchen, D. J., Jr., Ireland, D., & Snow, C. C. (2007). Strategic entrepreneurship, collaborative innovation, and wealth creation. *Strategic Entrepreneurship Journal, 1*(3–4), 371–385.
41. Ridder, D. D., Finkenauer, C., Lensvelt-Mulders, G., & Stok, M. (2011). Taking stock of self-control a meta-analysis of how trait self-control relates to a wide range of behaviors. *Personality and Social Psychology Review, 16*(1), 76–99.
42. Dahlander, L., & Gann, D. M. (2010). How open is innovation? *Research Policy, 39*(6), 699–709.
43. Chesbrough, H., Vanhaverbeke, W., & West, J. (2006). *Open innovation: Researching a new paradigm* (1st ed.). Oxford University Press.
44. Powell, W. W., Koput, K. W., & Doerr, S. L. (1996). Interorganizational collaboration and the locus of innovation: Networks of learning. *Biotechnology, Administrative Science Quarterly, 41*(1), 116–145.
45. Von Hippel, E. (1988). *Sources of innovation, 1st*. Oxford University Press.
46. Bellini, F. (2017). *The socio-economic impact of technological innovation: Models and analysis of the digital technologies for cultural and creative industries*. Eurokleis Press.
47. Michelino, F., Cammarano, A., Lamberti, E., & Caputo, M. (2017). Open innovation for start-ups: A patent-based analysis of bio-pharmaceutical firms at the knowledge domain level. *European Journal of Innovation Management, 20*(1), 112–134.
48. Usman, M., & Vanhaverbeke, W. (2017). How start-ups successfully organize and manage open innovation with large companies. *European Journal of Innovation Management, 20*(1), 171–186.
49. Hall, J., Daneke, G., & Lenox, M. J. (2010). Sustainable development and entrepreneurship: Past contributions and future directions. *Journal of Business Venturing, 25*(5), 439–448.
50. Pacheco, D. F., Dean, T. J., & Paynec, D. S. (2020). Escaping the green prison: Entrepreneurship and the creation of opportunities for sustainable development. *Journal of Business Venturing, 25*(5), 464–480.
51. MSCI ESG and SFDR Index Metrics Calculation Methodology, December 2021. Accessed May 25, 2022, from https://www.msci.com/documents/1296102/26144308/ESG-SFDR-Index-Metrics-Calc-Methodology.pdf
52. Giudici, G., Guerini, M., & Rossi-Lamastra, C. (2019). The creation of cleantech startups at the local level: The role of knowledge availability and environmental awareness. *Small Business Economics, 52*(4), 815–830.
53. Isaak, R. (2002). The making of the Ecopreneur. *Greener Management International, 38*, 81–91.
54. Leendertse, J., Rijnsoever, F. J., & Eveleens, C. P. (2021). The sustainable start-up paradox: Predicting the business and climate performance of start-ups. *Business Strategy and the Environment, 30*(2), 1019–1036.
55. Bjørnåli, E. S., & Ellingsen, A. (2014). Factors affecting the development of clean-tech start-ups: A literature review. *Energy Procedia, 58*, 43–50.
56. Calel, R., & Dechezleprêtre, A. (2016). Environmental policy and directed technological change: Evidence from the European carbon market. *The Review of Economics and Statistics, 98*(1), 173–191.
57. Meyskens, M., & Carsrud, A. (2013). Nascent green-technology ventures: A study assessing the role of partnership diversity in firm success. *Small Business Economics, 40*(3), 739–759.
58. Warhurst, A. (2002). Sustainability indicators and sustainability performance management. *MMSD, 43*.

59. Joung, C. B., Carrell, J., Sarkar, P., & Fenga, S. C. (2012). Categorization of indicators for sustainable manufacturing. *Ecological Indicators, 24*, 148–157.
60. Samuelsson, M., & Davidsson, P. (2009). Does venture opportunity variation matter? Investigating systematic process differences between innovative and imitative new ventures. *Small Business Economics, 33*(2), 229–255.
61. Al-Ashaab, A., Golob, M., Urrutia, U. A., & Gourdin, M. (2015). Development and application of lean product development performance measurement tool. *International Journal of Computer Integrated Manufacturing, 29*(3), 342–354.

A Bibliometric Analysis of FabLabs Research

Rocco Agrifoglio, Concetta Metallo, Roberta Oppedisano, and Maria Ferrara

Abstract This study presents an overview regarding the currently literature on community-based workshops and Fabrication Labs (FabLabs) in management and administration. An online search was conducted using the Scopus database and a co-occurrence analysis (VCA) was performed using the VOSviewer software. The analysis revealed a dataset of 148 publications, in which the results showed the existence of three main clusters, and the relevance of research topics over time. This paper contributes to the literature by presenting a comprehensive review about FabLab research, in management and organization, and leads to further reflections on emerging research domains.

Keywords Community-based workshops · Fabrication laboratories · FabLabs · Bibliometric analysis · Co-occurrence analysis

1 Introduction

In recent years, rapid advances in technology have encouraged the development of social movements such as community-based workshops [1, 2]. These are innovative spaces where people can learn new knowledge and acquire skills in all fields, including digital. Moreover, individuals can product technologies, through collaborative projects involving art, design, engineering, and science. Indeed, the purpose of community-based workshops are the creation of collaborative and innovative projects, the mutual exchange of knowledge, and the sharing of digital fabrication technologies, via an open-source basis. In addition, intellectual and cultural diversity,

R. Agrifoglio · C. Metallo · R. Oppedisano (✉) · M. Ferrara
University of Naples "Parthenope", Naples, Italy
e-mail: rocco.agrifoglio@uniparthenope.it; concetta.metallo@uniparthenope.it; roberta.oppedisano@uniparthenope.it; maria.ferrara@uniparthenope.it

A. M. Braccini et al. (eds.), *Technologies for Digital Transformation*, Lecture Notes in Information Systems and Organisation 64,
https://doi.org/10.1007/978-3-031-52120-1_17

aims to grow knowledge [3], to all members of the space that has the freedom to replicate the skills and projects learnt in the collective space [4].

Today, the increase of community-based workshops is extending the possibilities for individuals, companies, and civil associations, to learn and use digital fabrication technologies. Collaborative spaces are becoming successful, since they involve people on voluntary base, that learn the use of digital fabrication technologies and platforms, also through networked sharing [5]. So, such place isn't only physical, but also digital spaces where people share abilities, experiences, ideas.

The development of community-based workshops has grown so rapidly that become, quickly, an international phenomenon. In the literature, many studies recognize to community-based workshops a central role in the network, because such spaces can address various topics ranging from issues of democracy and inclusiveness, sustainable production, consumption, relocation of production to debates on creative and innovative technologies [6–8].

Today, in many cities around the world, community-based workshops are sites recognized for their ability to recalibrate innovation processes, toward social and environmental goals, but also, places that reconfigure access and participation of the society, by including citizens in solving problems and issues interest [9].

Community-based workshops have attracted increased attention in the literature [5, 10, 11] due to public participation of citizens in regenerative planning processes. Moreover, scholars studied how solve the difficulties associated with the depopulation of rural areas. The latter, in fact, experience situations of economic, social, and environmental hardship. As a result, citizens, depopulate rural areas, in particularly, for the problems linked to unemployment [12].

The creation of community-based workshops in rural areas help to solve the problems linked to depopulation and unemployment [2]. Citizen involvement contributes to legitimate decision-making, improving outcomes and benefits such as social learning, social capital, and empowerment [13]. The involvement of populations in community-based workshops can be the solution to inclusive and sustainable rural regeneration processes that can generate benefits for both the social capital, but also, the natural and human capital of the territory [14].

Community-based workshops stimulate the economic and social revival of rural areas, to undertake inclusive and participatory planning processes, that support citizens [5]. Rural areas are resources to be preserved, maintained, and developed, which through community-based workshops can overcome modern barriers and facilitate public participation [10].

2 FabLabs

Community-based workshops provide access to a workshop and the sharing of tools and equipment that encourage innovation and collaboration between individuals or groups [15, 16]. Often, they are also referred to as 'maker communities' [17] because they bring together different categories of people: from hackèrs (born behind their bedroom PCs) to hobbyists (do-it-yourself enthusiasts in their garages).

Community-based workshops are associated with various other names, such as Hackerspaces, FabLabs and Makerspaces. In general, all forms of community-based workshops have the same basic idea: to easily share skills and knowledge with the public [1].

The names used to identify community-based workshops are often used synonymously. The spaces differ depending on the IT activity performed, the technology or the purpose of sharing. Specifically, hackerspaces are a group of computer programmers who deal specifically with computer science [18], while FabLabs are a collaborative space associated with 3D printers, laser cutters and other digital tools and equipment [19, 20].

Gershenfeld and his colleagues, were the first to create a standardized and equipped lab, under the name of FabLab, in 2001 [20, 21]. Today, FabLab movement estimates an increase in the number around 1750 FabLabs in 100 countries.

FabLabs (or Fabrication Laboratories) are collaborative spaces where people have free access to technologies, acquire new abilities that can share to the community [22]. In such meeting places, everyone can enrich their cultural background through the putting of their ideas into practice by making real prototypes [22]. Moreover, they are a facilitator in stimulating innovation [16] and in increase ideas and expertise, through the creation (individual) and co-creation (collective), of physical or digital products [23, 24]. FabLabs can build bridges among professionals in technology, design, education, entrepreneurs, architects, artists, and non-profit organizations [4]. Collaboration with people of different skills and backgrounds, combined with training and the use of equipment in the workshops, creates a creative and stimulating environment. In fabrication labs, the process of knowledge construction is democratized, and the application of new technologies is taught to everyone who wants to benefit from the space and equipment [4]. Furthermore, FabLabs increase dynamism, competition, and employment [25]. They provide huge opportunities for emerging countries dealing with obstacles related to the scarcity of productive resources and equipment for innovation and growth [16, 26, 27].

3 Research Methodology

Building upon the previous literature on systematic and bibliometric analysis [28, 29]. The review methodology used in this study employs two approaches. An SLR approach to reliably search, evaluate, and select the most relevant research articles [28]. Furthermore, in a second phase 2, it analyses the articles selected in the first phase through VCA [29]. to identify emerging research domains. The two approaches improve the analysis and lead to more reliable results.

We conducted a VOSviewer Co-occurrence Analysis (VCA) for achieving more reliable findings. Figure 1 shows the research schema used to perform the co-occurrence analysis.

As Fig. 1 shows, we conducted a bibliometric analysis to provide an overview of existing literature about on FabLabs in managerial and organization fields. Data was collected using one of the most inclusive platforms for online searches, such as

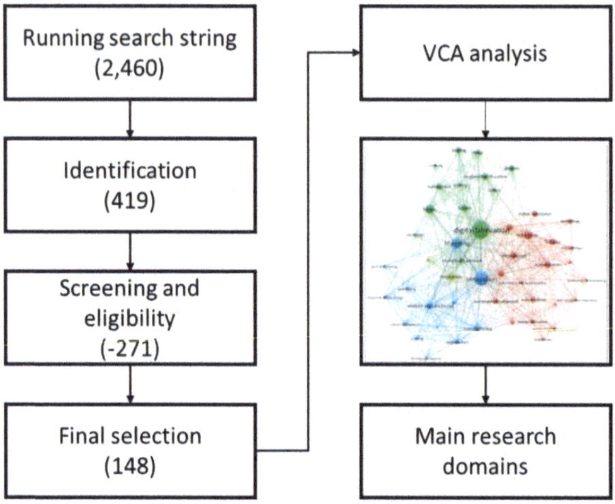

Fig. 1 The co-occurrence analysis schema

Scopus. In particular, we conducted an online search in February 2022 by using the following subject terms identified analyzing the managerial literature on FabLabs: "fablab*" (alternatively "fab lab*", "fabrication lab*", "fabrication laboratory", "digital fabrication", and "makerspace*") in title, abstract, and keywords.

The online search enables us to identify a total of 2,460 documents, of which 419 in (1) social sciences and (2) business, management, and accounting areas.

To eliminate duplicates, we performed a screening process. Subsequently, we also performed an eligibility process to remove articles that did not correspond to the selected subject areas. Finally, the last screening process led us to exclude papers not written in English. The final dataset consisted of 148 publications from 2011 to February 2022.

Then, we conducted a VCA using one of the most used software tools for bibliometrics, such as the VOSviewer. Using the software, we performed the descriptive statistics (publication trend, types and most attractive sources, and research methods) and the VCA.

4 Descriptive Statistics

The descriptive statistics enables us to obtain information on publication trend over the years (Fig. 2), the types of sources (Fig. 3) and a list of 10 most attractive sources (Table 1), as well as the methodology used in reviewed documents (Table 2).

The Fig. 2 shows a growth trend from 2001 to 2021 (excepting the 2014, 2017, and 2020 years), so proving the relevance of academic research on FabLabs in management and organizational fields.

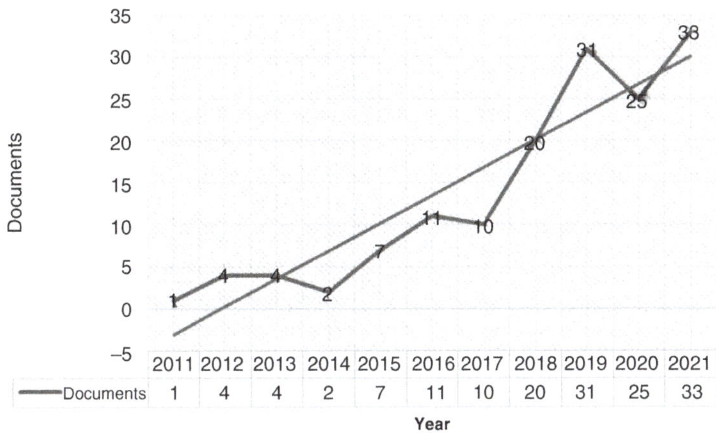

Fig. 2 Publication trend from 2011 to now

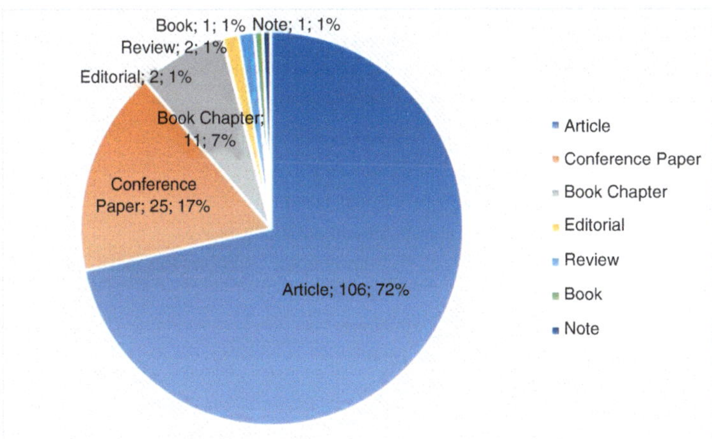

Fig. 3 Types of sources

The Fig. 3 shows the types of sources identified, such as articles (71.62%), conference proceedings and working papers (16.89%), book chapters (7.43%), editorial (1.35%), review (1.35%), book (0.68%), and note (0.68%).

The number of articles in the international peer-reviewed journals indicates that the topic is attractive not only for practitioners, but also for academics from management and organizational fields. Table 1 shows the relevance of research on FabLabs published by journals dealing with the management (Technological Forecasting and Social Change, 10; R&D Management, 5; Creativity and Innovation Management, 3; Journal of Manufacturing Technology Management, 2), education (International Journal of Child-Computer Interaction, 6; Frontiers in Education, 2; International Journal of Technology and Design Education, 2), and production,

Table 1 A list of 10 most attractive sources

Source	Count
Technological Forecasting and Social Change	10
International Journal of Child-Computer Interaction	6
R&D Management	5
Sustainability	5
Journal of Cleaner Production	3
Research for Development	3
Creativity and Innovation Management	3
Journal of Manufacturing Technology Management	2
Frontiers in Education	2
International Journal of Technology and Design Edu-	2

Table 2 The methodology used in reviewed documents

Method	Count	Percent
1. Experiment	6	4.05
2. Case study	34	22.97
3. Survey	15	10.14
4. Interview	28	18.92
5. Focus group	12	8.11
6. Document analysis	11	7.43
7. Ethnographic and observational	14	9.46
8. Mixed method	25	16.89
9. None	3	2.03
Total	148	

environmental, and sustainability topics (Sustainability, 5; Journal of Cleaner Production, 3; Research for Development, 3).

Table 2 shows that the most used methodologies in reviewed documents are (1) case study (34, 22.97%), (2) interview (28, 18.92%), (3) mixed methods (25, 16.89%), (4) survey (15, 10.14%), (5) ethnographic and observational (14, 9.46), (6) focus groups (12, 8.11%), (7) document analysis (11, 7.43%), and experiment (6, 4.05%).

5 Results of the VOSviewer Co-occurrence Analysis

Building upon the bibliometrics literature [29]; [28], we also performed the VCA analysis of our dataset aimed to identify the emerging research domains. The VCA analysis shown that network is composed of 864 keywords, of which 50 meet the threshold, 482 links, and 777 total link strength. The Fig. 4 shows the VCA results.

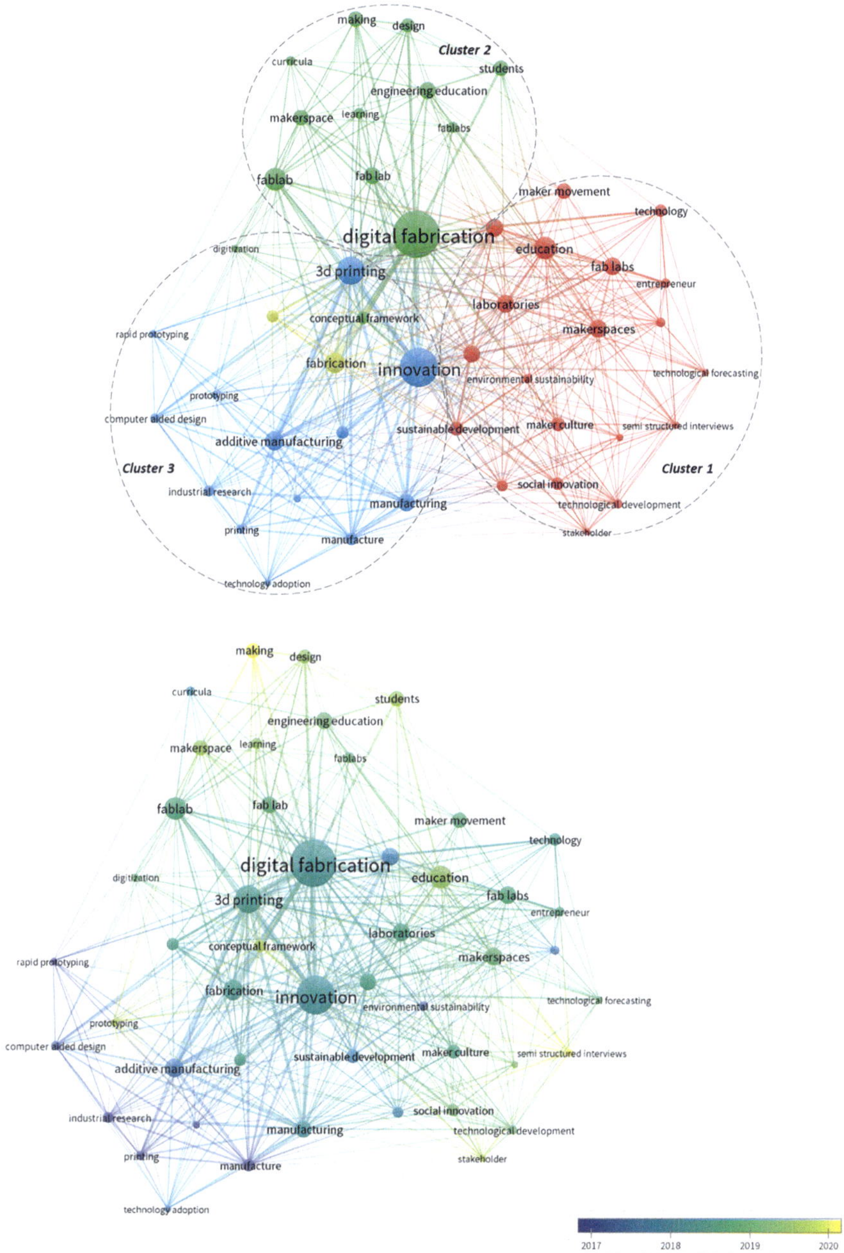

Fig. 4 VOSviewer co-occurrence analysis

The VCA enables us to identify three major clusters (Fig. 4), such as Cluster 1 (Red -20 items-), Cluster 2 (Green -13 items-), and Cluster 3 (Blue -13 items-), while a minor one, namely Cluster 4 (Yellow -2 items-), is not relevant for our analysis. Moreover, Fig. 4 also provides an overview on the relevance of trend keywords are relevant over the years.

6 Conclusion

The purpose of this study was to provide an overview of the current literature on laboratories and FabLabs regarding management and administration. Our survey revealed a growing body of literature on the topic, and we identified the existence of three main clusters based on the relevance of research topics over time. This paper provides a review of research on FabLabs and offers some insights into management and organisation. Findings show three main clusters that are: (1) FabLab drivers and consequences; (2) FabLab and learning process; and (3) FabLab and digital manufacturing processes.

6.1 Cluster 1: FabLab Drivers and Consequences

The first cluster is FabLab drivers and consequences that focuses on motives leading people to contribute to FabLabs as well as the several impacts for local communities. Papers in this cluster examine FabLab as enablers of innovative, learning, and collaborative settings, favoring social innovation and social entrepreneurship initiatives. In this way, FabLab allows to satisfy social needs or address social issues [30–32]. Moreover, some scholar highlighted as FabLab supports 'entrepreneurial action' [33], offering opportunities for fast learning for the individuals who might become entrepreneurs [34]. Research agrees that FabLabs bring environmental and social benefits and solve local problems [22, 35]. In fact, a research stream focused on how environmental and sustainability issue is constituted in FabLab ideology [1, 9, 36, 37].

6.2 Cluster 2: FabLab and Learning Process

The second cluster refers to the learning processes through FabLab. Literature considers FabLabs as new educational environments that combines existing knowledge allows to learn from others [38]. FabLabs encourage learning through interaction and relationships among members (such as students, teachers, independent inventors, or entrepreneurs), developing learning by doing [4]. A stream of research suggests applying FabLab as one pedagogical tool in formal education [39, 40].

Therefore, literature indicates FabLab as 'learning factories' [41] or FabLearn Labs (Chan, Blikstein, 2018), showing the role of educators who have started makerspaces in schools. For example, the initial project for digital fabrication in education, FabLab@School project, launched by Stanford University for K-12 schools or programs 'Learn2Teach, Teach2Learn' from MIT, that involves children into a FabLab [39]. Moreover, scholars highlighted FabLab as pedagogical tool in in academic education of STEM (science, technology, engineering, and mathematics) and design [39, 42, 43]. Papers in this cluster focus on the role of digital fabrication within of the core curriculum in schools and on individuation of specific educational methods [44].

6.3 Cluster 3: FabLab and Digital Manufacturing Processes

The third cluster refers to the digital manufacturing processes and analyses the FabLab as places where digital manufacturing is shared among users. People can use tools, infrastructure and methods of digital fabrication provided by FabLabs. This stream of research emphasizes the role of FabLab for providing access to digital manufacturing tools to small firms and helping them in the process of digital transition in the industry 4.0 era [45]. Moreover, FabLabs are considered as new organizational forms that allow post-industrial production and forms of peer production [46]. In this way, for some scholars FabLab is an enabler of an emergent 'industrial revolution' [36, 47] because allows democratization of manufacturing as well as personal and small-scale manufacturing. In fact, users can create customized products tailored to local and personal needs. Within FabLabs people have access to production tools and knowledge to manufacture objects for hobby, personal or commercial purposes [48, 49]. Finally, some papers investigate FabLabs business model [27, 50, 51], analyzing role and characteristics of FabLabs between several countries [20, 45].

7 Limitations and Future Prospects

The present work has some limitations that should be considered for further research. Firstly, the dataset is limited to the selection of scientific contributions related to the fields of management and organization and written in English, as well as publications related to the topics of management and organization.

Furthermore, another limitation is related to the online search database used to select the publications (Scopus); in fact, the use of other databases (such as Web of Science WoS) would be appropriate. In any case, the article can be a good starting point for framing the phenomenon and providing a comprehensive review of past research, thus being particularly suitable for the development of a research agenda, which is the next step in our research project on FabLabs. In any case, we believe this study is useful for researchers and practitioners who want to understand the state-of-the-art literature on FabLabs and the main implications in managerial and organizational contexts.

References

1. Hielscher, S., & Smith, A. (2014). *Community-based digital fabrication workshops: A review of the research literature*.
2. Liang, C. A., Munson, S. A., & Kientz, J. A. (2021). Embracing four tensions in human-computer interaction research with marginalized people. *ACM Transactions on Computer-Human Interaction (TOCHI), 28*(2), 1–47.
3. Blikstein, P. (2014). Digital fabrication and 'making' in education. In *FabLab* (pp. 203–222). Transcript-Verlag.
4. Maravilhas, S., & Martins, J. (2019). Strategic knowledge management in a digital environment: Tacit and explicit knowledge in fab labs. *Journal of Business Research, 94*, 353–359.
5. Giraud, T., Di Loreto, I., & Tixier, M. (2020). The making of accessibility to rural place for blind people: The relational design of an interactive map. In *Proceedings of the 2020 ACM designing interactive systems conference* (pp. 1419–1431).
6. Bauwens, M. (2006). The political economy of peer production. *Post-autistic Economics Review* (37), article 3, ss. 33–44.
7. Schor, J. B., & White, K. E. (2010). *Plenitude: The new economics of true wealth*. Penguin Press.
8. Söderberg, J. (2013). Automating amateurs in the 3D printing community: Connecting the dots between 'deskilling' and 'user-friendliness'. *Work Organisation, Labour and Globalisation, 7*(1), 124–139.
9. Smith, A., & Seyfang, G. (2013). Constructing grassroots innovations for sustainability. *Global Environmental Change, 23*(5), 827–829.
10. Harrington, C., Erete, S., & Piper, A. M. (2019). Deconstructing community-based collaborative design: Towards more equitable participatory design engagements. In *Proceedings of the ACM on human-computer interaction, 3(CSCW)* (pp. 1–25).
11. HuiHui, J., Barber, N. R., Casey, W., Cleage, S., Dolley, D. C., Worthy, F., & Dillahunt, T. R. (2020). Community collectives: Low-tech social support for digitally engaged entrepreneurship. In *Proceedings of the 2020 CHI conference on human factors in computing systems* (pp. 1–15).
12. de Luca, C., López-Murcia, J., Conticelli, E., Santangelo, A., Perello, M., & Tondelli, S. (2021). Participatory process for regenerating rural areas through heritage-led plans: The RURITAGE community-based methodology. *Sustainability, 13*(9), 5212.
13. Laurian, L. (2009). Trust in planning: Theoretical and practical considerations for participatory and deliberative planning. *Planning Theory and Practice, 10*, 369–391.
14. Egusquiza, A., Zubiaga, M., Gandini, A., Luca, C. D., & Tondelli, S. (2021). Systemic innovation areas for heritage-led rural regeneration: A multilevel repository of best practices. *Sustainability, 13*(9), 5069.
15. Tremblay, D. G., & Scaillerez, A. (2020). Coworking spaces: New places for business initiatives? *Journal of Innovation Economics Management, 1*, 39–67.
16. Wolf, P., Harboe, J., Sudbrack Rothbarth, C., Gaudenz, U., Arsan, L., Obrist, C., & van Leeuwen, M. (2021). Non-governmental organisations and universities as transition intermediaries in sustainability transformations building on grassroots initiatives. *Creativity and Innovation Management., 30*, 596–618.
17. Ree, R. (2011). *3D printing: Convergences, frictions, fluidity* (Doctoral dissertation).

18. Schrock, A. R. (2014). "Education in disguise": Culture of a hacker and maker space. *Inter-Actions: UCLA Journal of Education and Information Studies, 10*(1). Retrieved from https://escholarship.org/uc/item/0js1n1qg
19. de Boer, J. (2015). *The business case of FryskLab, Europe's first mobile library FabLab*. Library hi tech.
20. Rejeb, H. B., & Roussel, B. (2021). Perspectives on the evolution of a fabrication laboratory in an emerging country: A comparative lexicometric study of European FabLabs. *Journal of Manufacturing Technology Management*.
21. Gershenfeld, N., Manzoni, I., & Romoli, J. (2007). *Fab: dal personal computer al personal fabricator*. Le Scienze.
22. Gershenfeld, N. (2012). How to make almost anything: The digital fabrication revolution. *Foreign Affairs, 91*, 43.
23. Astrachan, O., Hambrusch, S., Peckham, J., & Settle, A. (2009). The present and future of computational thinking. *ACM SIGCSE Bulletin, 41*(1), 549–550.
24. Yasar, O., & Landau, R. H. (2003). Elements of computational science and engineering education. *SIAM Review, 45*(4), 787–805.
25. Gorji, M. B., & Rahimian, P. (2011). The study of barriers to entrepreneurship in men and women. *Australian Journal of Business and Management Research, 1*(9), 31.
26. Oladele-Emmanuel, B. D., Rejeb, H. B., & Redlich, T. (2018). *Strategic management: SWOT analysis of the African*.
27. Savastano, M., Bellini, F., D'Ascenzo, F., & Scornavacca, E. (2017). Fablabs as platforms for digital fabrication services: A literature analysis. In *International conference on exploring services science* (pp. 24–37). Springer.
28. Ali, I., & Gölgeci, I. (2019). Where is supply chain resilience research heading? A systematic and co-occurrence analysis. *International Journal of Physical Distribution & Logistics Management., 49*, 793–815.
29. van Eck, N., & Waltman, L. (2009). Software survey: VOSviewer, a computer program for bibliometric mapping. *Scientometrics, 84*(2), 523–538.
30. Guerra, A. G., & de Gómez, L. S. (2016). From a FabLab towards a social entrepreneurship and business lab. *Journal of Cases on Information Technology (JCIT), 18*(4), 1–21.
31. Rayna, T., & Striukova, L. (2019). Open social innovation dynamics and impact: Exploratory study of a fab lab network. *R&D Management, 49*(3), 383–395.
32. Schonwetter, T., & Van Wiele, B. (2020). Social entrepreneurs' use of fab labs and 3D printing in South Africa and Kenya. *The African Journal of Information and Communication, 26*, 1–24.
33. Aldrich, H. E. (2014, August). The democratization of entrepreneurship? Hackers, makerspaces, and crowdfunding. In *Annual meeting of the academy of management* (Vol. 10, pp. 1–7).
34. Mortara, L., & Parisot, N. (2018). How do fab-spaces enable entrepreneurship? Case studies of 'makers'–entrepreneurs. *International Journal of Manufacturing Technology and Management, 32*(1), 16–42.
35. Seo-Zindy, R., & Heeks, R. (2017). Researching the emergence of 3D printing, makerspaces, hackerspaces and fablabs in the global south: A scoping review and research agenda on digital innovation and fabrication networks. *The Electronic Journal of Information Systems in Developing Countries, 80*(1), 1–24.
36. Anderson, C. (2012). *Makers: The new industrial revolution*. Random House.
37. Kohtala, C. (2017). Making "making" critical: How sustainability is constituted in fab labideology. *The Design Journal, 20*(3), 375–394.
38. Kohtala, C., & Bosqué, C. (2014). *The story of MIT-Fablab Norway: Community embedding of peer production*.
39. Blikstein, P., & Krannich, D. (2013). The makers' movement and FabLabs in education: Experiences, technologies, and research. In *Proceedings of the 12th international conference on interaction design and children* (pp. 613–616).

40. Pitkänen, K., Iwata, M., & Laru, J. (2019). Supporting fab lab facilitators to develop pedagogical practices to improve learning in digital fabrication activities. In *Proceedings of the FabLearn Europe 2019 conference* (pp. 1–9).
41. Abele, E., Metternich, J., Tisch, M., Chryssolouris, G., Sihn, W., ElMaraghy, H., & Ranz, F. (2015). Learning factories for research, education, and training. *Procedia CIRP, 32*, 1–6.
42. Haldrup, M., Hobye, M., & Padfield, N. (2018). The bizarre bazaar: FabLabs as hybrid hubs. *CoDesign, 14*(4), 329–344.
43. Mostert-Van Der Sar, M., Mulder, I., Remijn, L., & Troxler, P. (2013). Fablabs in design education. In *DS 76: Proceedings of E&PDE 2013, the 15th International Conference on Engineering and Product Design Education, Dublin, Ireland*, 05–06.09. 2013 (pp. 629–634).
44. Angrisani, F., Ascione, G., D'Onofrio, L., & Manzo, G. (2020). Duality and distance formulas in Lipschitz–Hölder spaces. *Rendiconti Lincei-Matematica e Applicazioni, 31*(2), 401–419.
45. Santos, G., Murmura, F., & Bravi, L. (2018). Fabrication laboratories: The development of new business models with new digital technologies. *Journal of Manufacturing Technology Management., 29, 1332–1357.*
46. Shea, P., & Gu, X. (2018). Makerspaces and urban ideology: The institutional shaping of fab labs in China and Northern Ireland. *Journal of Peer Production, 1*(12), 1–16.
47. Gershenfeld, N. A. (2005). *Fab: The coming revolution on your desktop—from personal computers to personal fabrication*. Basic Books (AZ).
48. Hudson, N., Alcock, C., & Chilana, P. K. (2016). Understanding newcomers to 3D printing: Motivations, workflows, and barriers of casual makers. In *Proceedings of the 2016 CHI conference on human factors in computing systems* (pp. 384–396).
49. Yildirim, N., McCann, J., & Zimmerman, J. (2020). Digital fabrication tools at work: Probing professionals' current needs and desired futures. In *Proceedings of the 2020 CHI conference on human factors in computing systems* (pp. 1–13).
50. Menichinelli, M. (2011). Business models for fab labs. *openp2pdesign. org.*
51. Troxler, P., & Schweikert, S. (2010). Developing a business model for concurrent enterprising at the fab lab. In *2010 IEEE international technology management conference (ICE)* (pp. 1–8). IEEE.

The Metaverse: Digital Innovation in the Fashion Industry—A Systematic Literature Review

Grillo Michelle and Bonomi Sabrina

Abstract The growing interest in the metaverse is continuously increasing in recent years and involves many economic sectors. Primarily the fashion sector has long understood the potential of digital platforms and the advantages of being present in the main online gaming ones. Many fashion brands have entered meaningful partnerships with video game companies in recent years, "dressing" the avatars with their clothing. Regarding the metaverse, the fashion sector has taken up the challenge by creating the first Metaverse Fashion Week. After New York, Milan, and Paris, the fashion houses have landed on the Decentraland platform for a week of all-digital fashion shows and events. This work aims to do a systematic literature review to explore state-of-the-art relating to the digital innovation of fashion in the metaverse, in both business and social relations dimensions, on virtual gaming platforms and not strictly to find future research fields.

Keywords Fashion · Metaverse · Innovation · Gamification · Digital platforms

1 Introduction

Recent virtual world developments have offered opportunities for the digital transformation of business and social relations. In a hyper-connected world, social networks and game platforms have become the main tools to which people relate and give life to a community where users are increasingly active and create a new way of being together. Business stakeholders wanted to increase business value by

G. Michelle (✉) · B. Sabrina
Università eCampus, Novedrate, Como, Italy
e-mail: michelle.grillo@studenti.uniecampus.it; sabrina.bonomi@uniecampus.it

A. M. Braccini et al. (eds.), *Technologies for Digital Transformation*, Lecture Notes in Information Systems and Organisation 64,
https://doi.org/10.1007/978-3-031-52120-1_18

integrating real-world businesses with a rising metaverse concept. Traditional simulation games, social communities, and virtual communication activities to build business models were leveraged in different metaverse features to do new businesses [1].

The concept of virtual communities identifies the ability to pioneer new technologies and enchantment for imaginary worlds in fans' communities, stimulating new cultural productions [2]. The strategies of many companies that have long invested in digital focus on the value of youth subcultures that come to life within online communities.

The fashion sector considered virtual communities attractive even before the pandemic, concentrating on a vision increasingly at their service. Many fashion brands tried to link solidly with new communities, especially gamers; great brands, mainly luxury, and sportswear, built agreements and partnerships with the leading companies to meet new audiences in virtual spaces [3].

Due to the crisis caused by Covid 19, the fashion industry was inevitably forced to turn to virtual, redefining business models; digital innovation led brands to experiment with increasingly immersive technologies to drive the interest of big names in the metaverse [4].

The metaverse has attracted tremendous interest in developing related technologies. The term derives from science fiction literature [5] and is configured as an immersive space to be accessed through the augmented reality viewer or the PC with software; it must have the videogame imagination firmly in mind. Various metaverses now could represent the new frontier of social relations to convey stories and aggregate communities [6].

The fashion industry has been pushing towards its development for months; In March 2022, many fashion houses met in the Fashion District of the Decentraland Metaverse for the first Metaverse Fashion Week (MVFW), 4 days of events and showed that followed the famous New York's, Milan's, and Paris' face to face one. Simultaneously, the fast-fashion brand Mango opened its store in the Museum District of Decentraland. The Mango initiative is exciting; metaverse operators were primarily brands of the luxury sector; the presence of a brand that works with a broader audience can disseminate the metaverse idea on a large scale.

In this sense, the interaction between fashion and the metaverse is a fascinating area of investigation. The purpose of this work is to explore the current state of the art through an analysis of the most relevant aspects concerning fashion and the metaverse, including both game platforms (PG) and no game platforms (NPG), to prepare for future research in this field [7].

The paper presents an overview of the fashion sector, focusing on the relationships with virtual platforms, from games to metaverse, then describes the state of the art about digital innovation and the fashion industry, introducing the research questions and identifying the relevant articles on the topic's aspects. The third paragraph presents the systematic literature review process through the PRISMA method and content analysis; the discussion and conclusions are at the end.

2 Fashion and Digital

Fashion expresses and cements an era's culture, interacting in different sectors, from the economy to entertainment, even if someone considers it an evanescent phenomenon; clothing illustrates the elementary and fundamental perception of the human being and changes profoundly over time.

According to Simmel, the central knot of style is a model that satisfies the need for social support [8, p. 19], expressed through the need for cohesion on the one hand and differentiation on the other [8, p. 27]. Therefore, fashion becomes an instrument of individualization and cohesion in the group and social mobility, an element of differentiation of age and gender.

According to Barthes' theory, this study examines the relationship between fashion and the digital: style does not exist except through the apparatuses, technologies, and communication systems that build its meaning [9]. Theoretical categories of the early twentieth century are reinvented in the contemporary world, particularly in the virtual platforms of video games and the metaverse, to understand their evolutionary lines and relationships with the offline world.

The study intends to focus on the presence of fashion houses in the metaverse by including both game platforms (PG) and no-game platforms (NPG) within the metaverse, a recent and strongly growing phenomenon during the lockdown.

2.1 Fashion and Virtual Platforms: From Game to Metaverse

On April 27, 2021, Time inserted Nintendo in the list of the hundred most influential companies capable of exerting a substantial global impact. It created numerous communities thanks to the Nintendo Switch console and its flagship video game, Animal Crossing: New Horizon, was defined as "the game of lockdown" for the ability to make friends meet in times of social distancing, becoming a resource for socializing and increasing sales beyond all expectations.

The entire video games sector grew in 2020 and registered a turnover of over one hundred and eighty billion, confirming the growth trend in the first half of 2021, driven above all by online, which increased by 13.3% [10]; the boom in online communities of multiplayer players and the consecration of dedicated social networks cate to online games helped, becoming a new space to meet and socialize.

The immersive video game experience goes beyond the medium, finding space in other social environments; today, we talk about gamification or the act of introducing game elements into systems that are not starting [10]; very interesting is the so-called game bait, which concerns the fast and accelerated growth of cultural products inspired by the aesthetic ecosystem of the world of video games [11].

The virtual space of video games has especially conquered the world of fashion, becoming today what the Bois de Boulogne of early twentieth-century Paris was for the diffusion of aesthetic taste and activities related to consumption [12]. As the metropolis has long been the nourishment necessary for fashion, today, the metaverse becomes the new headquarters where fashion companies intercept new audiences and establish solid relationships.

The fashion "gamification" process horizons along two evolutionary lines.

On the one hand, companies create video games to provide a playful shopping experience. For example, in 2018, Hermes made it possible to download the Saint Hermes game; Burberry entered the world of video games through the B-Bounce game, where points accumulated allow one to win collector's items [13]. In 2019, Gucci launched the "Gucci Arcade" platform with a section dedicated to video games from the 70s and 80s, and Louis Vuitton was stimulated to play Endless Runner [14].

On the other hand, fashion houses consolidated partnerships with videogame companies to insert their products within virtual environments. Burberry, for example, designed two skins for the Honor of King mobile game [15]. Valentino, together with photographer Karen Chung, created, within the Animal Crossing game, a reality populated by islands in which to build houses and shops and shop for various items from the men's and women's collections. The first virtual fashion show was organized on Animal Crossing, producing a 3-min video on Youtube, where the looks of Craig Green, Gucci, Bottega Veneta, and Chanel were treading the catwalk, made entirely by gamers and kindly made available by fashion houses [16].

The experience of online fashion shows within videogames, which began during the pandemic, started a series of initiatives increasingly oriented to keep the presence of fashion houses alive within the virtual dimension; especially the new non-fungible token (Nft) market represented a new challenge and opportunity to be seized [17].

Fashion houses soon used them to increase brand awareness and promote products; they interact and include more and more users in their community, incorporating the metaverse, which concerns PNG, so much so that in March 2022, the first Metaverse Fashion Week was organized [18]. After New York, Paris, and Milan, avatars, models and digital models, and clothes in Nft have passed on the digital platform of Decentraland for a week of fashion shows, exhibitions, and events entirely digital.

Decentraland and many other online virtual reality platforms such as Sandbox, Mona, Rove, Spatial, and Somnium Space would represent the first metaverse model created on blockchain systems and accessible from browsers or desktops mobile applications [6]. They are spaces very close to the future metaverse in which a user, through his avatar, can immerse himself, interact, socialize, and participate in events in a digital world [6]. Some businessmen declared that business meetings would occur in the metaverse within 3 years [19], and interest in it has grown decisively because they understand the potential beyond the playful dimension [20].

It is taking a total change in how people interact with the Internet, in an "other" space connected to the physical one, in the development of which many companies from every sector are investing economic resources [21].

Today, therefore, the metaverse could be defined as a permanent and highly scalable network of virtual worlds in which individuals can work, socialize, buy, and play, and whose goal is an evolution of the Internet that points to virtual reality without borders physicists [22].

3 Fashion and Digital Innovation: State of the Art

The positioning of fashion houses on PGs and NPGs is a recent phenomenon. Existing research on the relationship between fashion and digital currently offers extensive literature on the relationship between fashion and social networks, specifically on the construction of storytelling by companies operating in the luxury sector.

These studies can represent an important starting point for understanding the narration of fashion houses within the metaverse from a transmedia perspective [2].

Much of the research has so far dealt with the influences that the interaction between users and fashion houses within social networks can exert in increasing preferences and brand loyalty, as will show below.

Interesting studies have been carried out in recent years on the relationship between fashion and digital with a view to sustainability. This investigation focuses on using apps to purchase used clothing or rent clothes. Other studies instead concern using digital technologies to create 3D models of fashion items before actual realization.

However, due to the novelty of the phenomenon, the literature on the relationship between fashion and the metaverse still needs to be made more prominent. As the phenomenon grows, it is necessary to recognize this void as a valuable area of investigation.

The idea is to gradually proceed from a general overview to understand the state of the art towards analyzing the fashion houses on virtual gaming platforms and those not strictly gaming; this kind of study often fails partly outside the single research field [7].

Firstly, the identification of the types of targets and the understanding of the influence that fashion houses within the virtual platforms can exert regarding brand awareness and purchasing choices. Then, it leads to an analysis of what kind of transformations in the imaginary can involve the presence of fashion houses within virtual platforms.

The main research questions are, therefore:

1. What is the state of the art relating to the fashion world within virtual gaming and non-gaming platforms?
2. Which are the fashion houses on virtual platforms, and which are in the metaverse?
3. What primary targets do fashion houses intercept on virtual platforms and spaces?

4. What influence can fashion houses exert on users regarding brand awareness?
5. What kind of innovations can fashion houses exert in online and offline interactions within platforms?

However, the speculated research questions could change or be improved due to the novelty of the topic and the speed of digital technology from year to year.

4 A Systematic Literature Review

4.1 Methodology

Firstly, due to the exploratory nature of this study, we proceeded to select the research carried out through a systematic review of the literature to make the results nearing completion accurate and transparent and prepare for future research [7]. A systematic review is a qualitative literature review that employs detailed, rigorous, and explicit methods based on one or more research questions or a focused purpose.

We chose the PRISMA methodology because it is a codified procedure with a checklist, recognizable, repeatable by everyone, reliable within the scientific community [23] but more straightforward and intuitive than others, and in line with the aim of the paper [24]. Following this methodology, we described why the review was done, the selection of articles listed, the search procedure and the related inclusion and exclusion criteria applied, and what we found [23]. The process takes place in three phases: a review protocol—sequential steps to collect, know and comprehend literature—the analysis and synthesis of the results, and the evaluation of the quality of literature [25], as shown in Fig. 1 [26].

The research used at least two databases [24], in our case Scopus and Google Scholar, to analyze indexed and non-indexed works because there may be exciting but still need indexed papers in a new field of study. The main keyword combinations were "fashion" and "digital,"; "Fashion" and "video games,"; "Fashion" and "metaverse,"; "Fashion" and "Nft,"; "fashion" and "digital" and "metaverse."

The search started on March 2022 with the insertion in the Scopus search engine, combining the keywords "Fashion" and "Digital," which gave a total number of results equal to 5949 [26]. Then we delimited the search field in a specific time range, indexed paper from 2020 onwards due to the strong acceleration of companies operating in fashion on PG and PNG in conjunction with the Covid-19 pandemic. This choice led to a significant reduction in the search result, from 5959 to 980 results, from which we excluded publications that are not strictly relevant disciplines (i.e., Molecular Biochemistry and Biology, Neuroscience, Physics, and Astronomy) [26], thus obtaining 314 results. The exact search string was then entered as a query in Google Scholar, getting zero results.

The keywords "Fashion" and "Nft" were added in May, leading to 26 results [26]. Again, the data relating to other research fields were excluded, reaching only

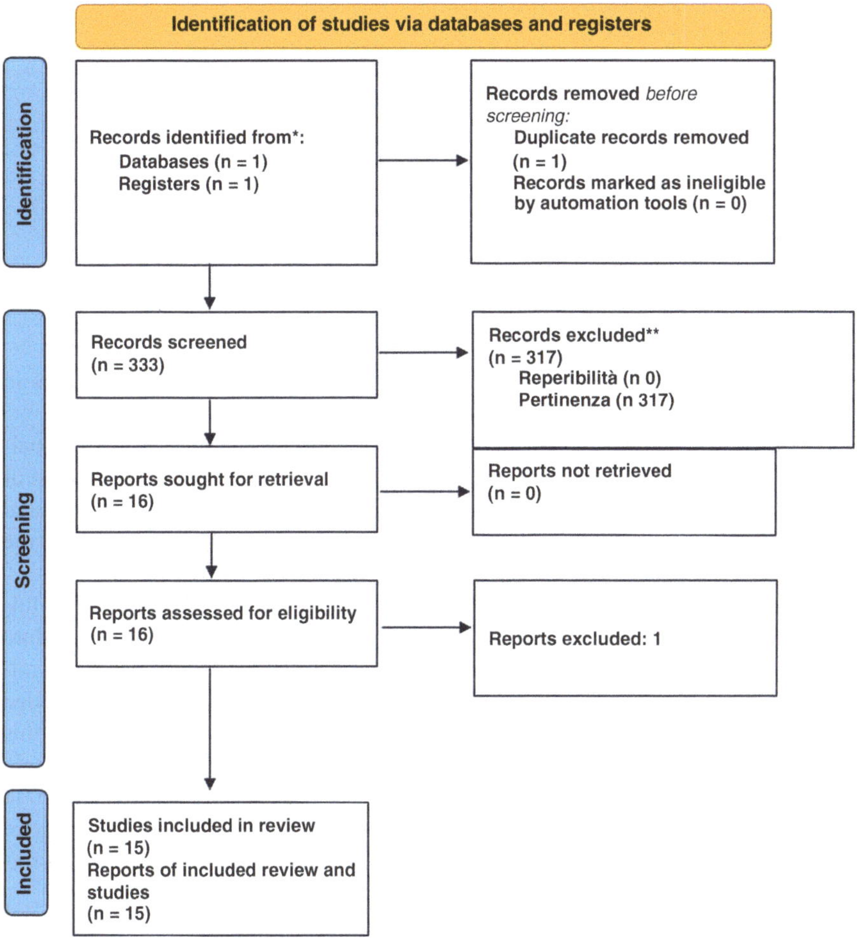

Fig. 1 Prisma method: the selection process (Authors' elaboration from [23, 26])

five results. The exact research string was repeated as a query on Google Scholar, generating 0 results.

The keywords "fashion" and "videogames" were then entered, and 12 results were recorded, limiting the choice to Social Science, Art and Humanity, Psychology, Environmental Sciences, Economics, Econometrics, and Finance, Neuroscience resulted in five effects.

The keywords "fashion" and "metaverse" were entered in the search bar of the Scopus database, generating only five results [26]; only two if we added "and digital." The exact strings were then entered as a query on Google Scholar, causing 0 marks for the first two and two for adding the third.

At the end of the research phase, the data collected from the two databases were exported to Excel to screen and eliminate any duplicates in the next step.

Table 1 Selection criteria (Source [25])

Availability (0–1 points)	Relevance (0–5 points)
0 points: Not available	A score of 0 was assigned for irrelevant results
	A score of 1–2 points was assigned for partially relevant or, in any case, partially relating to the research topic
1 points: Available	An average score of 3 points was assigned to the results consistent with the research topic
	A score of 4–5 points was attributed to the results strictly linked to the specific themes of the research question in which useful and important case studies where proposed

We then use the following indicators (see Table 1) with related descriptors to select the most accurate results for this search:

The PRISMA checklist is not a quality assessment instrument to gauge the quality of a systematic review [24]; all these articles were read thoroughly, and a list of well-defined selection criteria was made. Finally, the synthesis of each piece and preliminary information about the conducted research addressed challenges, and the main findings are presented in the next section [26].

We read the title and abstract of all the works identified in our research, thus following the inclusion and exclusion criteria (see Table 1). In particular, the procedure adopted for selecting the existing literature was based on two indicators: the availability of the material and the relevance. Time indicators have not yet been included since the topic is very recent. A score was associated with each hand. For this research, fully available studies were selected, and a binary score was used where the desired results had a score of 1. Regarding relevance, a score ranging from 0 to 5 was applied, applying an inclusion and exclusion criterion; only studies assigned a score of 3 or higher were selected, so only works relevant to the research questions indicated could be chosen [26].

In most cases, the selection or elimination of studies was straightforward, although in some cases, the text required careful and complete reading to reach the final decision. In cases where the title and the abstract seemed potential and eligible for paper inclusion, we looked at the full-text version, which was also helpful for the content analysis (see Table 2).

Ultimately, we ordered the selected papers from the more recent to the older ones.

4.2 Results

Through the systematic literature review, 15 indexed results were selected (see Fig. 1 and Table 2); the non-indexed results, on the other hand, achieved a relevance score of zero.

Table 2 Main results (Source: Authors)

Paper	Relevance (0–5)	Availability (0–1)	Keywords	Summary
Breiter, D., & Siegfried, P. (2022). The Metaverse: Exploring Consumer's Expectations, Their Attitudes, and its Meaning to the Fashion Industry	4	1	"Metaverse" and "Digital" and "Fashion"	The purpose of the paper is to identify consumers' expectations and attitudes towards Metaverse. It also examines the role played by the Meta Group in mass adaptation and the way in which the company makes possible the use of consumer opinion on the project
Choi, K. H. (2022). 3D dynamic fashion design development using digital technology and its potential in online platforms. Fashion and Textiles, 9(1), 1–28	3	1	"Fashion" and "Digital"	The paper concerns the realization of ten 3D models realized by a stylist and a group of graphic artists with the software CLO3D and Aftereffects, introducing the concept of dynamic fashion. The study highlights how dynamic fashion, using colors and patterns can give life to new forms of expression and aesthetics
Joy, A., Zhu, Y., Peña, C., & Brouard, M. (2022). Digital future of luxury brands: Metaverse, digital fashion, and non-fungible tokens. Strategic Change, 31(3), 337–34	5	1	"Fashion" and "Metaverse"	The article, with practical examples of the luxury brands such as Gucci and news startup DressX, theorized the attraction of NFT collectibles. The article addresses the Metaverse and offers an overview of the brands that have invested in it and the opportunities related to the new market space
Sayem, A. S. M. (2022). Digital fashion innovations for the real world and metaverse. International Journal of Fashion Design, Technology and Education, 15(2), 139–141	0	1	"Fashion" and "Digital"	The editorial presents a special issue about fashion and Metaverse, considering the parallel world in virtual reality as a new horizon of digital fashion. It clusters the innovations in digital fashion into two of the four possible themes: digital design and e-prototyping, and digital business and promotion

(continued)

Table 2 (continued)

Paper	Relevance (0–5)	Availability (0–1)	Keywords	Summary
Silvestri, B. (2022). How Virtual and Augmented Reality Are Reshaping the Fashion Industry During the Covid-19 Pandemic. In Extended Reality Usage During COVID 19 Pandemic (pp. 39–54). Springer, Cham	3	1	"Fashion" and "Digital"	The study explores the use of Virtual reality (VR) and augmented reality (AR) technologies. The paper starts from the idea that fashion is a field that is attentive and receptive to new technologies, whose use improves the relationship experiences between customers and brands. Specifically, the article addresses the issue of changing the fashion industry during the Covid-19 pandemic through the use of VR and AR in an experiential marketing logic
Jaradat, A., Ali, O., & AlAhmad, A. (2022). Blockchain Technology: A Fundamental Overview. In Blockchain Technologies for Sustainability	3	1	"Fashion" and "Digital"	The article covers blockchain technology, its basic features, components, categories, and architectures. The essential features are: trust, decentralization, persistence, anonymity; audibility, showing its application in various fields, from finance to business and education. The article also focuses on issues related to AI and Digital Privacy

Table 2 (continued)

Paper	Relevance (0–5)	Availability (0–1)	Keywords	Summary
Lau, O., & Ki, C. W. C. (2021). Can consumers' gamified, personalized, and engaging experiences with VR fashion apps increase in-app purchase intention by fulfilling needs?. Fashion and Textiles, 8(1), 1–22	4	1	"Fashion" and "Digital"	The paper examines how augmented reality can influence purchases in ecommerce apps. The study takes place on the gaming platform for smartphones Taobao Life, connected to the marketplace Taobao, within the game is possible customize your avatar. The study explores the extent to which the Taobao app provides consumers with a sophisticated and personalized experience that is engaging and satisfying consumers' needs for expertise, autonomy, and relationality, and whether this meets with positive purchasing behavior
Noris, A., Nobile, T. H., Kalbaska, N., & Cantoni, L. (2021). Digital fashion: A systematic literature review. A perspective on marketing and communication. Journal of Global Fashion Marketing, 12(1), 32–46	3	1	"Metaverse" and "Digital" and "Fashion"	This paper is about a systematic literature review conducted in July 2019 using keywords "digital" and "fashion" in five research databases. This study provides an overview of the state of the art of digital fashion studies, with particular attention to communication and marketing pursuit
Rehman, W., e Zainab, H., Imran, J., & Bawany, N. Z. (2021, December). Nfts: Applications and challenges. In 2021 22nd International Arab Conference on Information Technology (ACIT) (pp. 1–7). IEEE	3	1	"Fashion" and "NFT"	This research presents an overview of NFT and its technologies namely blockchain. Further, there are presents numerous platforms for buying and selling NFT across many sectors including education, fashion, sport, and digital art

(continued)

Table 2 (continued)

Paper	Relevance (0–5)	Availability (0–1)	Keywords	Summary
Rhee, H. L., & Lee, K. H. (2021). Enhancing the Sneakers Shopping Experience through Virtual Fitting Using Augmented Reality. Sustainability, 13(11), 6336	3	1	"Fashion" and "Digital"	The paper examines the relationship between the satisfaction of the virtual fitting experience in VR, brand advocacy, the intention to purchase online and the intention to buy offline
Särmäkari, N. (2021). Digital 3D Fashion Designers: Cases of Atacac and The Fabricant. Fashion Theory, 1–30	4	1	"Fashion" and "Digital"	The article frames the phenomenon of digital fashion through the research of two case studies: Atacac and the Fabricant. The aim of the article is to frame the phenomenon of digital fashion in the sociological perspective starting from an overview of fashion 4.0
Tripathi, G., Tripathi Nautiyal, V., Ahad, M. A., & Feroz, N. (2021). Blockchain Technology and Fashion Industry-Opportunities and Challenges. Blockchain Technology: Applications and Challenges, 201–220	4	1	"Fashion" and "NFT"	The paper explores the various aspects of blockchain in the fashion and textile industry highlighting the benefits that it could bring. The work, also, discusses the challenges of blockchain integration into the existing processes of the fashion and textile industry. The paper addresses the use of blockchain systems to protect intellectual property and focuses on sustainability by highlighting how efforts to cut costs and make fashion accessible have an impact on social and environmental sustainability. Finally, it offers an overview of the organizations that use blockchain in the fashion industry

Table 2 (continued)

Paper	Relevance (0–5)	Availability (0–1)	Keywords	Summary
Kim, H. Y., Lee, Y., Cho, E., & Jung, Y. J. (2020). Digital atmosphere of fashion retail stores. Fashion and Textiles, 7(1), 1–17	2	1	"Fashion" and "Digital"	This paper examines how the digital atmosphere can influence the consumer decision-making process in a fashion store. Especially with the use of ITC systems in retail stores to improve customer interaction (digital signage, display, and touch screen). The investigation of consumer behavior in a digital atmosphere is developed using the AIDSAS model (attention—interest—desire—research—action—action) (Hall, 1924)
Núñez-Gómez, P., Sánchez-Herrera, J., & Pintado-Blanco, T. (2020). Children's Engagement with Brands: From Social Media Consumption to Brand Preference and Loyalty. Sustainability, 12(22), 9337	2	1	"Fashion" and "Digital"	This study focuses on the empirical verification of the processes of consumption of children. The study focuses particularly on social networks and shows that the interaction of children with digital media has a significant effect on the increase and generation of brand preferences and loyalty
Särmäkari, N., & Vänskä, A. (2020). Open-source philosophy in fashion design: Contesting authorship conventions and professionalism. In Design Research Society International Conference (pp. 2410–2426). Design Research Society	4	1	"Fashion" and "Digital"	This article addresses the issue of fashion and the use of open-source platforms in a philosophical perspective. Examining some case studies: Atc, Minuji, and Self-Assembly, highlight the idea of challenging the traditional paradigm of fashion developing an alternative using open-source platforms. In all cases, there are some common issues such as the importance of transparency, product longevity, and sustainability

(continued)

Table 2 (continued)

Paper	Relevance (0–5)	Availability (0–1)	Keywords	Summary
Behr, O. (2018). Fashion 4.0–digital innovation in the fashion industry. Journal of Technology and innovation management, 2(1), 1–9	3	1	"Fashion" and "Digital"	This article provides a comprehensive overview of respective developments and product concepts within the field of Smart Clothes, examined from three survey perspectives (1) Sport and health, (2) environmental monitoring, organ perception and exoskeleton, as well as (3) communication and interaction

From our analysis, there is a vast amount of literature relating to the keywords "Fashion" and "Digital," which focus on internet studies and social media studies; of the 314 results, only 11 met the established relevance criteria.

Of the results generated by the keywords "Fashion" and "Nft," only 2 item could be selected. For the keywords "Fashion" and "Metaverse," a highly relevant but not available article was identified. In contrast, by adding the word "innovation," two papers were found highly suitable.

Finally, the results generated by the keywords "Fashion" and "Videogame" showed that no paper reached the minimum relevance score.

4.3 Content Analysis and Discussion

Paper	Method	Research questions	Main findings	Conclusion
Breiter, D., & Siegfried, P. (2022) [27]	Qualitative analysis through surveys	The paper follows 7 assumptions: H1 Consumers do not know enough about Metaverse, then make the judgment more difficult; H2 Meta entering the Metaverse increased interest in the topic; H3 Users have strong concerns about parts of the Metaverse; H4 The required technology is not mainstream ready (main reason: design, price, and possible use); H5 The Metaverse will increase the interest in digital clothing and its willingness to consume said goods; H6 The distribution channel Metaverse will be strongly accepted, especially when compared to Online-Shopping; H7 Participants have already spent money on digital clothing	The main findings show that Meta and Metaverse are considered critical, the technology required has not yet reached mainstream use, but interest is present	Potential users are not yet or partially ready for the Metaverse and they have shown concern about the security of private information, the decline of humans and possible mental interaction health problems, like losing touch with reality. Some consumers are willing to pay for digital clothes, some even spending a total of over 100 € on said products. However, this research shows that the adaption of consuming digital clothing still has a long way to go, with most consumers opposing the idea

Paper	Method	Research questions	Main findings	Conclusion
Choi, K. H. (2022) [28]	Qualitative analysis using focus group	The study investigates the potential of 3D fashion	The article addresses the social aspects and commercial possibilities, as well as the perceptions, attitudes, and behaviors of users toward 3D Fashion. What finally emerges is that software programs like CLO3D, Marvelous Designer and Dc Suite are used by both fashion and game designers	Focus group participants agreed that 3D virtual simulation systems will be needed in fashion soon, the potential of which concerns sustainability, co-creation, and design
Joy, A. et al. (2022) [29]	Qualitative analysis: ethnographic	The paper introduces two questions: the young consumers, that essentially live online, buy more fashion products in digital than in the real world? And then, how can the fashion industry strategize for the coexistence of digital collections and physical goods?	The article addresses the next changes in the fashion industry in the metaverse, illustrating the experience of some brands such as Gucci and Dolce and Gabbana and the digital fashion start-up DressX	The study traces a new academic territory that investigates the relationship between new technologies and fashion theorizing the fashion trends in the Metaverse by listing the advantages of the new consumption space
Silvestri, B. (2022) [31].	Qualitative analysis: interview	How virtual reality has changed the fashion industry during the Covid 19 Pandemic?	Through an overview of the use of VR technologies by some brands, observing the work of two companies, the Obsess and the Invrion that deal with creating virtual stores and showrooms, it emerges that the Covid has accelerated the process of using immersive technologies in the fashion industry	The study shows how Covid 19 has brought about significant change in the fashion industry, helping to accelerate the digitization process. The adoption of XR technology is a resource to ensure the competitiveness of a technologically advanced market

Paper	Method	Research questions	Main findings	Conclusion
Jaradat, et al. (2021) [32]	Literature Review	What are the achievable and anticipated benefits of the execution of blockchain technology for the government, financial, manufacturing, and healthcare sectors? What are the crucial challenges confronted in the execution of blockchain technology for the government, financial, manufacturing, and healthcare sectors? What are the recent and mutual areas of blockchain-enabled government, financial, manufacturing, and healthcare sector functionality? What arc thc outcomes of previous studies and their execution in guiding the forthcoming investigation?	The results aim to support professionals, practitioners, and stakeholders who wish to implement and manage transformation projects related to blockchain in their sectors. Moreover, help these possible blockchain users to understand the implied factors associated with blockchain as a support for the decision-making processes of their organizations	The review study presented shows important theoretical contributions to IT in general and blockchain research specifically. Contributes to IT literature by enriching studies on blockchain; most recent These studies have examined big data, social media, and cloud. While little is known about blockchain technology, this study adds a meaningful classification framework related to the advantages of the blockchain, its differences, and its functions

Paper	Method	Research questions	Main findings	Conclusion
Lau, O., & Ki, C. W [33]	Qualitative analysis with online survey	The paper develops around the following research questions: Do the gamification, customization, and engagement elements of VR fashion apps satisfy consumers' intrinsic needs for competence, autonomy, and relatedness, respectively? If so, does this fulfill of intrinsic needs (i.e., competence, autonomy, and relatedness) shape consumers' positive behavioral intention (i.e., the intentions to continuously use the VR app and make in-app purchases)?	Through empirical research, through Dynata and a set of 251 responses, it emerged that the more the sense of challenge and gratification is rewarded, the more it affects the purchase in the app. The study shows that the desire for autonomy is satisfied when consumers experience customization in VR fashion apps. Finally, highlights that the need for relationships is met when the consumer feels a sense of social presence and social support when using VR applications	The results show that VR apps can have a positive marketing effect because they meet the intrinsic needs of consumers' skills and autonomy by employing gamification in their applications. The study provides important new insights into literature and it is particularly interesting to understand the future of fashion
Noris, et al. (2021) [34]	Systematic literature review	What is the state of the art of digital fashion?	The results show that digital fashion is increasingly attracting the interest of both academics and practitioners, when referring to the category communication and marketing	Future research could further study the bibliographical elements recovered from the analysis of the research methods adopted by scholars. This could be useful for identifying which methods are mostly used to advance fashion research and to achieve penetrating results

Paper	Method	Research questions	Main findings	Conclusion
Rehman, et al.(2021) [35]	Qualitative analysis: ethnographic	What are the che and the challengers in the adoption of NFT?	The paper highlights the challenge linked by NFT technology from the perspective of security, privacy, environmental impact, ownership, governance, and property rights	The development of NFTs covers many fields. The increasing widespread use of NFTs, comes with many challenges including lack of industry-wide security standards for smart contracts, uncertainty of intellectual property rights, fraud risks by means of artist impersonation, transparency that violates user security, privacy, and adverse environmental effects due to a large amount of energy consumption

Paper	Method	Research questions	Main findings	Conclusion
Rhee, H. L., & Lee, K. H. (2021) [36].	Qualitative analysis: survey	The study develops around eight hypotheses: H1. High VF experience satisfaction has a positive impact on brand advocacy. H2. High satisfaction with VF experience improves customers' purchase intention in mobile apps. H3. High satisfaction with VF experience improves purchase intention in offline stores. H4. Brand advocacy formed after the VF experience has a positive impact on mobile purchase intentions. H5. Brand advocacy formed after the VF experience has a positive effect on offline purchase intentions. H6. VF experience satisfaction has a positive effect on mobile purchase intention. Through brand advocacy. H7. VF experience satisfaction has a positive effect on offline purchase intention through brand advocacy. H8. The relationship between VF experience satisfaction, brand advocacy, and mobile and offline purchase intentions is stronger in the high-involvement group.	The study revealed that the satisfaction of the VF experience based on AR has an important influence on the formation of brand advocacy and on the purchase intention in mobile apps. Such experiences can make the relationship with the retailer more intimate and customers who feel positive emotions will become the spokesperson of a particular brand of sales in their community	This study has several implications. First, it confirms that there is a significant relationship between the emotions that a customer experiences in the use of VR technologies and his behavior. It also suggests that the degree of satisfaction with the VF experience and brand promotion can be important for an organic connection between multiple channels through the VF experience

Paper	Method	Research questions	Main findings	Conclusion
Särmäkari, (2021) [37]	Qualitative analysis: interview	The paper starts from two questions, how and why Atac and The Fabricant are building their fashion design business on 3D digital design? How are these companies redefining the culture of fashion design and the figure of fashion design?	The research gets 3 important themes: sociotechnical sinks; professional pride in the digital fashion sector and how these companies are redefining the culture of fashion design	The study opens new research questions about how digital clothing could become effective enough to induce large-scale consumption, and how would the technological mediation of materials changes the relationships and knowledge of the material
Tripathi et al. (2021) [38]	Qualitative analysis: ethnographic	What are the various aspects of the use of blockchain technology in the fashion industry?	The paper shows the blockchain's potential to address issues related to the fashion supply chain by facilitating transparency and traceability. Eliminating intermediaries can help sustainability, improving the various social, economic, and environmental aspects, as well as ensuring clearness and protection of intellectual property	The paper shows the potential and developments of the blockchain applied to the fashion industry that also horizons in terms of security and the fight against counterfeiting

Paper	Method	Research questions	Main findings	Conclusion
Kim, et al. (2020) [39]	Qualitative analysis through interviews	Can the use of ITC devices in retail stores, such as touch screens and digital signage, improve customer interaction and influence customer decision making?	The study showed that the digital atmosphere in shops affects the mental and emotional state of consumers during shopping. Moreover, the effect of the digital atmosphere on consumer perceptions changes from retail to luxury	The digital atmosphere has a greater effect on consumer cognition (attention), influence (interest), reason for purchase (desire), and intention of behaviour (research, purchase, sharing) in sports shops and luxury stores. Sports brands could install digital devices in their stores to create a digital atmosphere to accelerate consumer decision-making. One limitation of the study is that it did not compare consumer behaviour in retail stores with a digital atmosphere and without digital technology

Paper	Method	Research questions	Main findings	Conclusion
Núñez-Gómez et al. (2020) [40]	Qualitative analysis: survey	The working hypotheses are: H1 The consumption of digital content has positive and significant effects on a child's participation in the valuation of said content. H2 The participation of a child in the assessment of digital content has a positive and significant effect on the creation of new content. H3 The creation of new digital content by the child has a positive and significant effect on brand preference. H4 The creation of new digital content by the child has a positive and significant effect on brand loyalty. H5 Brand preference has a positive and significant effect on the generation of loyalty	The study focused on the interaction between children in social network environments and shows that this interaction contributed to the growth of preference and brand loyalty. In addition, the effect is more intense in children between 12 and 14 years	This study concluded that marketing communications on virtual platforms and particularly on social media affect all aptitude elements. Therefore, the greater the consumption of content a brand seen on social media, the greater the involvement of the child with that brand, strengthening their preference and establish links that may intentionally last over time and build loyalty
Särmäkari, N., & Vänskä, A. (2020) [41]	Qualitative analysis: interview	Can open-source platforms for the creation of digital clothes subvert the traditional idea of the designer?	The paper presents 3 case studies and shows that the use of open-source platforms for the realization of clothing represents an alternative to the traditional concept of fashion designers. In particular, the article subverts the traditional concept of a designer not applicable in the digital context	Open-source platforms can challenge the old paradigm in the fashion industry while also ensuring transparency, product longevity, and sustainability

Paper	Method	Research questions	Main findings	Conclusion
Behr, O. (2018) [42]	Qualitative analysis: ethnographic	What are the potential of smart fashion products? What are the challenges of new business models?	Paper shows that to make smart clothing attractive to a wider part of the populace, and fully exploit its market potential; products must meet different needs: communicate identity, must have a competitive price, but also arouse positive emotions. In addition, businesses need to understand consumer expectations of smart clothes. It will not be enough to develop technologically advanced or aesthetically pleasing products, companies must combine compelling experiences and services with tasteful design and digital business models to build an emotional connection with their customers	This paper showed how advanced sensory technology, innovative components, and new ways of communication enable new product offerings with currently unknown capabilities in the fashion industry. To meet resulting requirements of the future Smart Clothes market, companies should reconsider their business models respecting their value proposition, value chain and revenue model

The literature review shows how the issue of digital fashion has been addressed in the academic field mainly from the point of view of design research by examining the new procedural, operational, technical, and economic aspects [28, 32, 34, 35, 37, 38, 41].

Other studies explored the opportunities and challenges of using blockchain and NFTs as tools to improve trust and security in the traditional fashion industry [29, 35, 38]. The idea addressed in some of these studies is that retail environments have radically changed over the past decade; in particular, there has been a shift towards online commerce, and the use of digital technologies, VR and AR, represent technologies that do not replace reality but enrich it by improving the shopping experience [29, 31, 33, 36, 39, 40] and metaverse can help consumers though most are wary [27]. More philosophical issues relating to the authorship of clothing creations through digital and 3D technologies, inclusion, and sustainability are addressed in other studies: [28, 37, 41]. The studies address the issue of sustainability understood from the economic and social perspective; in particular, the economic one aims to make fashion sustainable, balancing the social and environmental aspects [28, 38]. We excluded one of them [30] because it is an editorial. For our research questions, the two exciting topics were those that it does not address: digital human and metaverse and digital apparel and smart e-technology.

5 Conclusion

Of the selected results, only two articles [27, 29] can be considered relevant and in line with the research questions, offering a general and embryonic overview concerning the brands that have invested in the metaverse and consumer trends. However, it is believed that it could be an up-and-coming area of investigation.

The literature about the metaverse is increasingly explored; the studies about Metaverse's role in business innovation and change are little explored, but the cultural and relational aspects, pivotal in the fashion sector, are entirely missing.

Our study is still in its infancy, but after this first literature review, we can affirm that it could open a novel and promising stream of studies in this under-explored field, suitable for our research questions and future ones, particularly considering the empirically recorded links between fashion and gaming, especially following the first Metaverse fashion week.

Our study should be viewed with its limitations. First, our results build on the literature we could identify because the metaverse studies are still embryonic, continuously growing dispersedly in various Metaverse features. If we focus on digital innovation for the fashion sector, we can only sometimes reconcile and homogenize this yet fragmented field. Furthermore, we used only two databases, but we could add others.

Secondarily, our findings could be a foundation for empirical studies, which are much needed to accumulate additional knowledge on this recent topic in which enterprises are already investing, even if an irregular trend, finding new business opportunities, and creating innovative business models.

Acknowledgement This research received no external funding.

References

1. Kim, T., & Kim, S. (2021). Digital transformation, business model and the metaverse. *Journal of Digital Convergence, 19*(11), 215–224.
2. Jenkins, H. (2007). *Cultura Convergente, Apogeo, Santarcangelo di Romagna.*
3. Totaro, R. Dalle passerelle a Fortnite: quanta moda c'è nel metaverso. *Domus* 28/09/2021. Accessed 20/04/2022, from https://www.domusweb.it/it/design/gallery/2021/09/28/dalla-passerella-a-fortnite-quando-la-moda-si-fa-nel-metaverso.html
4. Rotolo. Il futuro della moda in un mondo sempre più virtuale. *Artribute* 7/11/2021. Accessed 17/04/2022, from https://www.artribune.com/progettazione/moda/2021/11/virtuale-digitale-futuro/
5. Stephenson, N. (1992). *Snow crash.* Milano.

6. Cosenza, V. Mappa del metaverso. *Vincos*, 16/04/2022. Accessed 20/04/2022, from https://vincos.it/2022/04/16/la-mappa-del-metaverso/
7. Webster, J., & Watson, R. T. (2002). Analyzing the past to prepare for the future: Writing a literature review. *MIS Quarterly*, xiii–xxiii.
8. Simmel, G. (1910). *Problemi fondamentali della filosofia*. Goschen.
9. Barthes, R. (2006). *Il senso della moda*. Einaudi.
10. Venini, M. Il settore del videogioco supera televisione, cinema e musica. *Financial Lounge.com* 26/04/2021. Accessed 21/04/2022, from https://www.financialounge.com/news/2021/04/26/videogiochi-superano-tv-cinema-musica/
11. Monahan, S. Video games have replaced music as the most critical aspect of youth culture. *Guardian* 11/01/2021. Accessed 10/03/2022, from https://www.theguardian.com/commentisfree/2021/jan/11/video-games-music-youth-culture
12. Codeluppi, V. (2007). *Dalla corte alla strada. Natura ed evoluzione sociale della moda*. Carocci.
13. https://it.burberry.com/b-bounce/
14. NSS Staff. Gucci svela la nuova sezione della sua app dedicata ai videogame in stile arcade. *Nssmeta.com*, 12/07/2019. Accessed 10/06/2022, from https://www.nssmag.com/it/pills/19113/gucci-app-arcade-videogames
15. Pantano, I. Burberry veste l'eroina del videogame Honor of King. *Vogue*, 23/03/2021. Access 09/06/2022, from https://www.nssmag.com/it/pills/19113/gucci-app-arcade-videogames
16. D'Amelio, M. Fashion gaming, tutti i brand che giocano con la moda. *IO Donna*, 29/05/2020. Accessed 10/06/2022, from https://www.iodonna.it/moda/news/2020/05/29/brand-videogiochi-sfilata-animal-crossing-gucci/
17. Morello, M. Unicità va cercando. Gli NFT e la moda. *Vogue*, 4/06/2021. Accessed 10/06/2022, from https://www.vogue.it/moda/article/nft-moda-kate-moss-gucci
18. Casadei, M. La fashion week debutta nel metaverso e fa il pieno di brand. *Il sole24ore*, 24/03/2022. Accessed 10/06/2022.
19. Devescovi, F. Il metaverso di Mark Zuckerberg: come cambierà il lavoro. *Ilsole24ore*, 30/11/2021. Accessed 09/06/2022, from https://alleyoop.ilsole24ore.com/2021/11/30/metaverso-zuckerberg/
20. Gates, B. Reason for optimism after a difficult year. *Gatesnote*, 07/12/2021. Accessed 8/06/2022, from https://www.gatesnotes.com/About-Bill-Gates/Year-in-Review-2021
21. Monaco, D. Da Microsoft a Tencent: tutte le aziende che stanno investendo nel metaverso. *Wired*, 03/11/2021. Accessed 07/06/2022, from https://www.wired.it/article/metaverso-microsoft-tencent-cina-facebook/
22. Ball, M. Framework for the metaverse. *MatthewBall*.vc 29/06/2021. Accessed 10/06/2022, from https://www.matthewball.vc/all/forwardtothemetaverseprimer
23. Page, M. J., McKenzie, J. E., Bossuyt, P. M., Boutron, I., Hoffmann, T. C., Mulrow, C. D., & Moher, D. (2021). The PRISMA 2020 statement: An updated guideline for reporting systematic reviews. *International Journal of Surgery, 88*, 105906.
24. Jahan, N., Naveed, S., Zeshan, M., & Tahir, M. A. (2016). How to conduct a systematic review: A narrative literature review. *Cureus, 8*(11), e864.
25. Levy, Y., & Ellis, T. J. (2006). A systems approach to conduct an effective literature review in support of information systems research. *Informing Science, 9*, 181–212.
26. Grillo, M., & Bonomi, S. (2022). Il metaverso e la digital innovation nel settore della moda. Una revisione della letteratura. *Rivista di ricerca e didattica digitale 4*(2), 70–99 – Studium editore.
27. Breiter, D., & Siegfried, P. (2022). The Metaverse: Exploring consumer's expectations, their attitudes, and it's meaning to the fashion industry. *eISSN*, 2683–5665.
28. Choi, K. H. (2022). 3D dynamic fashion design development using digital technology and its potential in online platforms. *Fashion and Textiles, 9*(1), 1–28.
29. Joy, A., Zhu, Y., Peña, C., & Brouard, M. (2022). Digital future of luxury brands: Metaverse, digital fashion, and non-fungible tokens. *Strategic Change, 31*(3), 337–343.

30. Sayem, A. S. M. (2022). Digital fashion innovations for the real world and metaverse. *International Journal of Fashion Design, Technology and Education, 15*(2), 139–141.
31. Silvestri, B. (2022). How virtual and augmented reality are reshaping the fashion industry during the Covid-19 pandemic. In *Extended Reality Usage During COVID 19 Pandemic* (pp. 39–54). Springer.
32. Jaradat, A., Ali, O., & AlAhmad, A. (2022). Blockchain technology: A fundamental overview. In *Blockchain technologies for sustainability* (pp. 1–24). Springer.
33. Lau, O., & Ki, C. W. C. (2021). Can consumers' gamified, personalized, and engaging experiences with VR fashion apps increase in-app purchase intention by fulfilling needs? *Fashion and Textiles, 8*(1), 1–22.
34. Noris, A., Nobile, T. H., Kalbaska, N., & Cantoni, L. (2021). Digital fashion: A systematic literature review. A perspective on marketing and communication. *Journal of Global Fashion Marketing, 12*(1), 32–46.
35. Rehman, W., Zainab, H., Imran, J., & Bawany, N. Z. (2021) Nfts: Applications and challenges. In *2021 22nd International Arab Conference on Information Technology (ACIT)* (pp. 1–7). IEEE.
36. Rhee, H. L., & Lee, K. H. (2021). Enhancing the sneakers shopping experience through virtual fitting using augmented reality. *Sustainability, 13*(11), 6336.
37. Särmäkari, N. (2021). Digital 3D fashion designers: Cases of Atacac and the fabricant. *Fashion Theory*, 1–30.
38. Tripathi, G., Tripathi Nautiyal, V., Ahad, M. A., & Feroz, N. (2021). Blockchain technology and fashion industry-opportunities and challenges. *Blockchain Technology: Applications and Challenges*, 201–220.
39. Kim, H. Y., Lee, Y., Cho, E., & Jung, Y. J. (2020). The digital atmosphere of fashion retail stores. *Fashion and Textiles, 7*(1), 1–17.
40. Núñez-Gómez, P., Sánchez-Herrera, J., & Pintado-Blanco, T. (2020). Children's engagement with brands: From social media consumption to brand preference and loyalty. *Sustainability, 12*(22), 9337.
41. Särmäkari, N., & Vänskä, A. (2020). Open-source philosophy in fashion design: Contesting authorship conventions and professionalism. In *Design Research Society International Conference* (pp. 2410–2426). Design Research Society.
42. Behr, O. (2018). Fashion 4.0–digital innovation in the fashion industry. *Journal of Technology and Innovation Management, 2*(1), 1–9.

“Look! This Is the Future of Cardiology”: Institutional Work and the Making of Telemedicine in Healthcare

Alberto Zanutto, Enrico Maria Piras, and Diego Ponte

Abstract This paper offers a critical perspective on the lack of widespread adoption of telemonitoring. By describing the processes that led from the first experimental adoption to the final codification of a clinical service, we show the complex ecology of actors, knowledge, and practices that are necessary to make the new telemonitoring service a part of the institutional fabric. Adopting a qualitative research design, organizational processes are investigated through the conceptual lens of institutional work, defined as the creative and rationally oriented activity of culturally competent actors aimed at adapting to dynamic conditions through which institutions are created, reproduced and destroyed. The work shows how different actors, using the resources at their disposal, act to modify healthcare institutions by redefining their role in a scenario characterized by increasing use of ICT tools in healthcare. Our work confirms how the institutionalization of change requires continuous “tuning” and its transformation into everyday operational practices. At the same time, we investigate why such innovation processes are difficult to replicate even within the same organization, arguing that in these healthcare contexts in which institutional work is successful, practices prevail in connecting discursive frameworks, limited implementation strategies and economic demands.

Keywords Institutional work · Remote monitoring · Telemedicine

A. Zanutto (✉)
University of Macerata, Macerata, Italy
e-mail: alberto.zanutto@unimc.it

E. M. Piras
Fondazione Bruno Kessler, Trento, Italy
e-mail: piras@fbk.eu

D. Ponte
University of Trento, Trento, Italy
e-mail: diego.ponte@unitn.it

A. M. Braccini et al. (eds.), *Technologies for Digital Transformation*, Lecture Notes in Information Systems and Organisation 64,
https://doi.org/10.1007/978-3-031-52120-1_19

1 Introduction

The reflection on telemedicine conducted over the last decades underlines how the introduction of technologies in healthcare allows actors involved to shape both the process of adoption and their role. From this point of view, the design and implementation phases are privileged vantage points to capture in vivo the processes of negotiation, cooperation and conflict that start when the actors involved are confronted with the opportunity to introduce the technologies in their working contexts.

At this moment all actors involved build representations of future technological situations [1] and it is possible to grasp the making of the definition of new models of service organization, the implementation of new work processes, and new forms of division of labor. Technological expectations shape scenarios of social and organizational changes built around new forms of technologically mediated relationships between health workers and patients. Many projects aimed at the adoption of new technologies, however, do not survive the piloting phase or end up being only partially deployed.

Remote cardiac monitoring is recursively presented as one of the building blocks of possible changes in traditional medical practices. Remote monitoring is regarded as a characterizing element of the replacement of the chronicity management model based on periodic visits with clinical encounters scheduled on as needed basis. Such new arrangement should be made possible by a continuous monitoring of implantable devices. The continuous process of automatic sending and screening of data has been heralded as a way to increase patients' trust while reducing the need for work performed by healthcare professionals.

Empirical analyses, however, show that telemonitoring, supported by remote visits, has a limited diffusion and is often the subject of experiments that do not go beyond the pilot testing phase on small numbers.

This paper seeks to offer a critical perspective on the lack of widespread adoption of telemonitoring in cardiology, starting with the analysis of a successful case. By offering a reconstruction of the processes that led from the first experimental adoption to the definitive codification of the service as a clinical service, the paper intends to show the complex ecology of actors, knowledge, and practices that are necessary to incardinate new services into the institutional fabric.

2 Contribution of Institutional Work

In complex organizations, the dynamics that determine a process of change and adoption of new technologies are multiple and cannot be traced back to a linear trajectory. It is often suggested in the ICT field to study the processes of technology diffusion to understand the adoption curves and the typical organizational configurations that enable them. A substantial amount of work has highlighted and explored these aspects, but from an organizational point of view, as Lawrence and Suddaby [2] suggest, the diffusion of a technology is often accompanied by a "black box" idea that does not help to understand the intrinsic organizational dimensions of these phenomena. Another particularly consistent problem with complex organizations stems from the nesting effect that each organizational dynamic brings with it. Each institutional actor brings with it a multiplicity of planes of responsibility at the level, micro and meso primarily, that can make the dynamics of technology diffusion contradictory, especially when the hierarchies of these dynamics are unclear [3].

The institutionalist perspective, and specifically institutional work, offers a set of conceptual tools that lend themselves particularly well to critical investigations of these processes. Institutional work is defined here as the creative and rationally oriented activity of culturally competent actors aimed at adapting to dynamic conditions through which institutions are created, reproduced and destroyed [4, 5]. This approach shows how different actors, using the resources at their disposal, act to change the institutions of which they are part and relates institutional change and everyday working practices.

In taking the perspective of institutional work, one can draw on a range of epistemological options that may even partially differ from one another. All these attempts attempt to address the issue of correspondence between actions and the institutions that contain them. However, as Modell [6] argues, the large body of studies on institutional work does not adequately and critically explore what happens within this construct when confronted with the reality of research fields. In the approaches most consistent with the tradition of institutionalism, the search for a certain isomorphism of dynamics to justify the managerial choices made always prevails, without however giving due weight to the situated and local dimensions. The seminal work of Lawrence and Suddaby [2] had already emphasized this aspect by opening up a plurality of approaches with which to study institutional work including, for example, actor-network theory. The nodes of these study approaches remain quite present over time with recurring trends that close the reflection within the scope of the scholars of this concept.

Aspects gaining relevance in the debate include on the one hand the question of the agency of institutional work [7] and the intentionality of actors [8], and on the other hand the power dynamics and attempts to manipulate it. These are all processes that are part of a phenomenological dynamic and need to consider the choices of individuals in relation to institutional agency [9].

Without entering here into the complex debate that has extensively explored institutional logics in recent years, the reflections around the behavior of individuals have appeared more complex and articulated. Amongst the various modelling proposed, however, it is difficult to understand the variations at the level of the individual precisely because of the membership of different social groups that may nourish different forms of reflexivity on different organizational situations [9, 10]. Thus, according to these studies, on the one hand, there is room for the contradiction fueled by institutional logics and their agency that reverberates in the subjects, on the other hand, attention must be focused on the limits of actors' understanding of institutional logics. This opens up the possibility of reinforcing the logics through everyday practices, or of activating new practices and breaking with habitual forms of agency, and thus they can mobilize other actors who share the same perceptions through reflexive processes. According to the outline of the review conducted by Modell [6], this dynamic can take hold and can generate new alliances by affirming 'reformist elites' actors' who take on new guiding assumptions for their actions that challenge traditional pre-existing institutional conditions.

This recognition allows us to dialectically consider the top-down and bottom-up dynamics that characterize these processes. In this paper, we intend to investigate a bottom-up dynamic of institutional work in order to understand under what conditions this reflexive path that overcomes and rearticulates institutional isomorphism can take place.

The work aims to answer two research questions. The first is to understand what the representations of telemedicine are for the different actors involved, with the aim of identifying possible elements of tension in the expectations associated with its massive introduction into clinical practice. The second question is what strategies the different actors deploy in order to seize the opportunities telemedicine offers them or to shield themselves from changes that are deemed to worsen their condition (Fig. 1).

3 Methodology

During the exploratory fieldwork phase, we considered a complex and multifaceted dynamic involving cardiology departments in the regional system to be promising. These departments have introduced new technologies to monitor patients with heart failure and were conducting further digitalization processes for new patients.

Cardiological monitoring is one of the issues of greatest concern in the healthcare systems. Problems arising from poor adherence to treatment and the non-linear trend in patients' attention to cardiological health (exercise, diet, therapy), is a source of hospitalization and worsening quality of life [11]. Therefore, the vulnerability of such patients requires specific measures to ensure adherence to follow-up therapies while preventing accessing the hospital.

Telephone calls and onsite visits are a time-consuming process and require specific skills as it generates a large amount of data that must be managed by trained staff limiting making it impossible to scale up the service [12].

Remote monitoring services were developed rapidly and widely implemented for these patients [13] and are regarded as effective, especially for patients with implantable devices. However, the interpretation of the organizational transformations seems much more complex and organizational resilience in these situations is one of the most difficult challenges to make the changes stable over time.

Cardiology was one of the fields of application of the technologies developed and the department of one hospital in the region was keen to redesign of service provision through some innovative systems supporting telemedicine.

The purpose of the empirical research was to capture the actors' choices about the implementation, the evolution, and the institutionalization of a telecardiological remote monitoring practice. We adopted a qualitative research design to flank the phases of the evolution of the project from its design to its piloting, from its refinement to the redesign and scale-up. To this aim, we conducted a longitudinal analysis involving the stakeholders in charge of the design of the remote monitoring system. For this analysis and for the purpose of this paper we will discuss the fieldwork related to a department of cardiology that first promoted this innovation in the region and at the Italian Association of Arrhythmology and Cardiostimulation (AIAC). A total of 21 informants have been interviewed (some of them twice) for a total of 30 semi-structured interviews, that were collected, recorded and verbatim transcribed. The research has been conducted in two distinct phases. In the summer of 2020, we focused on implementation in the cardiology department. In early 2021 and during the autumn we conducted other interviews with other stakeholders and with the founders of the telemonitoring service of the cardiology department and some actors who no longer work in the department. This second phase of the fieldwork gave us a more complete understanding actors' reflexivity and how they developed a new strategy to check over time of the implantable monitoring. In total the stakeholders involved were:

The political management

- General Director of Regional Health Department -
- Director of Innovation for health services at the Regional Health Department
- Director of Communication and IT services of Health Authority
- Director of Territorial Services (GPs) of Health Authority
- Director Clinical Governance

The technical management

- Director of a Research Centre for health technology innovation
- Project Manager of the provider of technological infrastructure
- 2 Project Managers of the multidisciplinary lab of technological innovation in health infrastructure

The department management

- Director of Cardiology Department
- 2 Doctors at Cardiology Department

The monitoring personnel

- 4 Nurses of telemonitoring service

For the sake of the present paper, our analysis relies on the interviews with the clinical governance, the department management and the monitoring personnel. The other interviews provided the background context in which the innovation took place.

4 Findings

The fieldwork allowed to deepen and clarify the role of the different stakeholders with respect to the context of the observed digital innovation. We identified that the technology used comes from a variety of actors. On the one hand, there are the implant vendors who provide their own dashboards, then there is the health authority which has produced a general dashboard for all implantable. This network of institutional infrastructures has opened the possibility for a series of actors to get into the flow of everyday practices that were able to change the flow itself [14].

In the beginning, around 2015, the team was beleaguered by the problem of check-ups for patients who had implantable heart rate control devices that imposed waiting times of around 6–8 months. At that time, implantable devices capable of recording and analysing cardiological data came onto the market that would allow remote consultation. The remote monitoring functionality, made technically possible by the devices, was, however, not practiced by the department except in what the director of the department described as a 'hobby form'.

A few selected patients were given the transponder that allowed the data to be sent to the cloud and from there to the doctors' dashboard. On these selected few patients, doctors could observe the data remotely, while all other patients with implantable devices had to travel in person to the department where their data was downloaded by the technical staff who analyzed it during the visit. The term 'hobby form' refers to the fact that the remote monitoring procedure was practiced without any training, without formalization and in an unplanned manner within the ward routines.

> We already had the technology in house because of a choice I had already made when I was working in Trento, for the tenders for the acquisition of diagnostic and therapeutic devices (ICDs, pacemakers, loop recorders, etc.), we chose in such a way that all this equipment was supplied already included in the price of the remote-control equipment. [Director].

The hobby phase allowed healthcare professionals to understand how it could change their daily work and the care relationship.

> We started out with nothing, there was no mandate but a futuristic vision, that is, with a view to the development of the technology's potential, because bringing 2,000 patients a year to the outpatient clinic is demanding, even to be able to manage it, you still have to spend time, you lose a lot more time, and you don't check on the patient every twenty days, every month according to the setting you could check him when you visited him, and also from the safety point of view telemedicine gave you an extra tool to go along with the outpatient visit, so we started and then slowly the legislation helped and covid even more when Covid started telemedicine got a huge boost, a lot. [Head nurse at the start of the trial].

These new modes could not do it alone, so work was needed to find the right person. A person who knew how to 'make these technologies talk' by feeding data into a new workflow. The search for this person was immediately complex because of the frontier skills he or she had to possess. What was needed was a nurse who could handle the computer equipment and could read it with reference to the specific cardiological skills involved in telemonitoring work. This search focused on a nurse who had been out of the ward for a few months due to physical health problems that had compromised his path on the ward because of the radiation risk to which operators in the operating theatre are subjected. The director recalls with particular satisfaction the work of researching and convincing this person, which lasted about a year.

> So, [with the appointment in this department] I came here and said let's get this technology [made available by procurement] going. The second step is how to implement it and we had to find the right people, the next step was to get an extra resource dedicated to this work and the tricky step was to find the right person. [Director]

But even this step alone was not sufficient to establish a recognized chain of institutional work within the organizational reality of the health authority. A third element was needed to make the work in the cardiology department truly institutional, the inclusion of telemonitoring in the regional and national nomenclature of planned activity. The director of the department explicitly speaks of a "third ingredient" after the technology and the people capable of "aligning" it with the other resources in the context.

> The following year [the human resource with the expected qualifications] arrived, and so we started with this project in 2015. So, we had the ingredients: we had the technology; we had the person; we were still missing a step, a third ingredient, which was codification, that is, moving towards a formalization of this activity. One of the big problems at a national level, but also at an international level, or at least at a European level for the lack of recognition of telemedicine activities, so one does these things but one does it on a voluntary basis, therefore with all that comes with it, something that is not quantified, someone who is not recognized, you have no cover, what you do you take on all the responsibilities... [Director]

The fieldwork has shown that in parallel with the internal work of the core group of people who have become active around the telemonitoring laboratory, work has progressively been developed to inform and validate the entire telemedicine process among the scientific community of reference for this type of medical expertise. Doctors participate in national scientific societies of electrophysiology and create awareness around the subject. Discussions are held in those contexts on the training needed by healthcare professionals to be able to set up a telecardiology service and to support its validity in other regional contexts. This work focuses attention to several key issues that guide the production of papers published in international journals of reference for the international community.

In the meantime, the work can really be consolidated, and the entire organizational machine has the basic elements to act in the context of cardiology telemonitoring. It soon became clear that this setup would soon have to deal with the issue of the sustainability of the tele-monitoring laboratory given the increasing enrolment of patients with implants. In addition, doctors and nurses began to be operational in the actual work of the tele-monitoring practices. As the nurse acquires skills in handling the dashboards of the various brands and submitting the various situations to the referring physician, it is immediately apparent that ongoing learning can lead to a major transformation in the distribution of competencies. It can be seen that the nurse can easily resolve an increasing proportion of monitored cases and require the intervention of the competent doctor only for particularly complex and difficult-to-manage cases. This progressive redefinition of competences is also solved by a particular management of the hospital information system so that the nurse is enabled to instruct “simple” cases directly on the central information system, making the centrality of his work evident even then.

> Yes. These choices here are mine and the director’s, but also mine, in short, in the sense that I have pushed very hard with the CED, with the information services, to allow the nurse and other competent persons, once they have acquired that certain competence, to be able to sign that report, let’s say, that report of the parameters... in which it does not state whether he is ill or not ill, [but] it states that those parameters are within the norm, that the impedance is right, that the frequency is correct, that there are no alterations... [Head nurse at the beginning of the trial].

The experience gradually becomes a national case. Delegations of health workers visit from other regions to analyze the model, which becomes a point of reference in view of possible replication in different territories. The Dedicated Telemonitoring Nurse develops a further competence as a trainer offered throughout the Italian health system for the specific scientific community dealing with implantable devices.

Finally, the initiative generated a new assessment with the patient, who had to recognize and accept the new organizational methods by making the management of telemonitoring data transparent, which was guaranteed in 2 3 days at most. The effect of this transformation generated among the patients immediately indicated an interest because an increase in the healthcare facility’s focus on cardiological pathology and implanted instruments for monitoring was guaranteed.

> We had made a pact with the patient, where the patient at enrolment signed a document that in any case of pain... goes to the emergency room, because if I transfer the data, and in addition to this we had given a time now I don’t remember if it was two days three working days, it was [important] to say [that] his data will be seen in x days, also because there were holidays, etc. The nurse in charge was on his own and we couldn’t think of doing h24 so there was a pact [between] nurse, doctor, department and patient on dates and times and how to handle any discomfort. [Lead nurse at the beginning of the trial].

5 Discussion

The fieldwork confirms how institutional work is the result of a complex set of activities that different actors on the organizational scene bring into play. The two main complexities can be indicated on the one hand in trying to align the everyday operational practices made possible by technology and on the other in convincing the institution to consider these new modalities as part of its own set of actions and services. We have also seen that the focal point where institutional work takes place is the situated context within which not only the agency of the actors involved in technological development acts, but also technology is a strategic ally with its own agency. The combination of these two tensions is not resolved in the simple adoption of new practices typical of a professional community but must consolidate into genuine institutional work that is capable of transforming the organization and transforming the rules that govern it, including the digital rules of dedicated information systems.

The story told by these field data confirms the hierarchical and incremental logic with which institutional work develops, which must be acted upon with recurring and repeated iterations in order to arrive at the complex objective of institutionalizing new organizational practices. Work from this point of view can no longer be considered as individual or even as a simple network alliance but must assume individual reflexivity as capable of a collective agency that can modify the institution itself. As we have seen, these actions cannot be replicated simply by informing the scientific community and organizational decision-makers but require for each area of reference a negotiation is continued support over time for change to take place.

6 Conclusions

The processes described above read through the conceptual lens of 'institutional work' [2], understood as the creative and rationally oriented activity of 'culturally competent' actors to adapt to dynamic conditions that constitute the mechanism by which institutions are created, reproduced, and destroyed [4, 5]. The paper aims to show how different actors, using the resources at their disposal, act to modify healthcare institutions by redefining their role in a scenario characterized by an increasing use of ICT tools in healthcare.

References

1. Borup, M., Brown, N., Konrad, K., & Van Lente, H. (2006). The sociology of expectations in science and technology. *Technology Analysis & Strategic Management, 18*(3–4), 285–298. https://doi.org/10.1080/09537320600777002
2. Lawrence, T., & Suddaby, R. (2006). Institutions and institutional work. In *Handbook of organization studies* (Vol. 2, pp. 215–254). https://doi.org/10.4135/9781848608030.
3. Blavoukos, S., & Bourantonis, D. (2017). Nested institutions. In J. A. Koops & R. Biermann (Eds.), *Palgrave handbook of inter-organizational relations in world politics* (pp. 303–317). Palgrave Macmillan. https://doi.org/10.1057/978-1-137-36039-7_14.
4. Currie, G., & White, L. (2012). Inter-professional barriers and knowledge brokering in an organizational context: The case of healthcare. *Organization Studies, 33*, 1333–1361. https://doi.org/10.1177/0170840612457617
5. Currie, G., Lockett, A., Finn, R., Martin, G., & Waring, J. (2012). Institutional work to maintain professional power: Recreating the model of medical professionalism. *Organization Studies, 33*(7), 937–962. https://doi.org/10.1177/0170840612445116
6. Modell, S. (2022). Accounting for institutional work: A critical review. *European Accounting Review, 31*(1), 33–58. https://doi.org/10.1080/09638180.2020.1820354
7. Troshani, I., Janssen, M., Lymer, A., & Parker, L. (2018). Digital transformation of business to government reporting: An institutional work perspective. *International Journal of Accounting Information Systems, 31*, 17–36. https://doi.org/10.1016/j.ac-cinf.2018.09.002

8. Nyland, K., Morland, C., & Burns, J. (2017). The interplay of managerial and non-managerial controls, institutional work, and the coordination of laterally dependent hospital activities. *Qualitative Research in Accounting & Management, 14*(4), 467–495. https://doi.org/10.1108/QRAM-08-2017-0076
9. Elder-Vass, D. (2010). *The causal power of social structures: Emergence, structure and agency*. Cambridge University Press. https://doi.org/10.1017/CBO9780511761720
10. Elder-Vass, D. (2015). Developing social theory using critical realism. *Journal of Critical Realism, 14*, 80–92. https://doi.org/10.1179/1476743014Z.00000000047
11. Kotseva, K., De Backer, G., De Bacquer, D., Rydén, L., Hoes, A., Grobbee, D., Maggioni, A., Marques-Vidal, P., Jennings, C., Abreu, A., Aguiar, C., Badariene, J., Bruthans, J., Castro Conde, A., Cifkova, R., Crowley, J., Davletov, K., Deckers, J., De Smedt, D., & EUROASPIRE Investigators. (2019). Lifestyle and impact on cardiovascular risk factor control in coronary patients across 27 countries: Results from the European Society of Cardiology ESC-EORP EUROASPIRE V registry. *European Journal of Preventive Cardiology, 26*(8), 824–835. https://doi.org/10.1177/2047487318825350
12. Ameri, P., & Angermann, C. (2020). Implementing structured heart failure outpatient monitoring and care in real life. *Journal of Cardiovascular Medicine, 21*(4), 315–317. https://doi.org/10.2459/JCM.0000000000000935
13. DeFilippis, E., Impink, S., Singell, M., Polzer, J., & Sadun, R. (2020). Collaborating during coronavirus: The impact of COVID-19 on the nature of work. *SSRN Electronic Journal*. https://doi.org/10.2139/ssrn.3654470
14. Zanutto, A., Ponte, D., & Piras, E. M. (2022). COVID-19 pandemic and new cardiology telemonitoring organization: How to cast the others. In S. Za, R. Winter, & A. Lazazzara (Eds.), *Sustainable digital transformation: Paving the way towards smart organizations and societies* (pp. 117–132). Springer International Publishing. https://doi.org/10.1007/978-3-031-15770-7_8

The manufacturer's authorised representative in the EU is Springer Nature Customer Service Centre GmbH, Europaplatz 3, 69115 Heidelberg, Germany. If you have any concerns regarding our products, please contact ProductSafety@springernature.com

Printed and bound by CPI Group (UK) Ltd, Croydon, CR0 4YY
01/10/2026
02225893-0008